Angel Sanctuary

story and art by **Kaori Yuki** vol.5

Whose love killed
the child of God?

The Story Thus Far

High school boy Setsuna Mudo has just destroyed the world. He's always been a troublemaker, but his worst sin was falling incestuously in love with his beautiful sister, Sara. However, his troubles aren't entirely his fault. He is the reincarnation of the Lady Alexiel, an angel who rebelled against Heaven and led the demons of Hell, the Evils, in a revolt. Her punishment was to be reborn into tragic life after tragic life. This time, her life is Setsuna.

But these days, God does not reign in Heaven, and the rule of the highest angels—child-like Metatron and strict dictator Sevothtarte—is shaky. The mad angel, Rosiel, sends his servants Katan and the selfish young female angel Kirie to Earth to reawaken the dormant Alexiel within Setsuna.

When Kirie murders Sara, it finally awakens Alexiel, but the violence of her divine resurrection destroys Tokyo. On the brink of death, Setsuna awakens when the angel Seraphita appears before him. The angel has frozen time the moment before Tokyo was destroyed, but explains that he couldn't save Sara because it was necessary for her to die and Alexiel to awaken. But the angel offers Setsuna some hope: He has seven days to journey into Hell and try to rescue his sister. At the end of seven days, he'll die forever. In Hell, Setsuna is guided by his old schoolmate and nemesis, Kato.

Meanwhile in Heaven, the Supreme Council is in chaos. In the confusion, mad Rosiel seizes power. The angel Sevothtarte instructs Dobiel to spy on Rosiel, but things go badly for his henchmen—they're devoured by Rosiel's servant Katan, who died in the Tokyo blast and has turned into a flesh-eating ghoul. In Hades, Setsuna thinks he sees Sara, but it's just a demon in disguise, so his hunt continues.

Contents

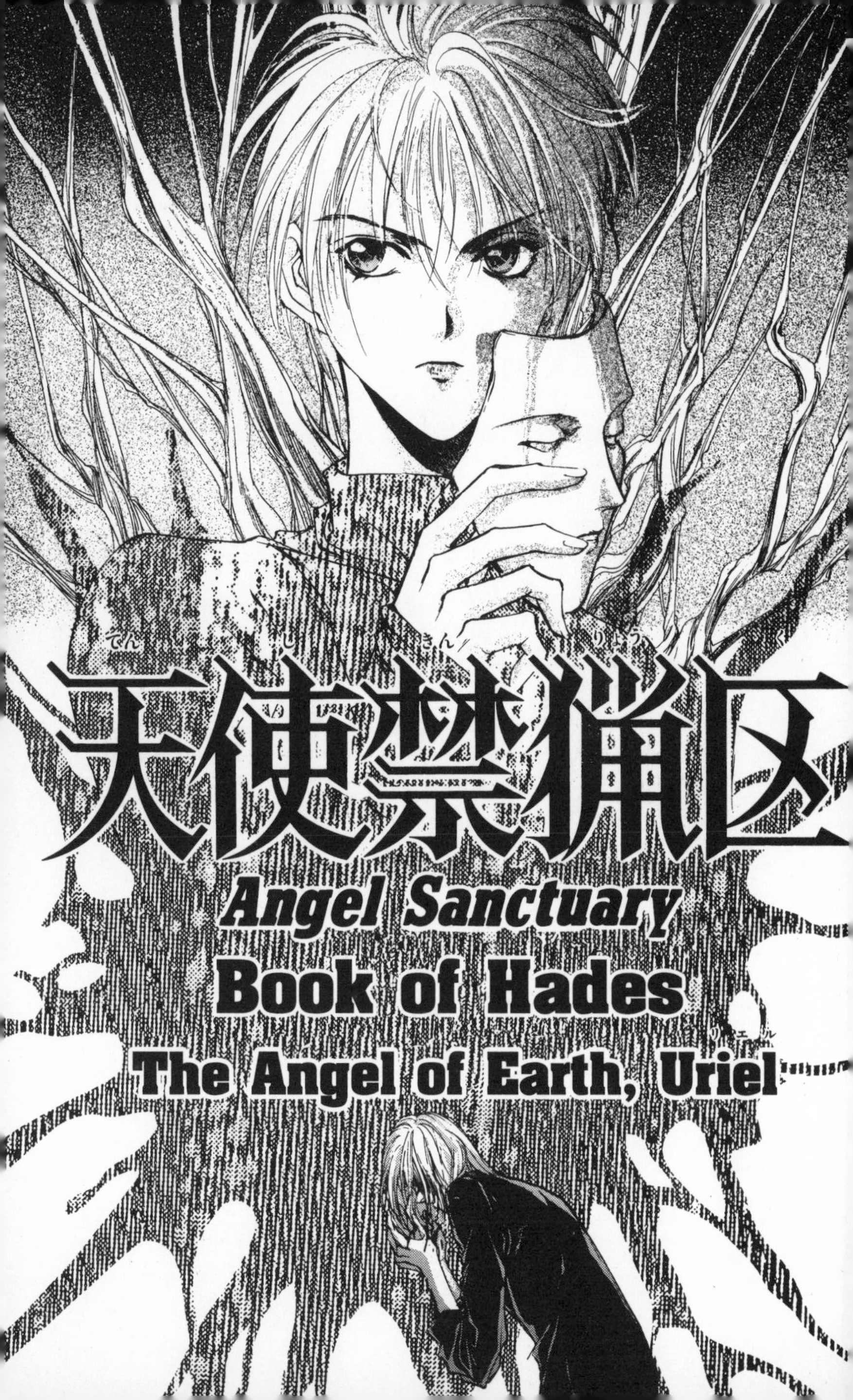
天使禁猟区
Angel Sanctuary
Book of Hades
The Angel of Earth, Uriel

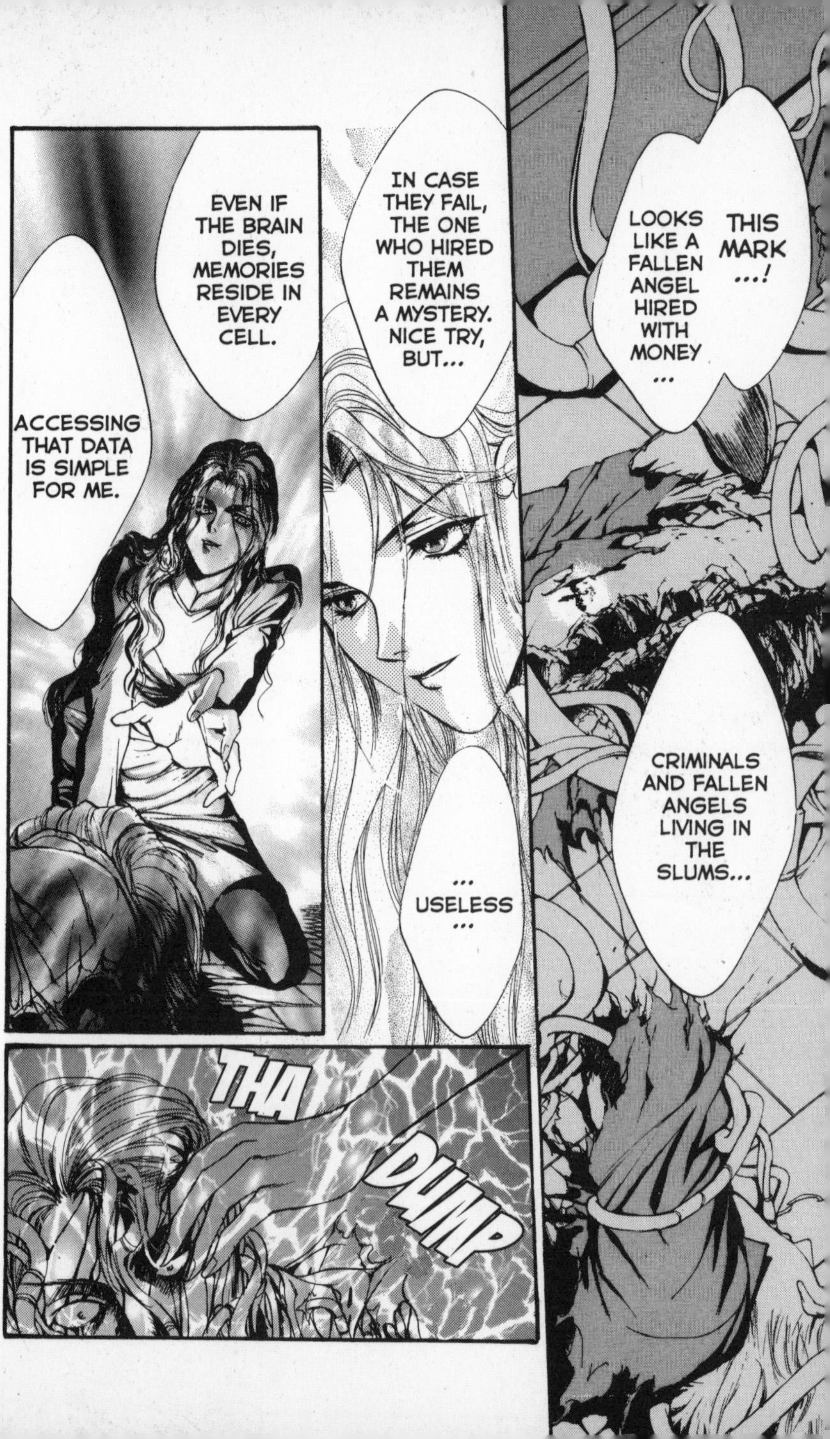
THIS MARK ...!
LOOKS LIKE A FALLEN ANGEL HIRED WITH MONEY ...
CRIMINALS AND FALLEN ANGELS LIVING IN THE SLUMS...
IN CASE THEY FAIL, THE ONE WHO HIRED THEM REMAINS A MYSTERY. NICE TRY, BUT...
... USELESS ...
EVEN IF THE BRAIN DIES, MEMORIES RESIDE IN EVERY CELL.
ACCESSING THAT DATA IS SIMPLE FOR ME.
THA DUMP

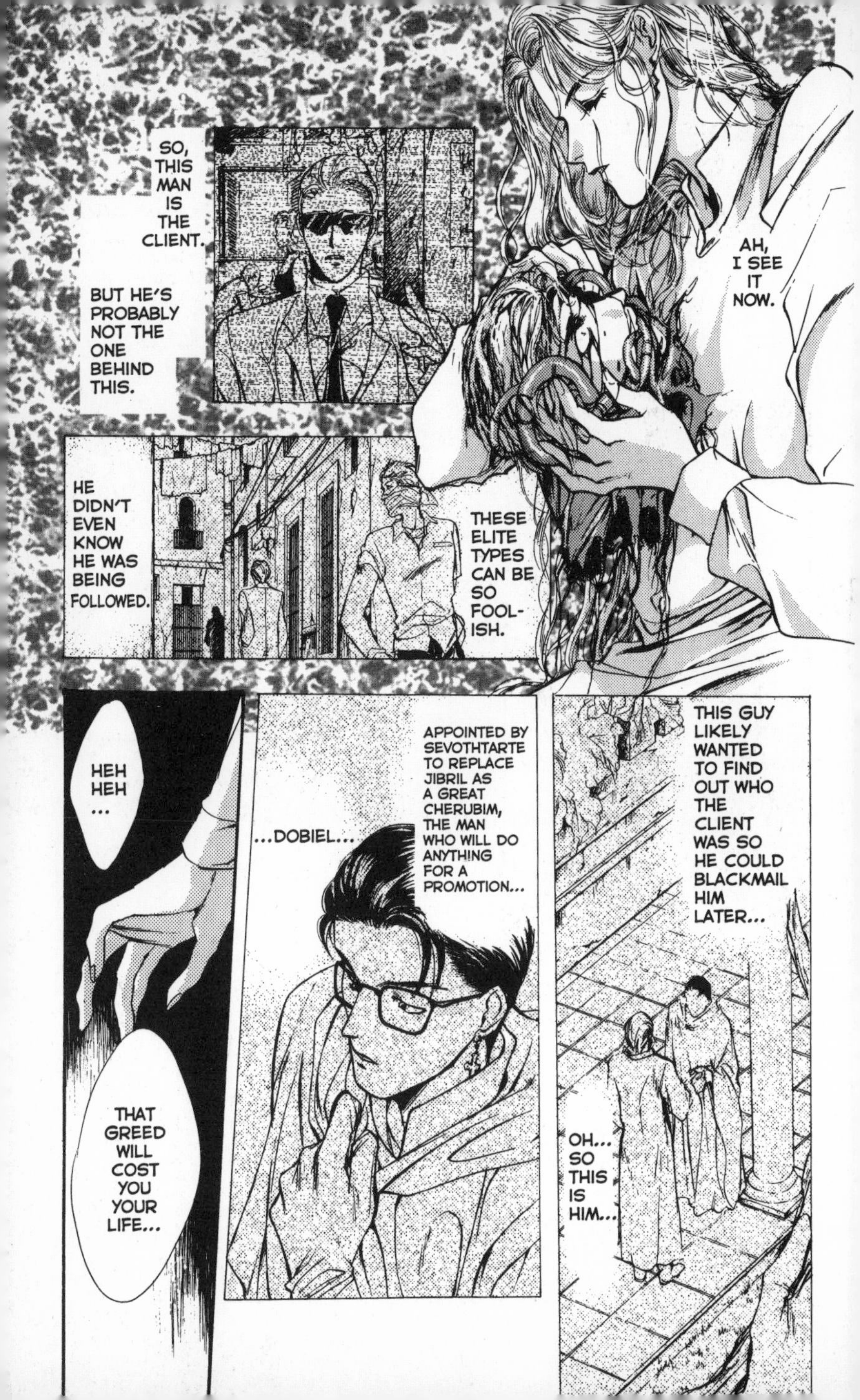
AH, I SEE IT NOW.
SO, THIS MAN IS THE CLIENT.
BUT HE'S PROBABLY NOT THE ONE BEHIND THIS.
THESE ELITE TYPES CAN BE SO FOOLISH.
HE DIDN'T EVEN KNOW HE WAS BEING FOLLOWED.
THIS GUY LIKELY WANTED TO FIND OUT WHO THE CLIENT WAS SO HE COULD BLACKMAIL HIM LATER...
OH... SO THIS IS HIM...
APPOINTED BY SEVOTHTARTE TO REPLACE JIBRIL AS A GREAT CHERUBIM, THE MAN WHO WILL DO ANYTHING FOR A PROMOTION...
...DOBIEL...
HEH HEH...
THAT GREED WILL COST YOU YOUR LIFE...

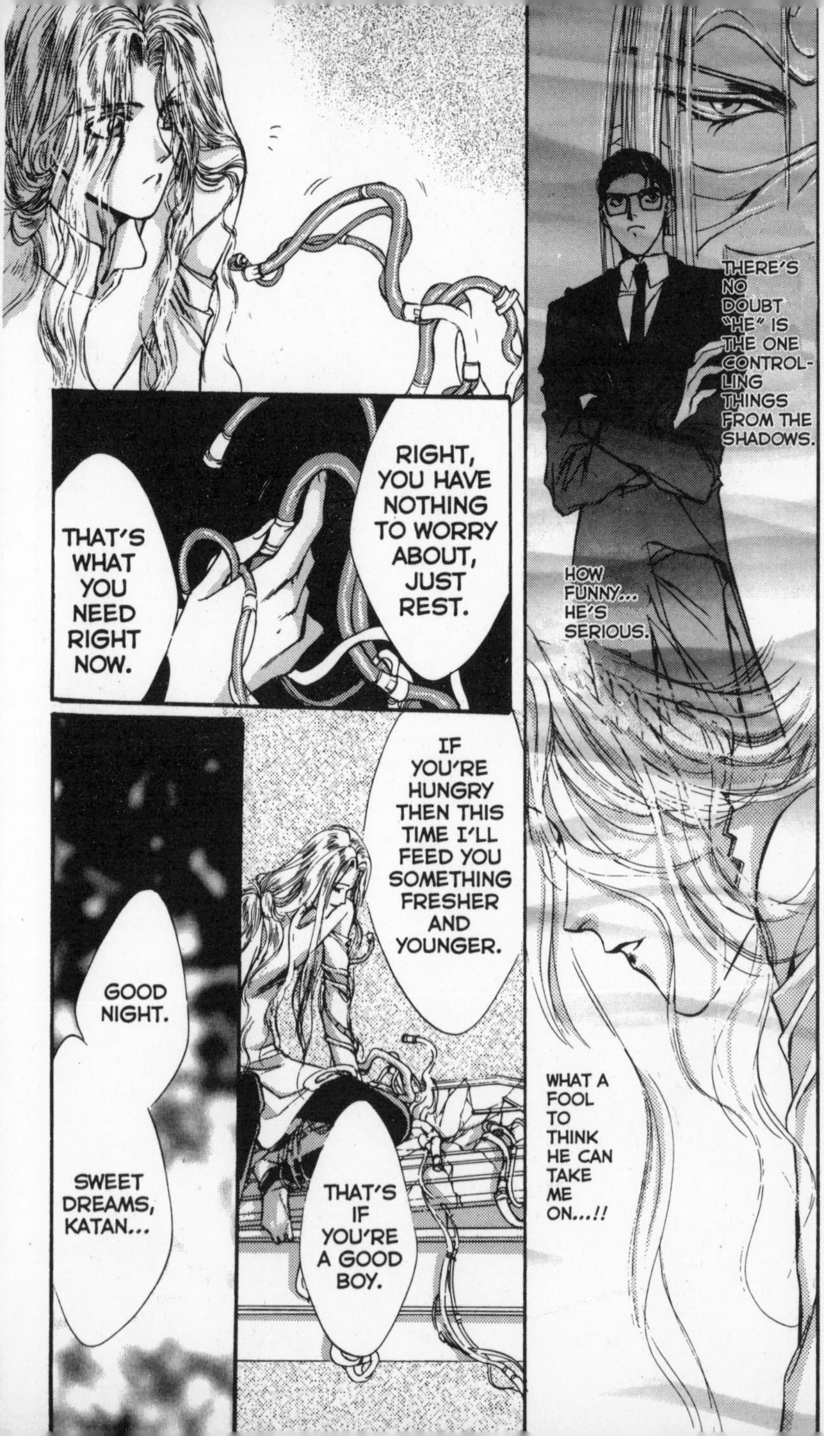
THERE'S NO DOUBT "HE" IS THE ONE CONTROLLING THINGS FROM THE SHADOWS.
HOW FUNNY... HE'S SERIOUS.
WHAT A FOOL TO THINK HE CAN TAKE ME ON...!!
RIGHT, YOU HAVE NOTHING TO WORRY ABOUT, JUST REST.
THAT'S WHAT YOU NEED RIGHT NOW.
IF YOU'RE HUNGRY THEN THIS TIME I'LL FEED YOU SOMETHING FRESHER AND YOUNGER.
THAT'S IF YOU'RE A GOOD BOY.
GOOD NIGHT.
SWEET DREAMS, KATAN...

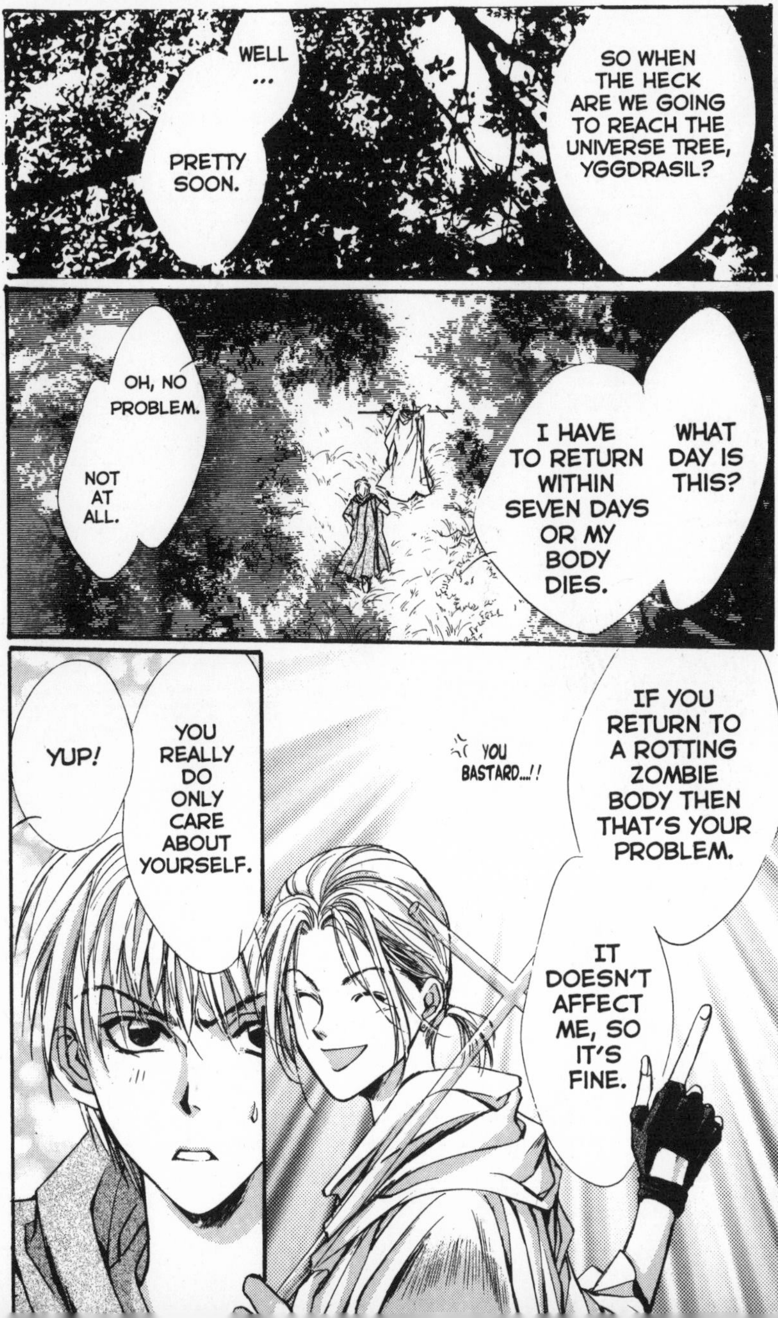
SO WHEN THE HECK ARE WE GOING TO REACH THE UNIVERSE TREE, YGGDRASIL?
WELL ...
PRETTY SOON.
WHAT DAY IS THIS?
I HAVE TO RETURN WITHIN SEVEN DAYS OR MY BODY DIES.
OH, NO PROBLEM.
NOT AT ALL.
IF YOU RETURN TO A ROTTING ZOMBIE BODY THEN THAT'S YOUR PROBLEM.
IT DOESN'T AFFECT ME, SO IT'S FINE.
YOU BASTARD...!!
YOU REALLY DO ONLY CARE ABOUT YOURSELF.
YUP!

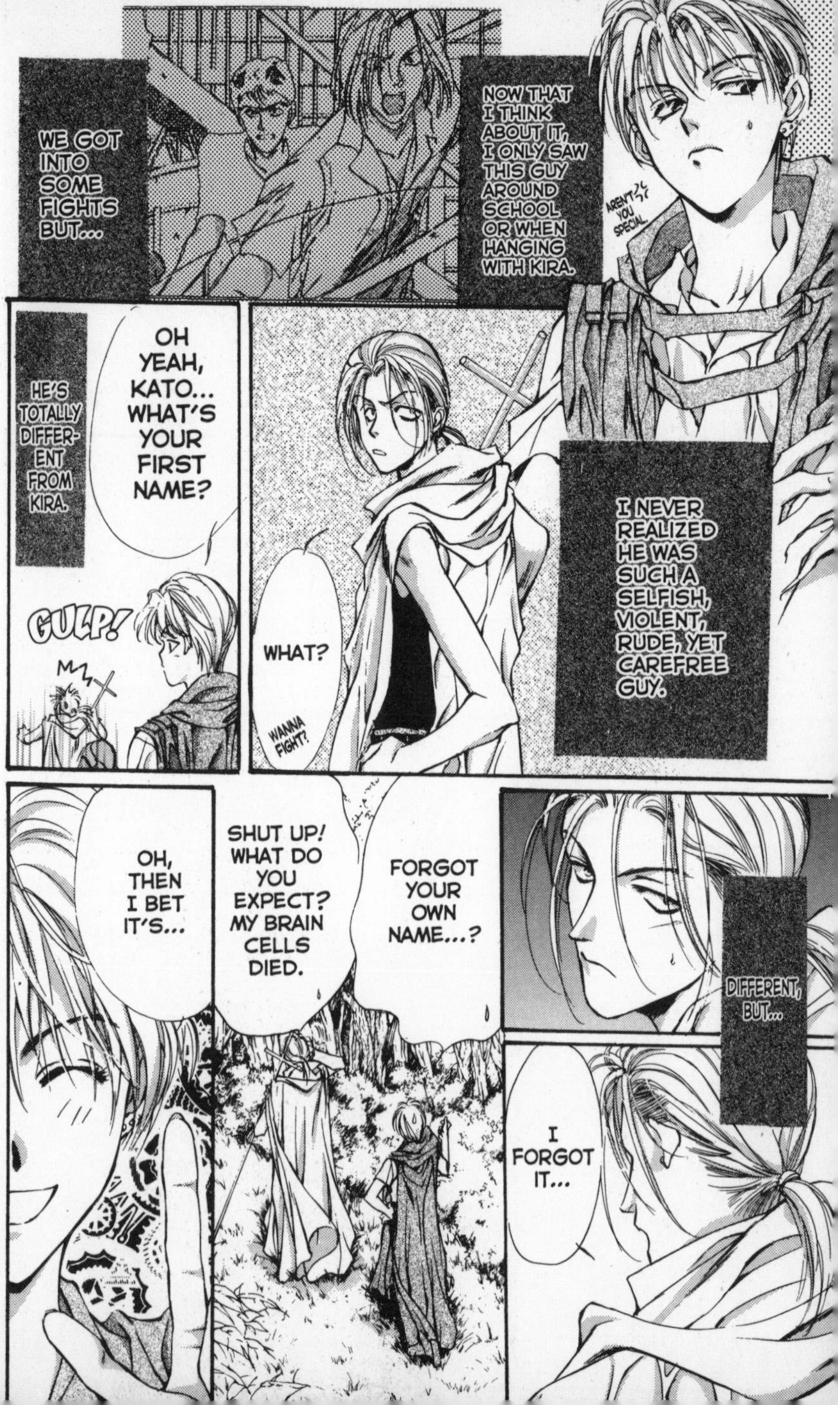
NOW THAT I THINK ABOUT IT, I ONLY SAW THIS GUY AROUND SCHOOL OR WHEN HANGING WITH KIRA.
AREN'T YOU SPECIAL
I NEVER REALIZED HE WAS SUCH A SELFISH, VIOLENT, RUDE, YET CAREFREE GUY.
WE GOT INTO SOME FIGHTS BUT...
WHAT?
WANNA FIGHT?
HE'S TOTALLY DIFFER-ENT FROM KIRA.
OH YEAH, KATO... WHAT'S YOUR FIRST NAME?
GULP!
DIFFERENT, BUT...
I FORGOT IT...
FORGOT YOUR OWN NAME...?
SHUT UP! WHAT DO YOU EXPECT? MY BRAIN CELLS DIED.
OH, THEN I BET IT'S...

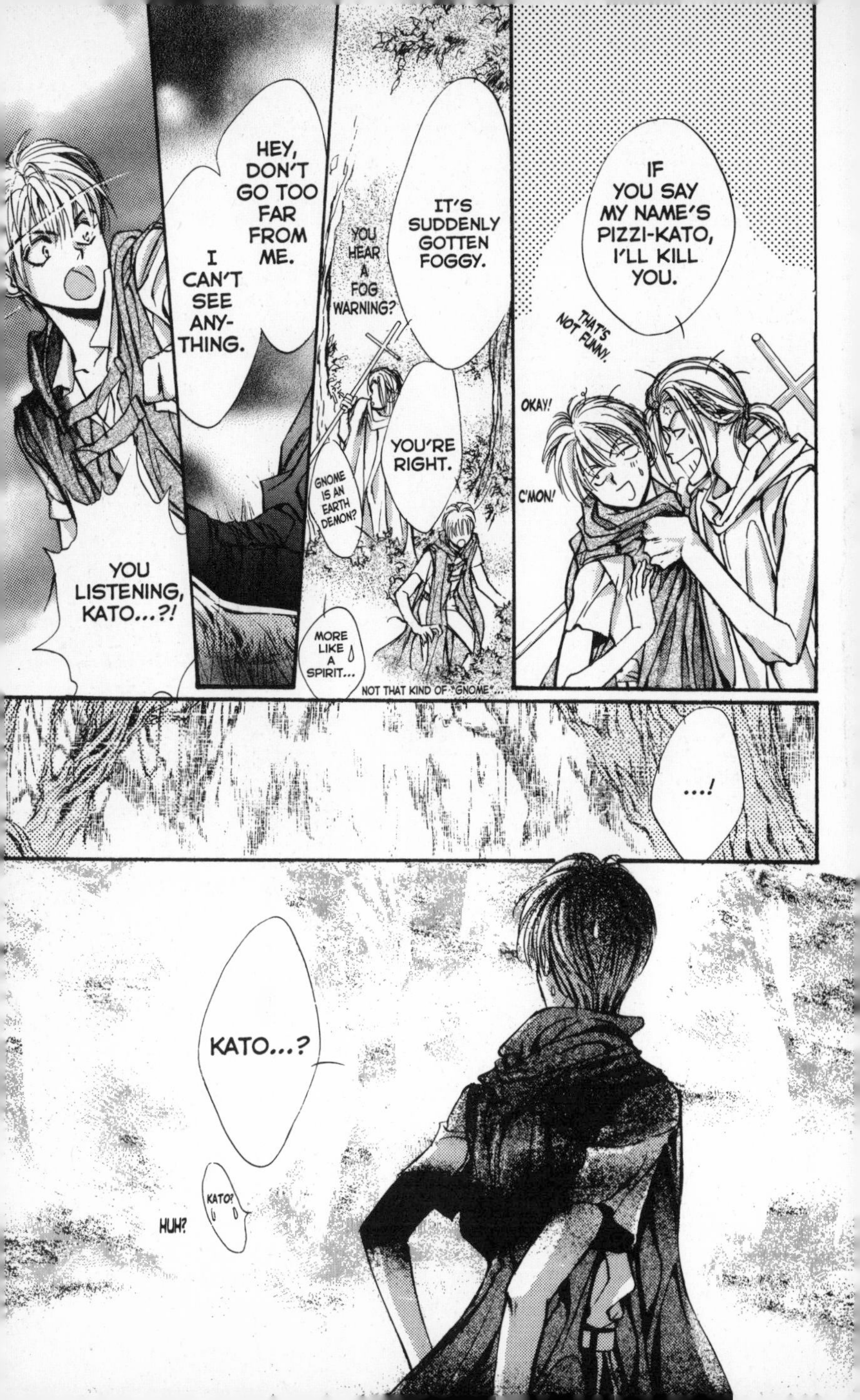
IF YOU SAY MY NAME'S PIZZI-KATO, I'LL KILL YOU.
THAT'S NOT FUNNY.
OKAY!
C'MON!
IT'S SUDDENLY GOTTEN FOGGY.
YOU HEAR A FOG WARNING?
YOU'RE RIGHT.
GNOME IS AN EARTH DEMON?
MORE LIKE A SPIRIT...
NOT THAT KIND OF "GNOME"...
HEY, DON'T GO TOO FAR FROM ME.
I CAN'T SEE ANY-THING.
YOU LISTENING, KATO...?!
...!
KATO...?
KATO?
HUH?

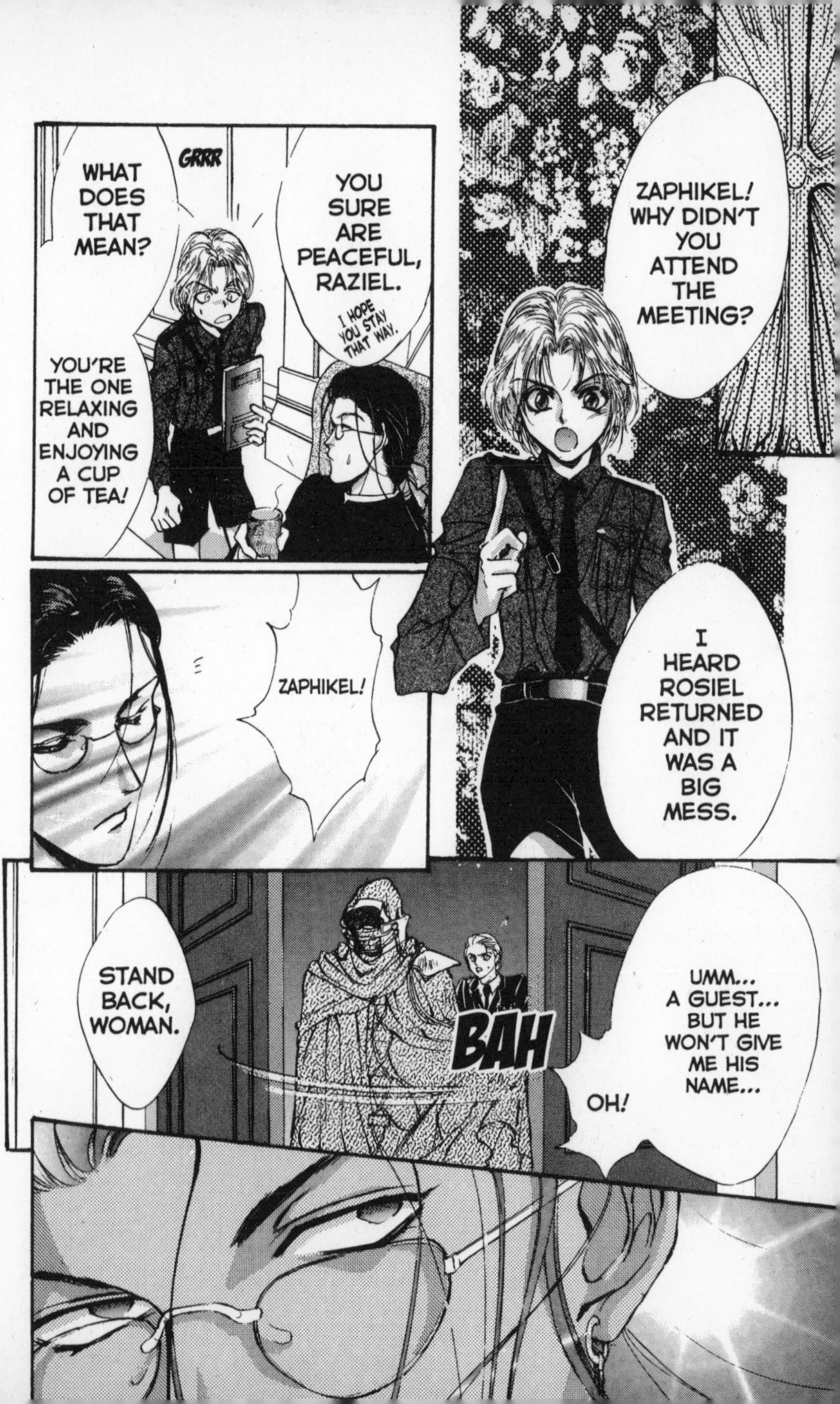

ZAPHIKEL! WHY DIDN'T YOU ATTEND THE MEETING?
I HEARD ROSIEL RETURNED AND IT WAS A BIG MESS.
YOU SURE ARE PEACEFUL, RAZIEL.
I HOPE YOU STAY THAT WAY.
GRRR
WHAT DOES THAT MEAN?
YOU'RE THE ONE RELAXING AND ENJOYING A CUP OF TEA!
ZAPHIKEL!
UMM... A GUEST... BUT HE WON'T GIVE ME HIS NAME...
OH!
BAH
STAND BACK, WOMAN.

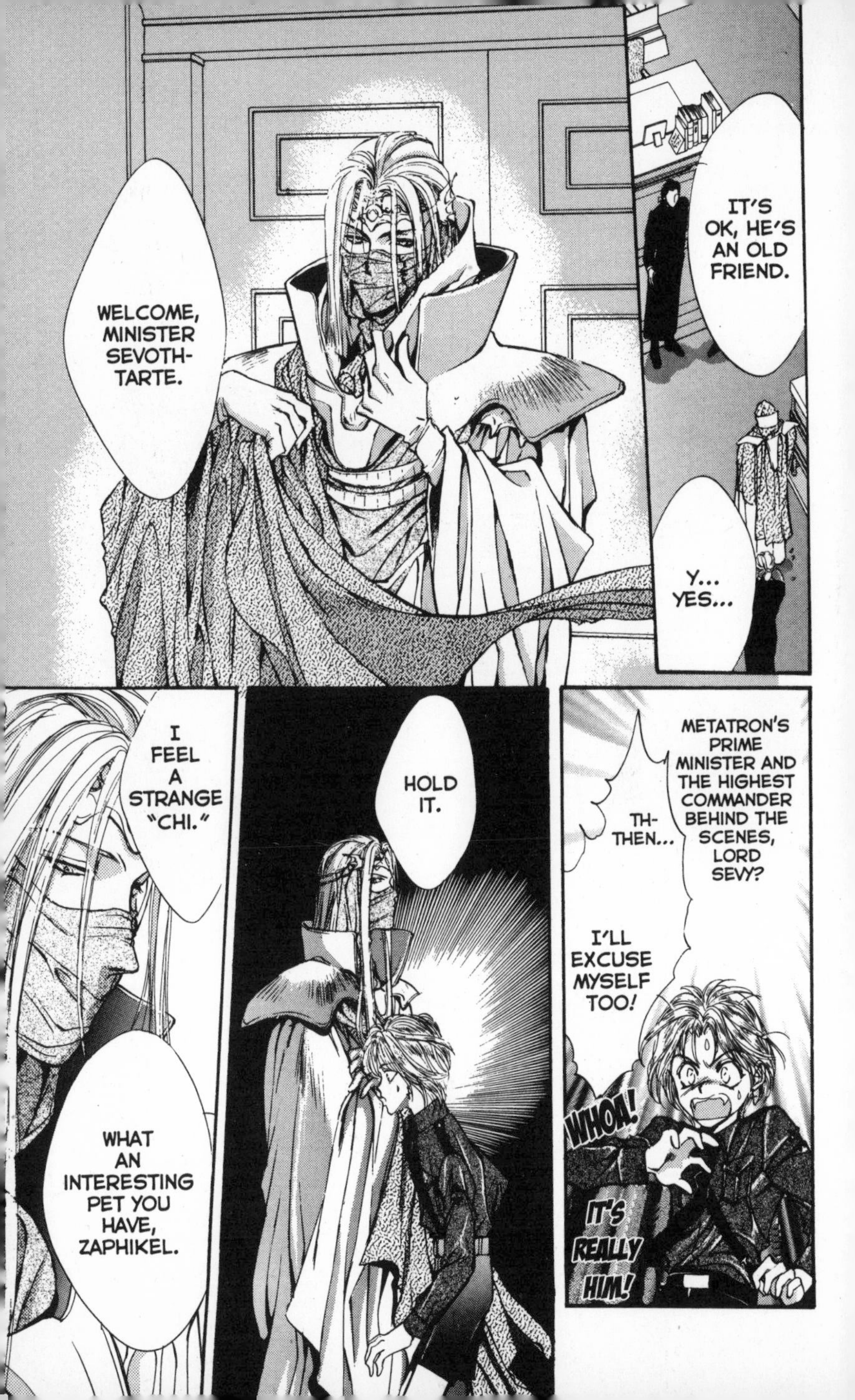
IT'S OK, HE'S AN OLD FRIEND.
Y... YES...
WELCOME, MINISTER SEVOTH-TARTE.
METATRON'S PRIME MINISTER AND THE HIGHEST COMMANDER BEHIND THE SCENES, LORD SEVY?
TH- THEN...
I'LL EXCUSE MYSELF TOO!
WHOA!
IT'S REALLY HIM!
HOLD IT.
I FEEL A STRANGE "CHI."
WHAT AN INTERESTING PET YOU HAVE, ZAPHIKEL.

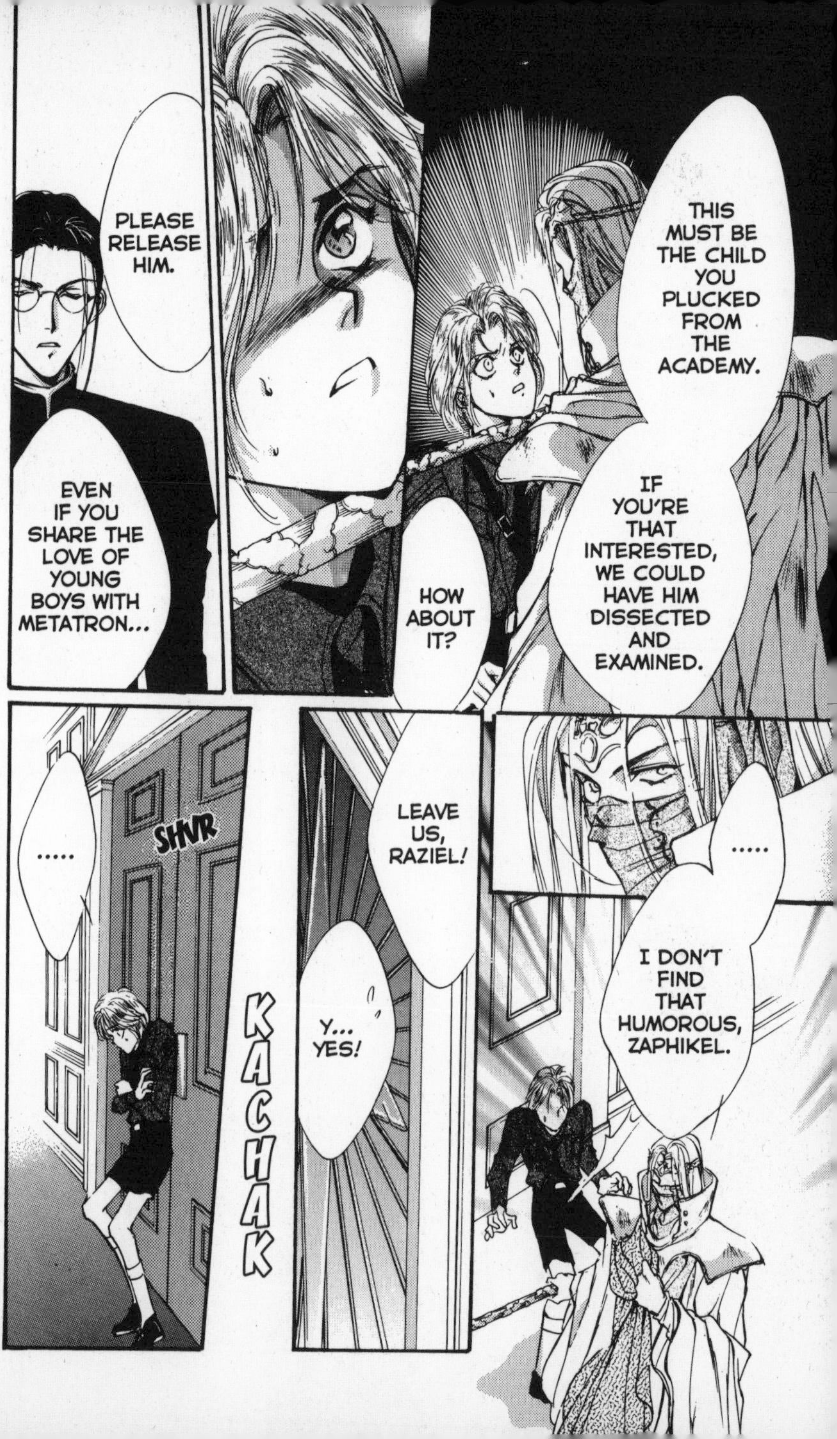
THIS MUST BE THE CHILD YOU PLUCKED FROM THE ACADEMY.
IF YOU'RE THAT INTERESTED, WE COULD HAVE HIM DISSECTED AND EXAMINED.
HOW ABOUT IT?
PLEASE RELEASE HIM.
EVEN IF YOU SHARE THE LOVE OF YOUNG BOYS WITH METATRON...
.....
I DON'T FIND THAT HUMOROUS, ZAPHIKEL.
LEAVE US, RAZIEL!
Y... YES!
KACHAK
.....
SHVR

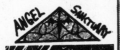

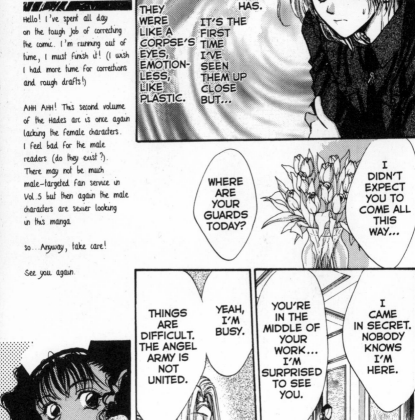

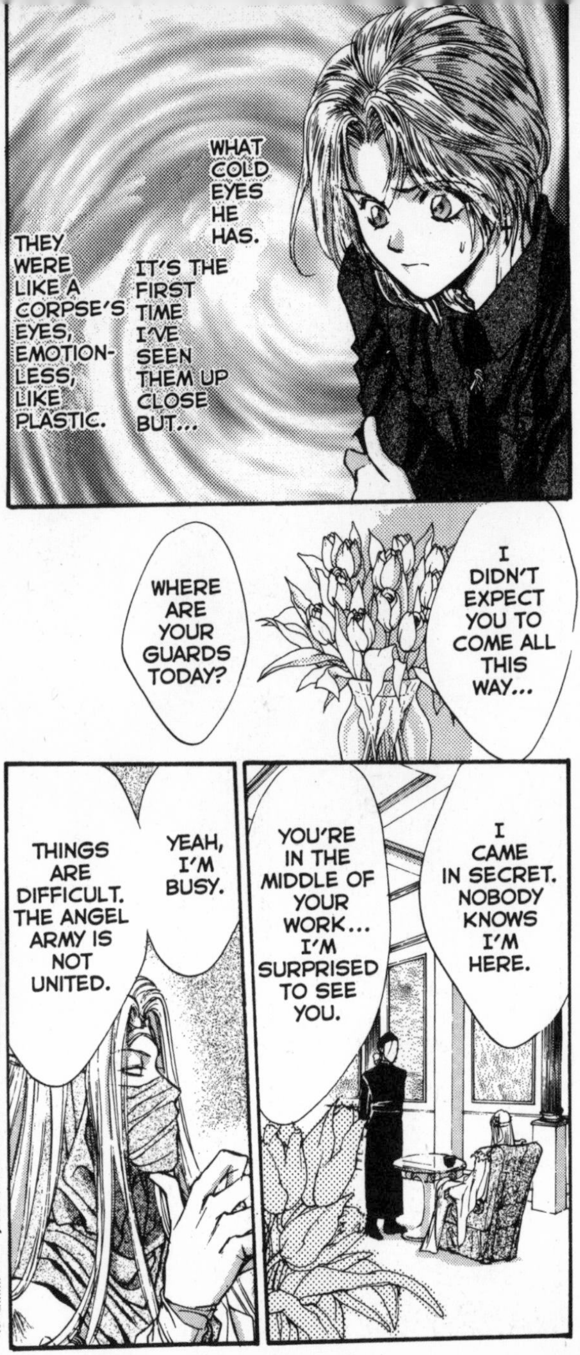
WHAT COLD EYES HE HAS.
IT'S THE FIRST TIME I'VE SEEN THEM UP CLOSE BUT...
THEY WERE LIKE A CORPSE'S EYES, EMOTION-LESS, LIKE PLASTIC.
I DIDN'T EXPECT YOU TO COME ALL THIS WAY...
WHERE ARE YOUR GUARDS TODAY?
I CAME IN SECRET. NOBODY KNOWS I'M HERE.
YOU'RE IN THE MIDDLE OF YOUR WORK... I'M SURPRISED TO SEE YOU.
YEAH, I'M BUSY.
THINGS ARE DIFFICULT. THE ANGEL ARMY IS NOT UNITED.

ANGEL SANCTUARY

Hello! I've spent all day on the tough job of correcting the comic. I'm running out of time, I must finish it! (I wish I had more time for corrections and rough drafts!)

AHH AHH! This second volume of the Hades arc is once again lacking the female characters. I feel bad for the male readers (do they exist?). There may not be much male-targeted fan service in Vol.5 but then again the male characters are sexier looking in this manga

so... Anyway, take care!

See you again.

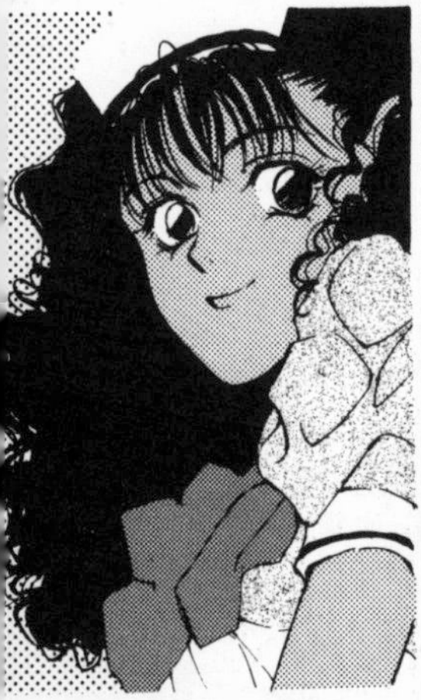

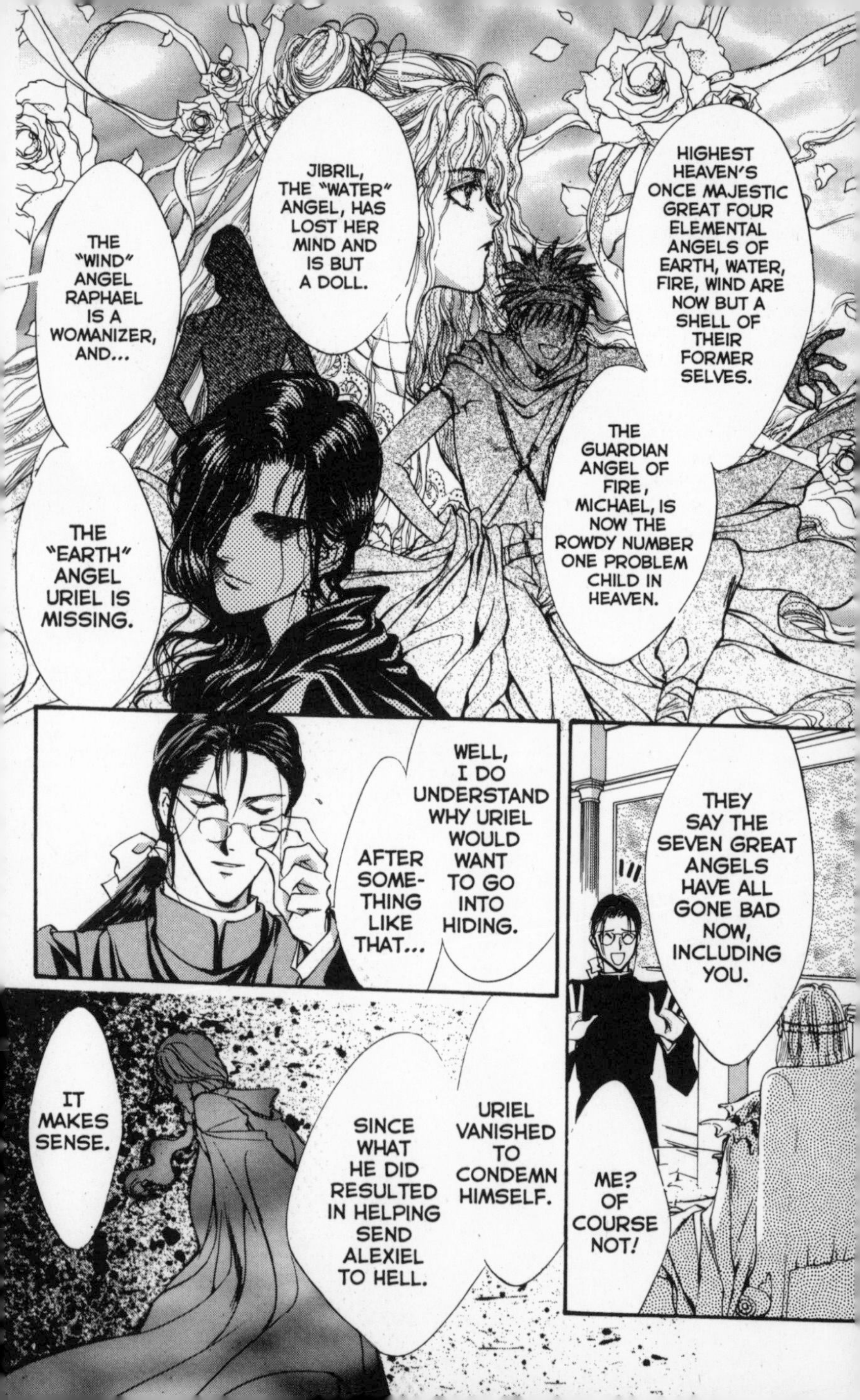
HIGHEST HEAVEN'S ONCE MAJESTIC GREAT FOUR ELEMENTAL ANGELS OF EARTH, WATER, FIRE, WIND ARE NOW BUT A SHELL OF THEIR FORMER SELVES.
THE GUARDIAN ANGEL OF FIRE, MICHAEL, IS NOW THE ROWDY NUMBER ONE PROBLEM CHILD IN HEAVEN.
JIBRIL, THE "WATER" ANGEL, HAS LOST HER MIND AND IS BUT A DOLL.
THE "WIND" ANGEL RAPHAEL IS A WOMANIZER, AND...
THE "EARTH" ANGEL URIEL IS MISSING.
THEY SAY THE SEVEN GREAT ANGELS HAVE ALL GONE BAD NOW, INCLUDING YOU.
ME? OF COURSE NOT!
WELL, I DO UNDERSTAND WHY URIEL WOULD WANT TO GO INTO HIDING.
AFTER SOME-THING LIKE THAT...
URIEL VANISHED TO CONDEMN HIMSELF.
SINCE WHAT HE DID RESULTED IN HELPING SEND ALEXIEL TO HELL.
IT MAKES SENSE.

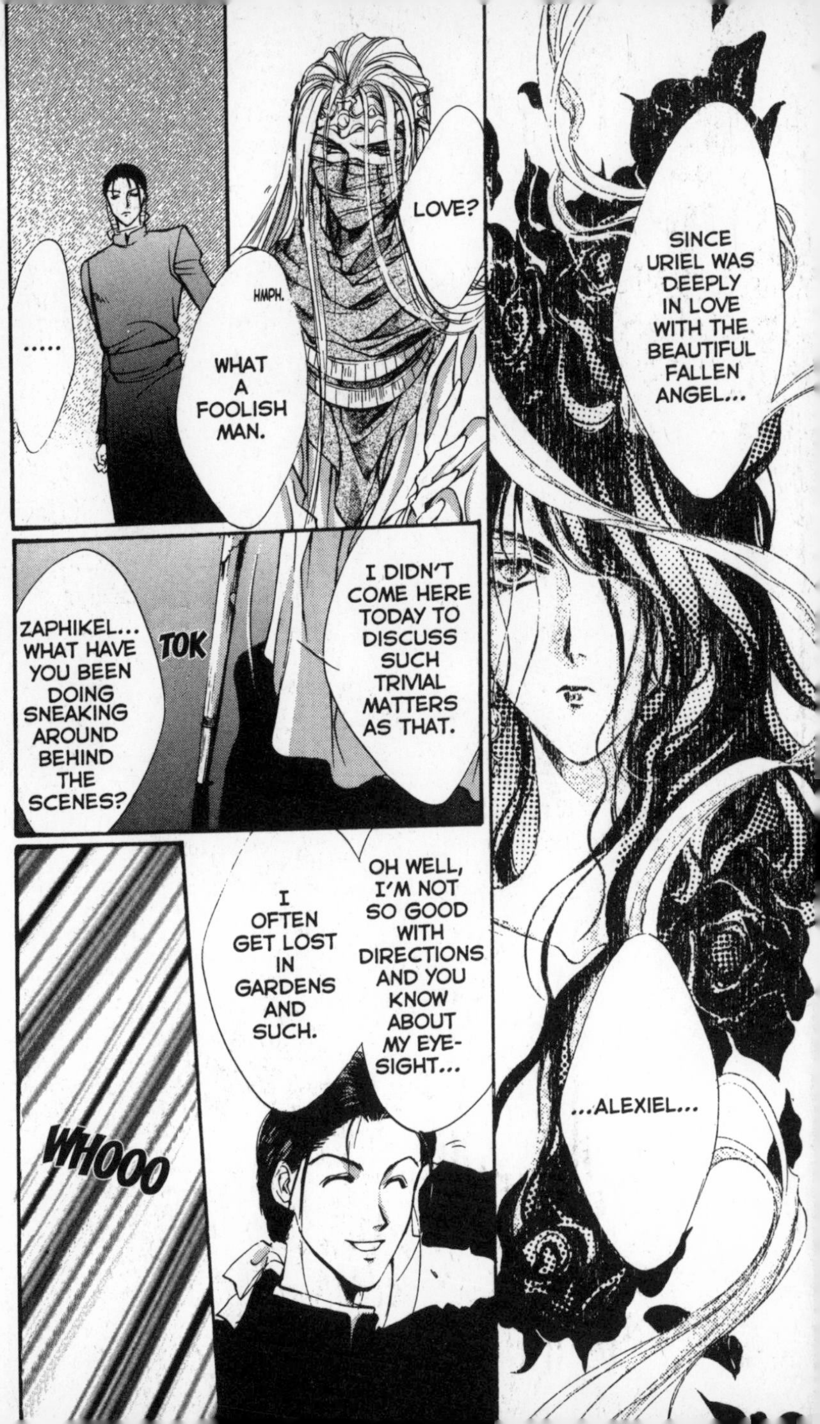
SINCE URIEL WAS DEEPLY IN LOVE WITH THE BEAUTIFUL FALLEN ANGEL...
...ALEXIEL...
LOVE?
HMPH.
WHAT A FOOLISH MAN.
.....
I DIDN'T COME HERE TODAY TO DISCUSS SUCH TRIVIAL MATTERS AS THAT.
TOK
ZAPHIKEL... WHAT HAVE YOU BEEN DOING SNEAKING AROUND BEHIND THE SCENES?
OH WELL, I'M NOT SO GOOD WITH DIRECTIONS AND YOU KNOW ABOUT MY EYE-SIGHT...
I OFTEN GET LOST IN GARDENS AND SUCH.
WHOOO

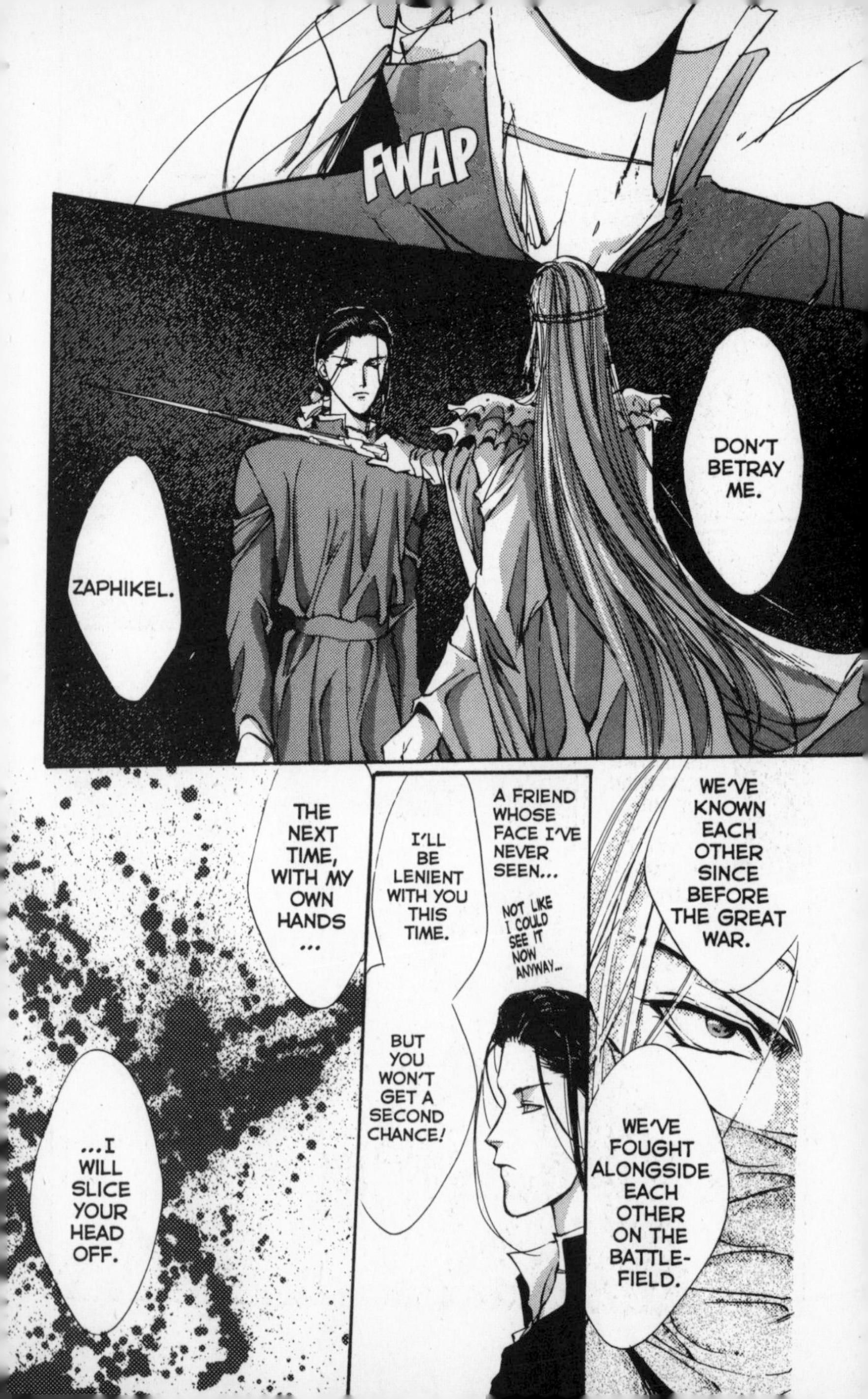
FWAP
DON'T BETRAY ME.
ZAPHIKEL.
WE'VE KNOWN EACH OTHER SINCE BEFORE THE GREAT WAR.
WE'VE FOUGHT ALONGSIDE EACH OTHER ON THE BATTLE-FIELD.
A FRIEND WHOSE FACE I'VE NEVER SEEN...
NOT LIKE I COULD SEE IT NOW ANYWAY...
I'LL BE LENIENT WITH YOU THIS TIME.
BUT YOU WON'T GET A SECOND CHANCE!
THE NEXT TIME, WITH MY OWN HANDS...
...I WILL SLICE YOUR HEAD OFF.

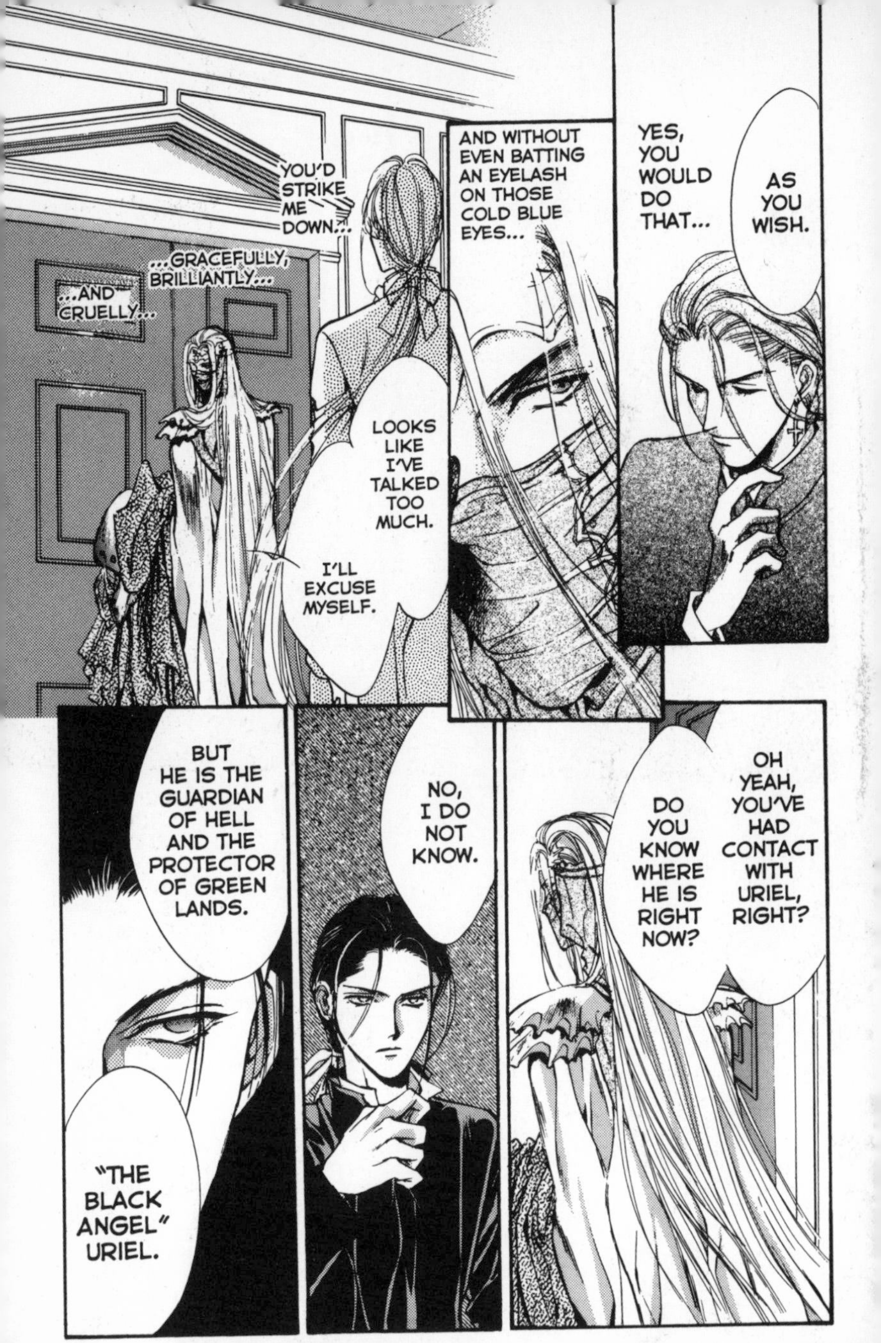
AS YOU WISH.
YES, YOU WOULD DO THAT...
AND WITHOUT EVEN BATTING AN EYELASH ON THOSE COLD BLUE EYES...
YOU'D STRIKE ME DOWN...
...GRACEFULLY, BRILLIANTLY...
...AND CRUELLY...
LOOKS LIKE I'VE TALKED TOO MUCH.
I'LL EXCUSE MYSELF.
OH YEAH, YOU'VE HAD CONTACT WITH URIEL, RIGHT?
DO YOU KNOW WHERE HE IS RIGHT NOW?
NO, I DO NOT KNOW.
BUT HE IS THE GUARDIAN OF HELL AND THE PROTECTOR OF GREEN LANDS.
"THE BLACK ANGEL" URIEL.

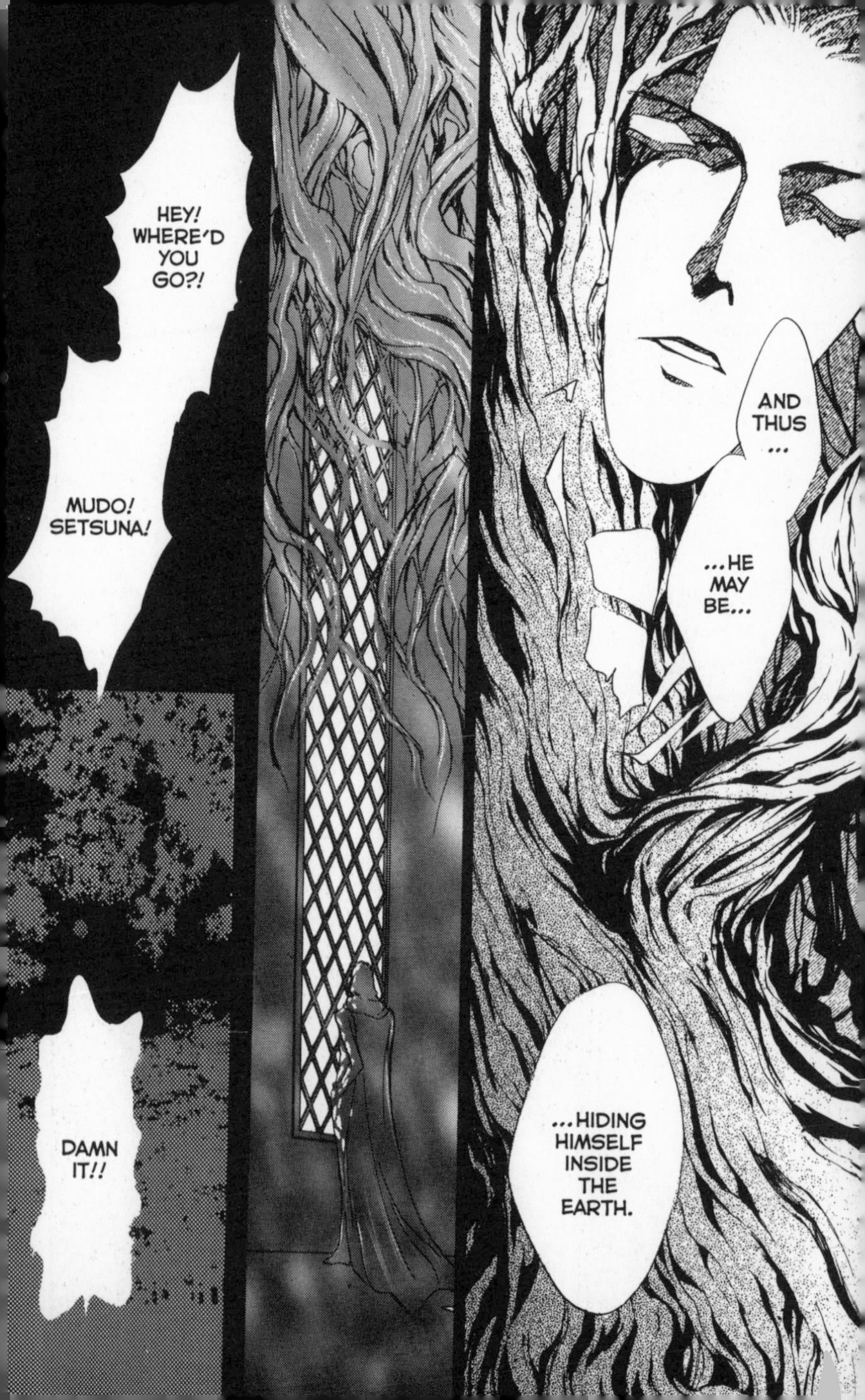
AND THUS...
...HE MAY BE...
...HIDING HIMSELF INSIDE THE EARTH.
HEY! WHERE'D YOU GO?!
MUDO! SETSUNA!
DAMN IT!!

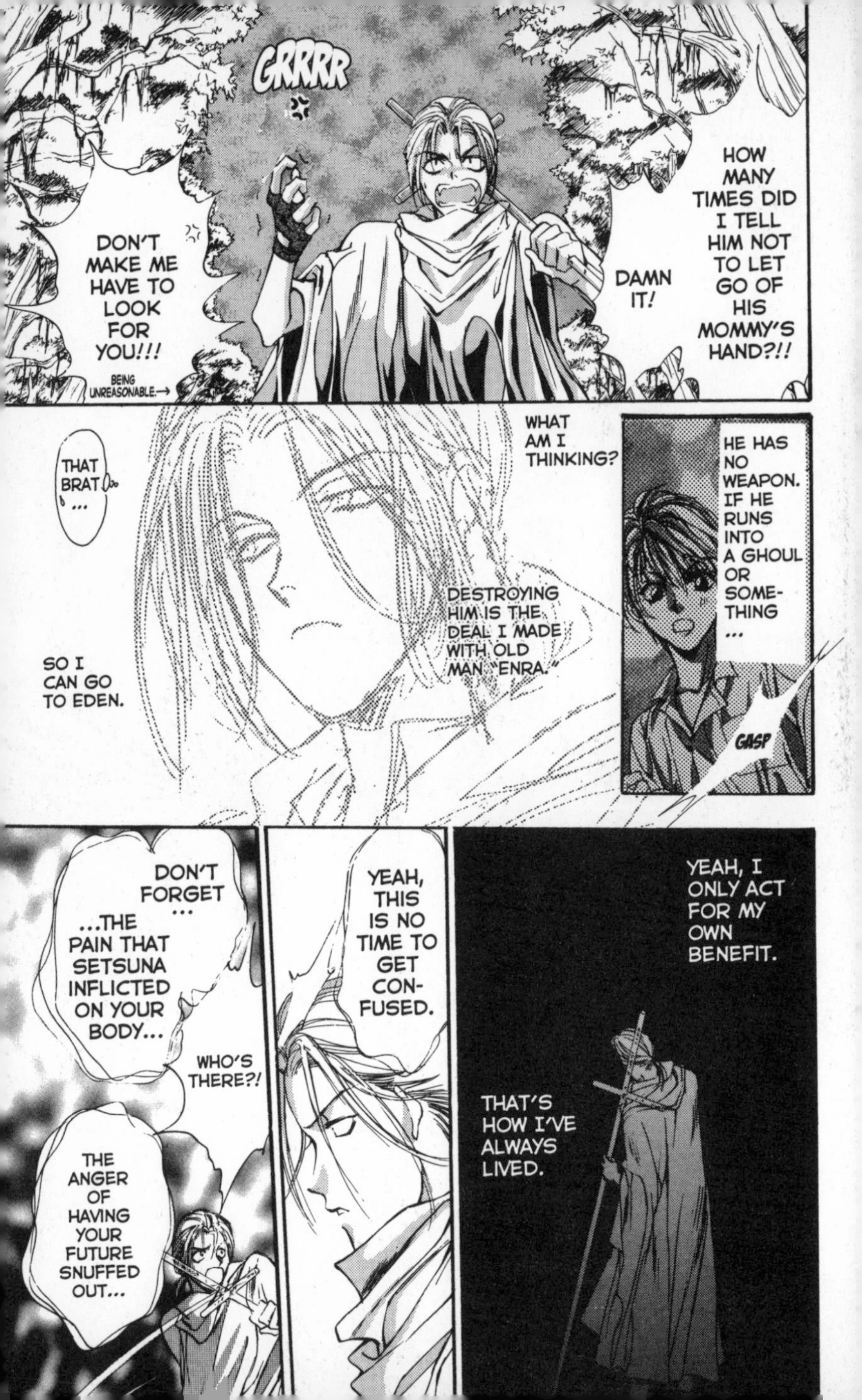
HOW MANY TIMES DID I TELL HIM NOT TO LET GO OF HIS MOMMY'S HAND?!!
DAMN IT!
GRRRR
DON'T MAKE ME HAVE TO LOOK FOR YOU!!!
BEING UNREASONABLE.→
HE HAS NO WEAPON. IF HE RUNS INTO A GHOUL OR SOME-THING...
GASP
WHAT AM I THINKING?
DESTROYING HIM IS THE DEAL I MADE WITH OLD MAN "ENRA."
THAT BRAT...
SO I CAN GO TO EDEN.
YEAH, I ONLY ACT FOR MY OWN BENEFIT.
THAT'S HOW I'VE ALWAYS LIVED.
YEAH, THIS IS NO TIME TO GET CON-FUSED.
DON'T FORGET... ...THE PAIN THAT SETSUNA INFLICTED ON YOUR BODY...
WHO'S THERE?!
THE ANGER OF HAVING YOUR FUTURE SNUFFED OUT...

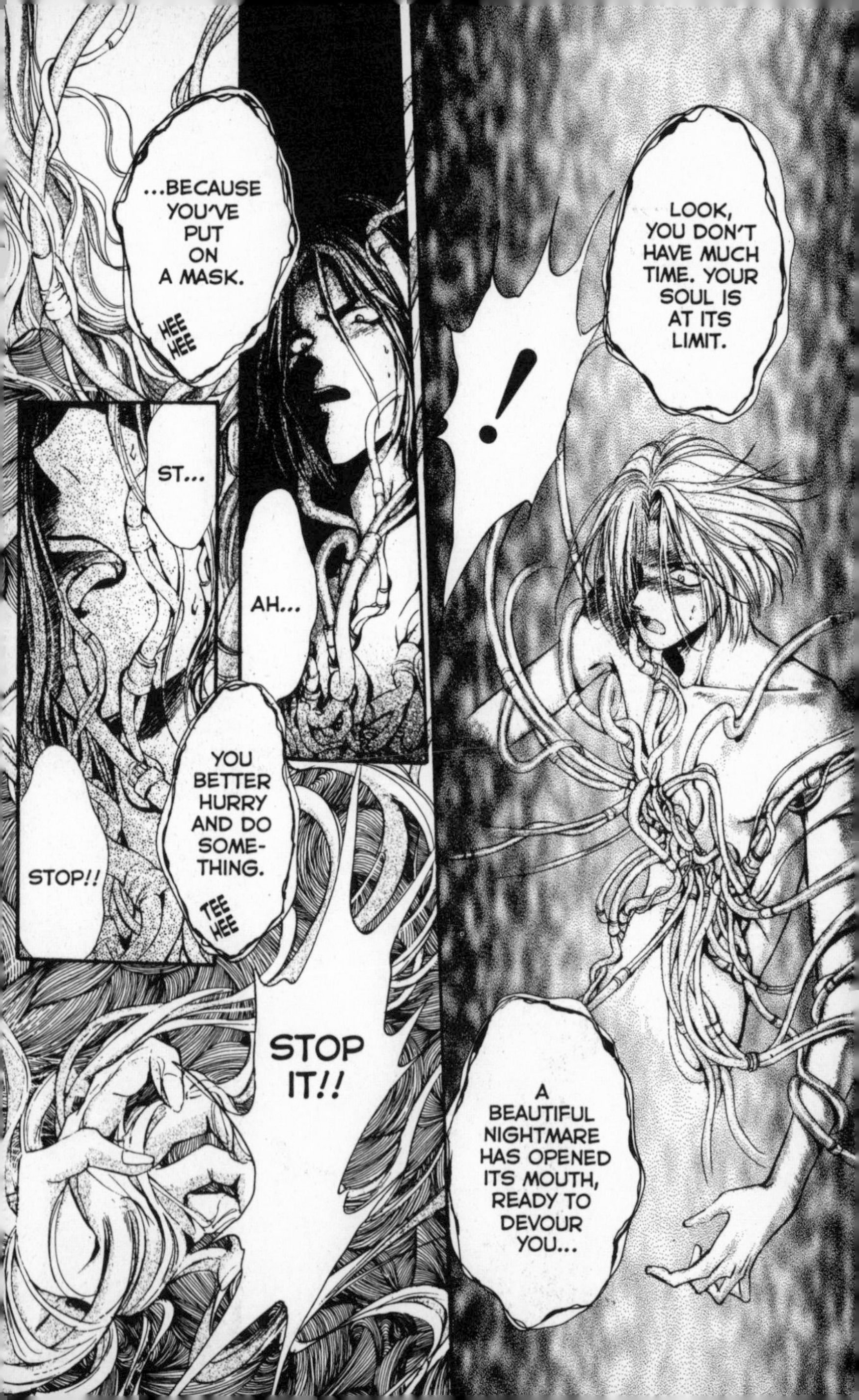
LOOK, YOU DON'T HAVE MUCH TIME. YOUR SOUL IS AT ITS LIMIT.
!
A BEAUTIFUL NIGHTMARE HAS OPENED ITS MOUTH, READY TO DEVOUR YOU...
...BECAUSE YOU'VE PUT ON A MASK.
HEE HEE
AH...
ST...
STOP!!
YOU BETTER HURRY AND DO SOME-THING.
TEE HEE
STOP IT!!

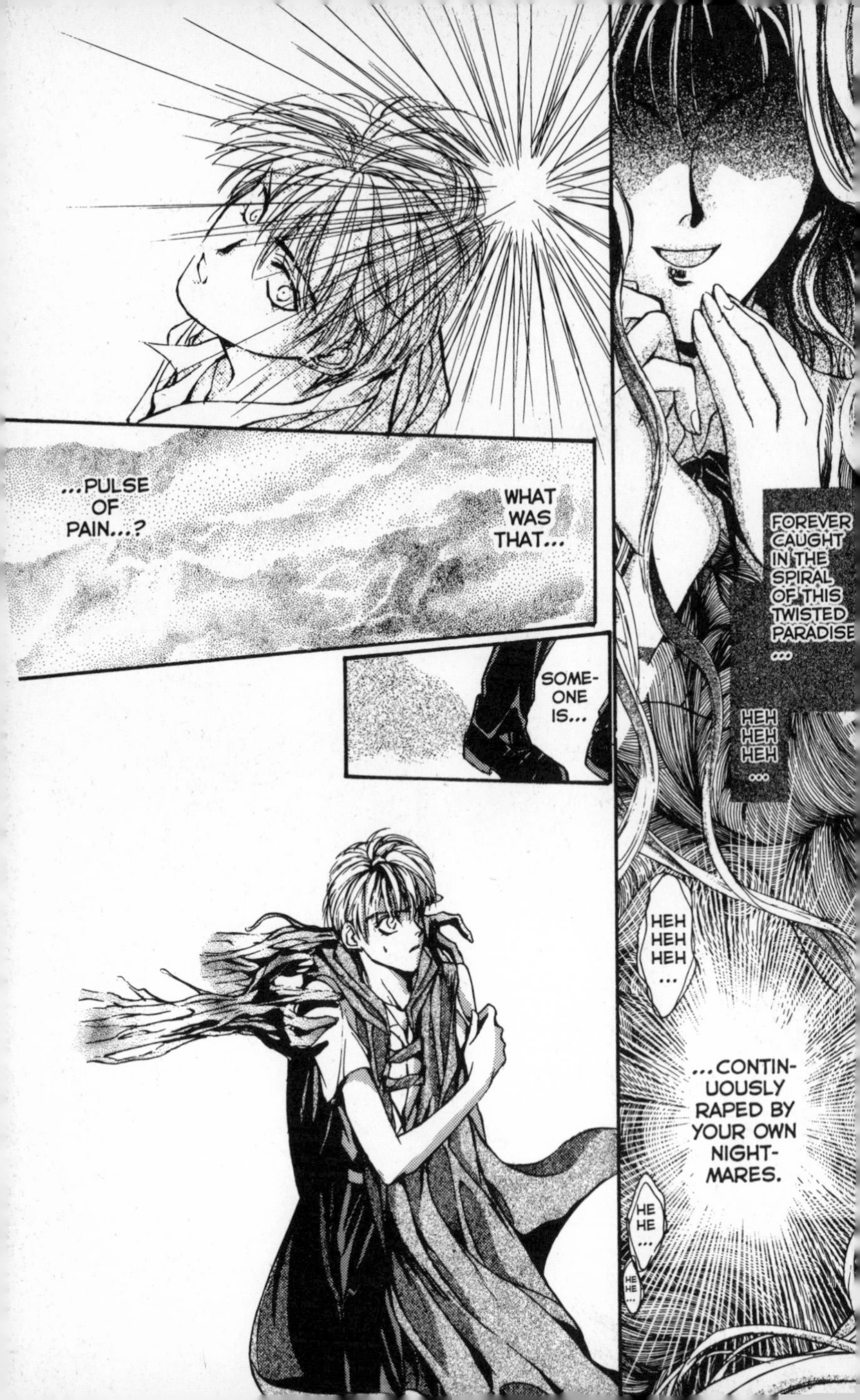
FOREVER CAUGHT IN THE SPIRAL OF THIS TWISTED PARADISE...
HEH HEH HEH...
HEH HEH HEH...
...CONTIN-UOUSLY RAPED BY YOUR OWN NIGHT-MARES.
HE HE...
HE HE...
WHAT WAS THAT...
...PULSE OF PAIN...?
SOME-ONE IS...

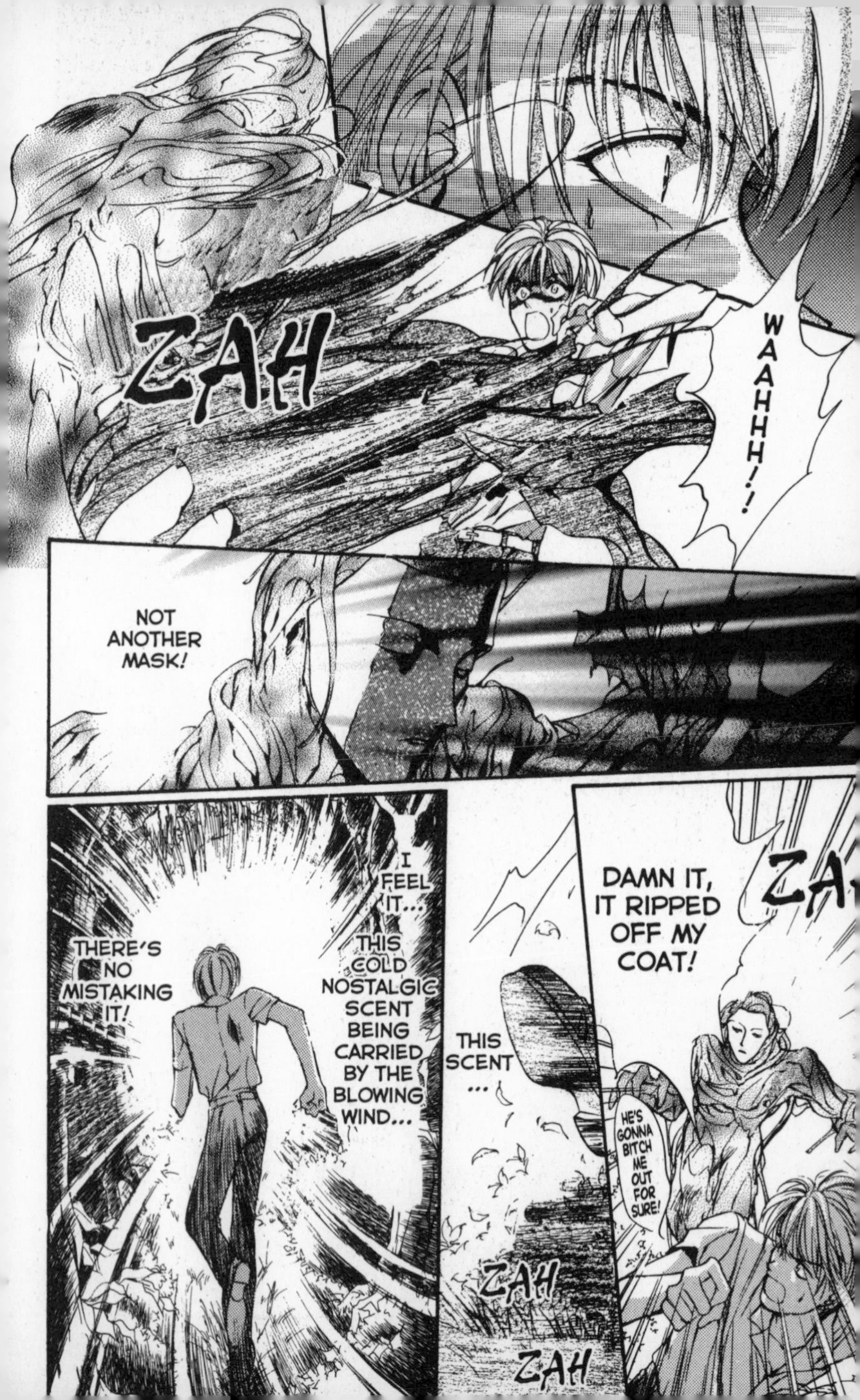
WAAHHH!!
ZAH
NOT ANOTHER MASK!
ZA
DAMN IT, IT RIPPED OFF MY COAT!
HE'S GONNA BITCH ME OUT FOR SURE!
THIS SCENT...
ZAH
ZAH
I FEEL IT...
THIS COLD NOSTALGIC SCENT BEING CARRIED BY THE BLOWING WIND...
THERE'S NO MISTAKING IT!

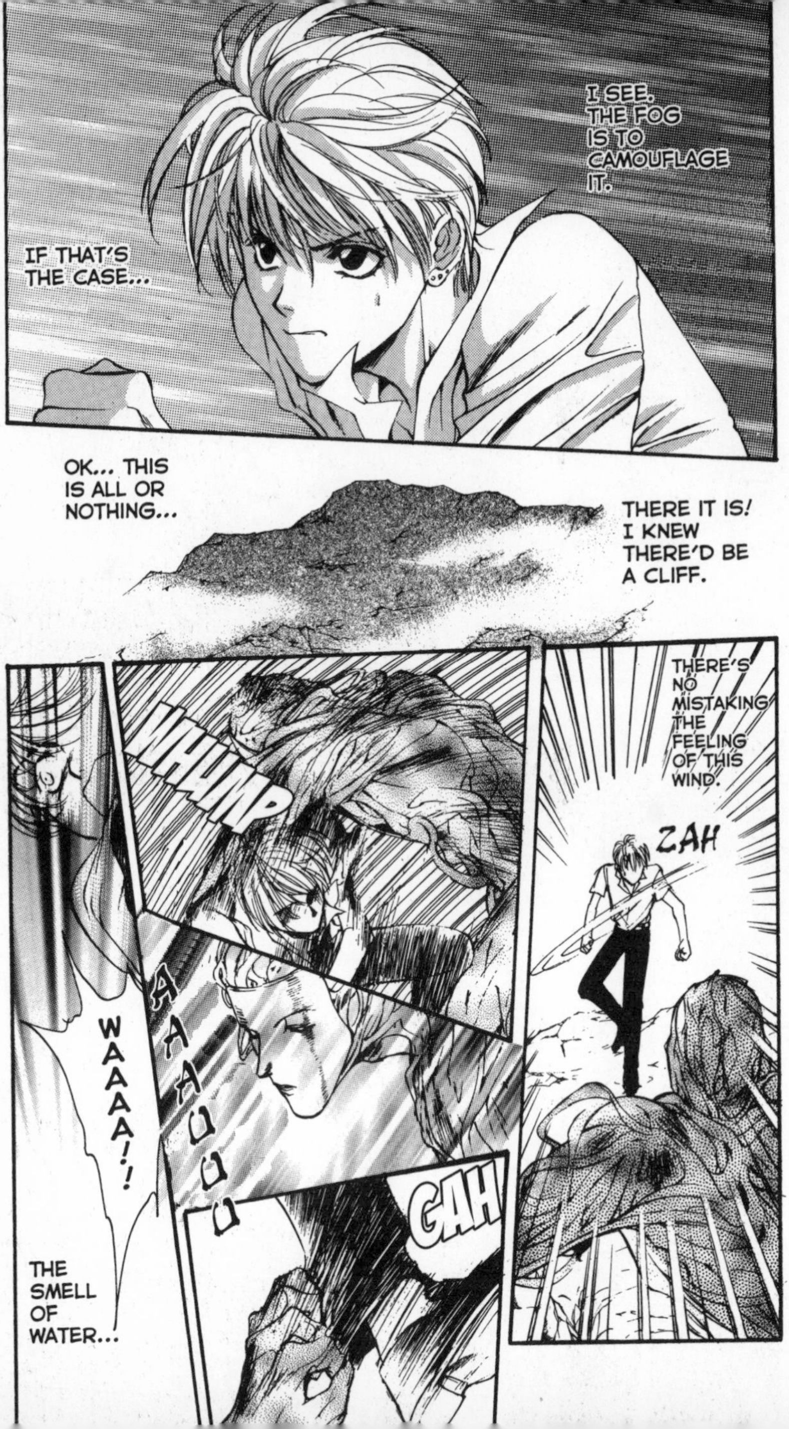
I SEE. THE FOG IS TO CAMOUFLAGE IT.
IF THAT'S THE CASE...
THERE IT IS! I KNEW THERE'D BE A CLIFF.
OK... THIS IS ALL OR NOTHING...
THERE'S NO MISTAKING THE FEELING OF THIS WIND.
ZAH
WHUMP
AAAUUU
GAH
WAAAAA!!
THE SMELL OF WATER...

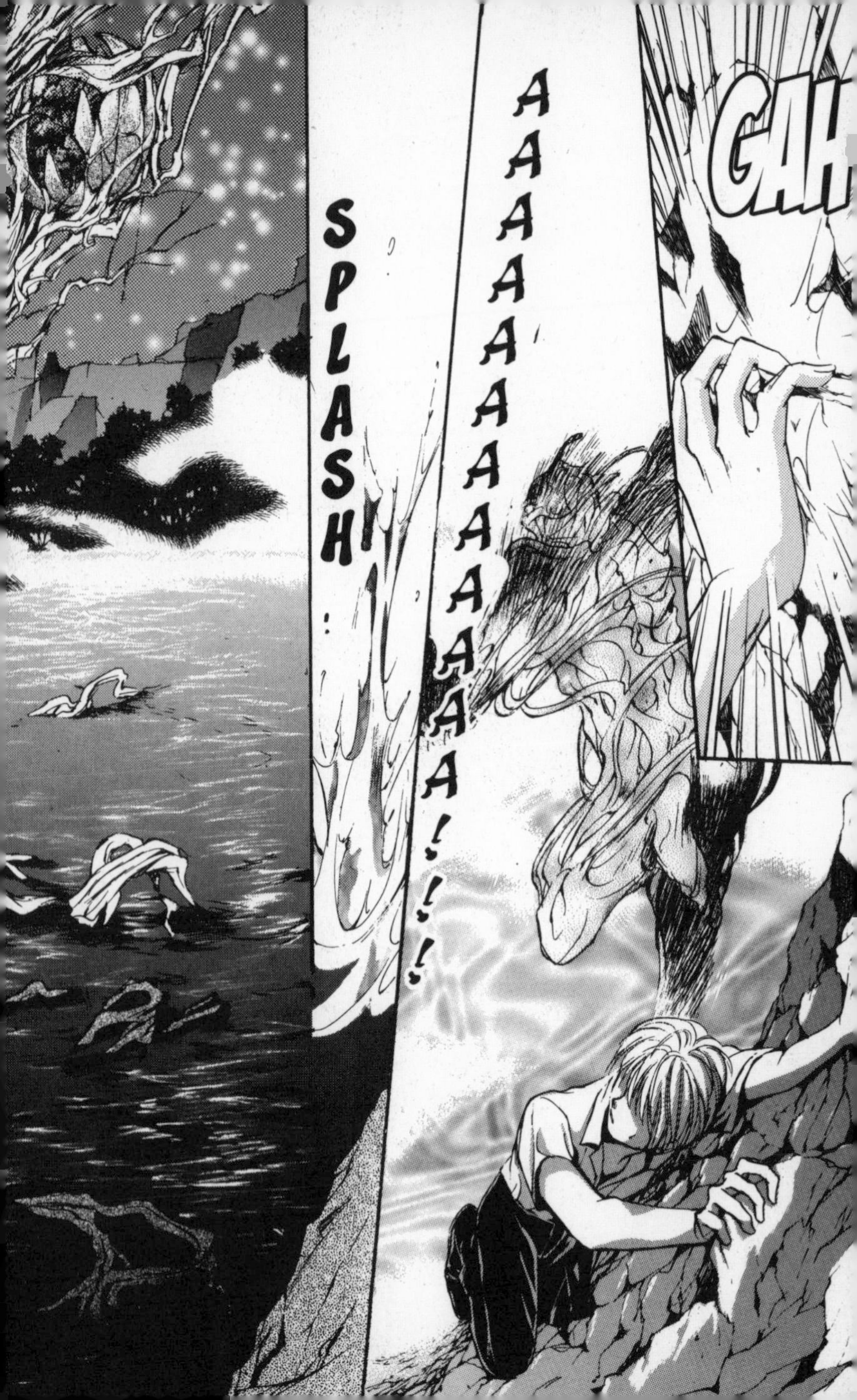
GAH
AAAAAAAAAAAA!!!
SPLASH

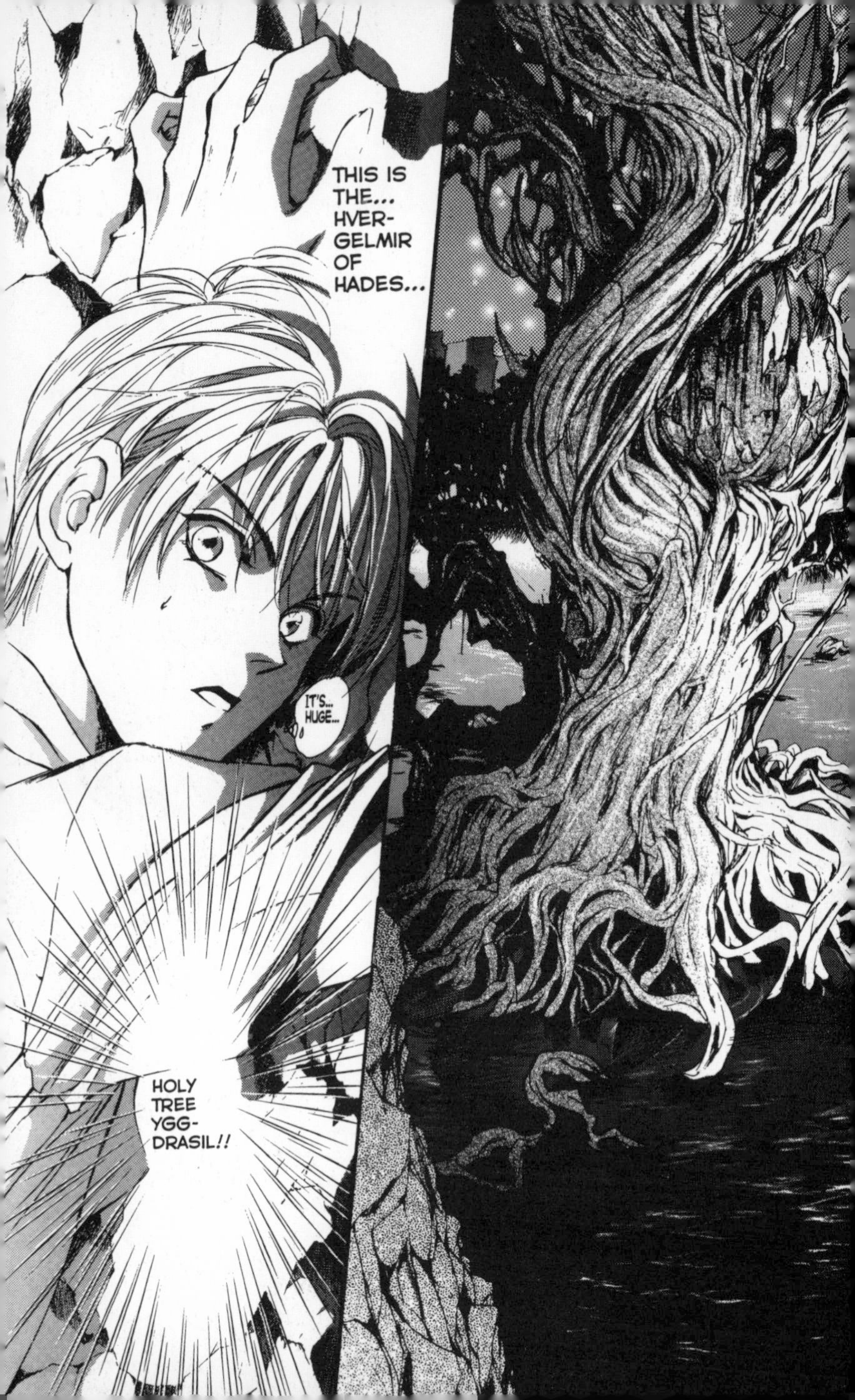
THIS IS THE... HVER-GELMIR OF HADES...
IT'S... HUGE...
HOLY TREE YGG-DRASIL!!

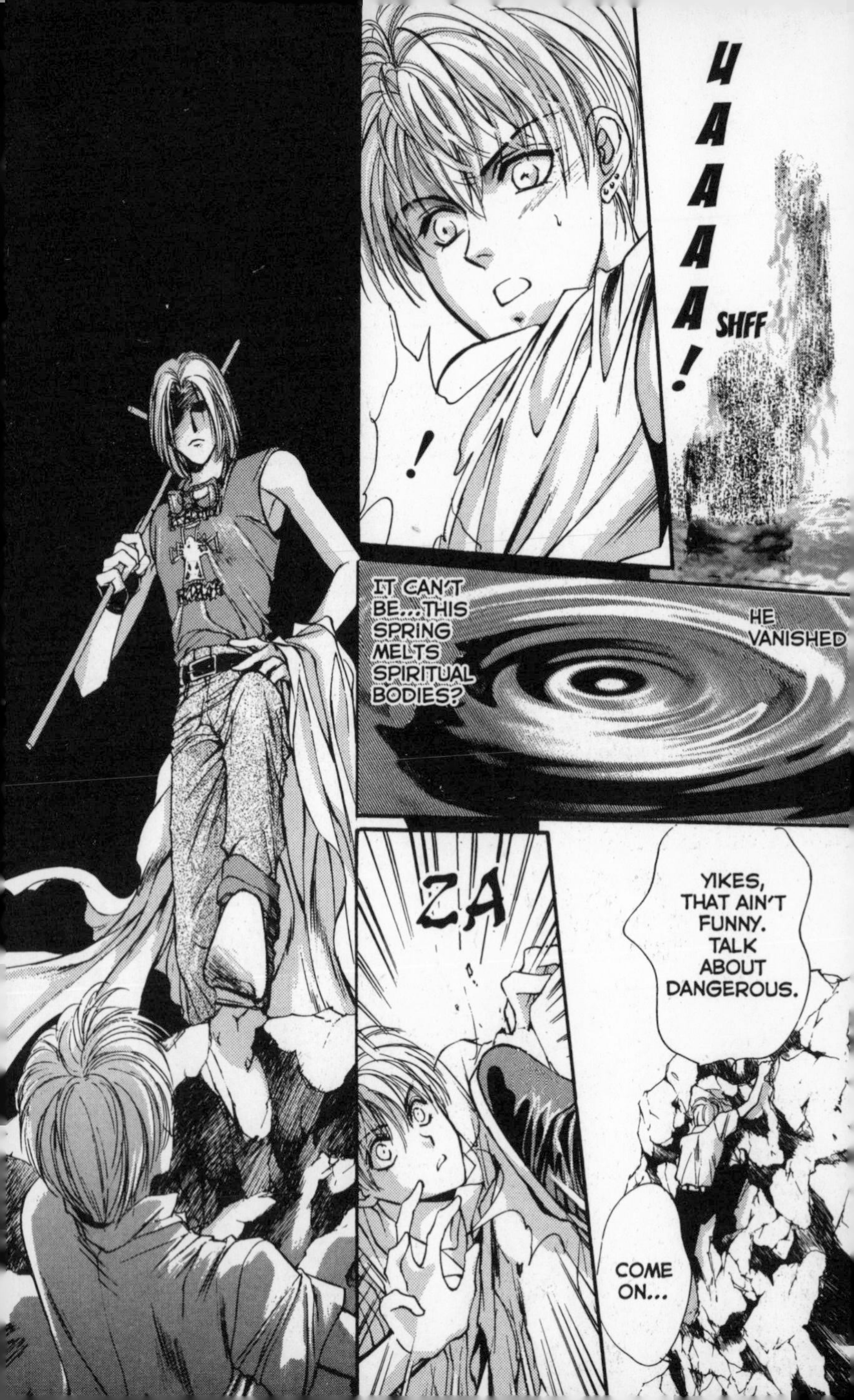
UAAAAA!
SHFF
!
HE VANISHED
IT CAN'T BE... THIS SPRING MELTS SPIRITUAL BODIES?
ZA
YIKES, THAT AIN'T FUNNY. TALK ABOUT DANGEROUS.
COME ON...

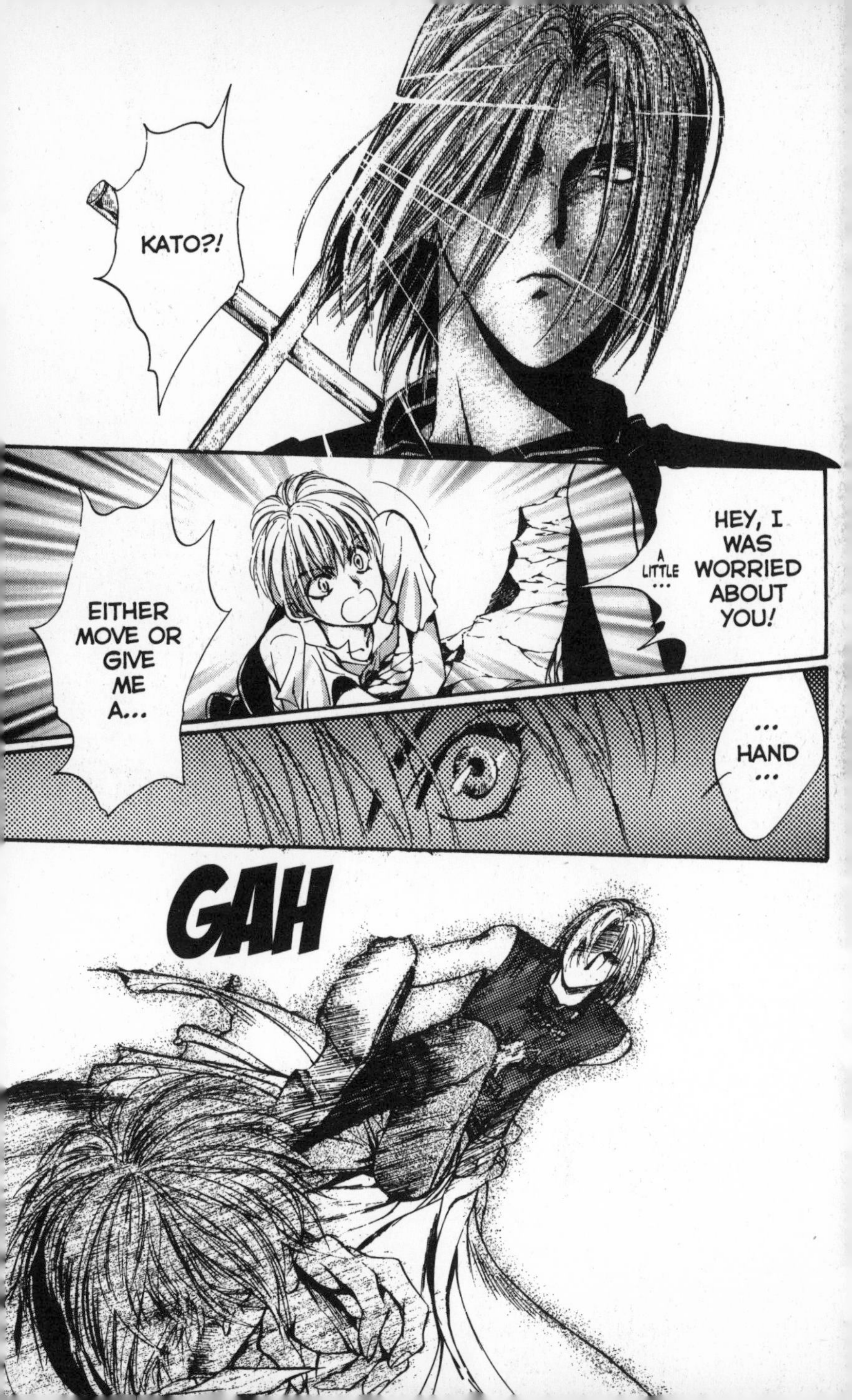
KATO?!
HEY, I WAS WORRIED ABOUT YOU!
A LITTLE ...
EITHER MOVE OR GIVE ME A...
... HAND ...
GAH

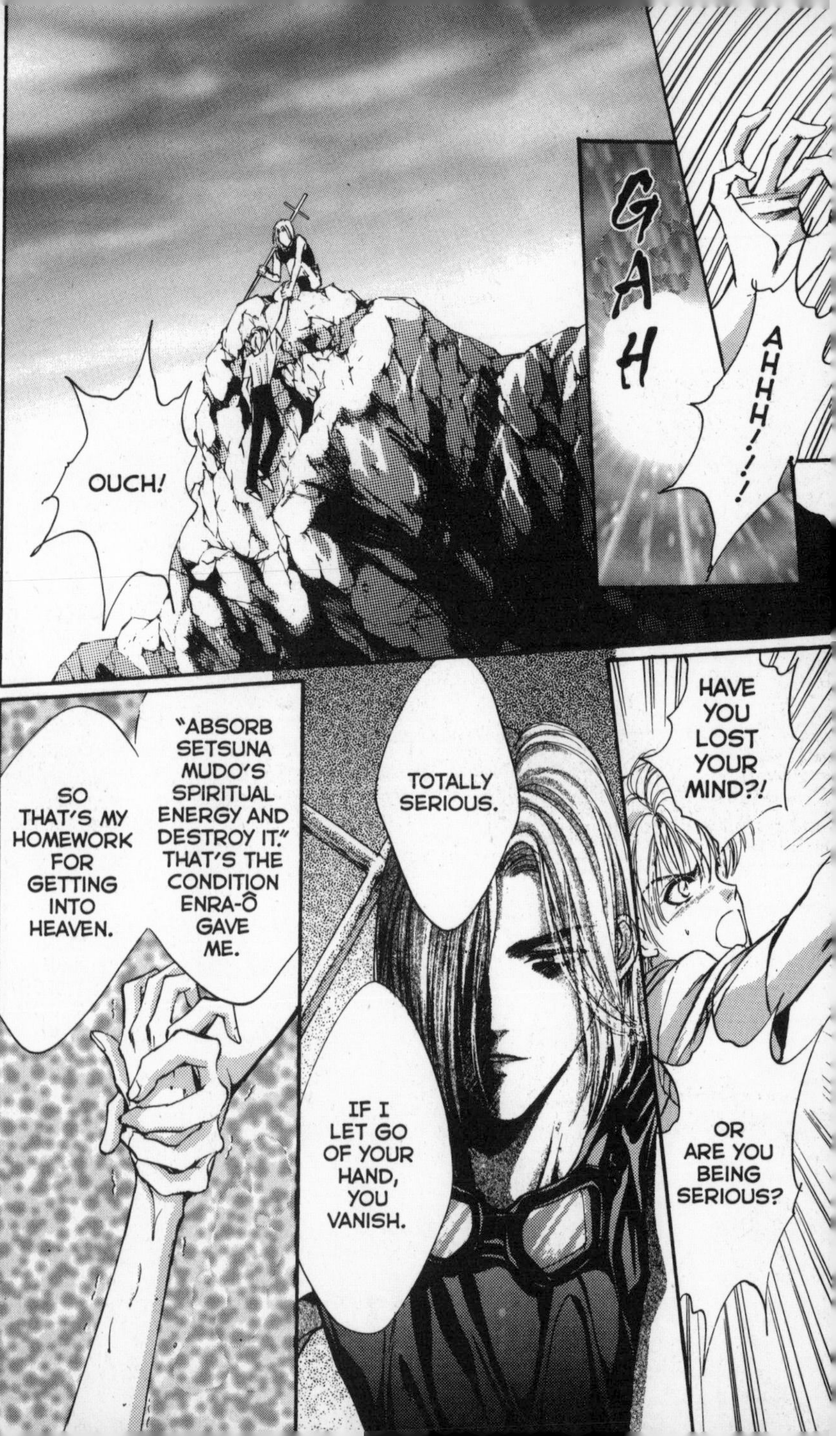
GAH
AHHH!!!
OUCH!
HAVE YOU LOST YOUR MIND?!
OR ARE YOU BEING SERIOUS?
TOTALLY SERIOUS.
IF I LET GO OF YOUR HAND, YOU VANISH.
"ABSORB SETSUNA MUDO'S SPIRITUAL ENERGY AND DESTROY IT." THAT'S THE CONDITION ENRA-Ô GAVE ME.
SO THAT'S MY HOMEWORK FOR GETTING INTO HEAVEN.

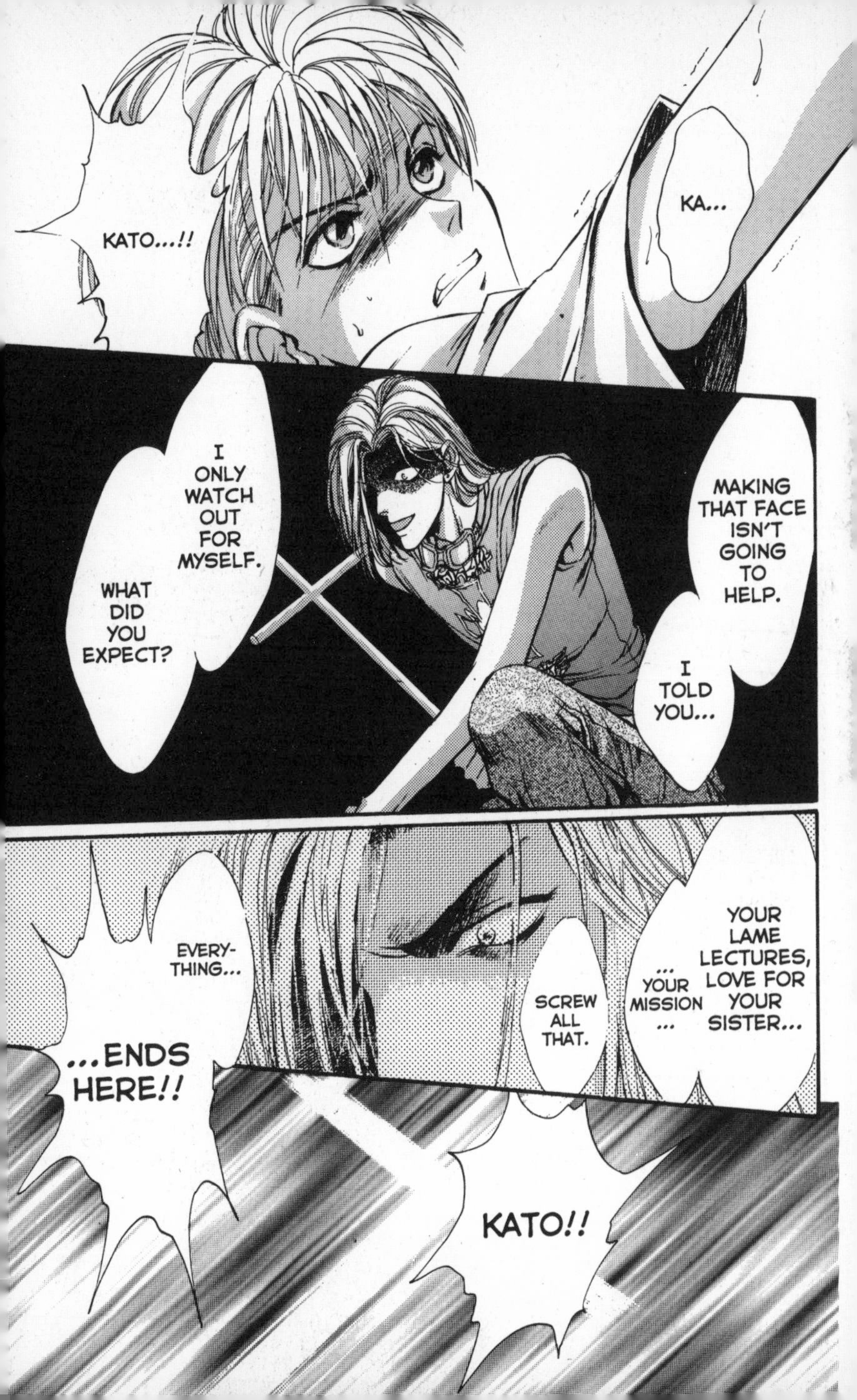
KA...
KATO...!!
MAKING THAT FACE ISN'T GOING TO HELP.
I TOLD YOU...
I ONLY WATCH OUT FOR MYSELF.
WHAT DID YOU EXPECT?
YOUR LAME LECTURES, LOVE FOR YOUR SISTER...
... YOUR MISSION ...
SCREW ALL THAT.
EVERY-THING...
...ENDS HERE!!
KATO!!

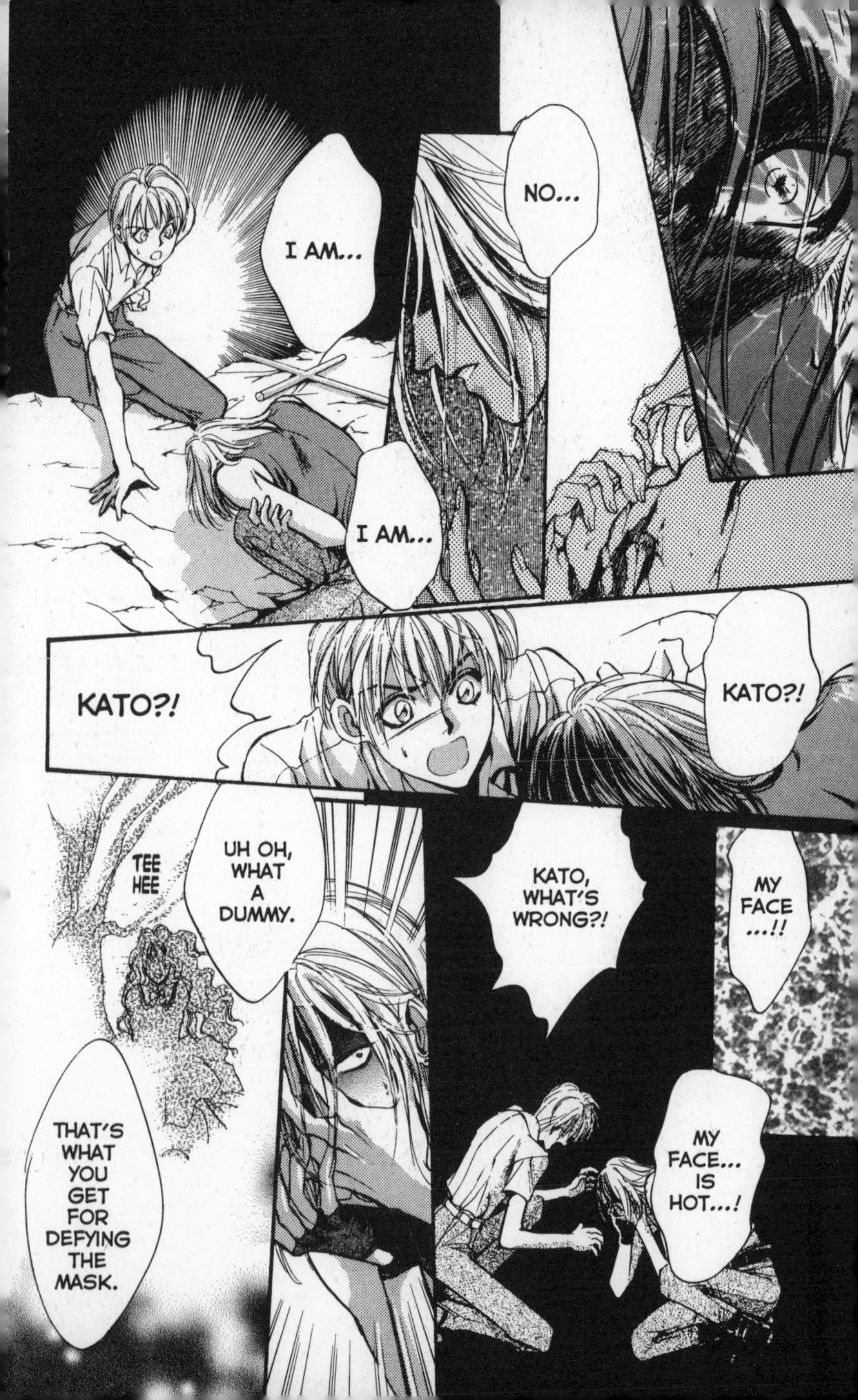
NO...
I AM...
I AM...
KATO?!
KATO?!
MY FACE ...!!
KATO, WHAT'S WRONG?!
MY FACE... IS HOT...!
UH OH, WHAT A DUMMY.
TEE HEE
THAT'S WHAT YOU GET FOR DEFYING THE MASK.

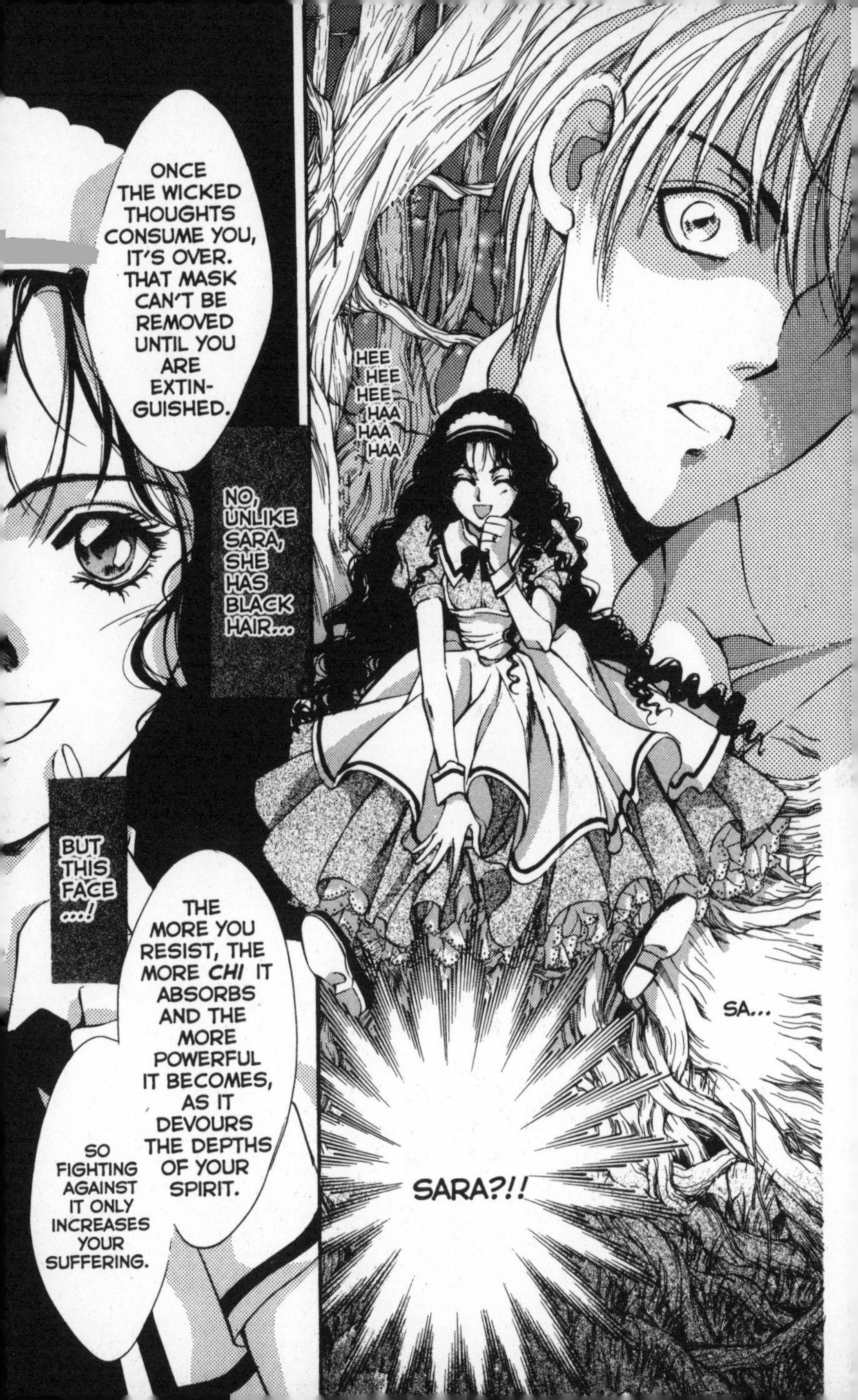
HEE HEE HEE HAA HAA HAA
SA...
SARA?!!
ONCE THE WICKED THOUGHTS CONSUME YOU, IT'S OVER. THAT MASK CAN'T BE REMOVED UNTIL YOU ARE EXTIN-GUISHED.
NO, UNLIKE SARA, SHE HAS BLACK HAIR...
BUT THIS FACE ...!
THE MORE YOU RESIST, THE MORE CHI IT ABSORBS AND THE MORE POWERFUL IT BECOMES, AS IT DEVOURS THE DEPTHS OF YOUR SPIRIT.
SO FIGHTING AGAINST IT ONLY INCREASES YOUR SUFFERING.

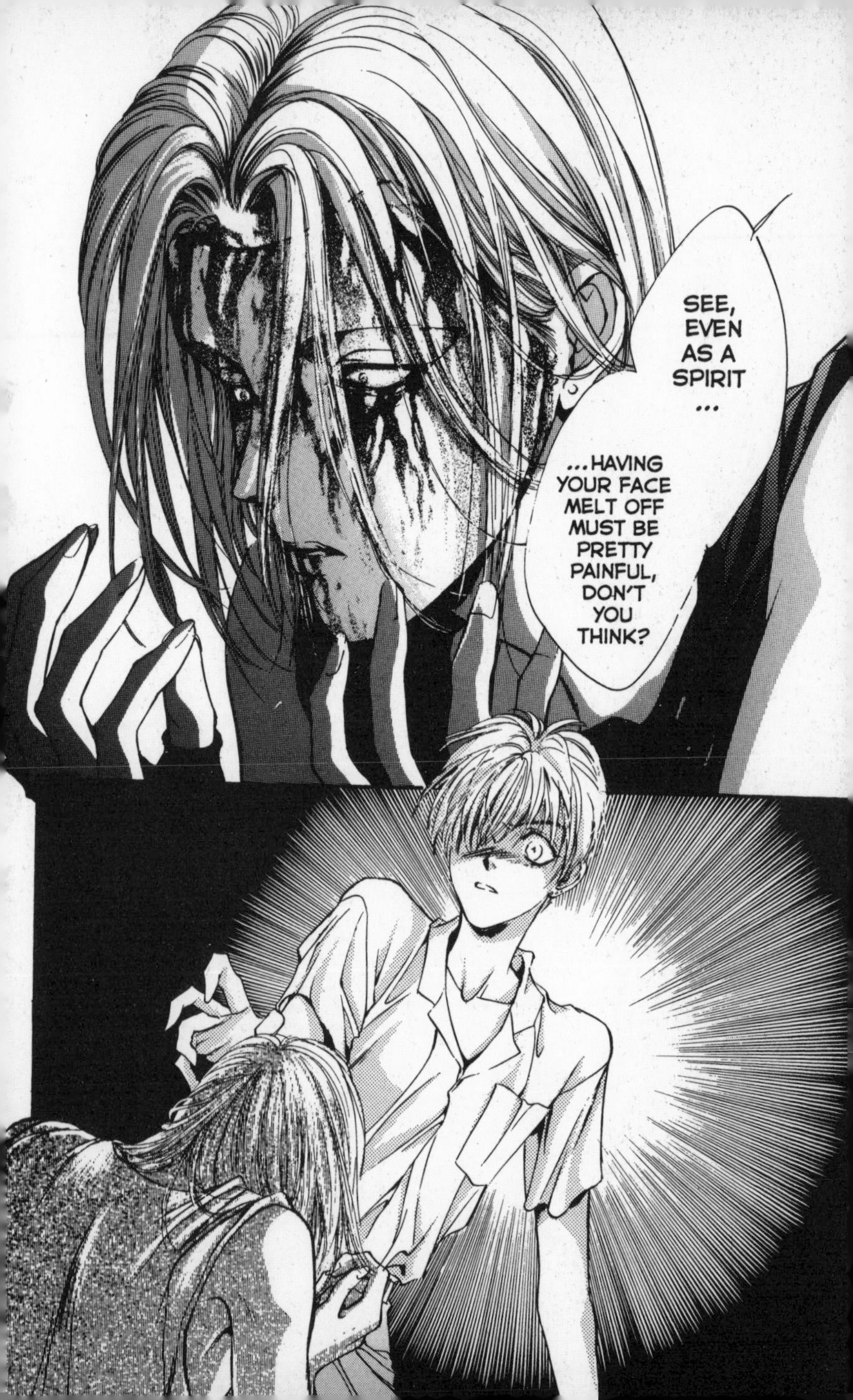
SEE, EVEN AS A SPIRIT ...
...HAVING YOUR FACE MELT OFF MUST BE PRETTY PAINFUL, DON'T YOU THINK?

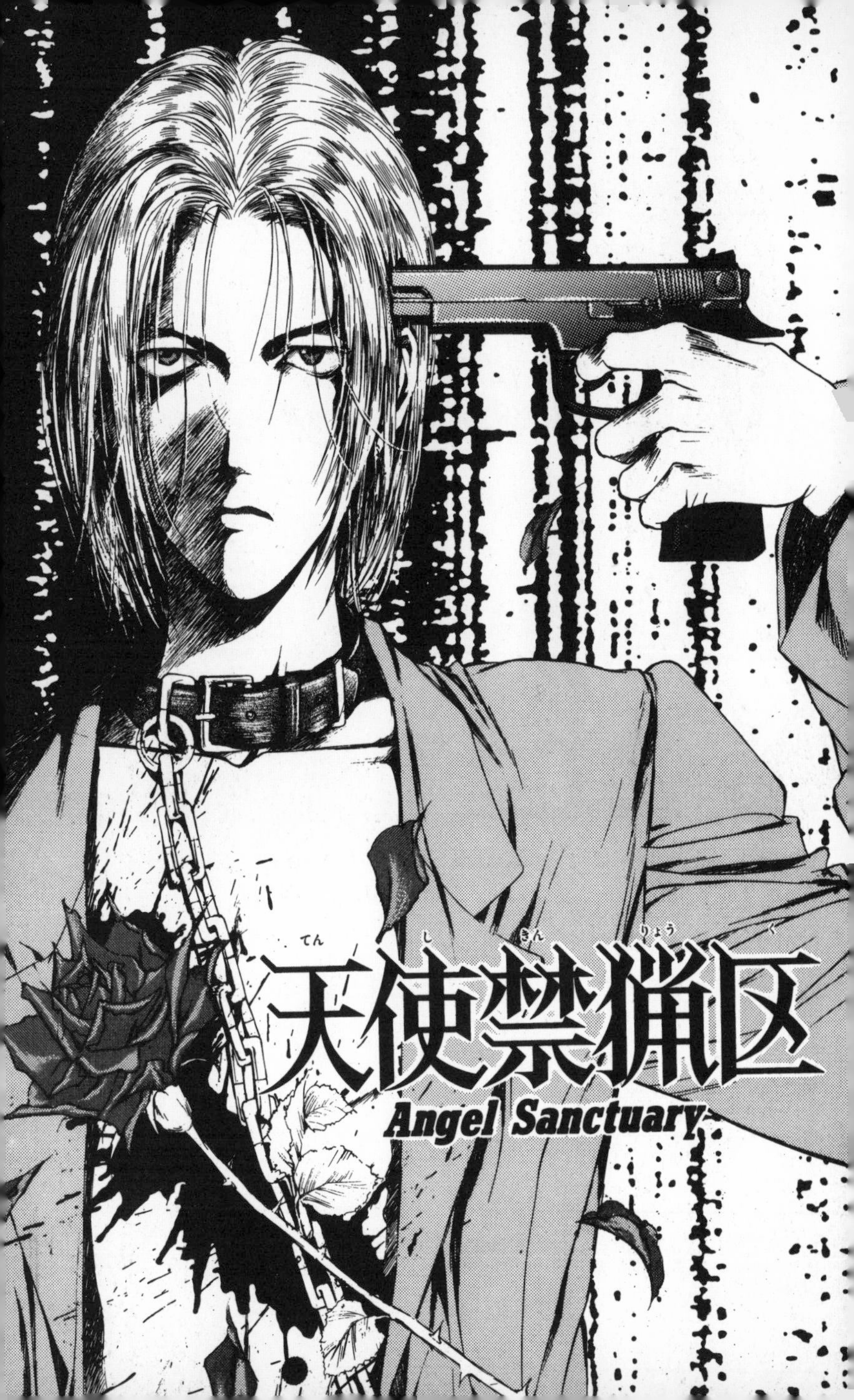
天使禁猟区
Angel Sanctuary

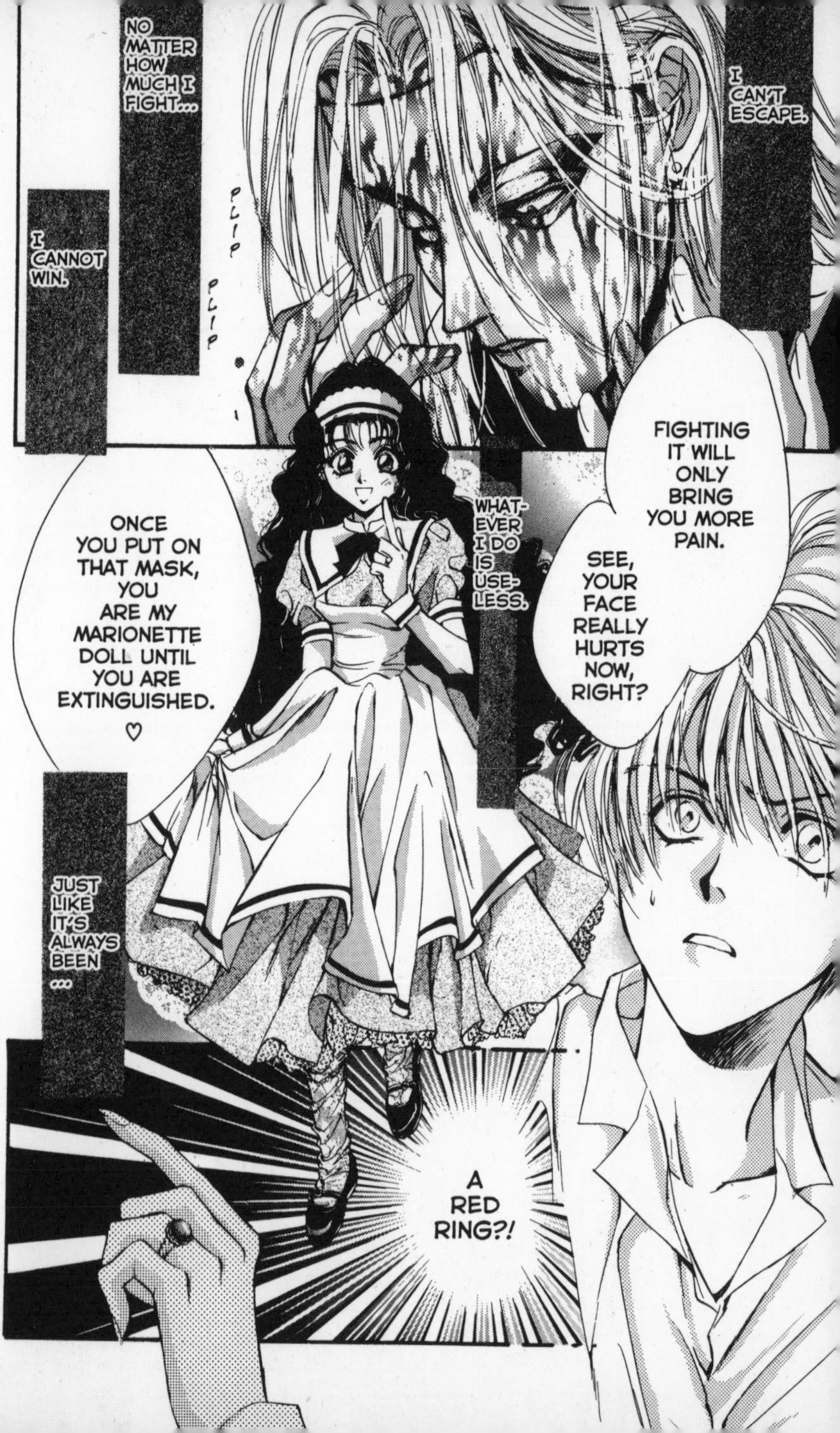
I CAN'T ESCAPE.
NO MATTER HOW MUCH I FIGHT...
PLIP PLIP
I CANNOT WIN.
FIGHTING IT WILL ONLY BRING YOU MORE PAIN.
SEE, YOUR FACE REALLY HURTS NOW, RIGHT?
WHAT-EVER I DO IS USE-LESS.
ONCE YOU PUT ON THAT MASK, YOU ARE MY MARIONETTE DOLL UNTIL YOU ARE EXTINGUISHED. ♡
JUST LIKE IT'S ALWAYS BEEN ...
A RED RING?!

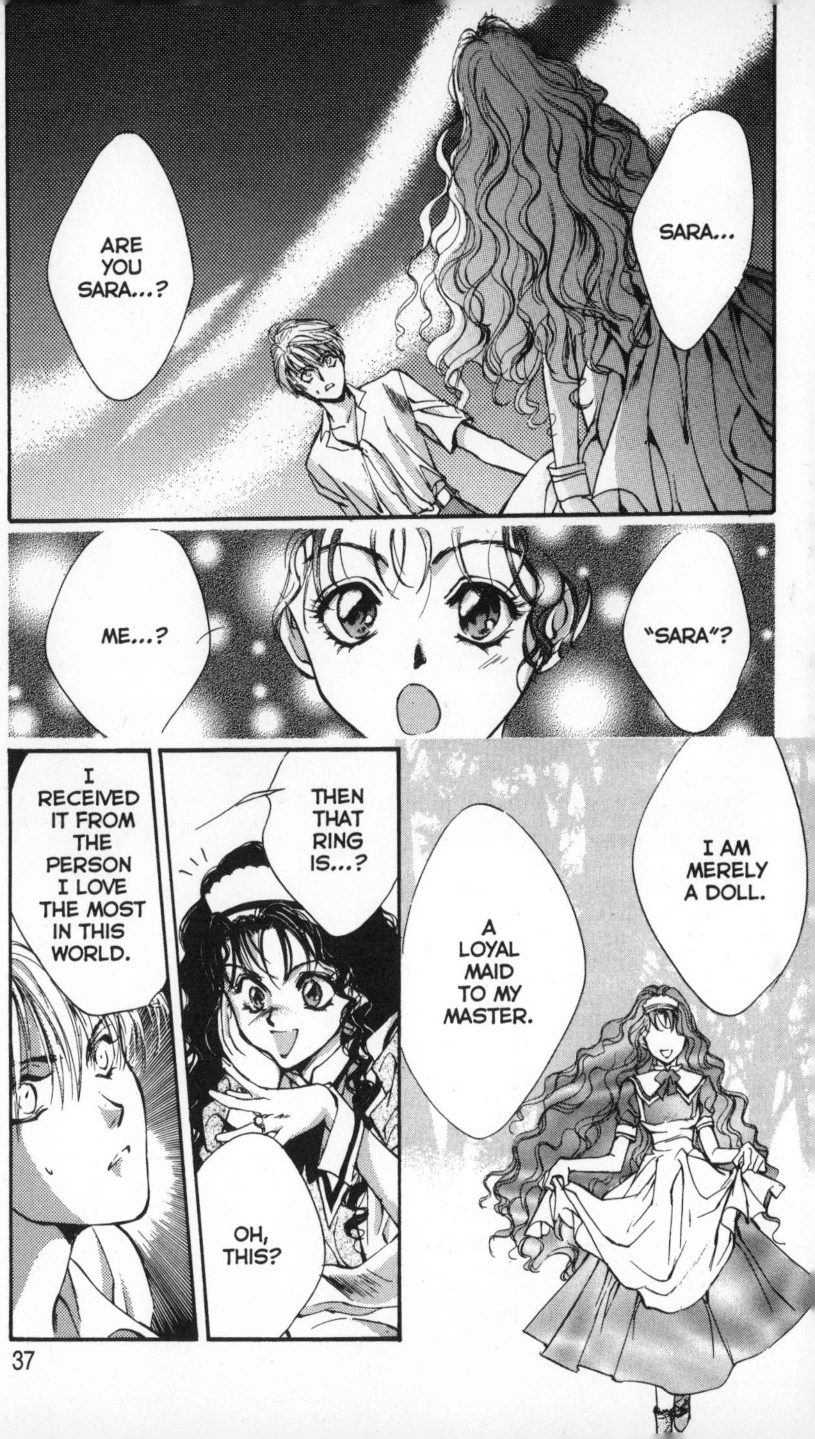
SARA...
ARE YOU SARA...?
"SARA"?
ME...?
I AM MERELY A DOLL.
A LOYAL MAID TO MY MASTER.
THEN THAT RING IS...?
OH, THIS?
I RECEIVED IT FROM THE PERSON I LOVE THE MOST IN THIS WORLD.

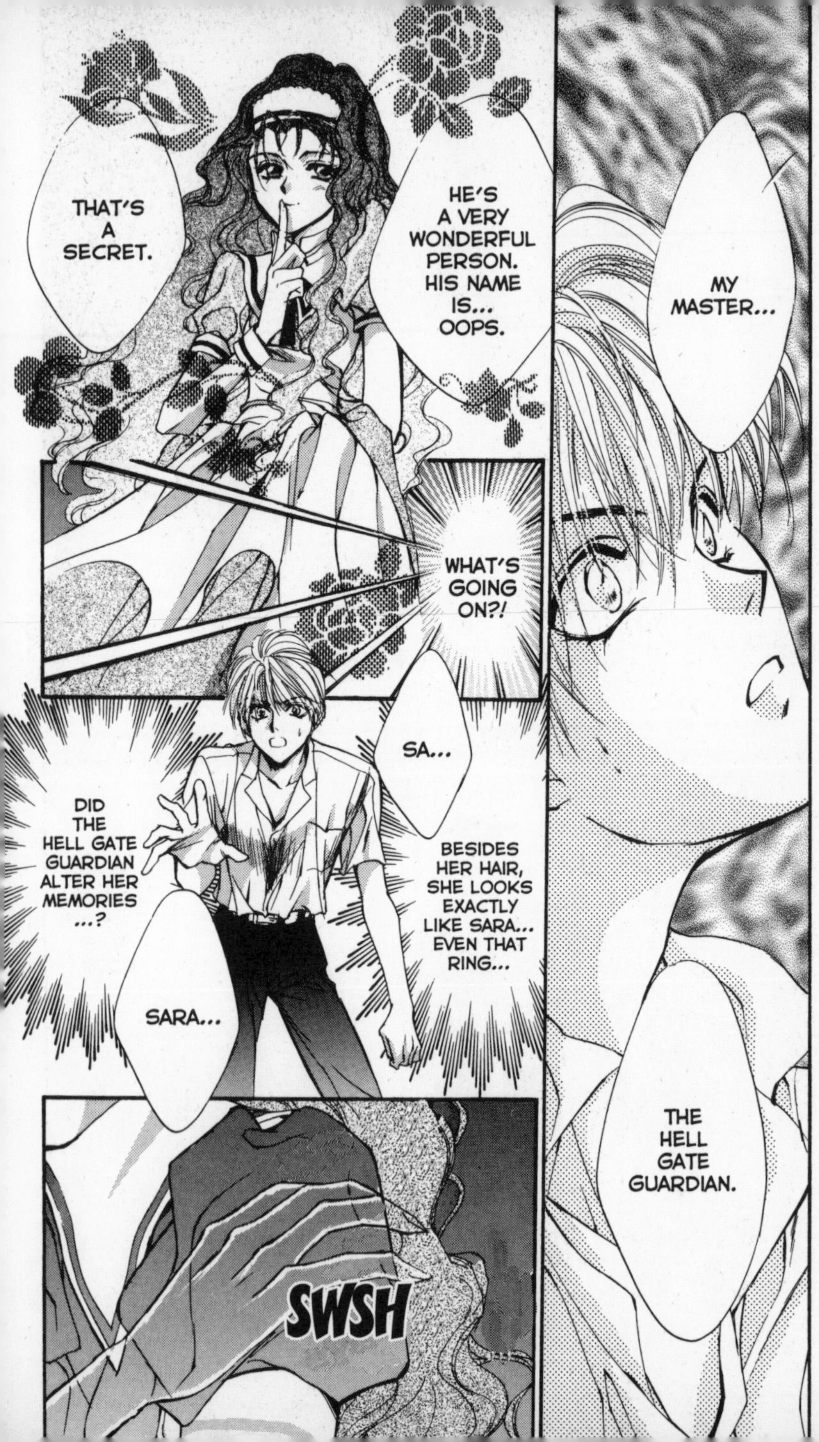
MY MASTER...
THE HELL GATE GUARDIAN.
HE'S A VERY WONDERFUL PERSON. HIS NAME IS... OOPS.
THAT'S A SECRET.
WHAT'S GOING ON?!
SA...
BESIDES HER HAIR, SHE LOOKS EXACTLY LIKE SARA... EVEN THAT RING...
DID THE HELL GATE GUARDIAN ALTER HER MEMORIES ...?
SARA...
SWSH

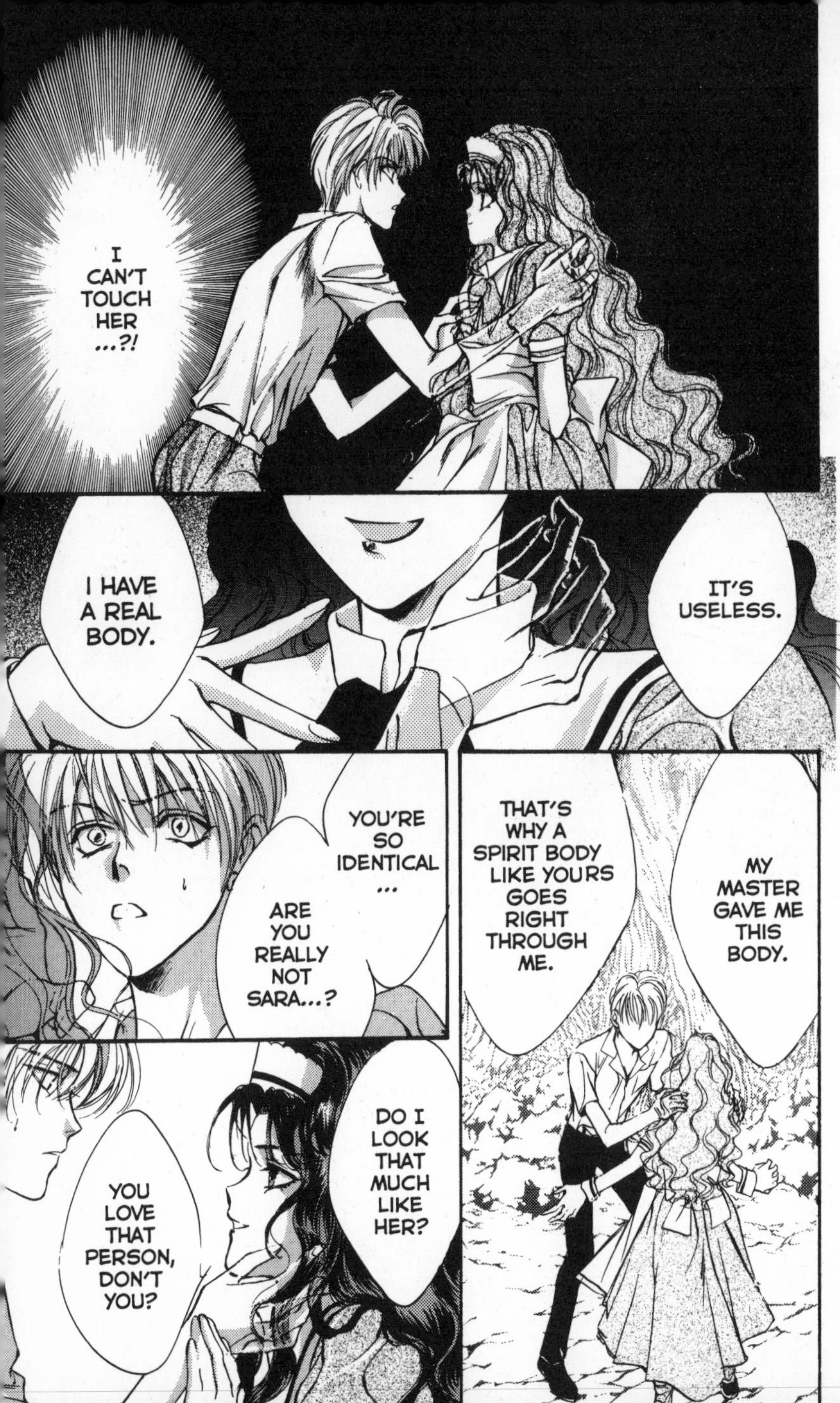
I CAN'T TOUCH HER ...?!
IT'S USELESS.
I HAVE A REAL BODY.
MY MASTER GAVE ME THIS BODY.
THAT'S WHY A SPIRIT BODY LIKE YOURS GOES RIGHT THROUGH ME.
YOU'RE SO IDENTICAL ...
ARE YOU REALLY NOT SARA...?
DO I LOOK THAT MUCH LIKE HER?
YOU LOVE THAT PERSON, DON'T YOU?

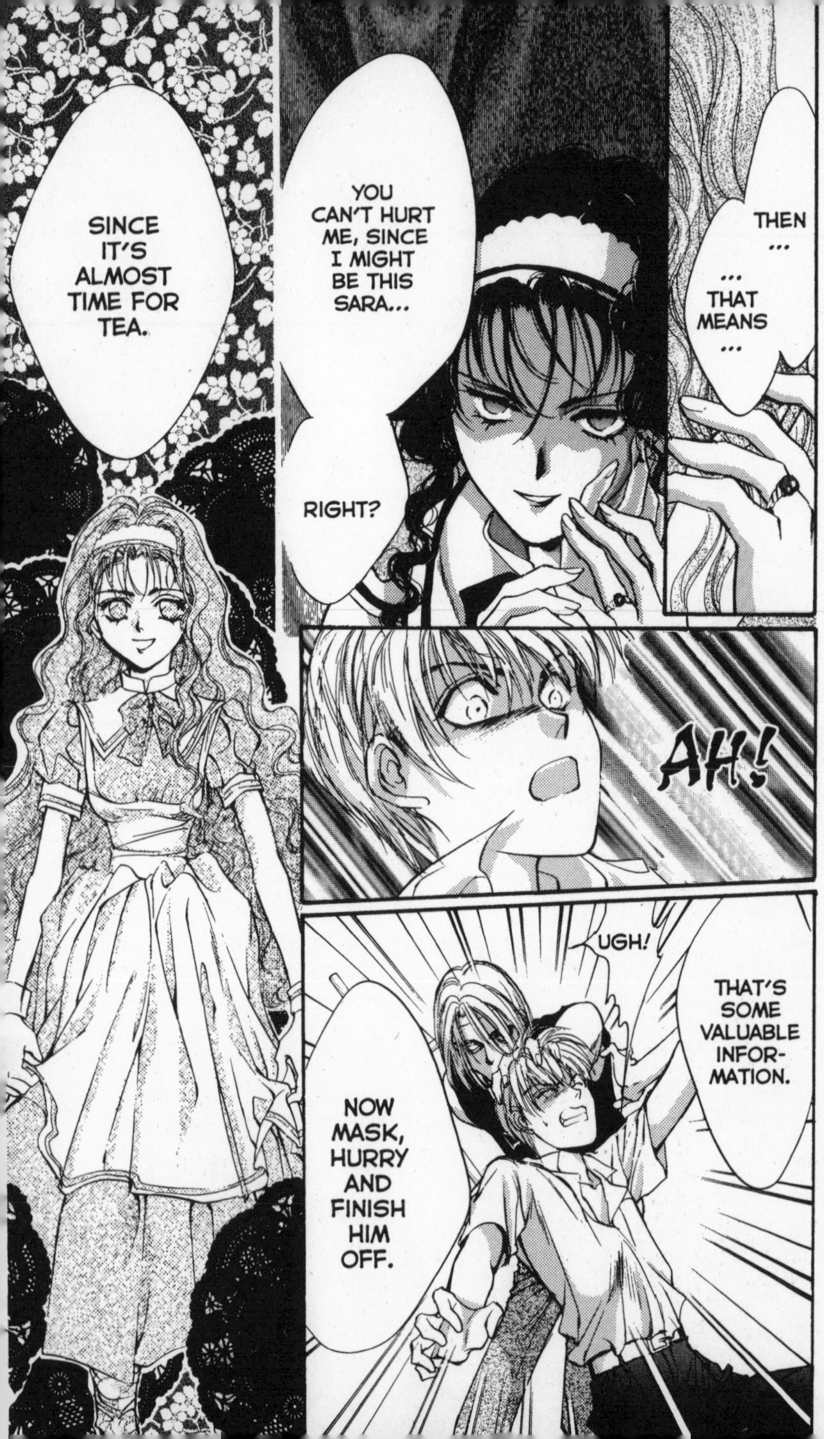
THEN ...
... THAT MEANS ...
YOU CAN'T HURT ME, SINCE I MIGHT BE THIS SARA...
RIGHT?
AH!
UGH!
THAT'S SOME VALUABLE INFOR-MATION.
NOW MASK, HURRY AND FINISH HIM OFF.
SINCE IT'S ALMOST TIME FOR TEA.

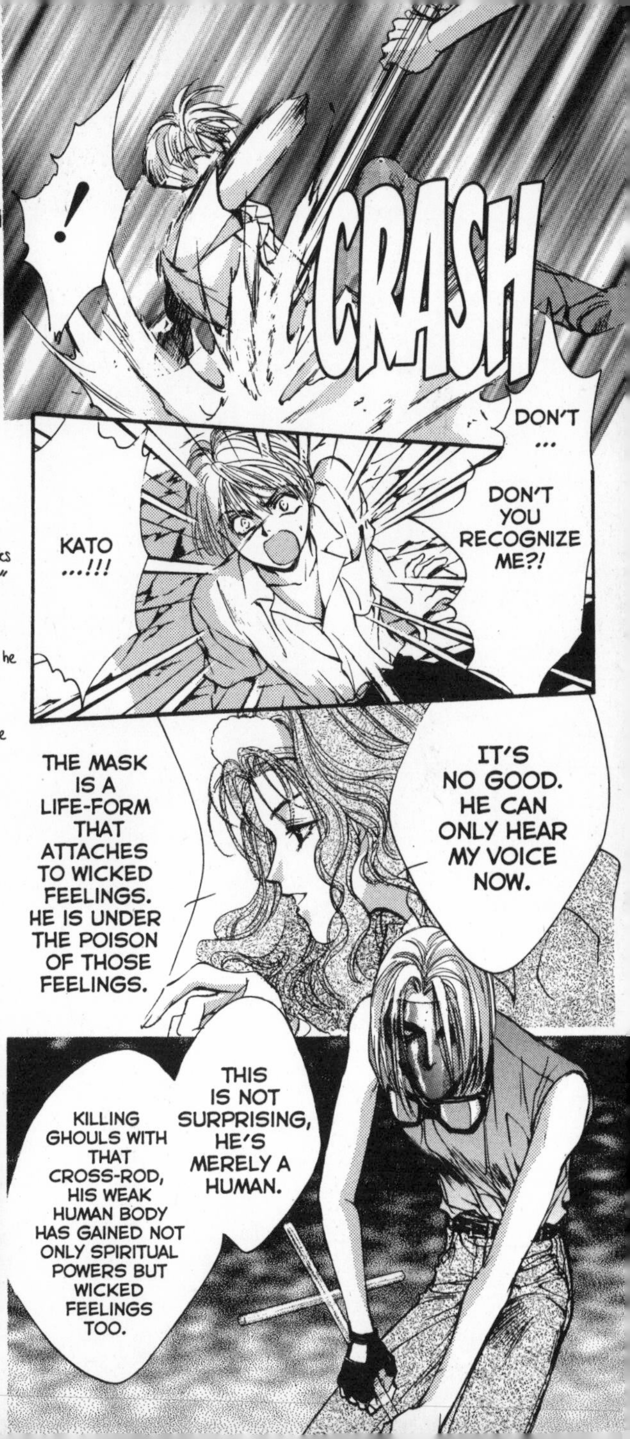
CRASH
!
DON'T ...
DON'T YOU RECOGNIZE ME?!
KATO ...!!!
IT'S NO GOOD. HE CAN ONLY HEAR MY VOICE NOW.
THE MASK IS A LIFE-FORM THAT ATTACHES TO WICKED FEELINGS. HE IS UNDER THE POISON OF THOSE FEELINGS.
THIS IS NOT SURPRISING, HE'S MERELY A HUMAN.
KILLING GHOULS WITH THAT CROSS-ROD, HIS WEAK HUMAN BODY HAS GAINED NOT ONLY SPIRITUAL POWERS BUT WICKED FEELINGS TOO.

"No matter how you think about it, Kato is gay," an assistant said to me. To which I responded with a resounding "Yes, you're right." Well, so many people share that opinion on him. "On the cover picture for chapter 5 of vol.4 where Kira is piercing the ears of Kato and Setsuna, is that the same room where Kira talks to Kato within the series?" I can't believe I get such specific questions like that! That's Kira's loft where he hides AND hangs out...

Not like it comes up in the actual series though.

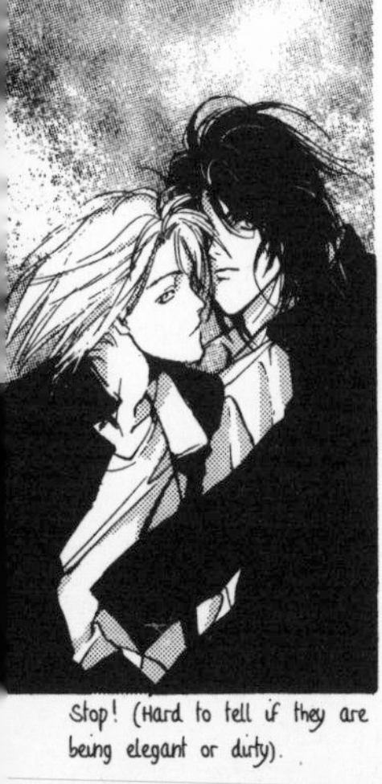

Stop! (Hard to tell if they are being elegant or dirty).

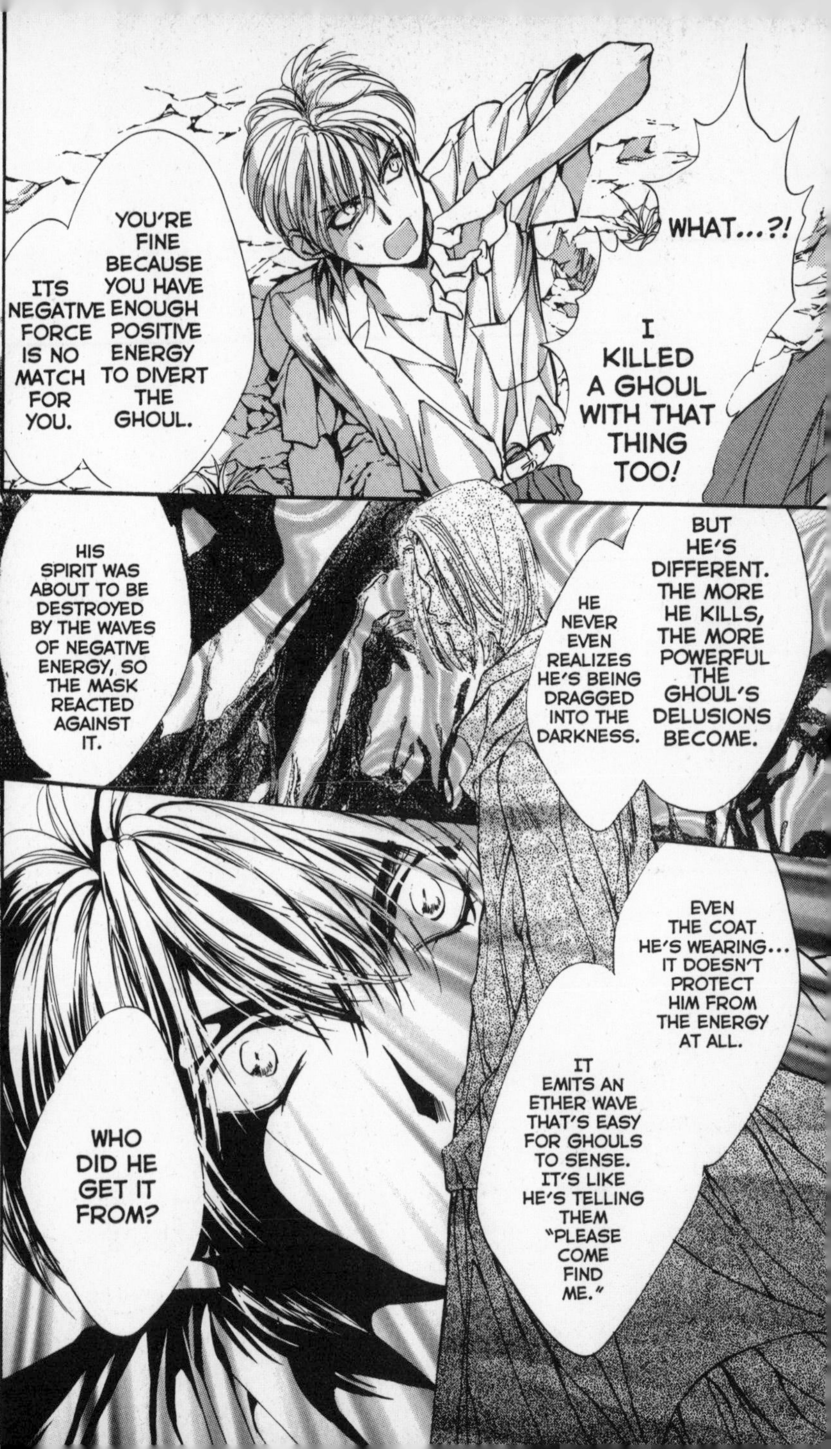
WHAT...?!
I KILLED A GHOUL WITH THAT THING TOO!
YOU'RE FINE BECAUSE YOU HAVE ENOUGH POSITIVE ENERGY TO DIVERT THE GHOUL.
ITS NEGATIVE FORCE IS NO MATCH FOR YOU.
BUT HE'S DIFFERENT. THE MORE HE KILLS, THE MORE POWERFUL THE GHOUL'S DELUSIONS BECOME.
HE NEVER EVEN REALIZES HE'S BEING DRAGGED INTO THE DARKNESS.
HIS SPIRIT WAS ABOUT TO BE DESTROYED BY THE WAVES OF NEGATIVE ENERGY, SO THE MASK REACTED AGAINST IT.
EVEN THE COAT HE'S WEARING... IT DOESN'T PROTECT HIM FROM THE ENERGY AT ALL.
IT EMITS AN ETHER WAVE THAT'S EASY FOR GHOULS TO SENSE. IT'S LIKE HE'S TELLING THEM "PLEASE COME FIND ME."
WHO DID HE GET IT FROM?

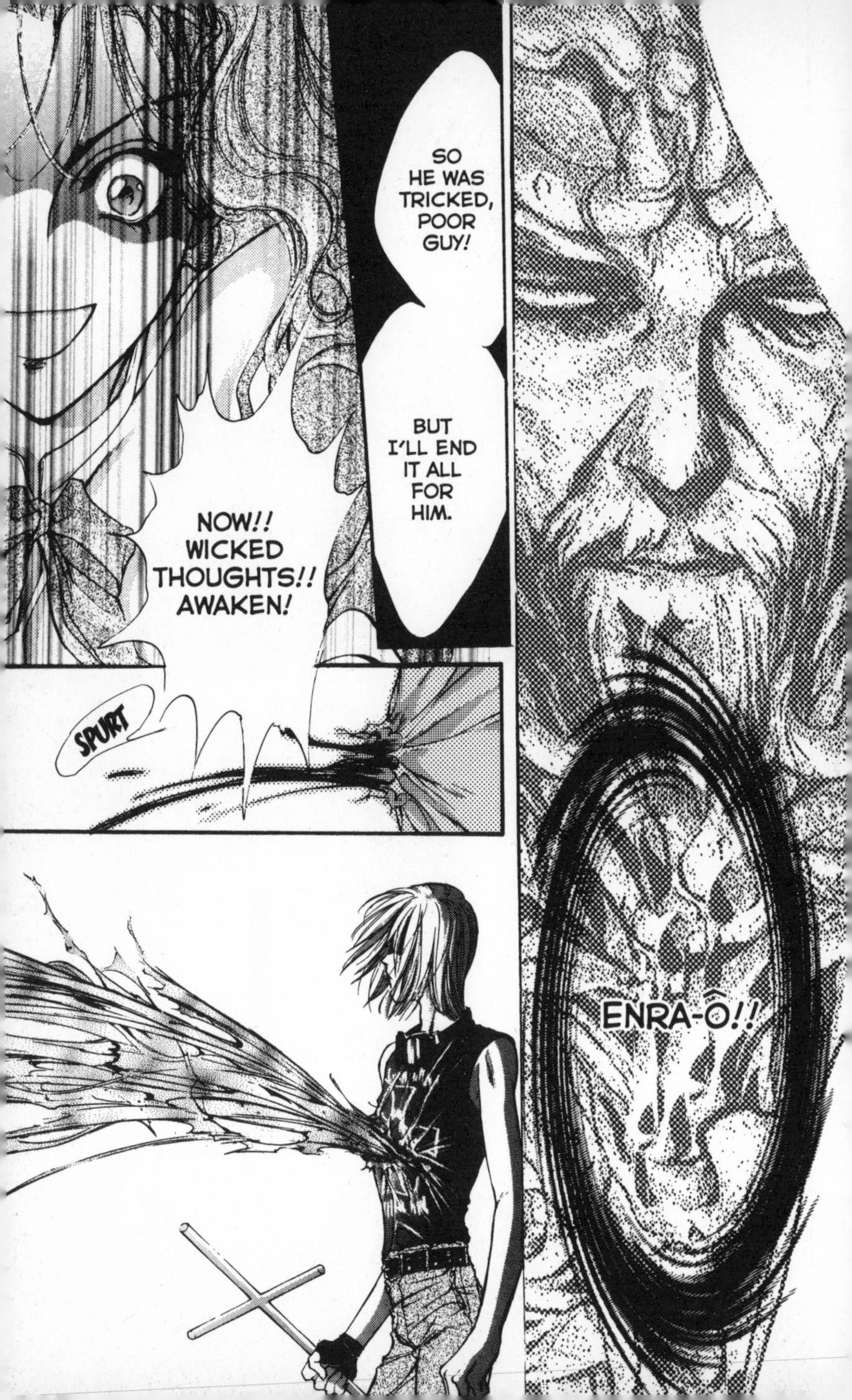
ENRA-Ô!!
SO HE WAS TRICKED, POOR GUY!
BUT I'LL END IT ALL FOR HIM.
NOW!! WICKED THOUGHTS!! AWAKEN!
SPURT

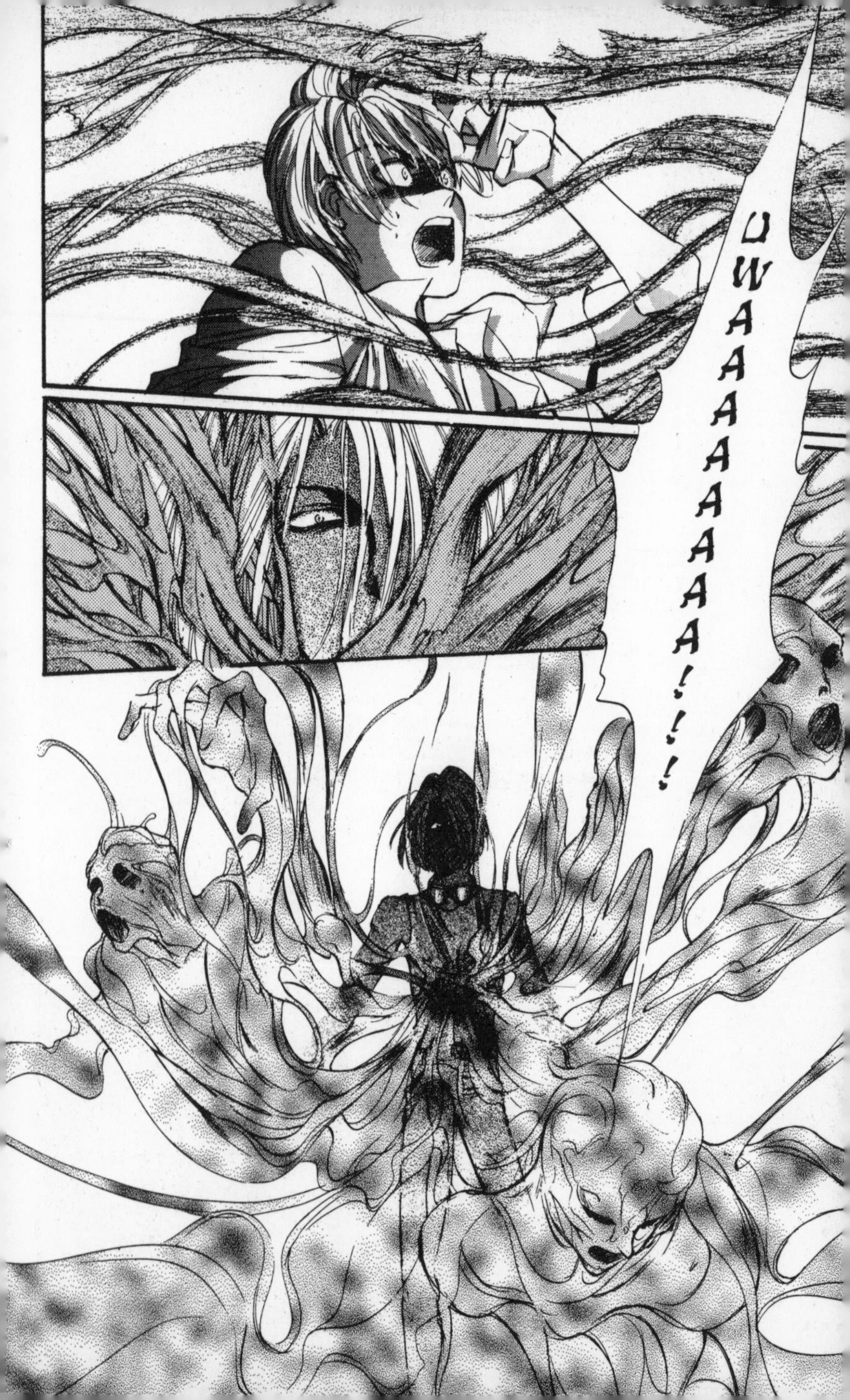
UWAAAAAAAAAAA!!!!

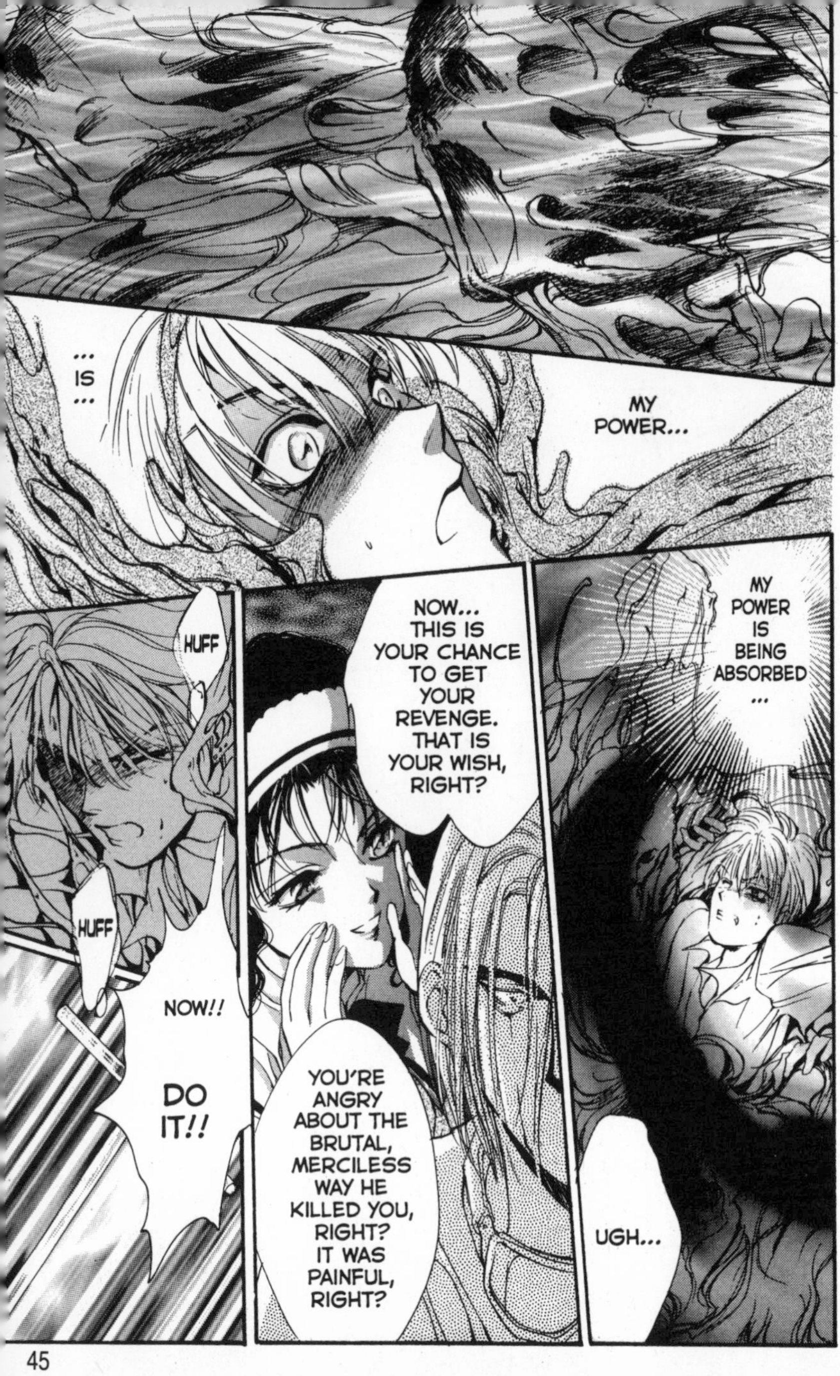
MY POWER...
... IS ...
MY POWER IS BEING ABSORBED ...
UGH...
NOW... THIS IS YOUR CHANCE TO GET YOUR REVENGE. THAT IS YOUR WISH, RIGHT?
YOU'RE ANGRY ABOUT THE BRUTAL, MERCILESS WAY HE KILLED YOU, RIGHT? IT WAS PAINFUL, RIGHT?
HUFF
HUFF
NOW!!
DO IT!!

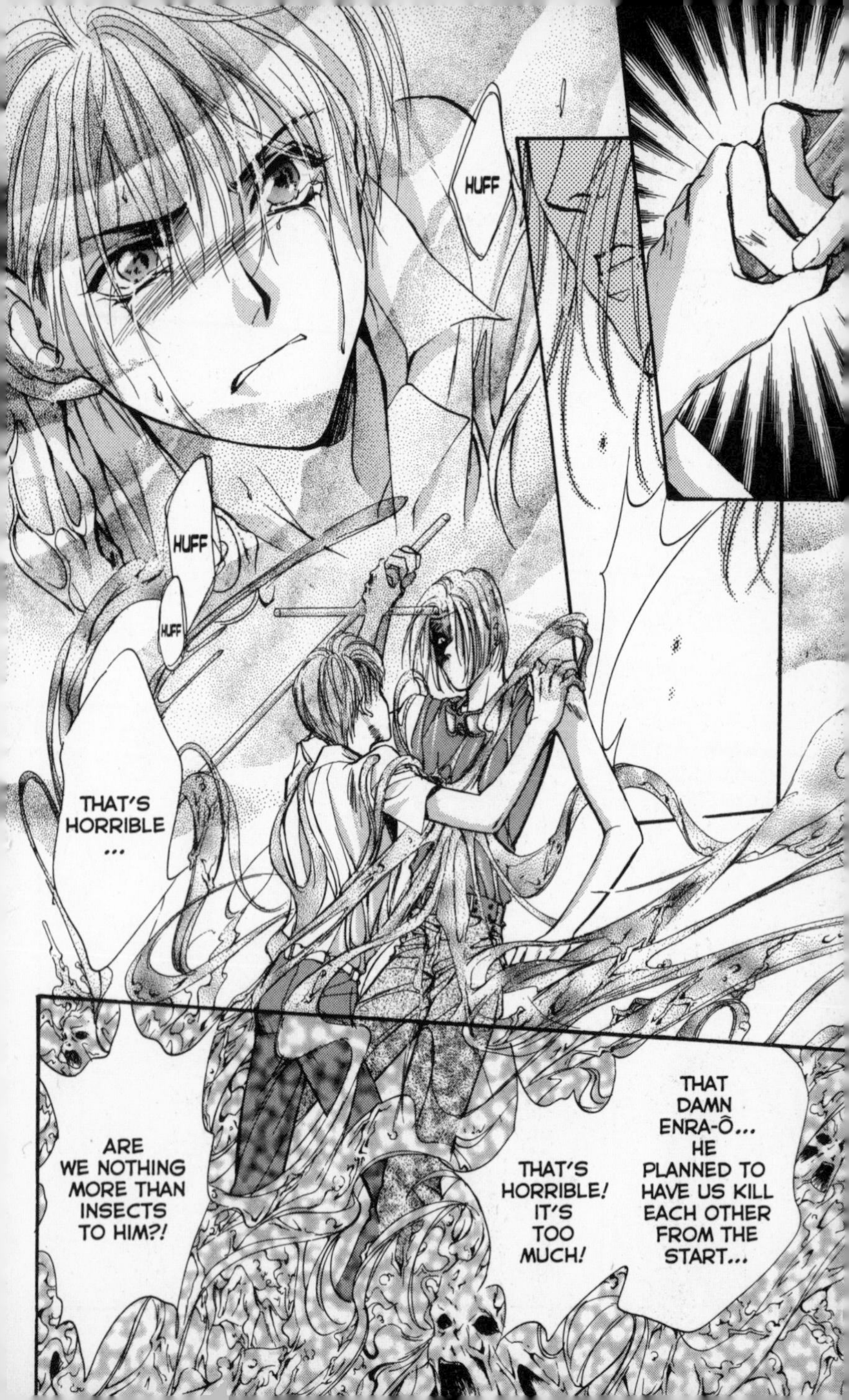
HUFF
HUFF
HUFF
THAT'S HORRIBLE ...
THAT DAMN ENRA-Ô... HE PLANNED TO HAVE US KILL EACH OTHER FROM THE START...
THAT'S HORRIBLE! IT'S TOO MUCH!
ARE WE NOTHING MORE THAN INSECTS TO HIM?!

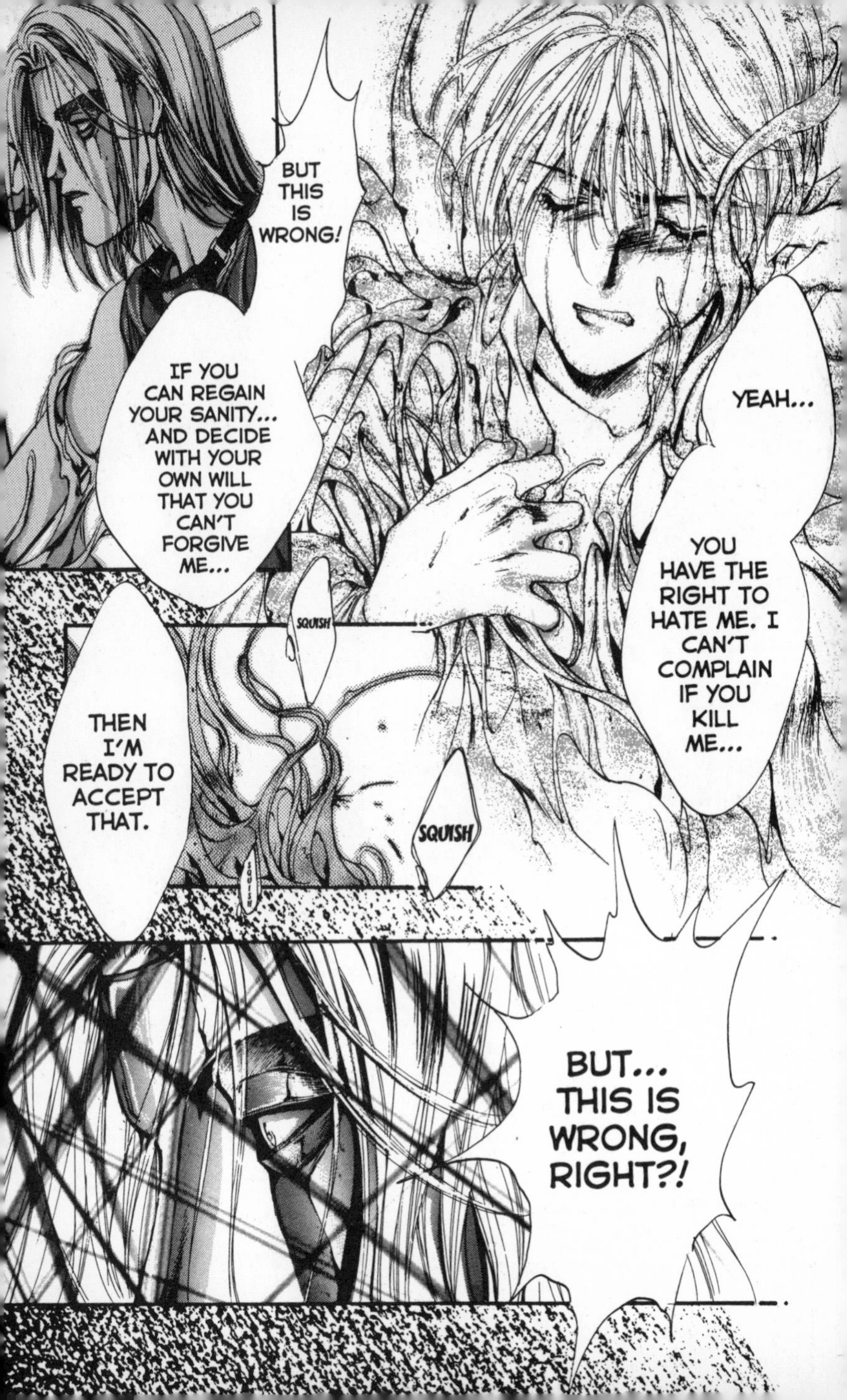
YEAH...
YOU HAVE THE RIGHT TO HATE ME. I CAN'T COMPLAIN IF YOU KILL ME...
BUT THIS IS WRONG!
IF YOU CAN REGAIN YOUR SANITY... AND DECIDE WITH YOUR OWN WILL THAT YOU CAN'T FORGIVE ME...
SQUISH
SQUISH
SQUISH
THEN I'M READY TO ACCEPT THAT.
BUT... THIS IS WRONG, RIGHT?!

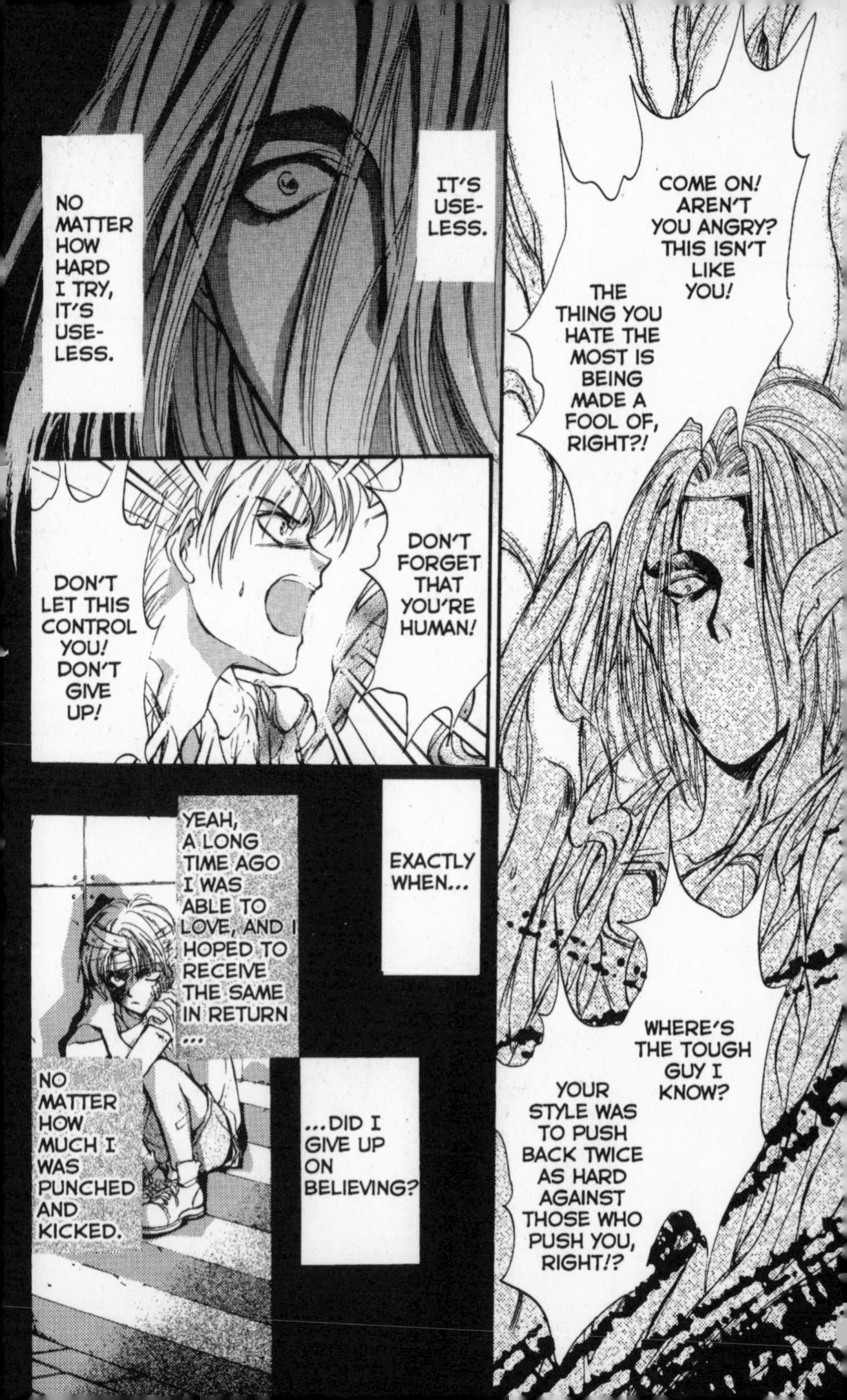
COME ON! AREN'T YOU ANGRY? THIS ISN'T LIKE YOU!
THE THING YOU HATE THE MOST IS BEING MADE A FOOL OF, RIGHT?!
WHERE'S THE TOUGH GUY I KNOW?
YOUR STYLE WAS TO PUSH BACK TWICE AS HARD AGAINST THOSE WHO PUSH YOU, RIGHT!?
IT'S USELESS.
NO MATTER HOW HARD I TRY, IT'S USELESS.
DON'T FORGET THAT YOU'RE HUMAN!
DON'T LET THIS CONTROL YOU! DON'T GIVE UP!
EXACTLY WHEN...
YEAH, A LONG TIME AGO I WAS ABLE TO LOVE, AND I HOPED TO RECEIVE THE SAME IN RETURN...
...DID I GIVE UP ON BELIEVING?
NO MATTER HOW MUCH I WAS PUNCHED AND KICKED.

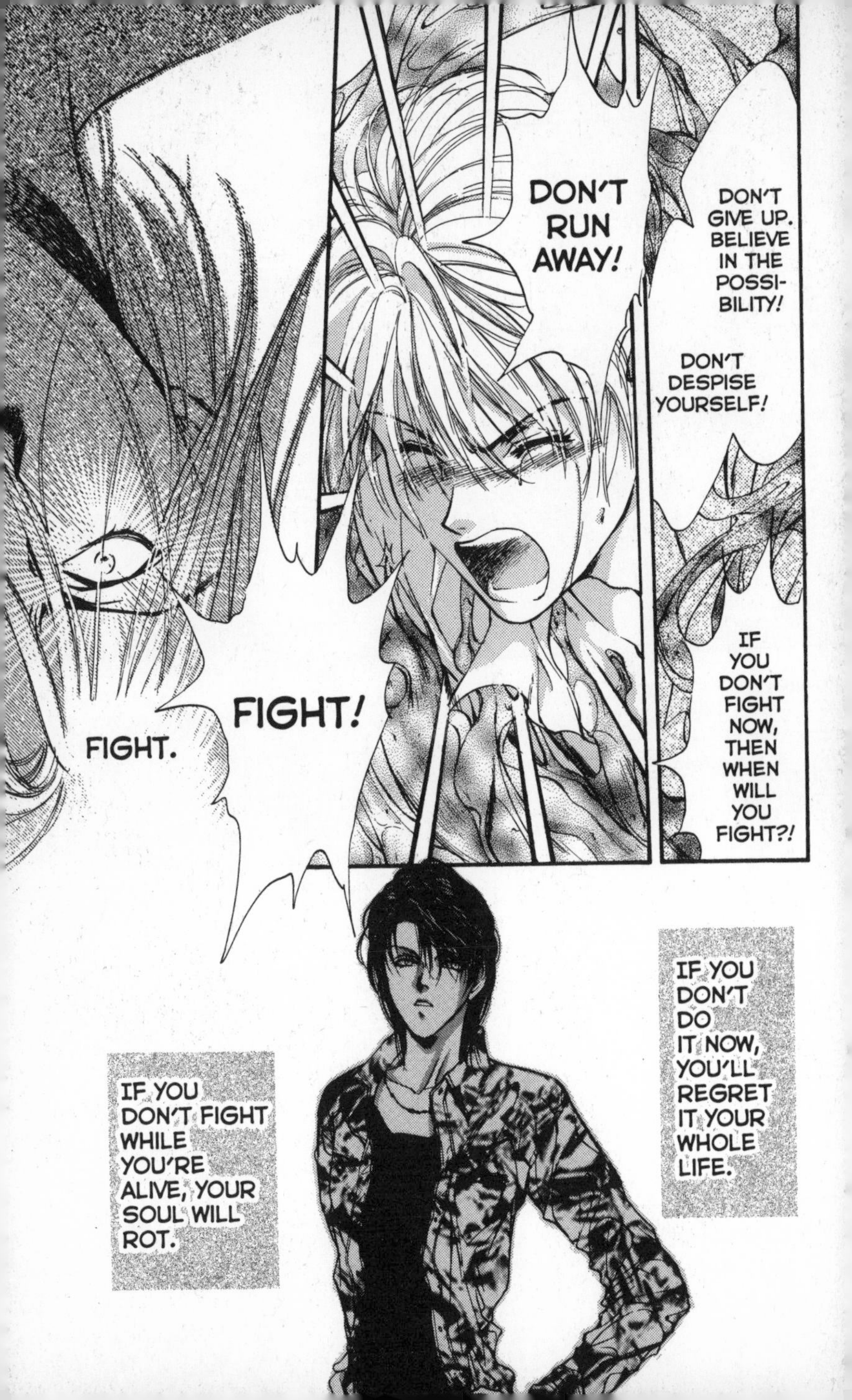

DON'T GIVE UP. BELIEVE IN THE POSSIBILITY!
DON'T DESPISE YOURSELF!
IF YOU DON'T FIGHT NOW, THEN WHEN WILL YOU FIGHT?!
DON'T RUN AWAY!
FIGHT!
FIGHT.
IF YOU DON'T DO IT NOW, YOU'LL REGRET IT YOUR WHOLE LIFE.
IF YOU DON'T FIGHT WHILE YOU'RE ALIVE, YOUR SOUL WILL ROT.

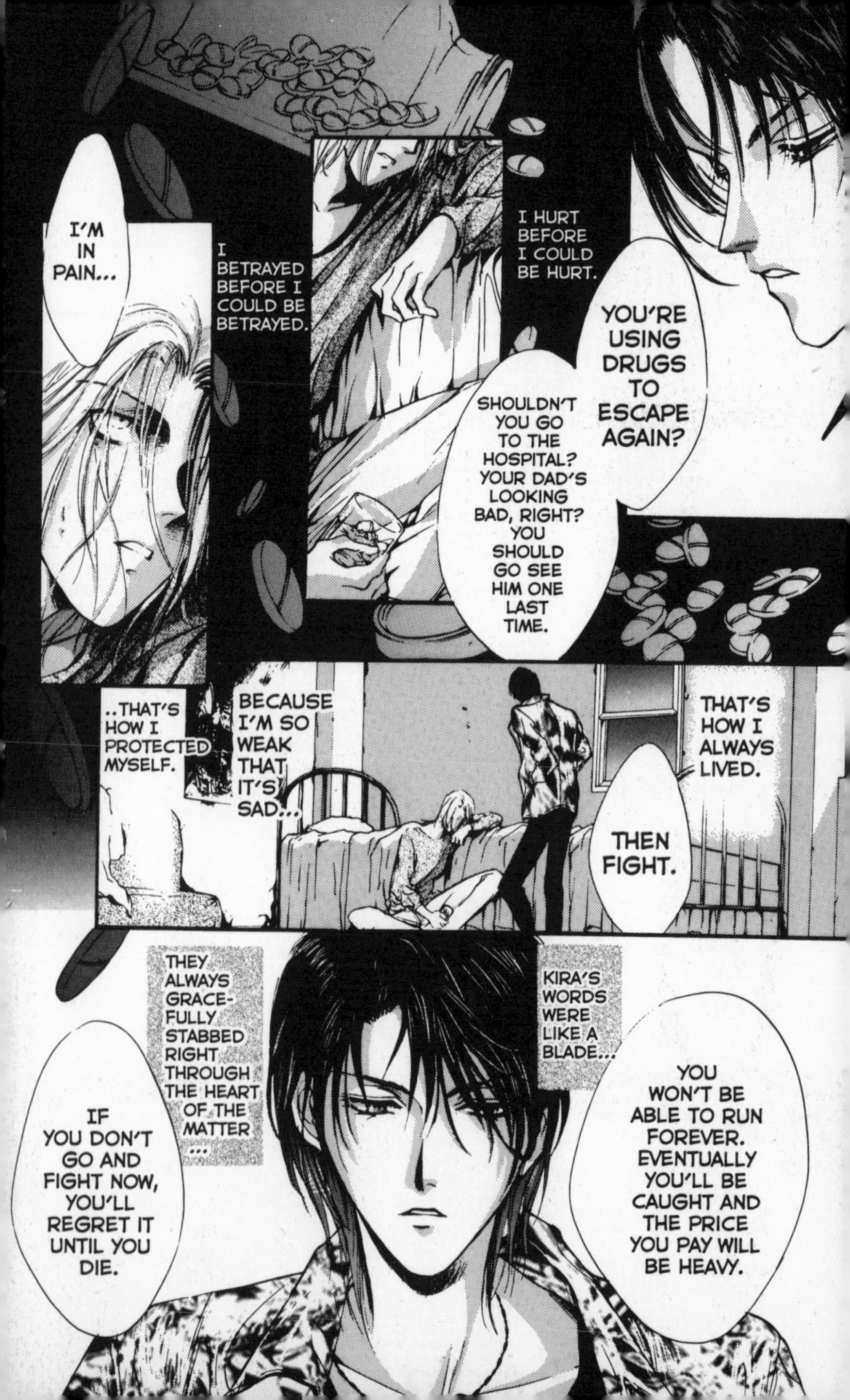
YOU'RE USING DRUGS TO ESCAPE AGAIN?
I HURT BEFORE I COULD BE HURT.
SHOULDN'T YOU GO TO THE HOSPITAL? YOUR DAD'S LOOKING BAD, RIGHT? YOU SHOULD GO SEE HIM ONE LAST TIME.
I BETRAYED BEFORE I COULD BE BETRAYED.
I'M IN PAIN...
THAT'S HOW I ALWAYS LIVED.
THEN FIGHT.
BECAUSE I'M SO WEAK THAT IT'S SAD...
..THAT'S HOW I PROTECTED MYSELF.
KIRA'S WORDS WERE LIKE A BLADE...
YOU WON'T BE ABLE TO RUN FOREVER. EVENTUALLY YOU'LL BE CAUGHT AND THE PRICE YOU PAY WILL BE HEAVY.
THEY ALWAYS GRACEFULLY STABBED RIGHT THROUGH THE HEART OF THE MATTER...
IF YOU DON'T GO AND FIGHT NOW, YOU'LL REGRET IT UNTIL YOU DIE.

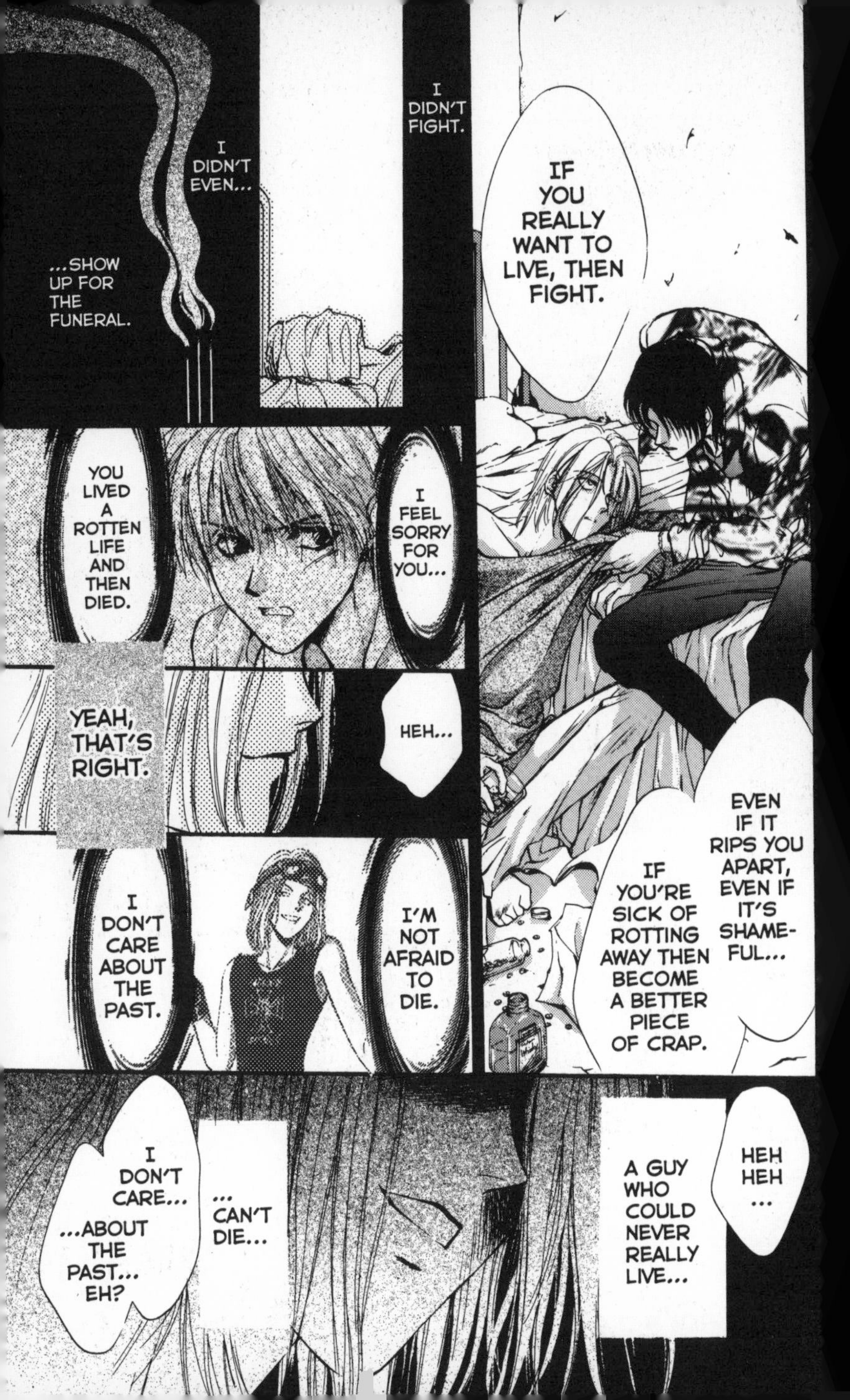
IF YOU REALLY WANT TO LIVE, THEN FIGHT.
EVEN IF IT RIPS YOU APART, EVEN IF IT'S SHAME-FUL...
IF YOU'RE SICK OF ROTTING AWAY THEN BECOME A BETTER PIECE OF CRAP.
I DIDN'T FIGHT.
I DIDN'T EVEN...
...SHOW UP FOR THE FUNERAL.
I FEEL SORRY FOR YOU...
YOU LIVED A ROTTEN LIFE AND THEN DIED.
HEH...
YEAH, THAT'S RIGHT.
I'M NOT AFRAID TO DIE.
I DON'T CARE ABOUT THE PAST.
HEH HEH...
A GUY WHO COULD NEVER REALLY LIVE...
...CAN'T DIE...
I DON'T CARE...
...ABOUT THE PAST... EH?

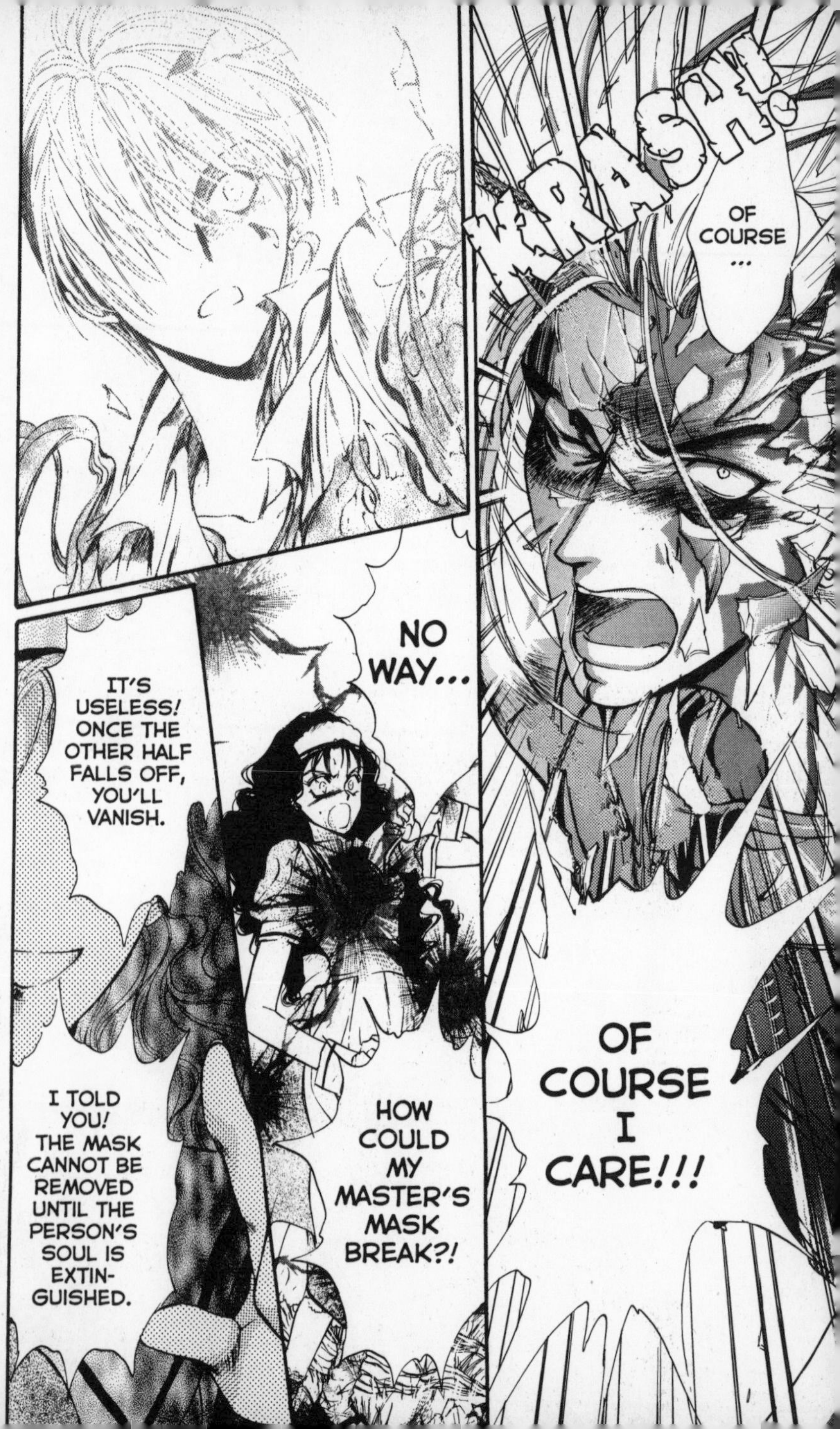
KRASH!
OF COURSE ...
OF COURSE I CARE!!!
NO WAY...
HOW COULD MY MASTER'S MASK BREAK?!
IT'S USELESS! ONCE THE OTHER HALF FALLS OFF, YOU'LL VANISH.
I TOLD YOU! THE MASK CANNOT BE REMOVED UNTIL THE PERSON'S SOUL IS EXTIN-GUISHED.

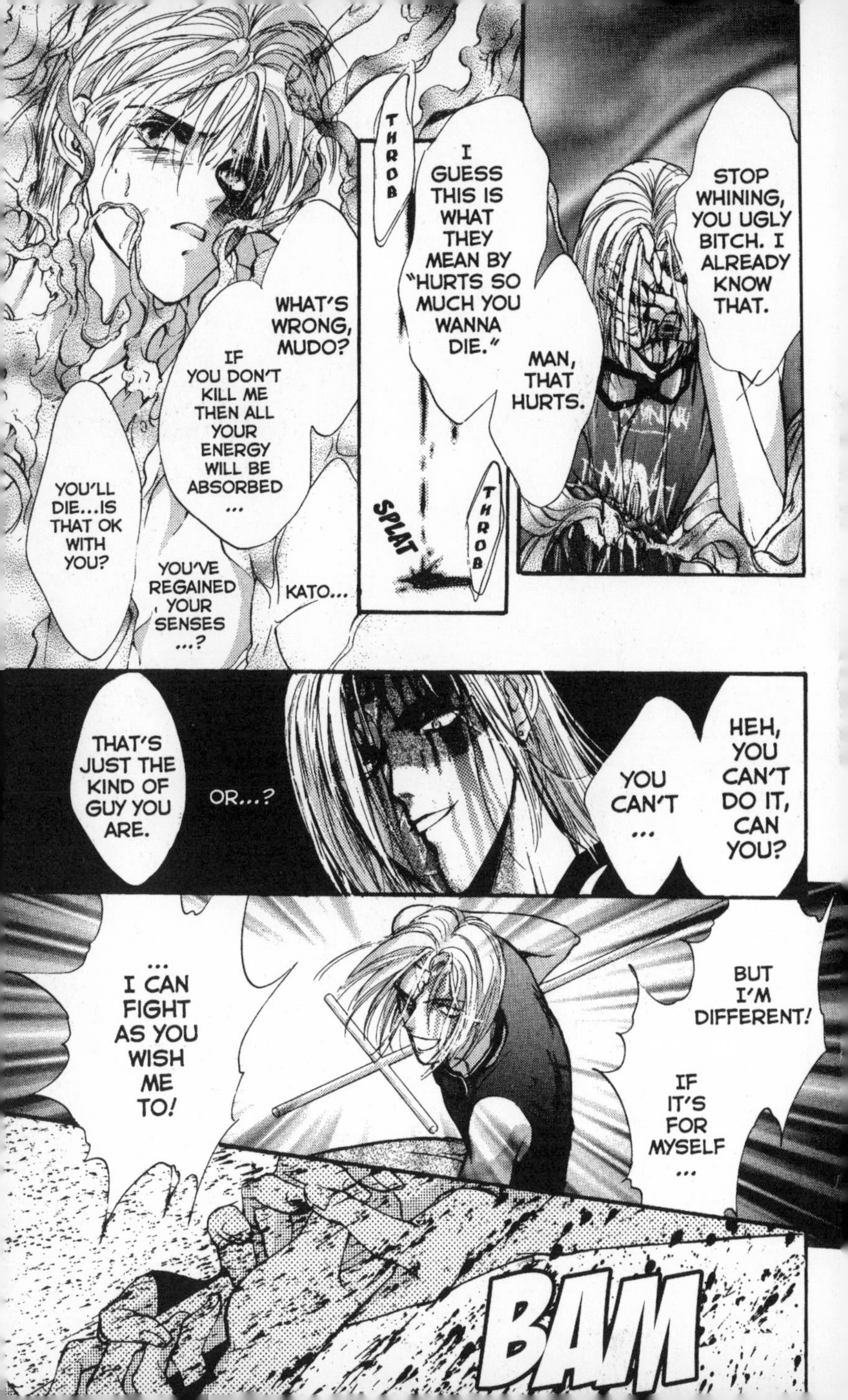
STOP WHINING, YOU UGLY BITCH. I ALREADY KNOW THAT.
MAN, THAT HURTS.
THROB
I GUESS THIS IS WHAT THEY MEAN BY "HURTS SO MUCH YOU WANNA DIE."
THROB
SPLAT
WHAT'S WRONG, MUDO?
IF YOU DON'T KILL ME THEN ALL YOUR ENERGY WILL BE ABSORBED ...
YOU'LL DIE...IS THAT OK WITH YOU?
KATO...
YOU'VE REGAINED YOUR SENSES ...?
HEH, YOU CAN'T DO IT, CAN YOU?
YOU CAN'T ...
OR...?
THAT'S JUST THE KIND OF GUY YOU ARE.
BUT I'M DIFFERENT!
IF IT'S FOR MYSELF ...
... I CAN FIGHT AS YOU WISH ME TO!
BAM

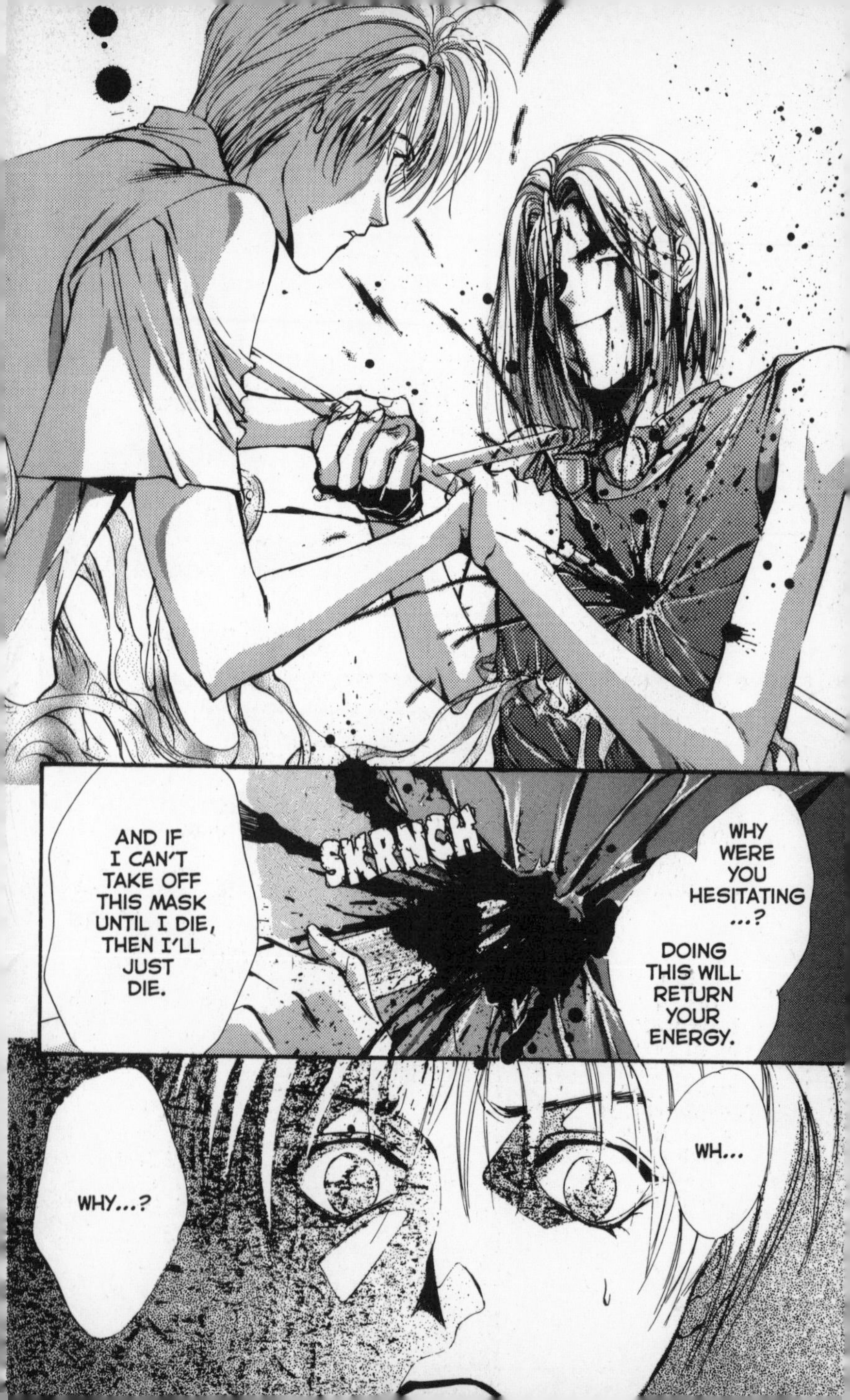
WHY WERE YOU HESITATING ...?
DOING THIS WILL RETURN YOUR ENERGY.
SKRNCH
AND IF I CAN'T TAKE OFF THIS MASK UNTIL I DIE, THEN I'LL JUST DIE.
WH...
WHY...?

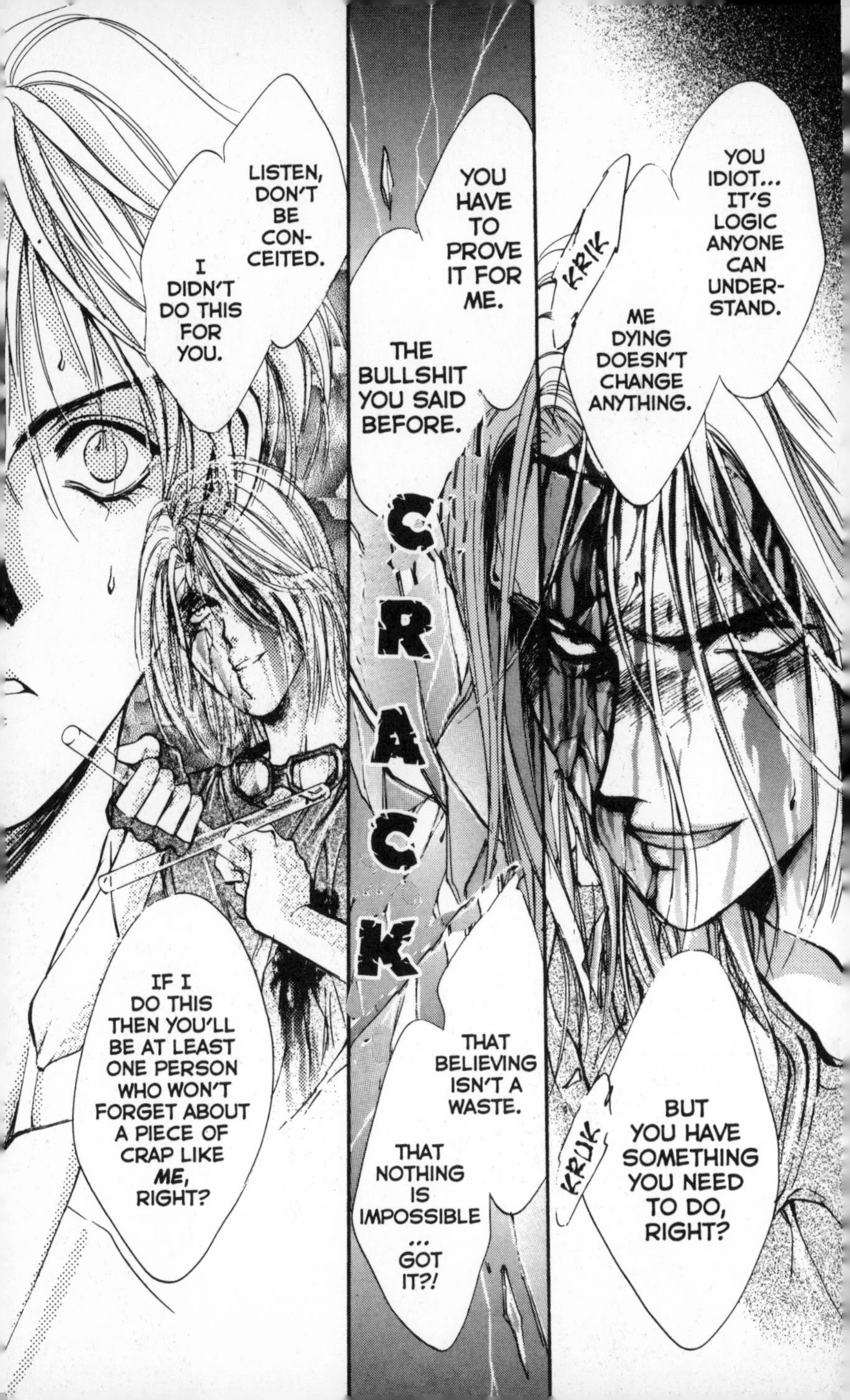
YOU IDIOT... IT'S LOGIC ANYONE CAN UNDERSTAND.
KRIK
ME DYING DOESN'T CHANGE ANYTHING.
KRUK
BUT YOU HAVE SOMETHING YOU NEED TO DO, RIGHT?
YOU HAVE TO PROVE IT FOR ME.
THE BULLSHIT YOU SAID BEFORE.
CRACK
THAT BELIEVING ISN'T A WASTE.
THAT NOTHING IS IMPOSSIBLE ... GOT IT?!
LISTEN, DON'T BE CONCEITED.
I DIDN'T DO THIS FOR YOU.
IF I DO THIS THEN YOU'LL BE AT LEAST ONE PERSON WHO WON'T FORGET ABOUT A PIECE OF CRAP LIKE *ME*, RIGHT?

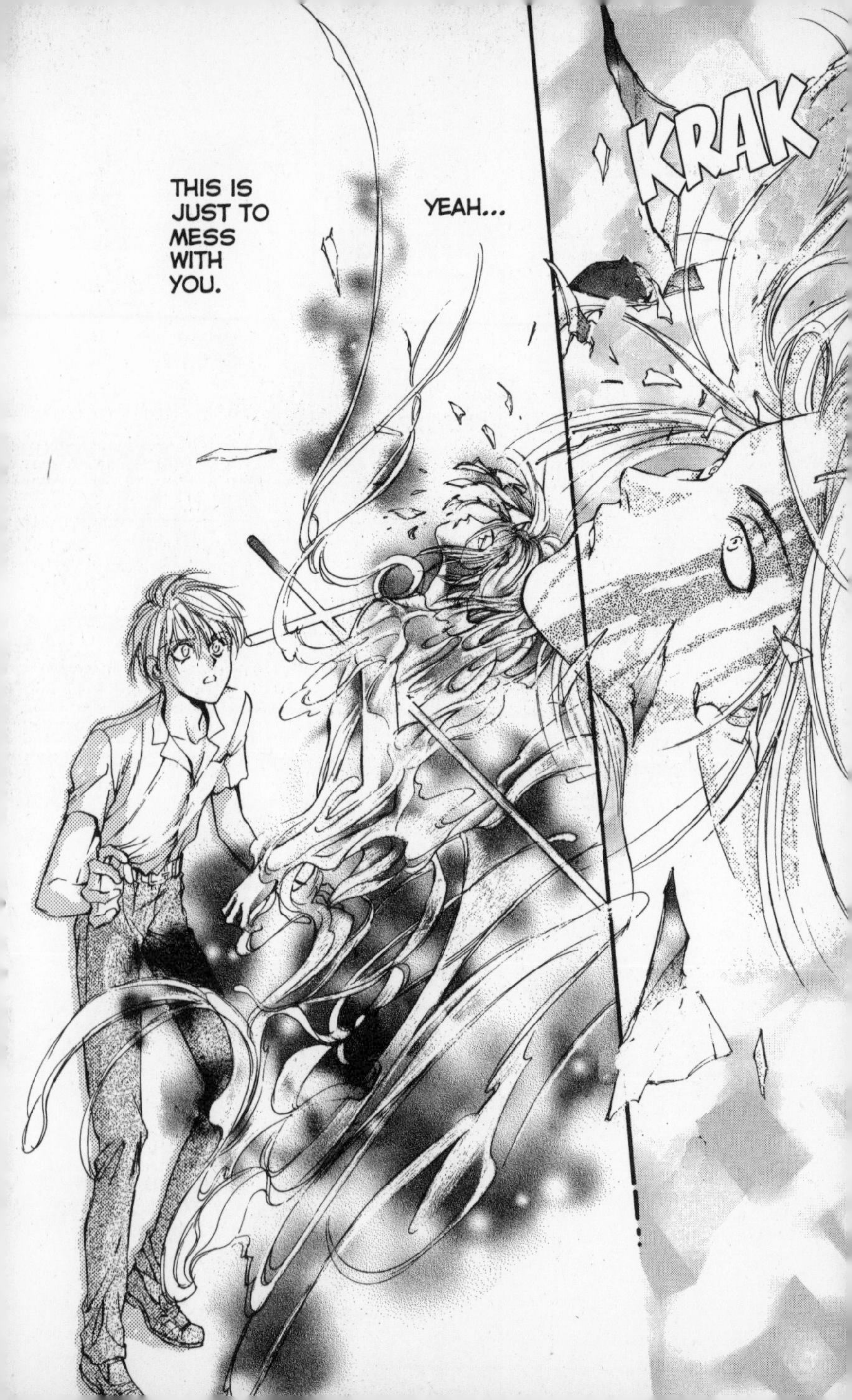
KRAK
YEAH...
THIS IS JUST TO MESS WITH YOU.

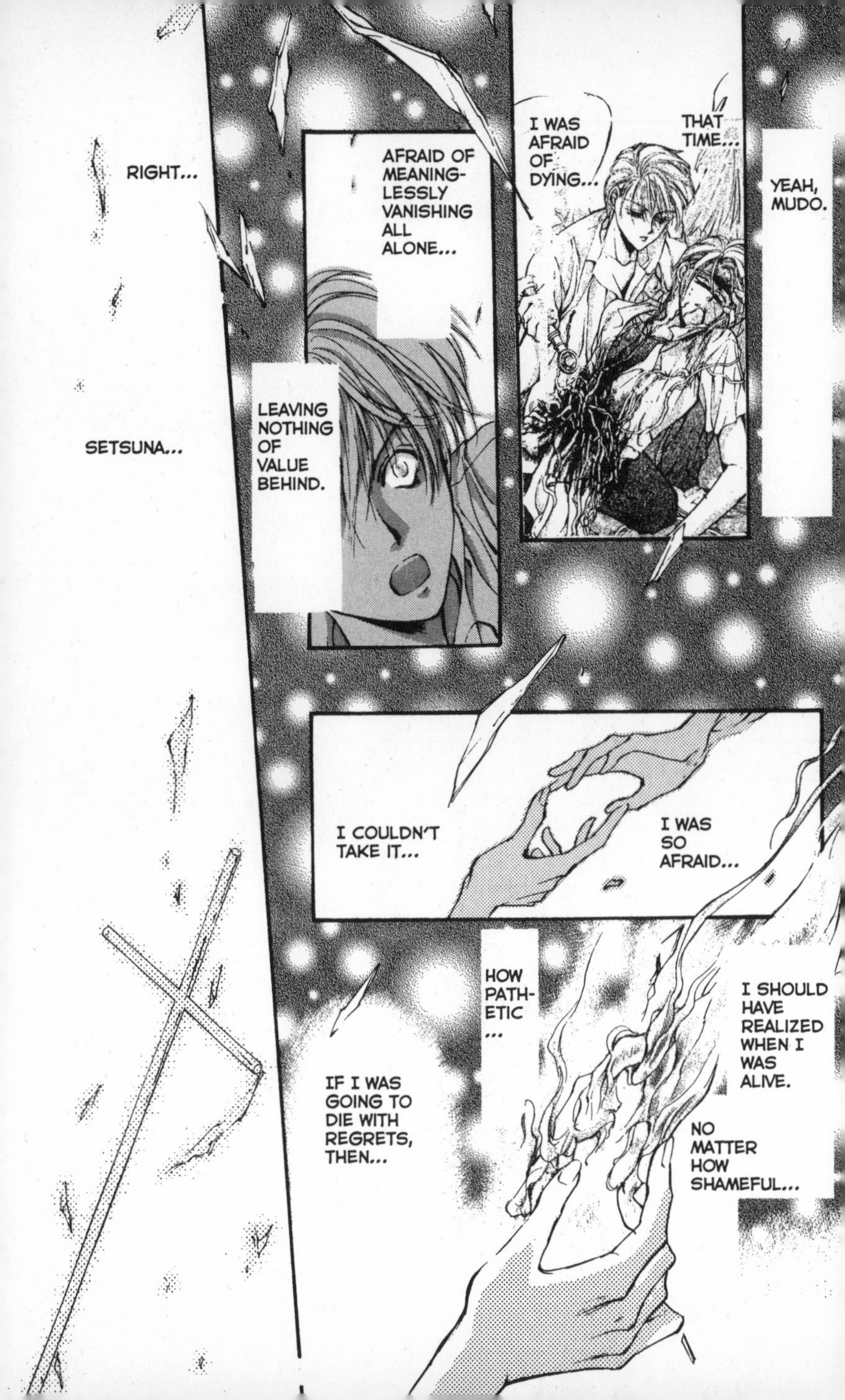

YEAH, MUDO.
THAT TIME...
I WAS AFRAID OF DYING...
AFRAID OF MEANING-LESSLY VANISHING ALL ALONE...
LEAVING NOTHING OF VALUE BEHIND.
I WAS SO AFRAID...
I COULDN'T TAKE IT...
I SHOULD HAVE REALIZED WHEN I WAS ALIVE.
NO MATTER HOW SHAMEFUL...
HOW PATH-ETIC...
IF I WAS GOING TO DIE WITH REGRETS, THEN...
RIGHT...
SETSUNA...

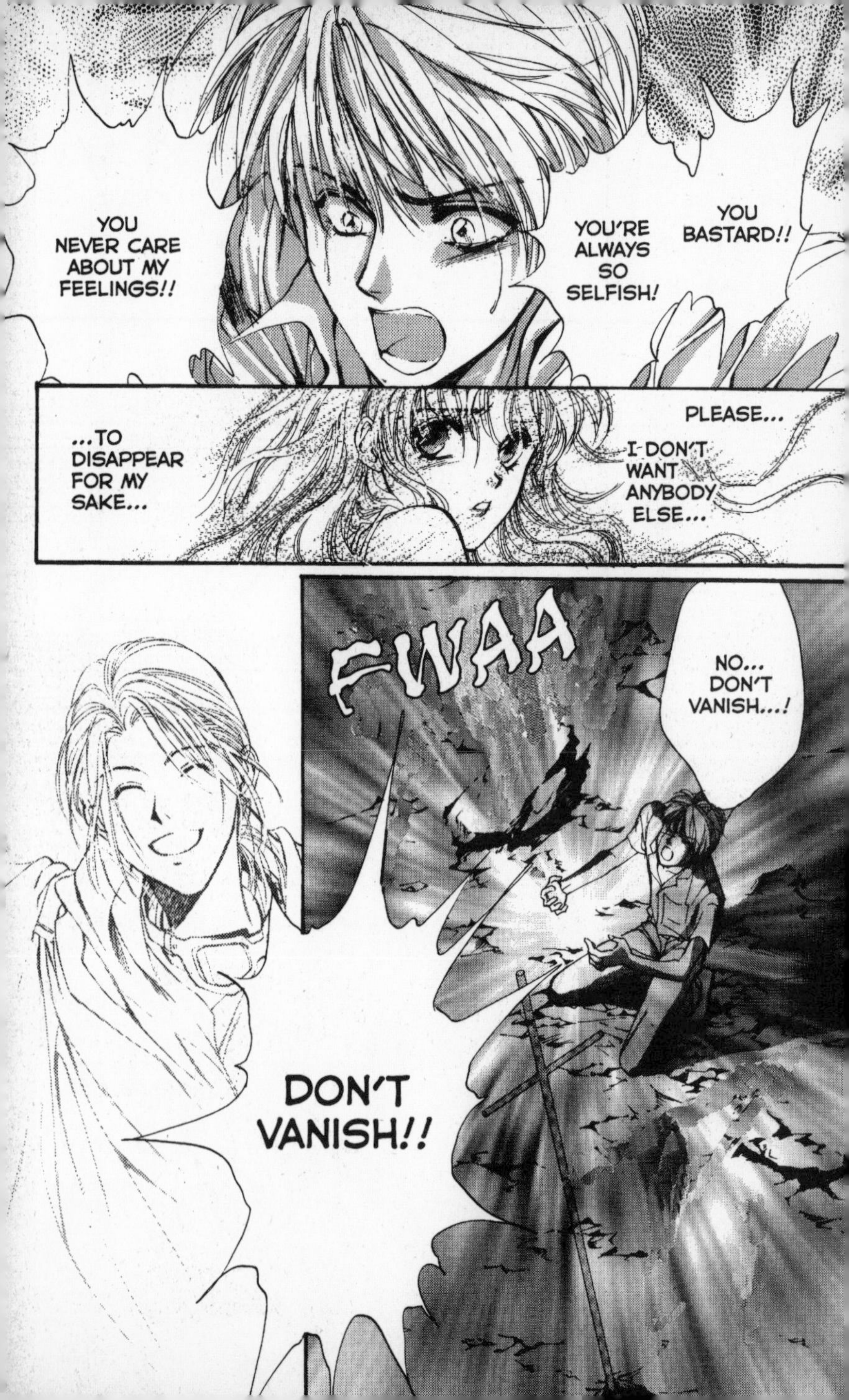
YOU BASTARD!!
YOU'RE ALWAYS SO SELFISH!
YOU NEVER CARE ABOUT MY FEELINGS!!
PLEASE...
I DON'T WANT ANYBODY ELSE...
...TO DISAPPEAR FOR MY SAKE...
FWAA
NO... DON'T VANISH...!
DON'T VANISH!!

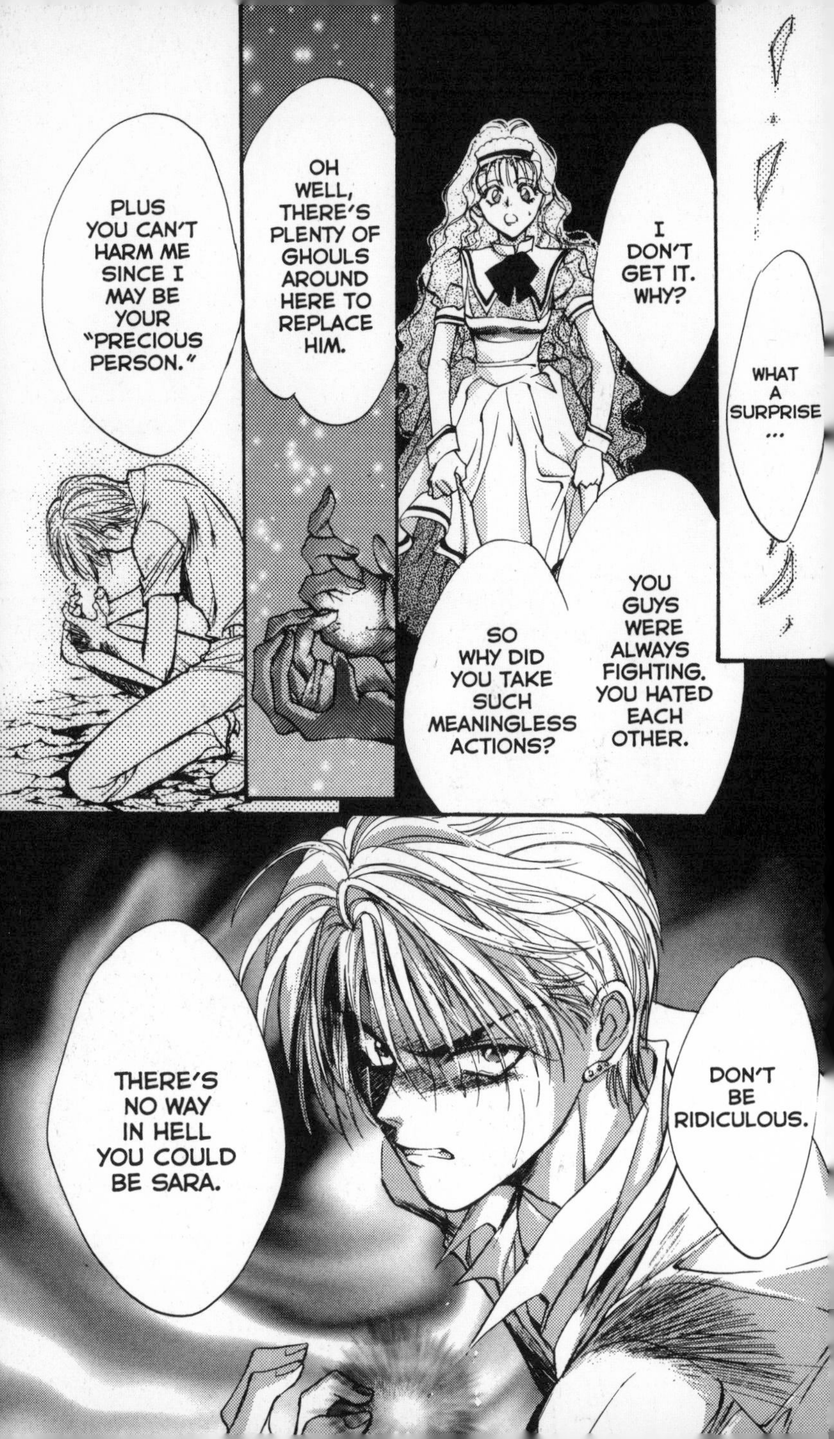
WHAT A SURPRISE...
I DON'T GET IT. WHY?
YOU GUYS WERE ALWAYS FIGHTING. YOU HATED EACH OTHER.
SO WHY DID YOU TAKE SUCH MEANINGLESS ACTIONS?
OH WELL, THERE'S PLENTY OF GHOULS AROUND HERE TO REPLACE HIM.
PLUS YOU CAN'T HARM ME SINCE I MAY BE YOUR "PRECIOUS PERSON."
DON'T BE RIDICULOUS.
THERE'S NO WAY IN HELL YOU COULD BE SARA.

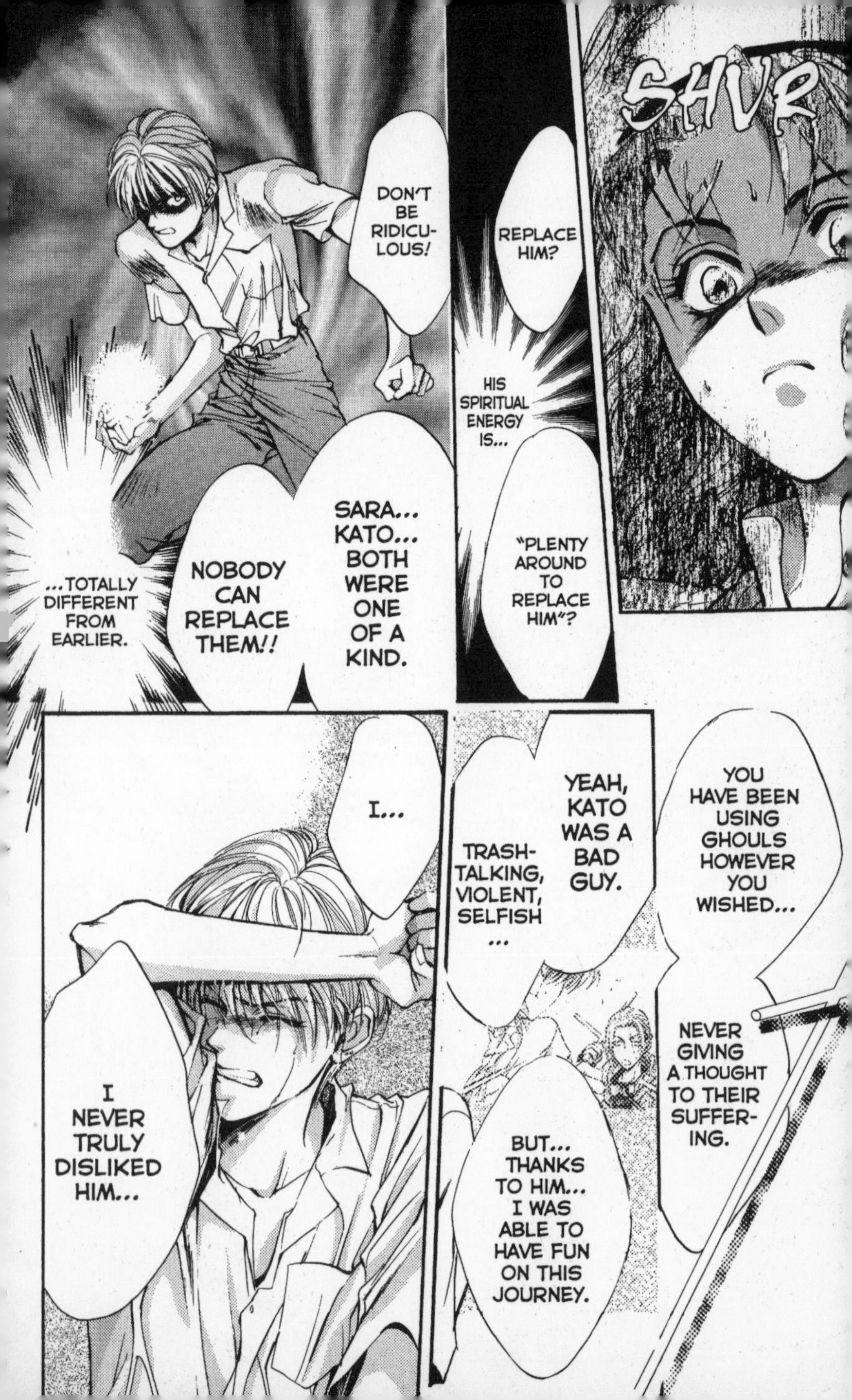
SHVR
REPLACE HIM?
HIS SPIRITUAL ENERGY IS...
"PLENTY AROUND TO REPLACE HIM"?
DON'T BE RIDICULOUS!
SARA... KATO... BOTH WERE ONE OF A KIND.
NOBODY CAN REPLACE THEM!!
...TOTALLY DIFFERENT FROM EARLIER.
YOU HAVE BEEN USING GHOULS HOWEVER YOU WISHED...
NEVER GIVING A THOUGHT TO THEIR SUFFERING.
YEAH, KATO WAS A BAD GUY.
TRASH-TALKING, VIOLENT, SELFISH...
BUT... THANKS TO HIM... I WAS ABLE TO HAVE FUN ON THIS JOURNEY.
I...
I NEVER TRULY DISLIKED HIM...

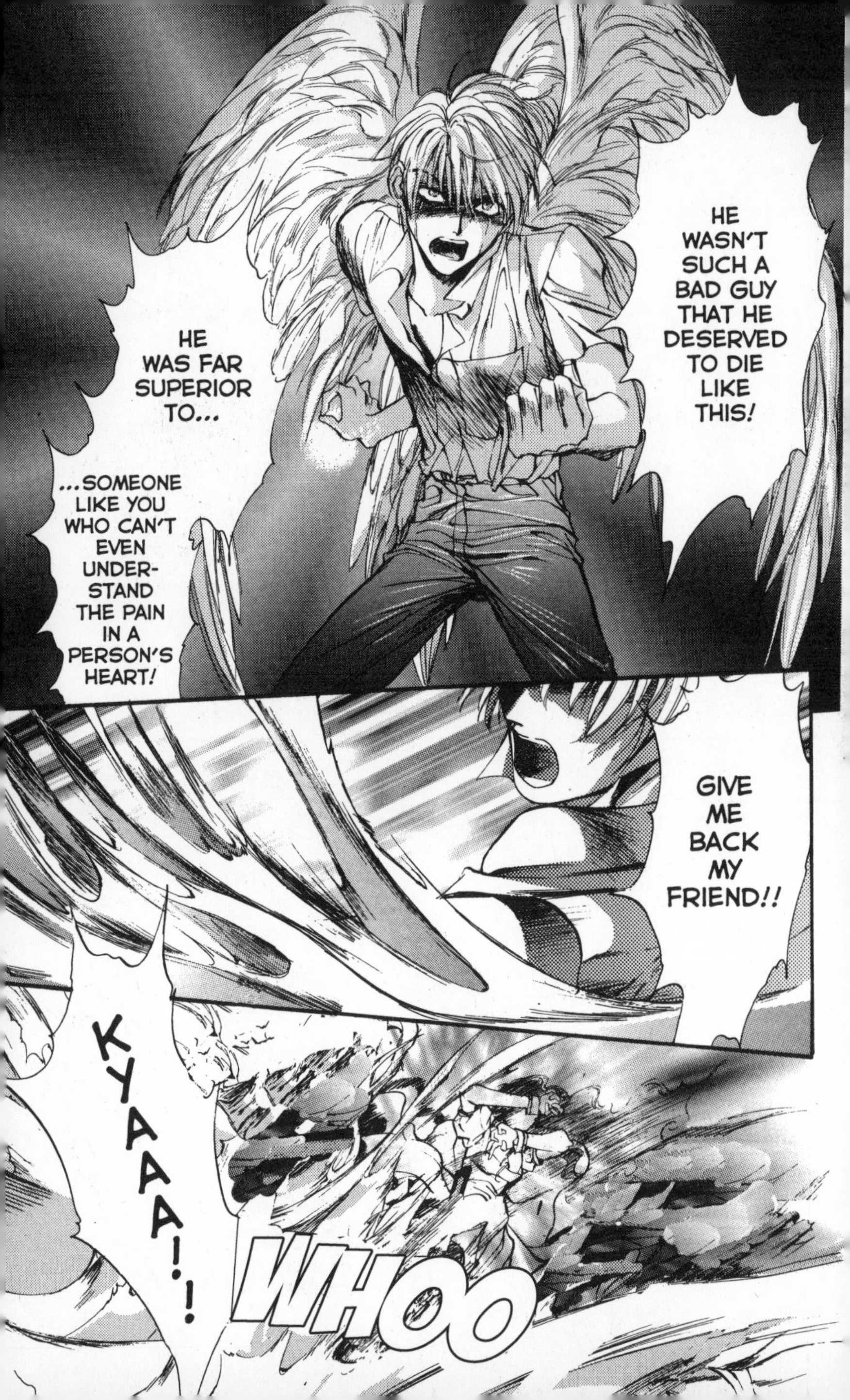
HE WASN'T SUCH A BAD GUY THAT HE DESERVED TO DIE LIKE THIS!
HE WAS FAR SUPERIOR TO...
...SOMEONE LIKE YOU WHO CAN'T EVEN UNDER-STAND THE PAIN IN A PERSON'S HEART!
GIVE ME BACK MY FRIEND!!
WHOO
KYAAA!!

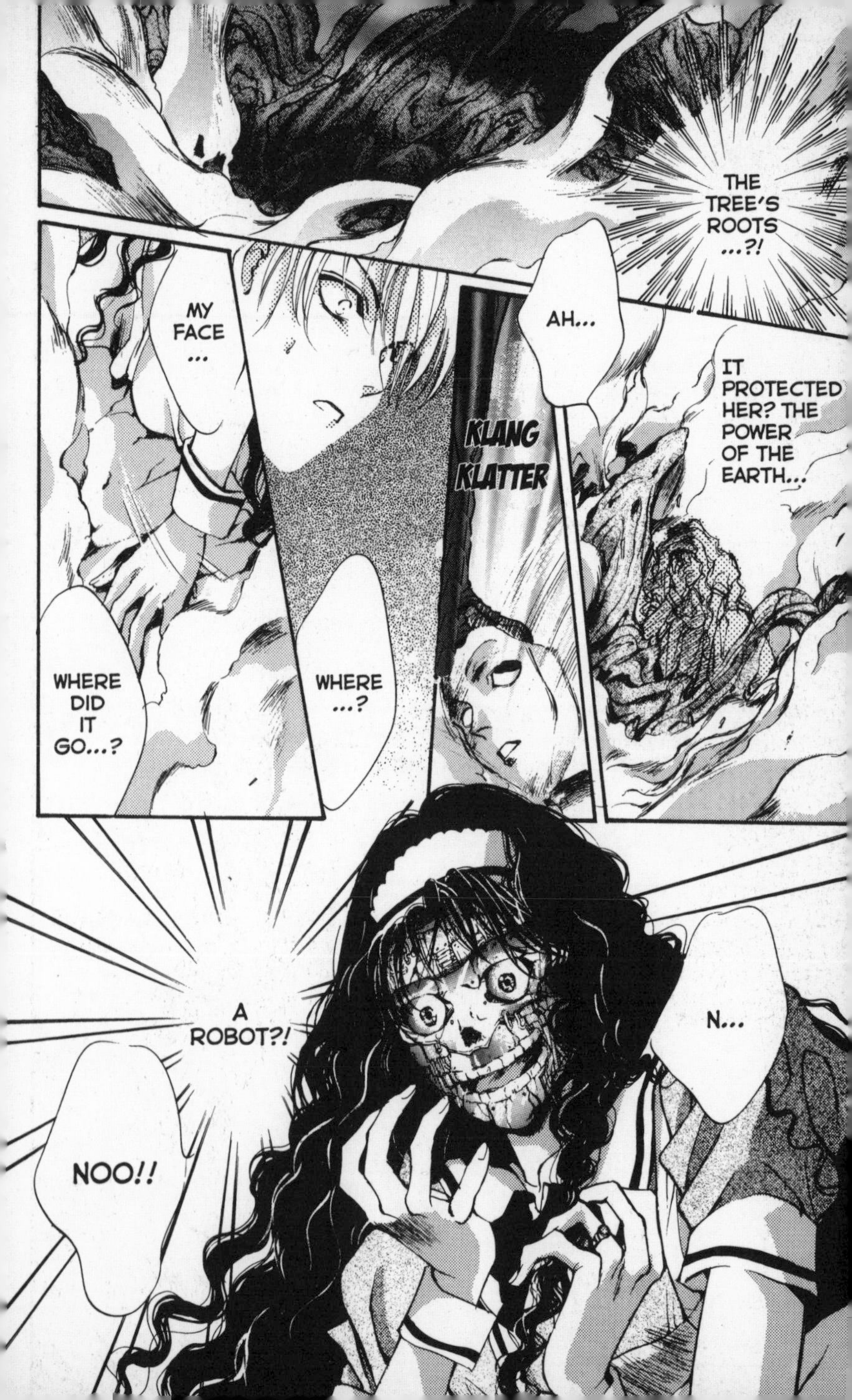
THE TREE'S ROOTS ...?!
AH...
IT PROTECTED HER? THE POWER OF THE EARTH...
KLANG KLATTER
WHERE ...?
MY FACE ...
WHERE DID IT GO...?
N...
A ROBOT?!
NOO!!

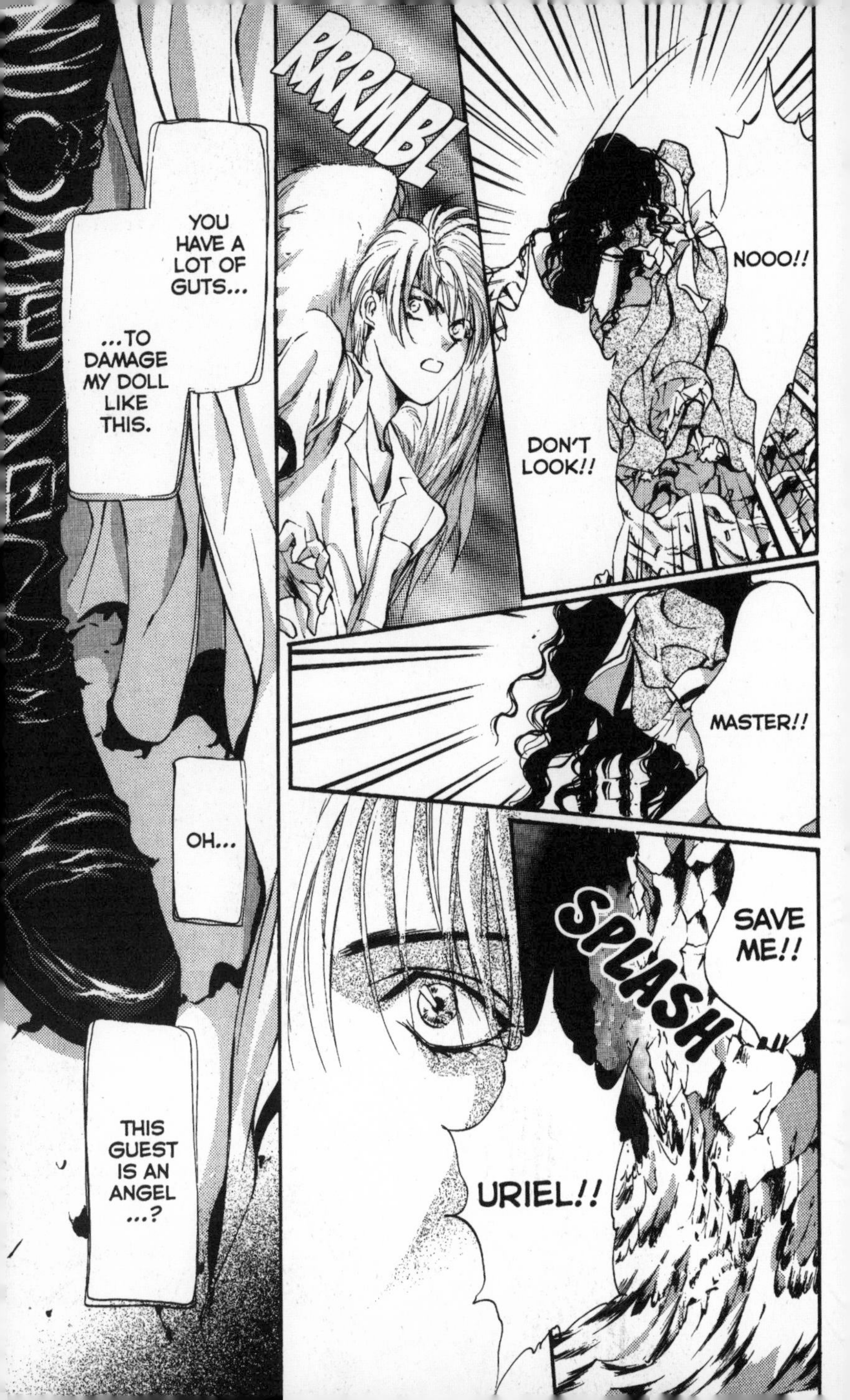
NOOO!!
DON'T LOOK!!
RRRMBL
MASTER!!
SAVE ME!!
SPLASH
URIEL!!
YOU HAVE A LOT OF GUTS...
...TO DAMAGE MY DOLL LIKE THIS.
OH...
THIS GUEST IS AN ANGEL ...?

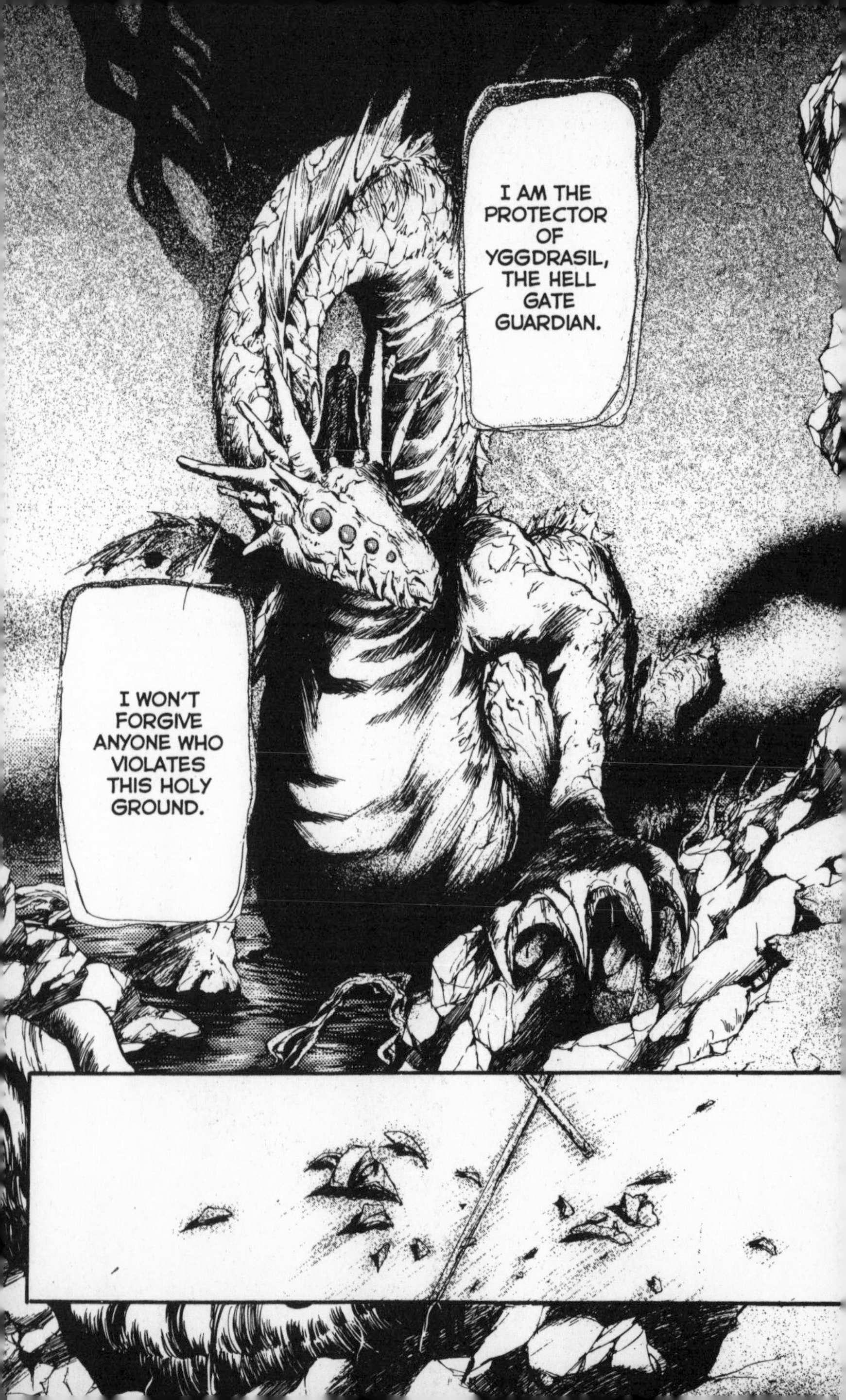
I AM THE PROTECTOR OF YGGDRASIL, THE HELL GATE GUARDIAN.
I WON'T FORGIVE ANYONE WHO VIOLATES THIS HOLY GROUND.

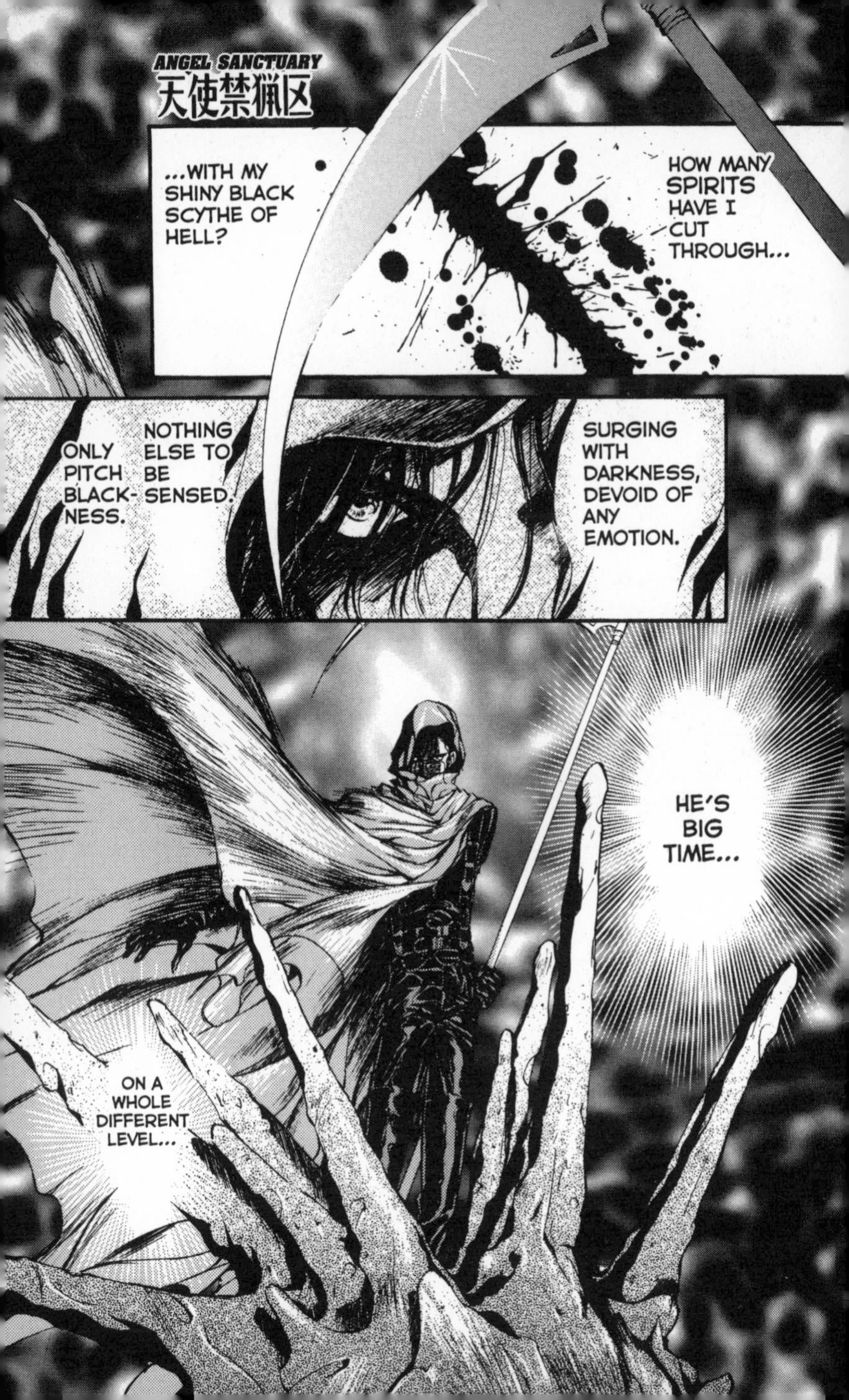
ANGEL SANCTUARY
天使禁猟区
HOW MANY SPIRITS HAVE I CUT THROUGH...
...WITH MY SHINY BLACK SCYTHE OF HELL?
SURGING WITH DARKNESS, DEVOID OF ANY EMOTION.
NOTHING ELSE TO BE SENSED.
ONLY PITCH BLACKNESS.
HE'S BIG TIME...
ON A WHOLE DIFFERENT LEVEL...

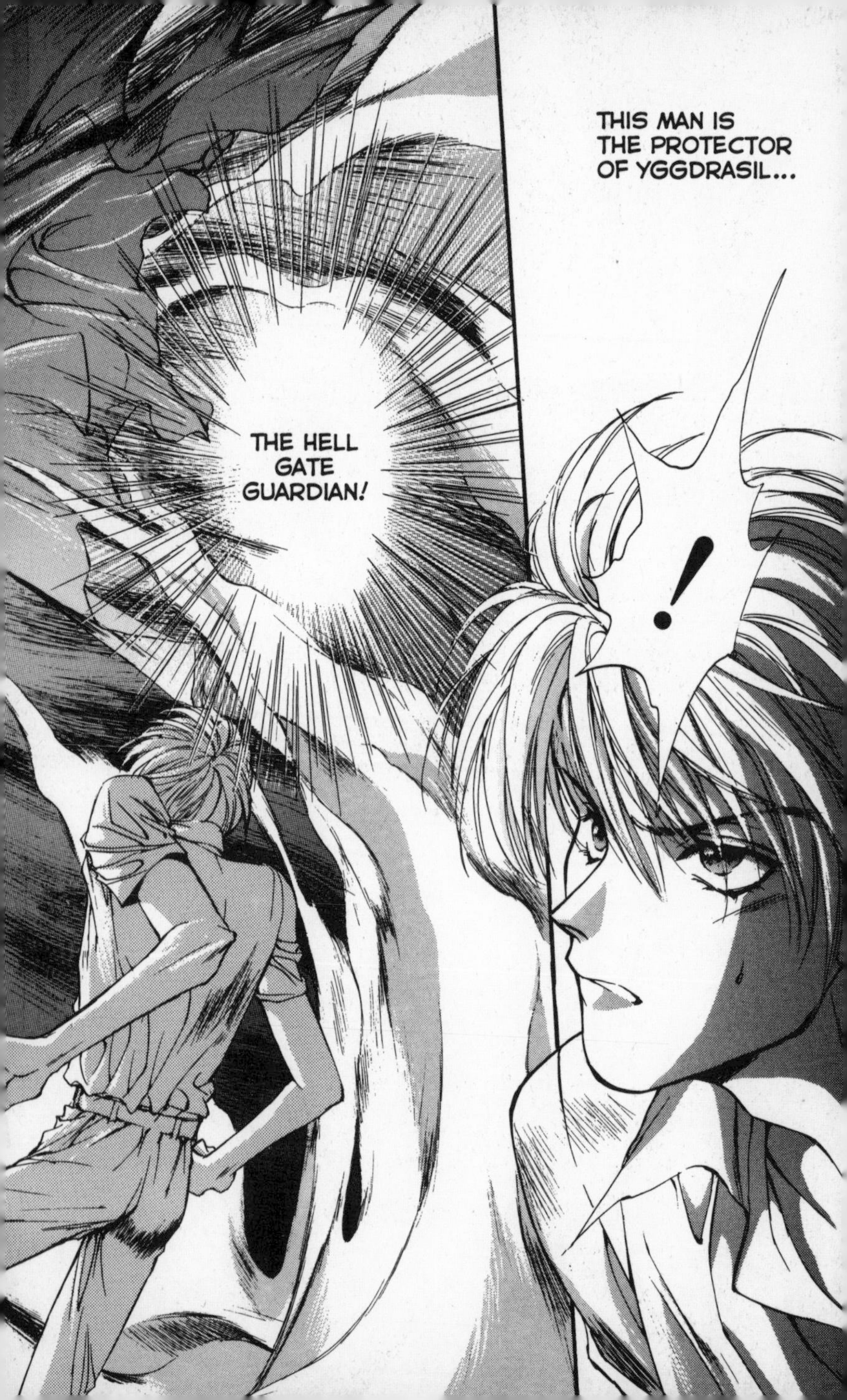
THIS MAN IS THE PROTECTOR OF YGGDRASIL...
!
THE HELL GATE GUARDIAN!

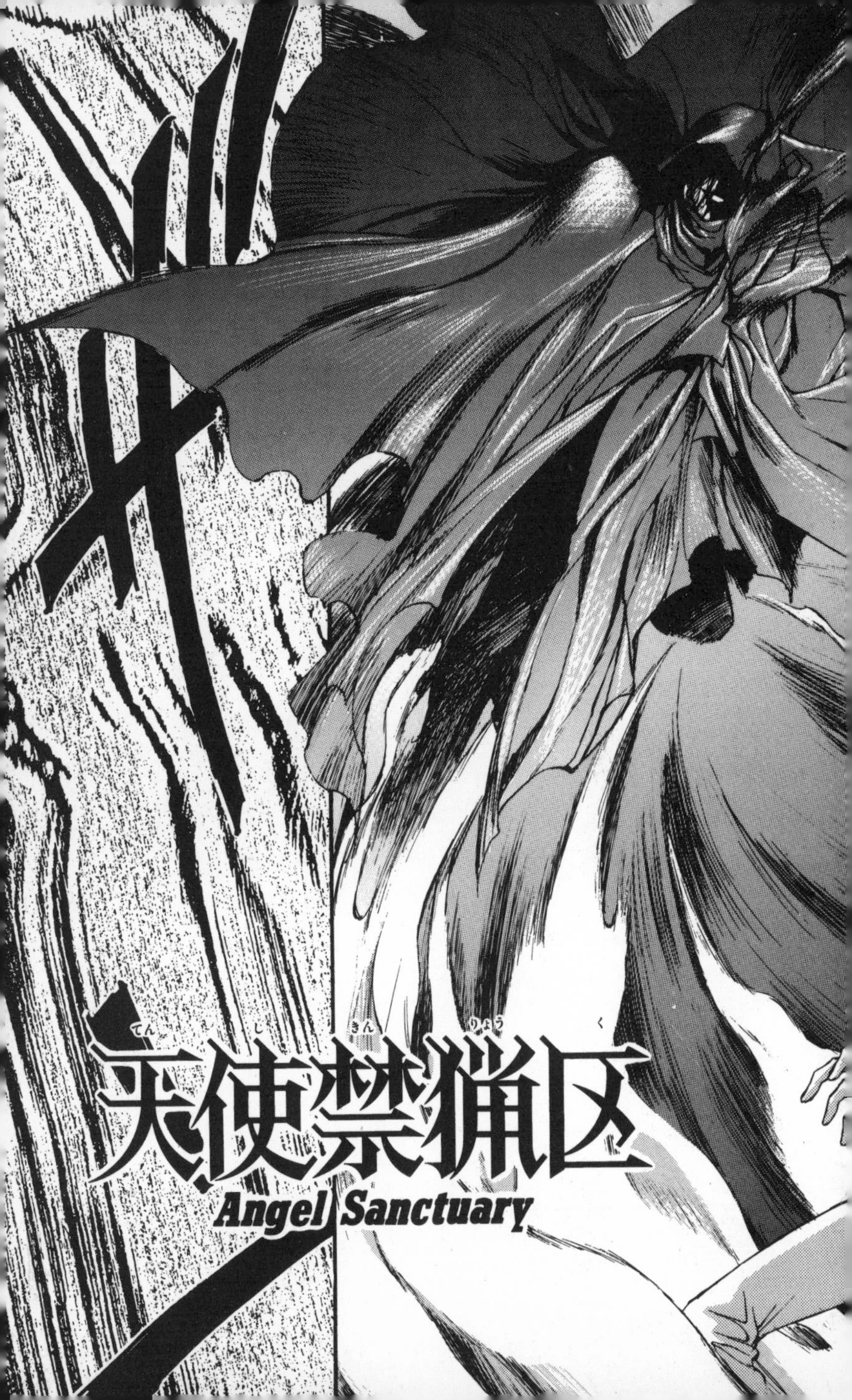
天使禁猟区
Angel Sanctuary

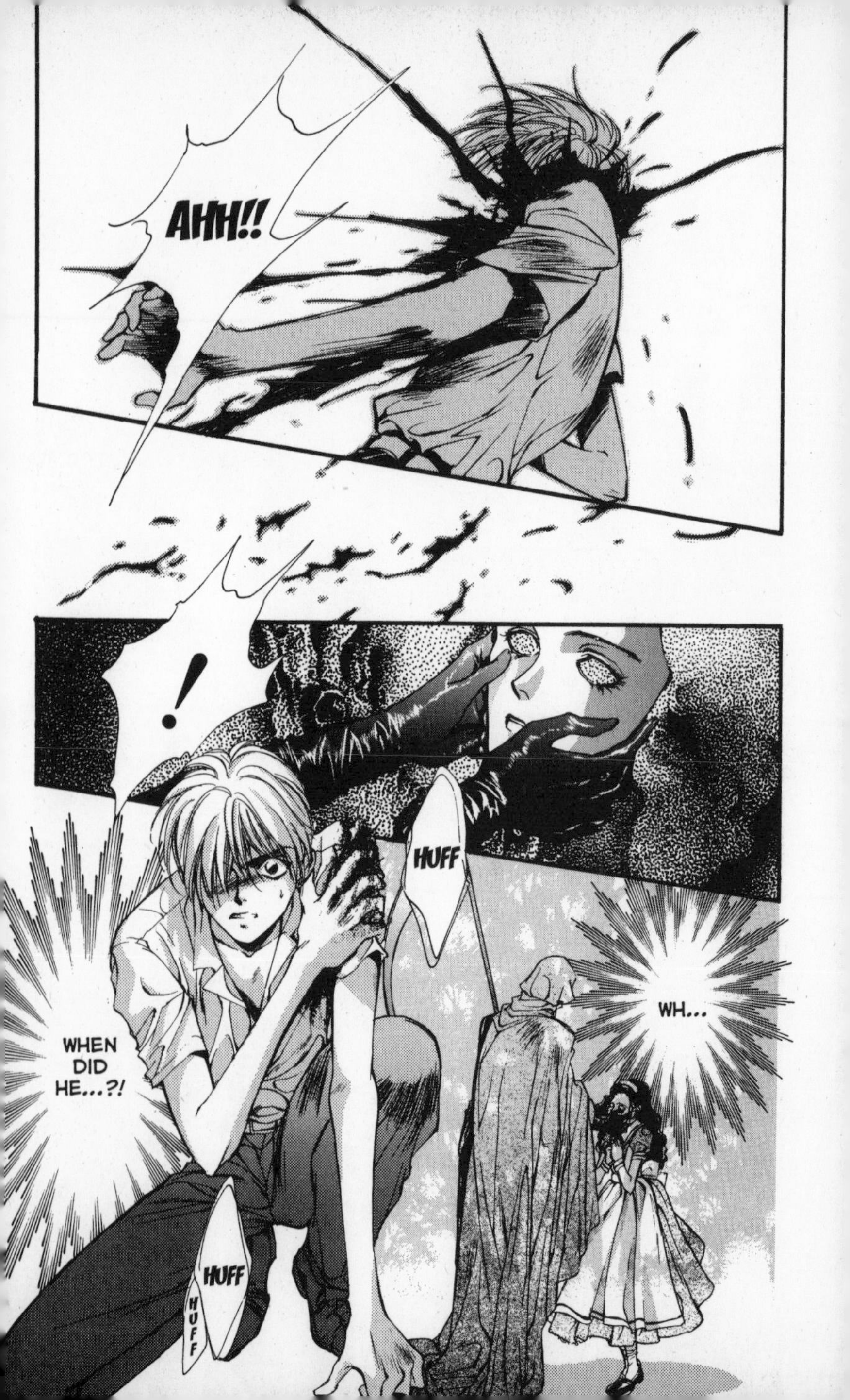
AHH!!
!
HUFF
WH...
WHEN DID HE...?!
HUFF
HUFF

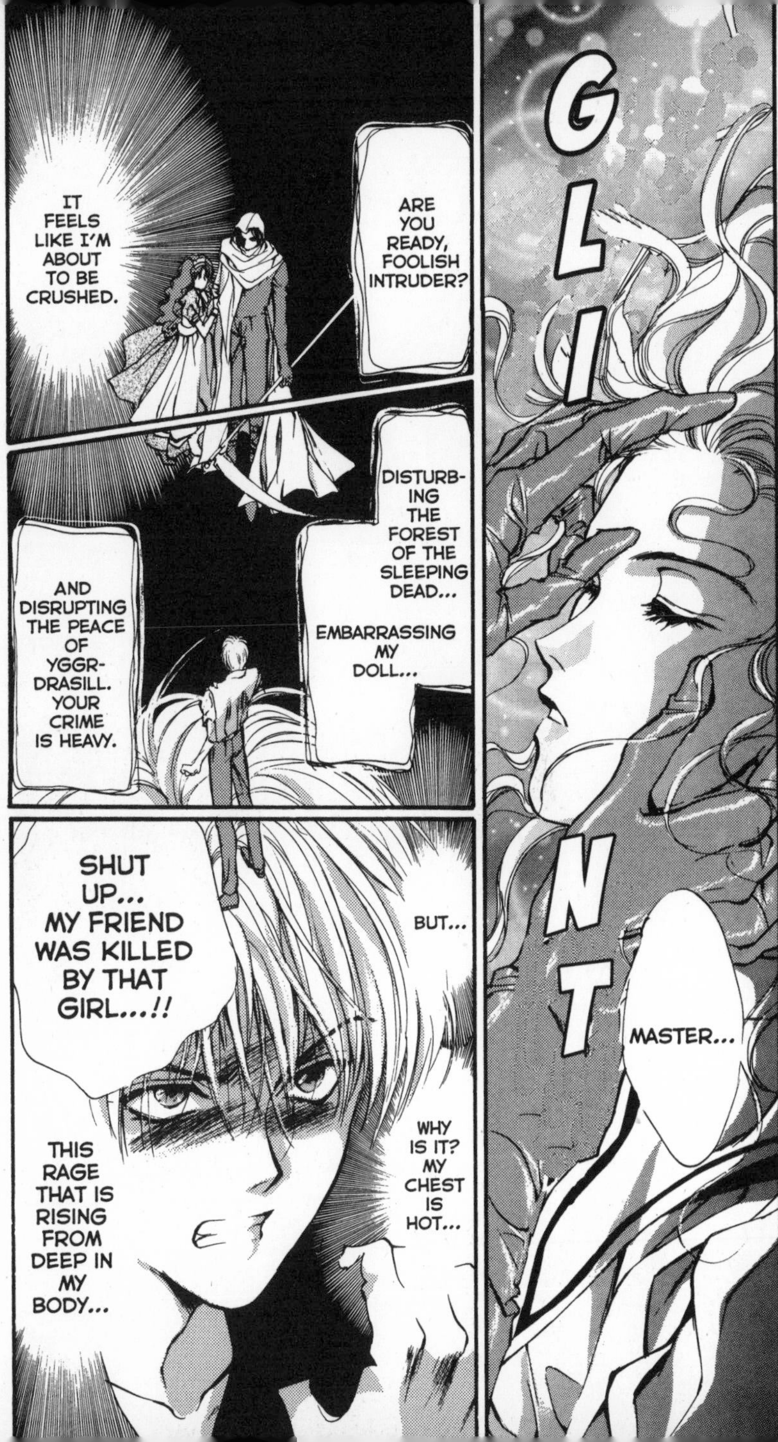
GLINT
MASTER...
ARE YOU READY, FOOLISH INTRUDER?
IT FEELS LIKE I'M ABOUT TO BE CRUSHED.
DISTURBING THE FOREST OF THE SLEEPING DEAD...
EMBARRASSING MY DOLL...
AND DISRUPTING THE PEACE OF YGGR-DRASILL. YOUR CRIME IS HEAVY.
BUT...
SHUT UP... MY FRIEND WAS KILLED BY THAT GIRL...!!
WHY IS IT? MY CHEST IS HOT...
THIS RAGE THAT IS RISING FROM DEEP IN MY BODY...

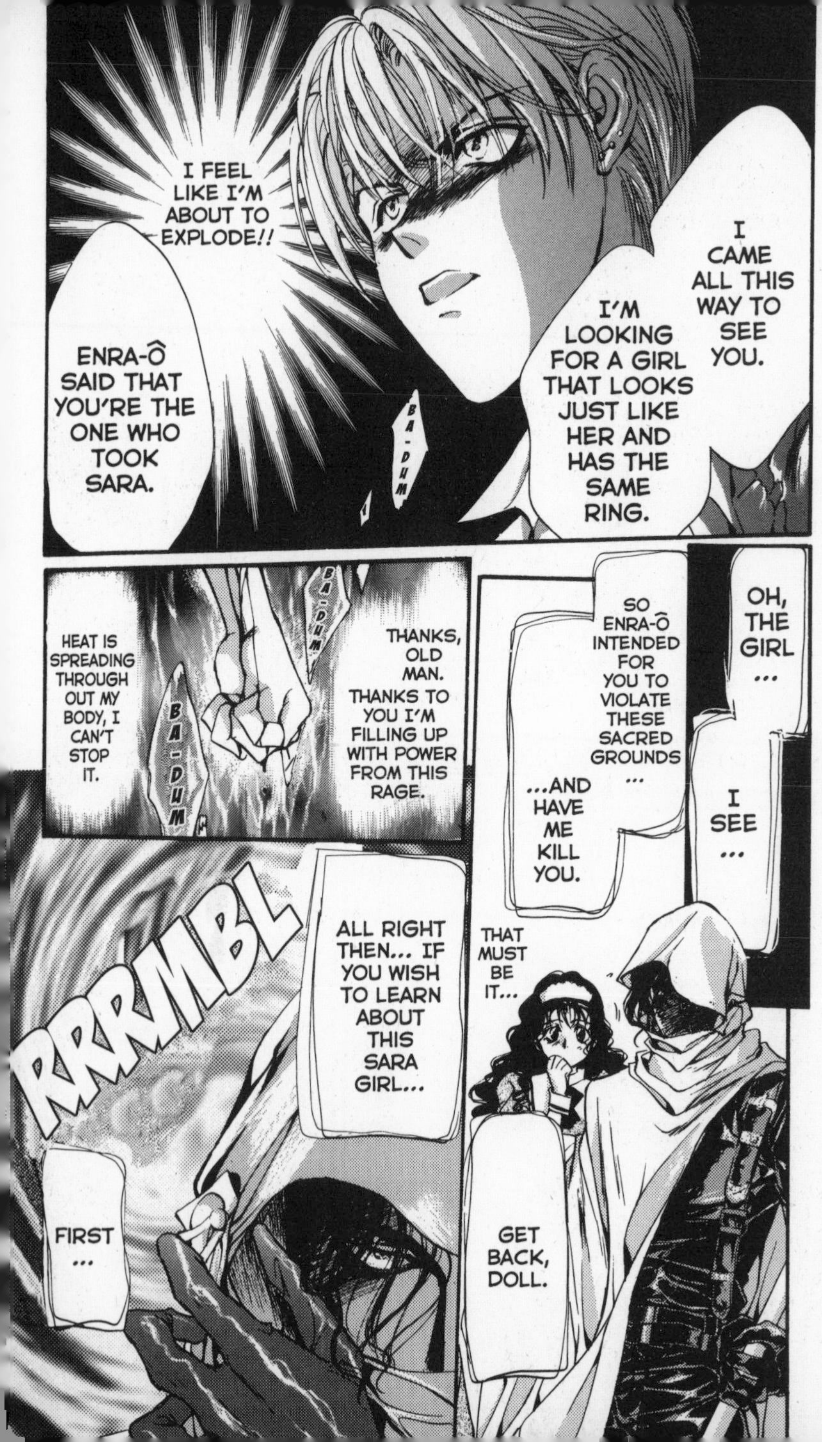
I CAME ALL THIS WAY TO SEE YOU.
I'M LOOKING FOR A GIRL THAT LOOKS JUST LIKE HER AND HAS THE SAME RING.
BA-DUM
I FEEL LIKE I'M ABOUT TO EXPLODE!!
ENRA-Ô SAID THAT YOU'RE THE ONE WHO TOOK SARA.
OH, THE GIRL...
I SEE...
SO ENRA-Ô INTENDED FOR YOU TO VIOLATE THESE SACRED GROUNDS...
...AND HAVE ME KILL YOU.
BA-DUM
THANKS, OLD MAN. THANKS TO YOU I'M FILLING UP WITH POWER FROM THIS RAGE.
BA-DUM
HEAT IS SPREADING THROUGH OUT MY BODY, I CAN'T STOP IT.
THAT MUST BE IT...
ALL RIGHT THEN... IF YOU WISH TO LEARN ABOUT THIS SARA GIRL...
RRRMBL
GET BACK, DOLL.
FIRST...

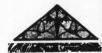

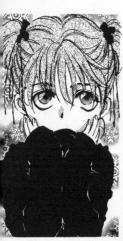

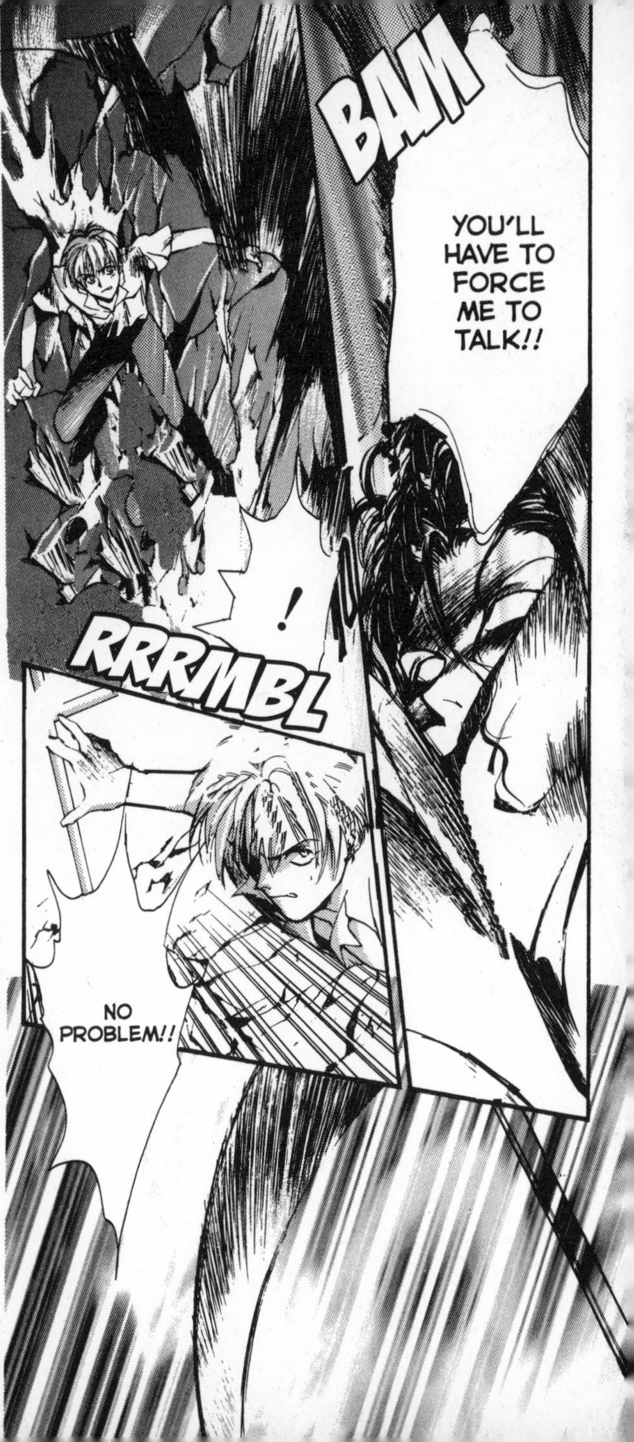
BAM
YOU'LL HAVE TO FORCE ME TO TALK!!
!
RRRMBL
NO PROBLEM!!

I actually didn't plan to include this battle between Uriel and Setsuna but I just needed to stretch the story one chapter so this is what happened. Now I'm glad I included it but when I was drawing it I was worried because I'm not used to doing action scenes. It took up a lot of time. (And the action isn't even that good)

This is around the time when drawing Rosiel got fun again. Huh? Why is that? Well, he's much easier than drawing dragons. And Yggdrasil was a major pain too.

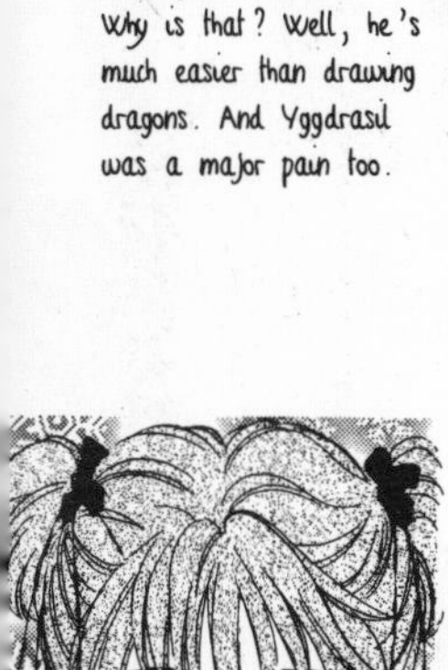

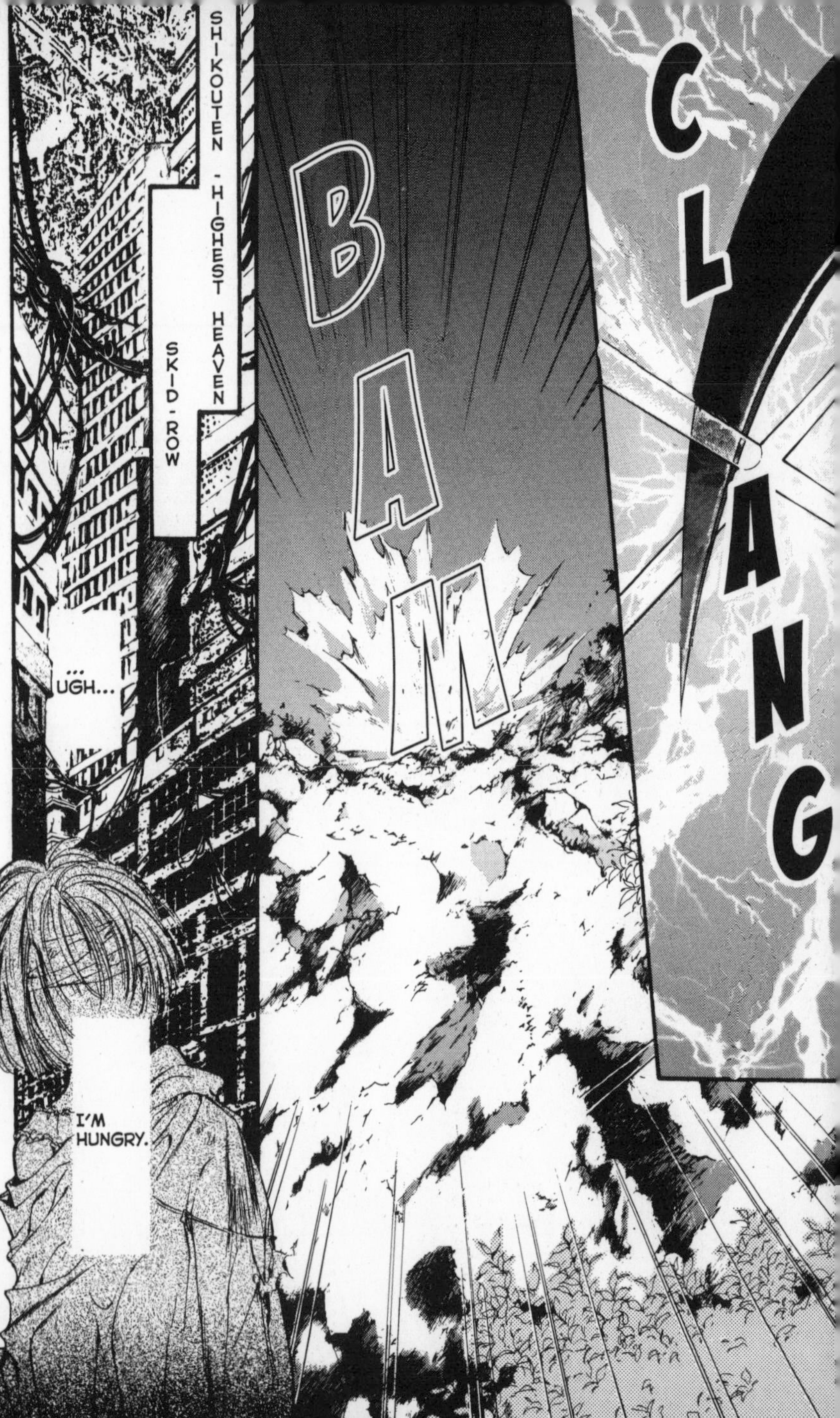
CLANG
BAM
SHIKOUTEN -HIGHEST HEAVEN
SKID-ROW
...UGH...
I'M HUNGRY.

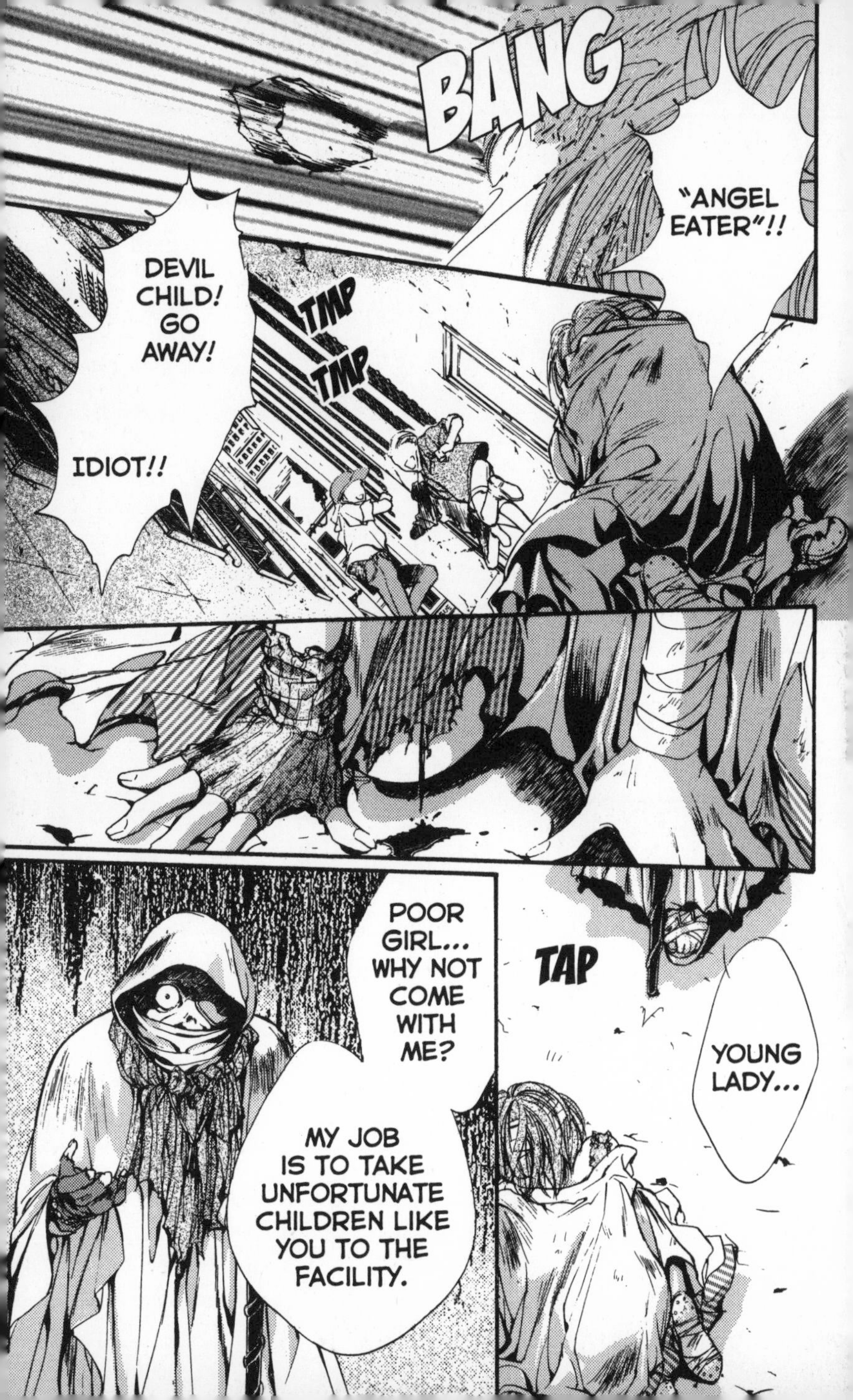
BANG
"ANGEL EATER"!!
DEVIL CHILD! GO AWAY!
TMP
TMP
IDIOT!!
TAP
YOUNG LADY...
POOR GIRL... WHY NOT COME WITH ME?
MY JOB IS TO TAKE UNFORTUNATE CHILDREN LIKE YOU TO THE FACILITY.

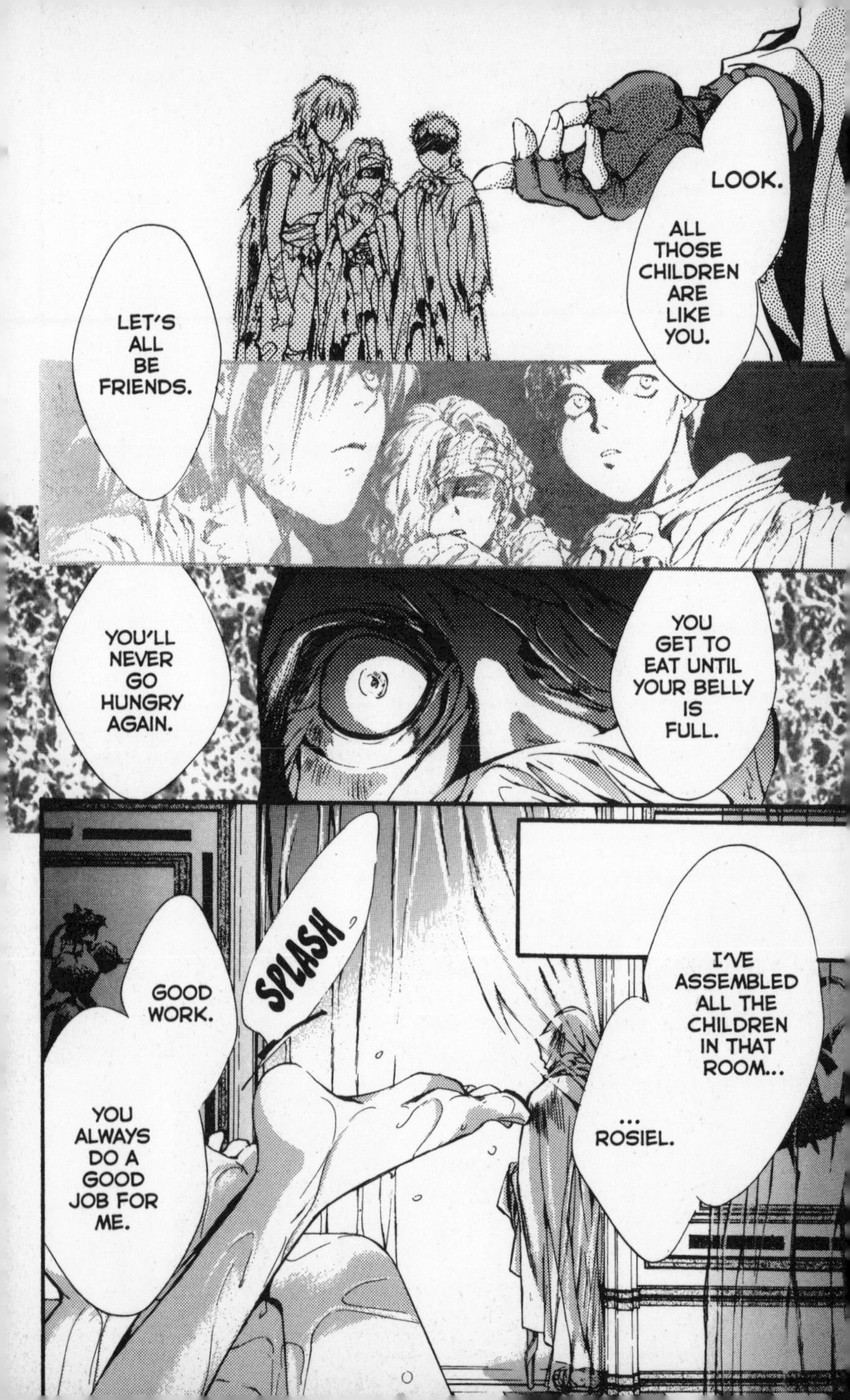
LOOK.
ALL THOSE CHILDREN ARE LIKE YOU.
LET'S ALL BE FRIENDS.
YOU GET TO EAT UNTIL YOUR BELLY IS FULL.
YOU'LL NEVER GO HUNGRY AGAIN.
I'VE ASSEMBLED ALL THE CHILDREN IN THAT ROOM...
... ROSIEL.
SPLASH
GOOD WORK.
YOU ALWAYS DO A GOOD JOB FOR ME.

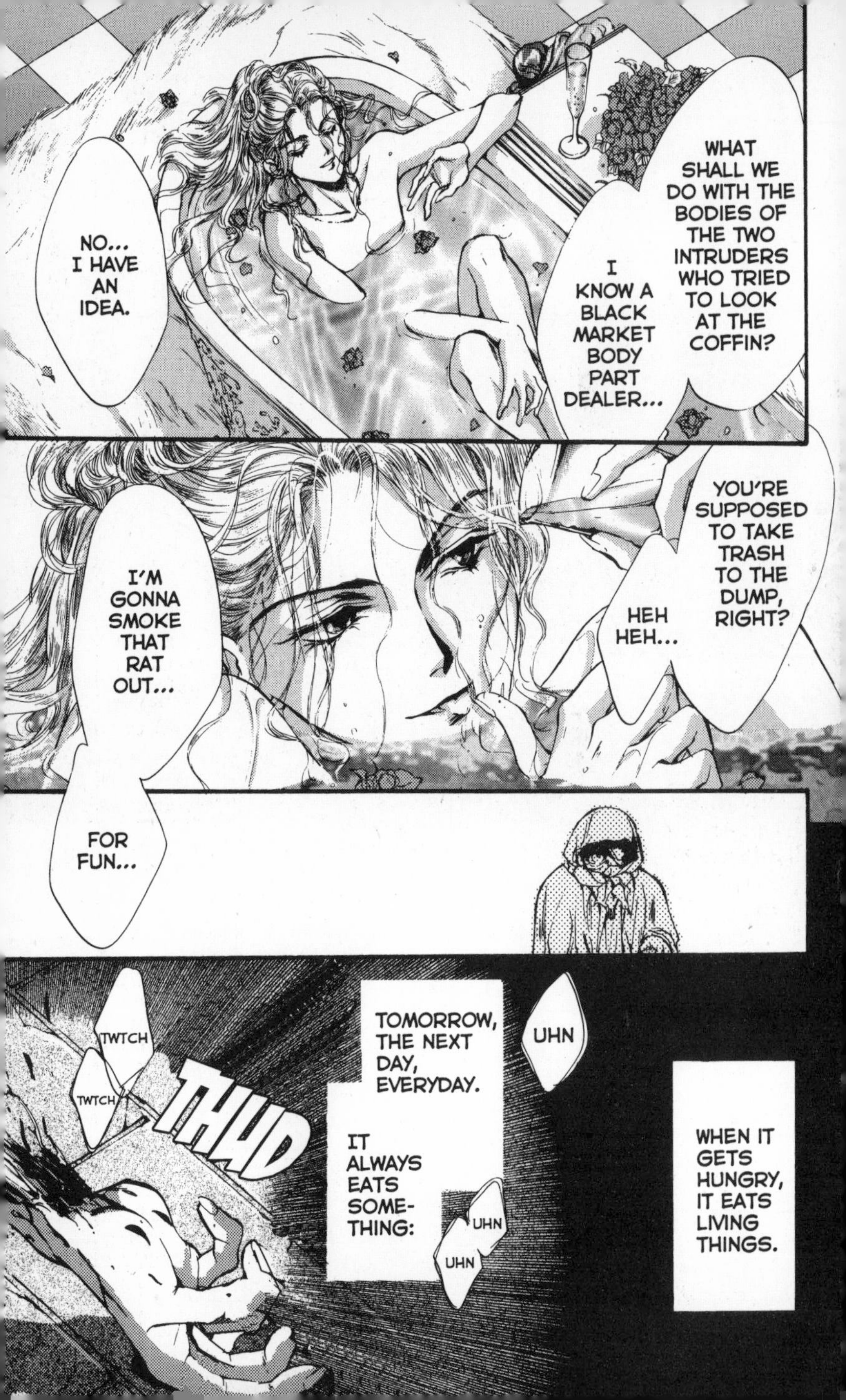
WHAT SHALL WE DO WITH THE BODIES OF THE TWO INTRUDERS WHO TRIED TO LOOK AT THE COFFIN?
I KNOW A BLACK MARKET BODY PART DEALER...
NO... I HAVE AN IDEA.
YOU'RE SUPPOSED TO TAKE TRASH TO THE DUMP, RIGHT?
HEH HEH...
I'M GONNA SMOKE THAT RAT OUT...
FOR FUN...
WHEN IT GETS HUNGRY, IT EATS LIVING THINGS.
UHN
TOMORROW, THE NEXT DAY, EVERYDAY.
IT ALWAYS EATS SOME-THING:
UHN
UHN
THUD
TWTCH
TWTCH

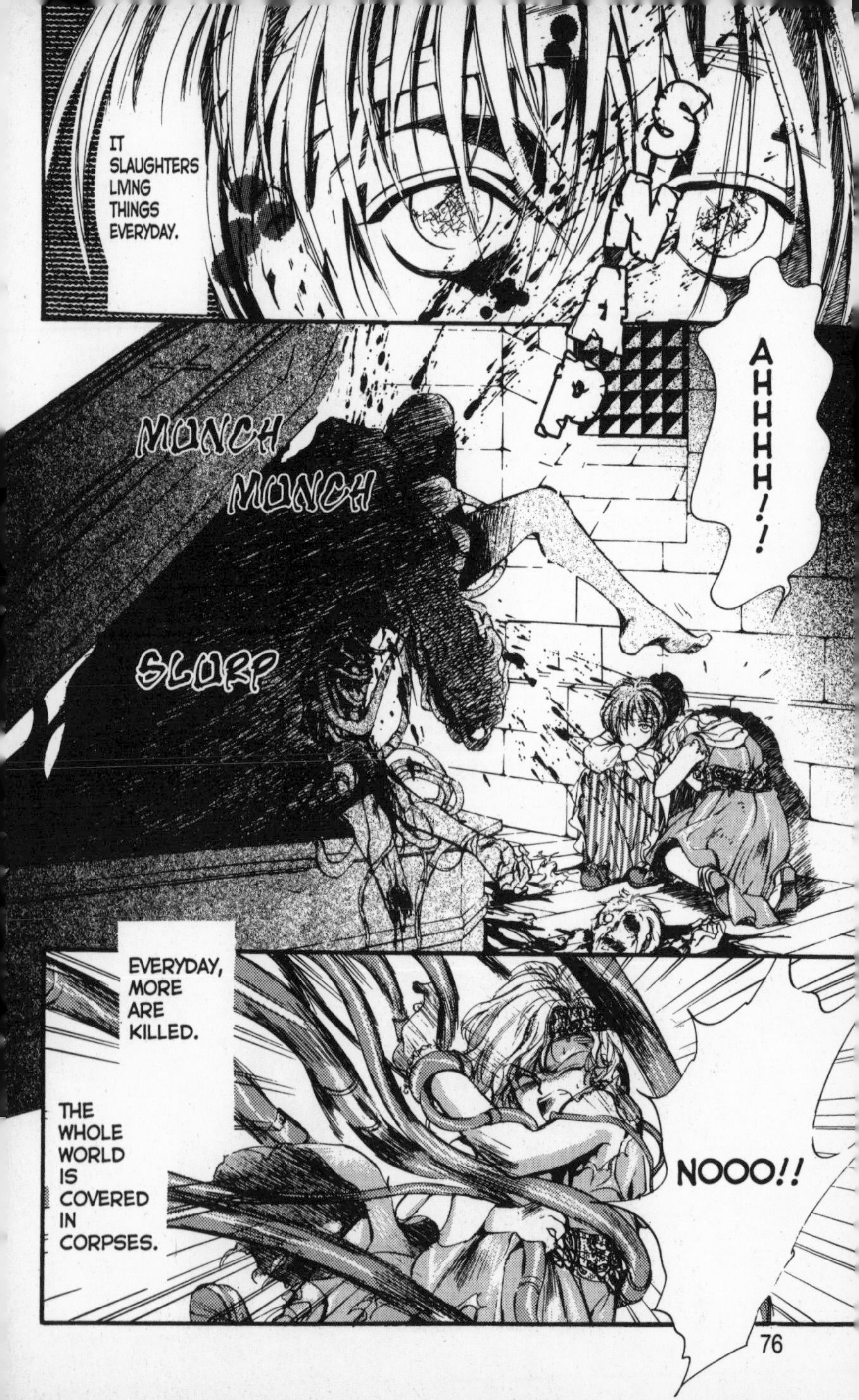
IT SLAUGHTERS LIVING THINGS EVERYDAY.
AHHHH!!
MUNCH
MUNCH
SLURP
EVERYDAY, MORE ARE KILLED.
NOOO!!
THE WHOLE WORLD IS COVERED IN CORPSES.

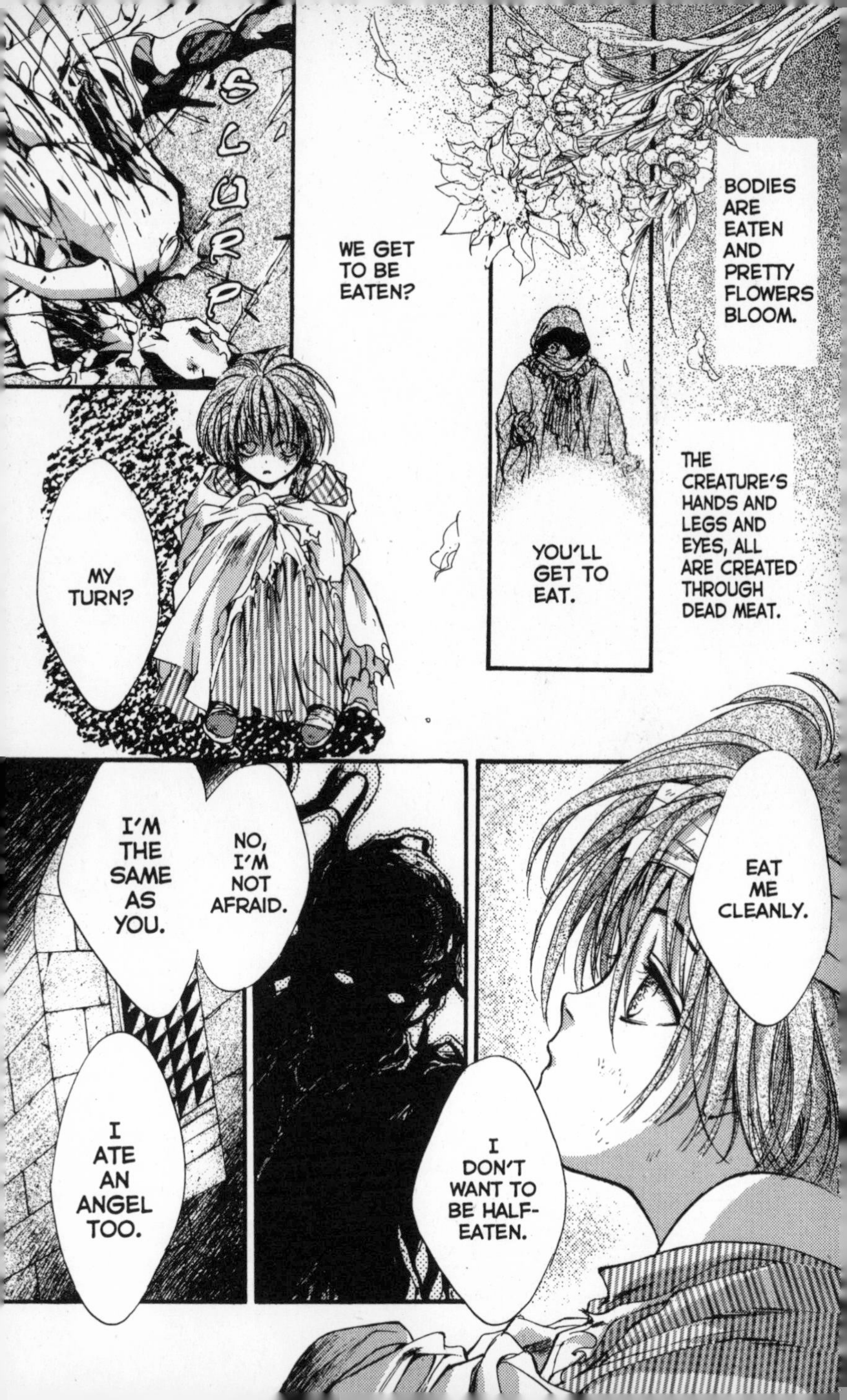
BODIES ARE EATEN AND PRETTY FLOWERS BLOOM.
THE CREATURE'S HANDS AND LEGS AND EYES, ALL ARE CREATED THROUGH DEAD MEAT.
YOU'LL GET TO EAT.
WE GET TO BE EATEN?
SLURP
MY TURN?
EAT ME CLEANLY.
I DON'T WANT TO BE HALF-EATEN.
NO, I'M NOT AFRAID.
I'M THE SAME AS YOU.
I ATE AN ANGEL TOO.

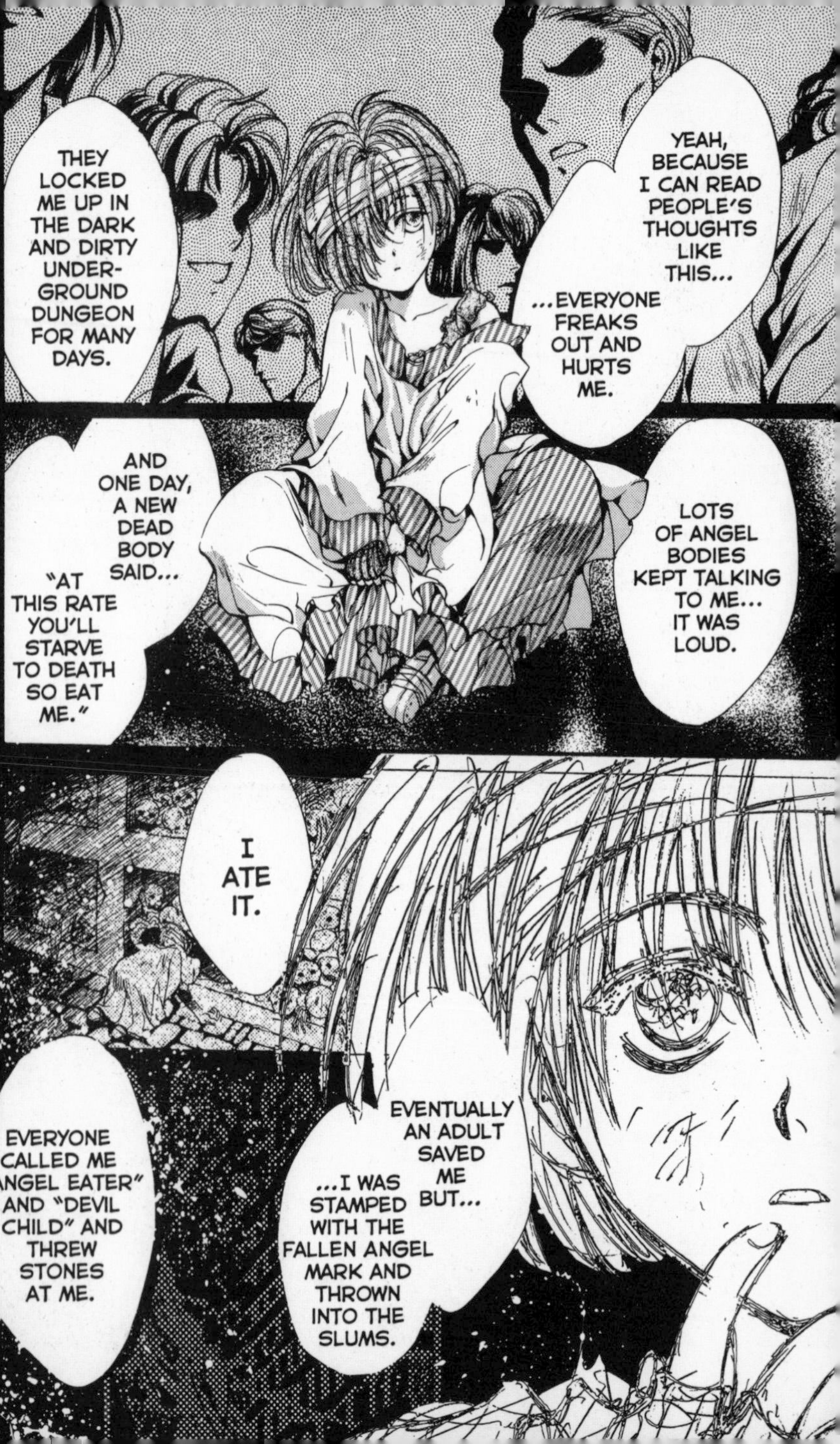

YEAH, BECAUSE I CAN READ PEOPLE'S THOUGHTS LIKE THIS...
...EVERYONE FREAKS OUT AND HURTS ME.
THEY LOCKED ME UP IN THE DARK AND DIRTY UNDER-GROUND DUNGEON FOR MANY DAYS.
LOTS OF ANGEL BODIES KEPT TALKING TO ME... IT WAS LOUD.
AND ONE DAY, A NEW DEAD BODY SAID...
"AT THIS RATE YOU'LL STARVE TO DEATH SO EAT ME."
I ATE IT.
EVENTUALLY AN ADULT SAVED ME BUT...
...I WAS STAMPED WITH THE FALLEN ANGEL MARK AND THROWN INTO THE SLUMS.
EVERYONE CALLED ME "ANGEL EATER" AND "DEVIL CHILD" AND THREW STONES AT ME.

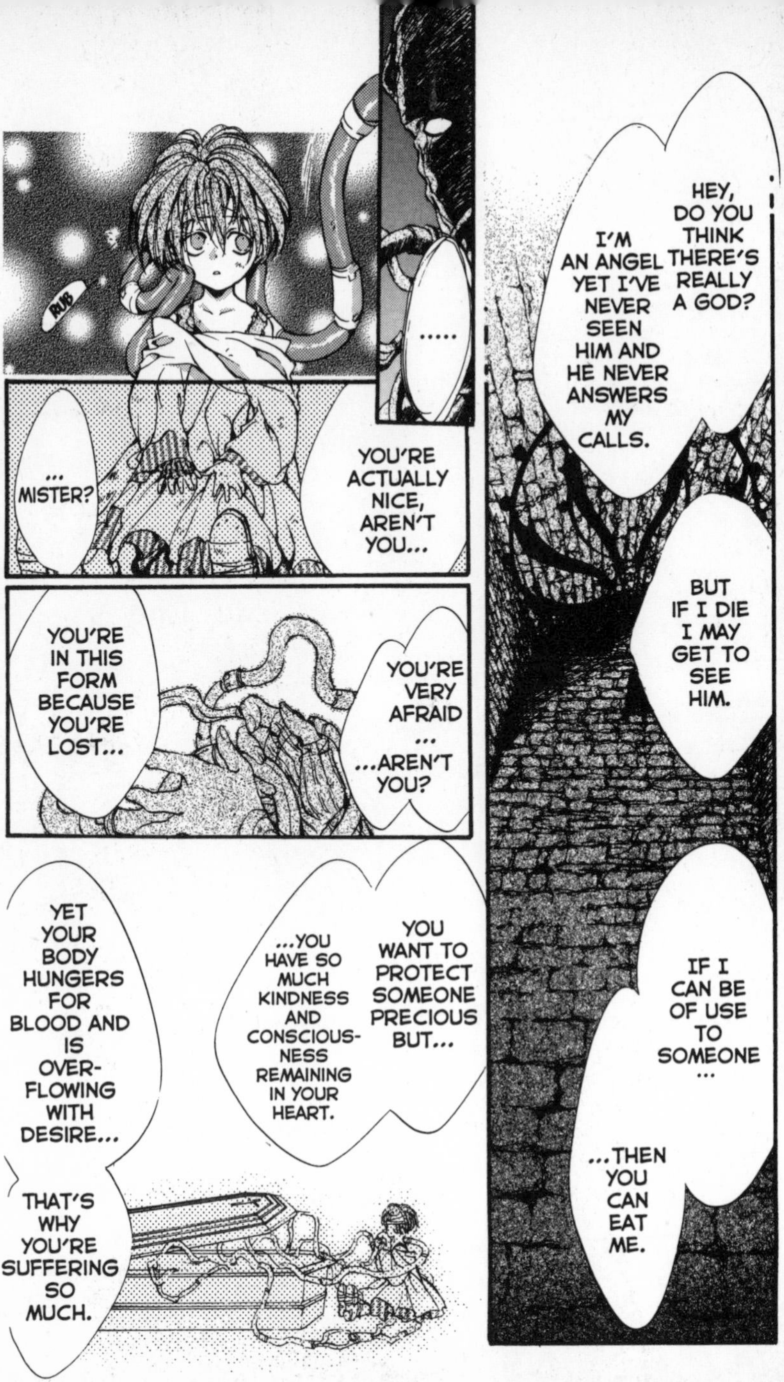
HEY, DO YOU THINK THERE'S REALLY A GOD?
I'M AN ANGEL YET I'VE NEVER SEEN HIM AND HE NEVER ANSWERS MY CALLS.
BUT IF I DIE I MAY GET TO SEE HIM.
IF I CAN BE OF USE TO SOMEONE ...
...THEN YOU CAN EAT ME.
.....
RUB
YOU'RE ACTUALLY NICE, AREN'T YOU...
... MISTER?
YOU'RE VERY AFRAID ... ...AREN'T YOU?
YOU'RE IN THIS FORM BECAUSE YOU'RE LOST...
YOU WANT TO PROTECT SOMEONE PRECIOUS BUT...
...YOU HAVE SO MUCH KINDNESS AND CONSCIOUS-NESS REMAINING IN YOUR HEART.
YET YOUR BODY HUNGERS FOR BLOOD AND IS OVER-FLOWING WITH DESIRE...
THAT'S WHY YOU'RE SUFFERING SO MUCH.

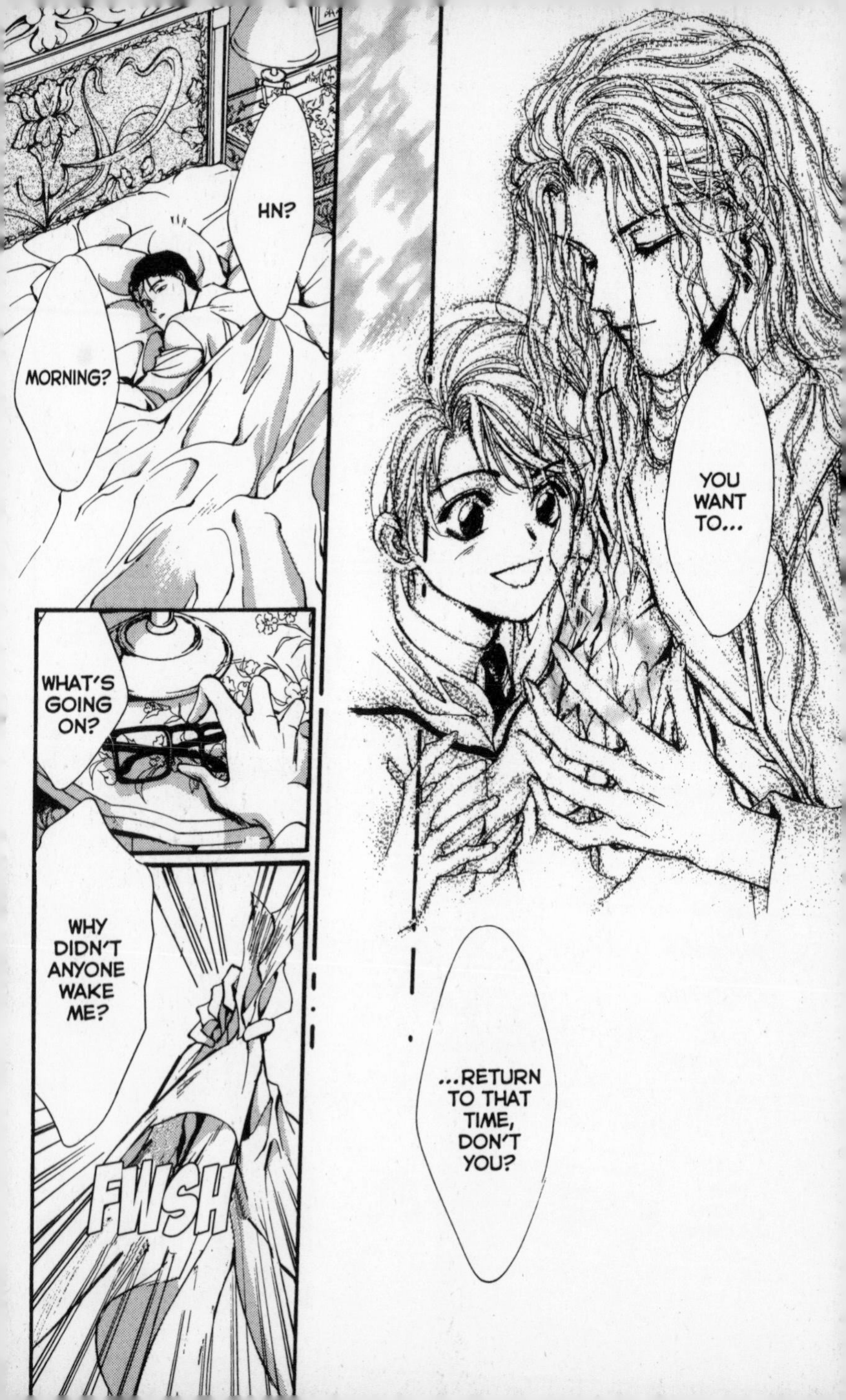
YOU WANT TO...
...RETURN TO THAT TIME, DON'T YOU?
HN?
MORNING?
WHAT'S GOING ON?
WHY DIDN'T ANYONE WAKE ME?
FWSH

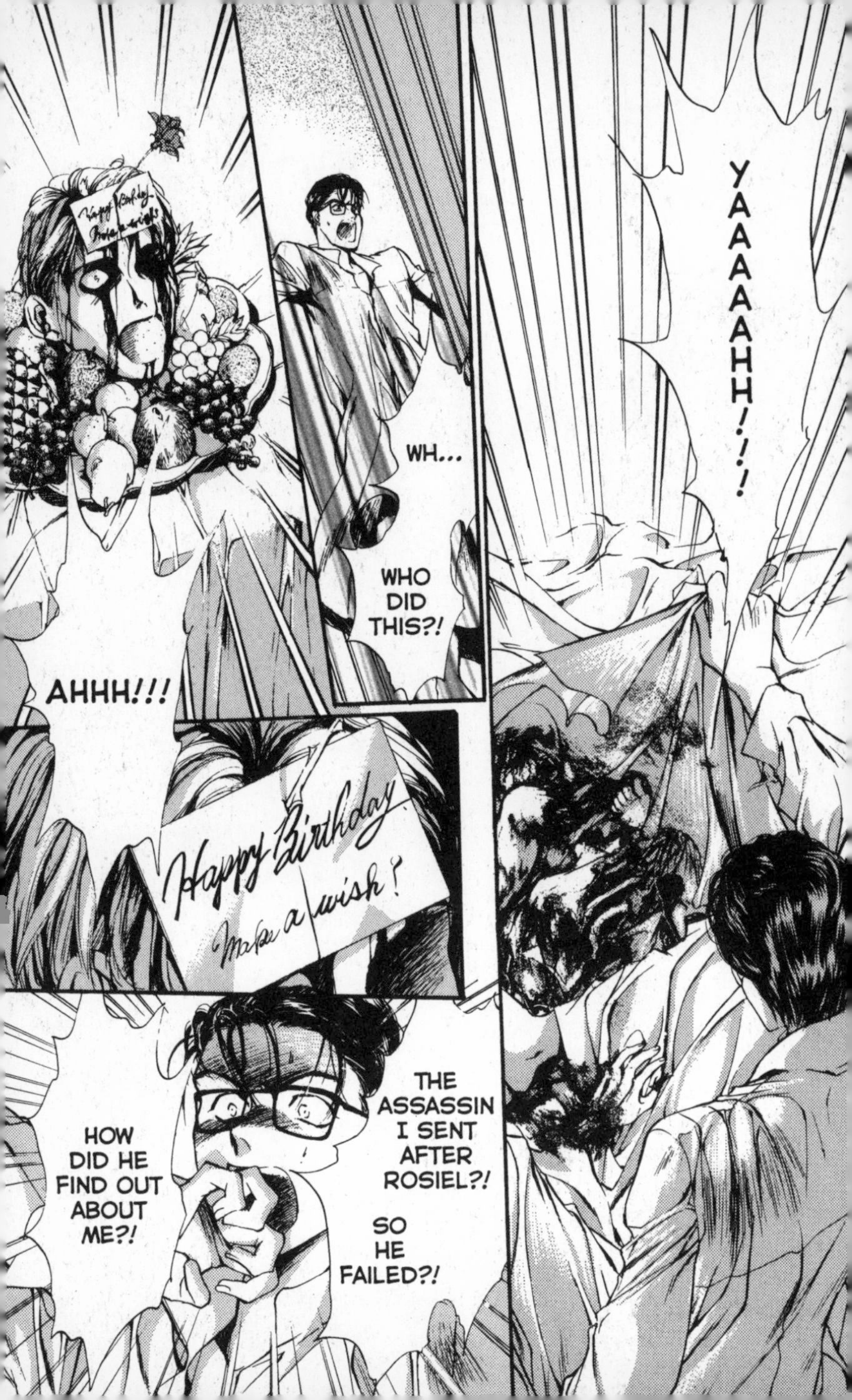
YAAAAAHH!!!
WH...
WHO DID THIS?!
AHHH!!!
Happy Birthday
Make a wish?
THE ASSASSIN I SENT AFTER ROSIEL?!
SO HE FAILED?!
HOW DID HE FIND OUT ABOUT ME?!

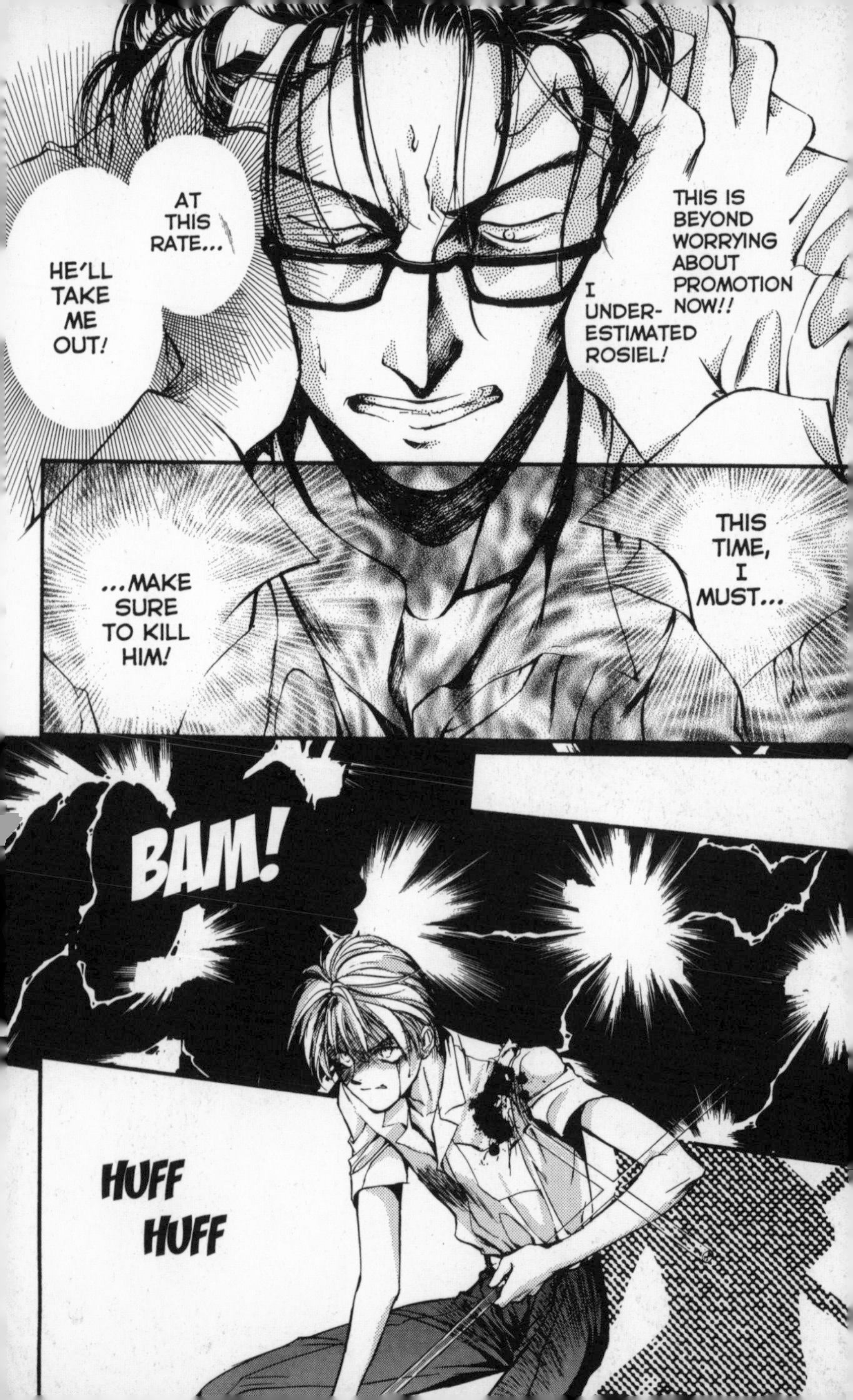
THIS IS BEYOND WORRYING ABOUT PROMOTION NOW!!
I UNDER-ESTIMATED ROSIEL!
AT THIS RATE...
HE'LL TAKE ME OUT!
THIS TIME, I MUST...
...MAKE SURE TO KILL HIM!
BAM!
HUFF HUFF

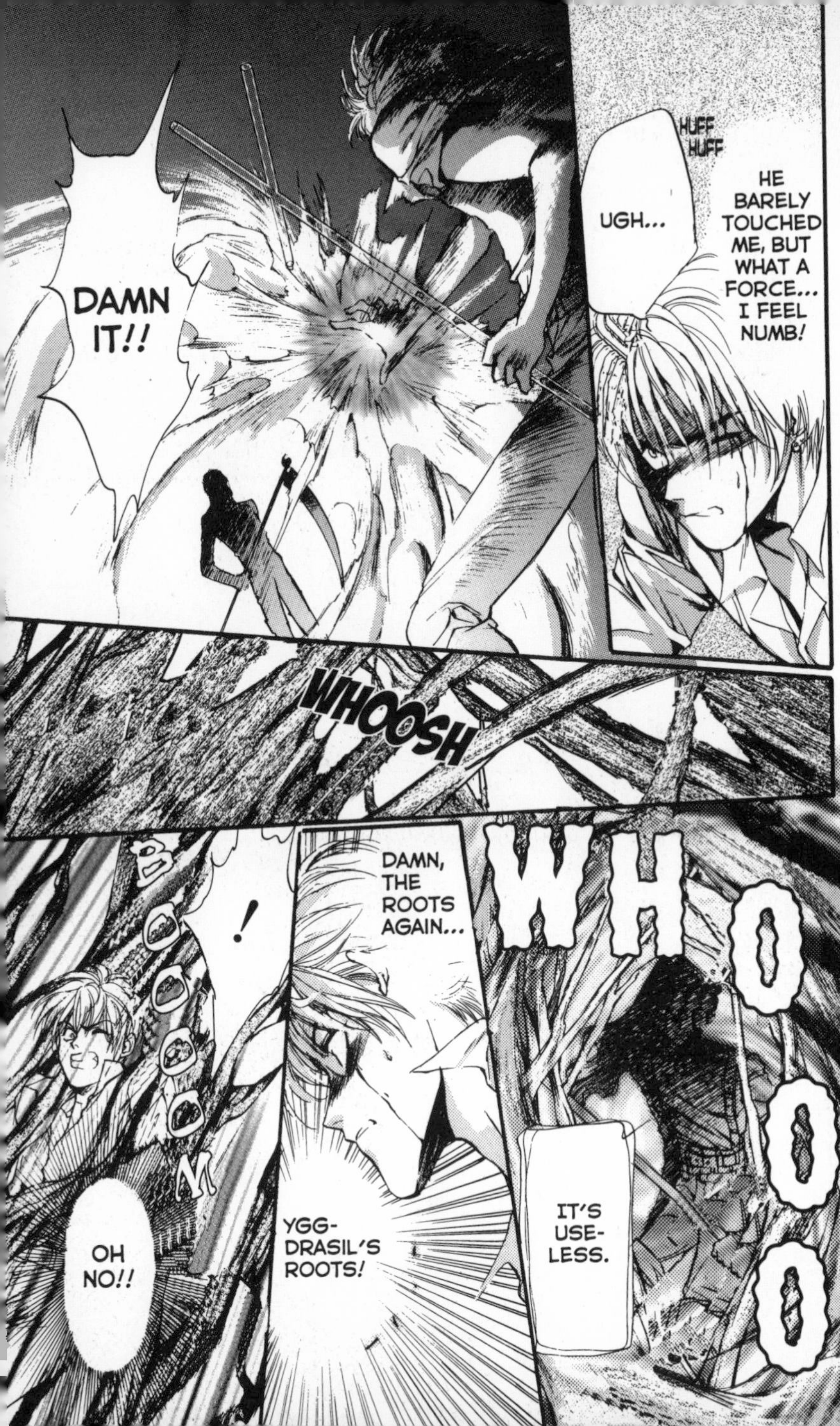
HUFF HUFF
UGH...
HE BARELY TOUCHED ME, BUT WHAT A FORCE... I FEEL NUMB!
DAMN IT!!
WHOOSH
WHOOOO
IT'S USE-LESS.
DAMN, THE ROOTS AGAIN...
YGG-DRASIL'S ROOTS!
BOOOOOM
!
OH NO!!

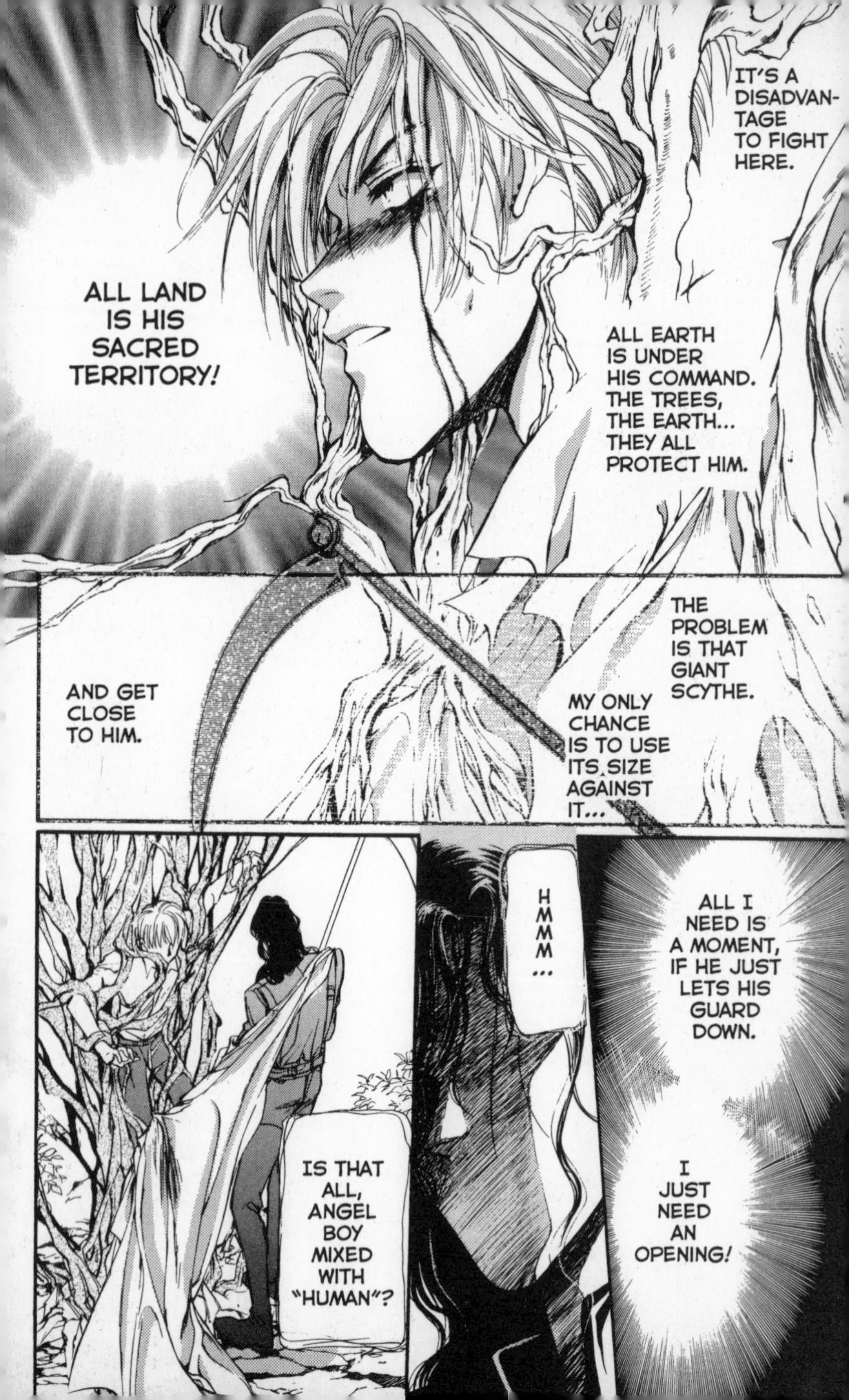
IT'S A DISADVAN-TAGE TO FIGHT HERE.
ALL EARTH IS UNDER HIS COMMAND. THE TREES, THE EARTH... THEY ALL PROTECT HIM.
ALL LAND IS HIS SACRED TERRITORY!
THE PROBLEM IS THAT GIANT SCYTHE.
MY ONLY CHANCE IS TO USE ITS SIZE AGAINST IT...
AND GET CLOSE TO HIM.
ALL I NEED IS A MOMENT, IF HE JUST LETS HIS GUARD DOWN.
I JUST NEED AN OPENING!
HMMM...
IS THAT ALL, ANGEL BOY MIXED WITH "HUMAN"?

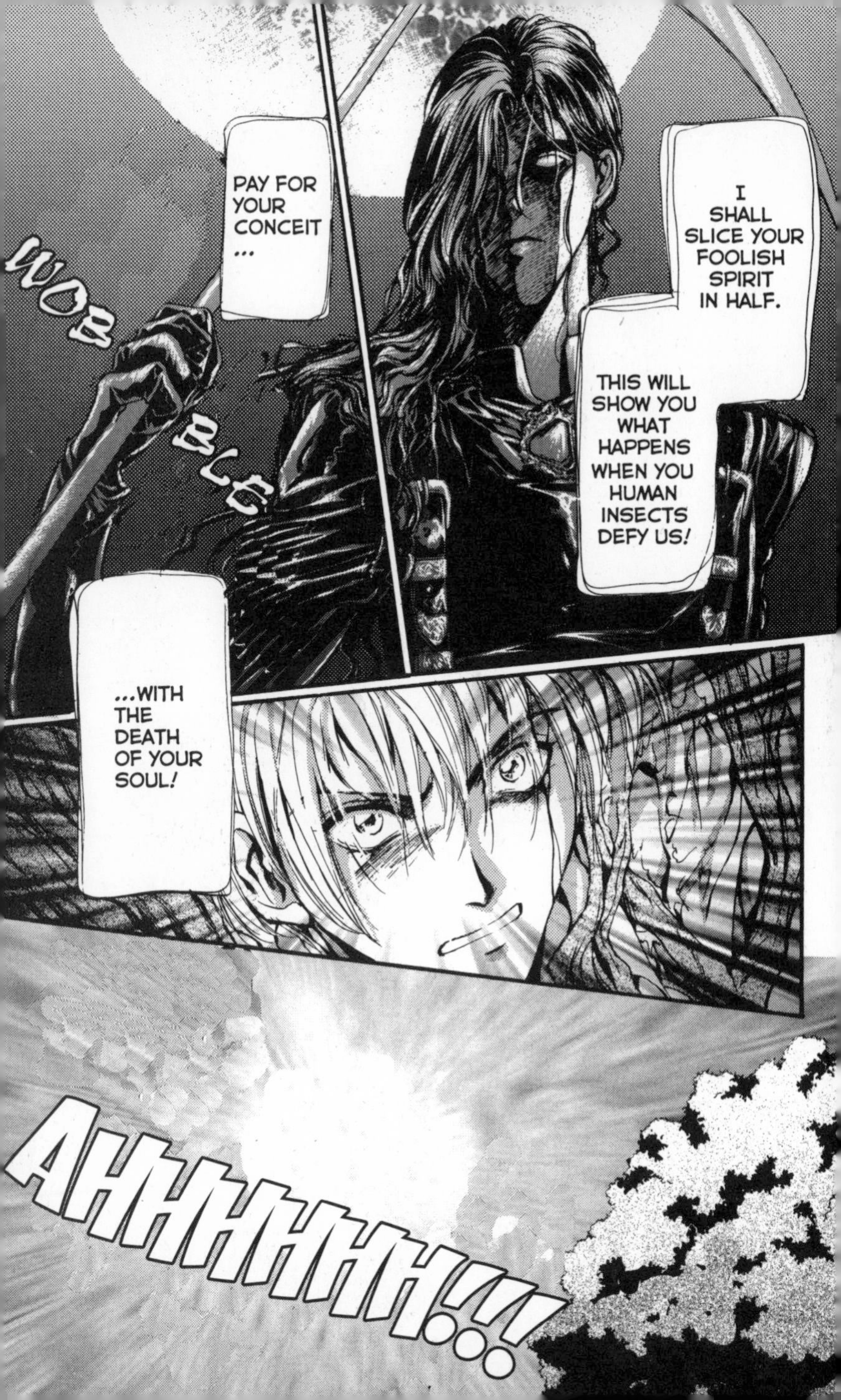
I SHALL SLICE YOUR FOOLISH SPIRIT IN HALF.
THIS WILL SHOW YOU WHAT HAPPENS WHEN YOU HUMAN INSECTS DEFY US!
PAY FOR YOUR CONCEIT ...
WOBBLE
...WITH THE DEATH OF YOUR SOUL!
AHHHHHH!!!...

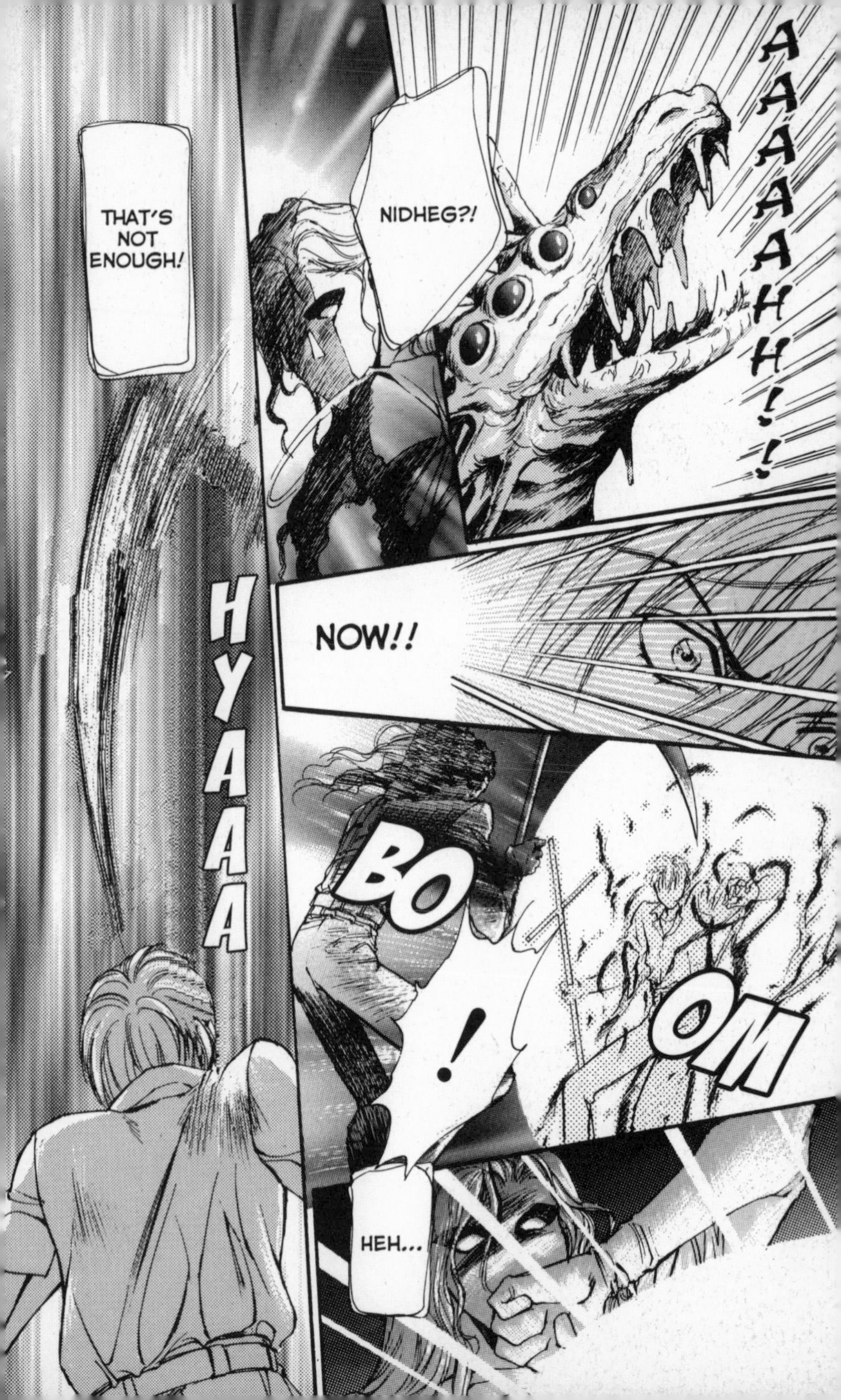
AAAAAHH!!
NIDHEG?!
NOW!!
BOOM
!
HEH...
THAT'S NOT ENOUGH!
HYAAAA

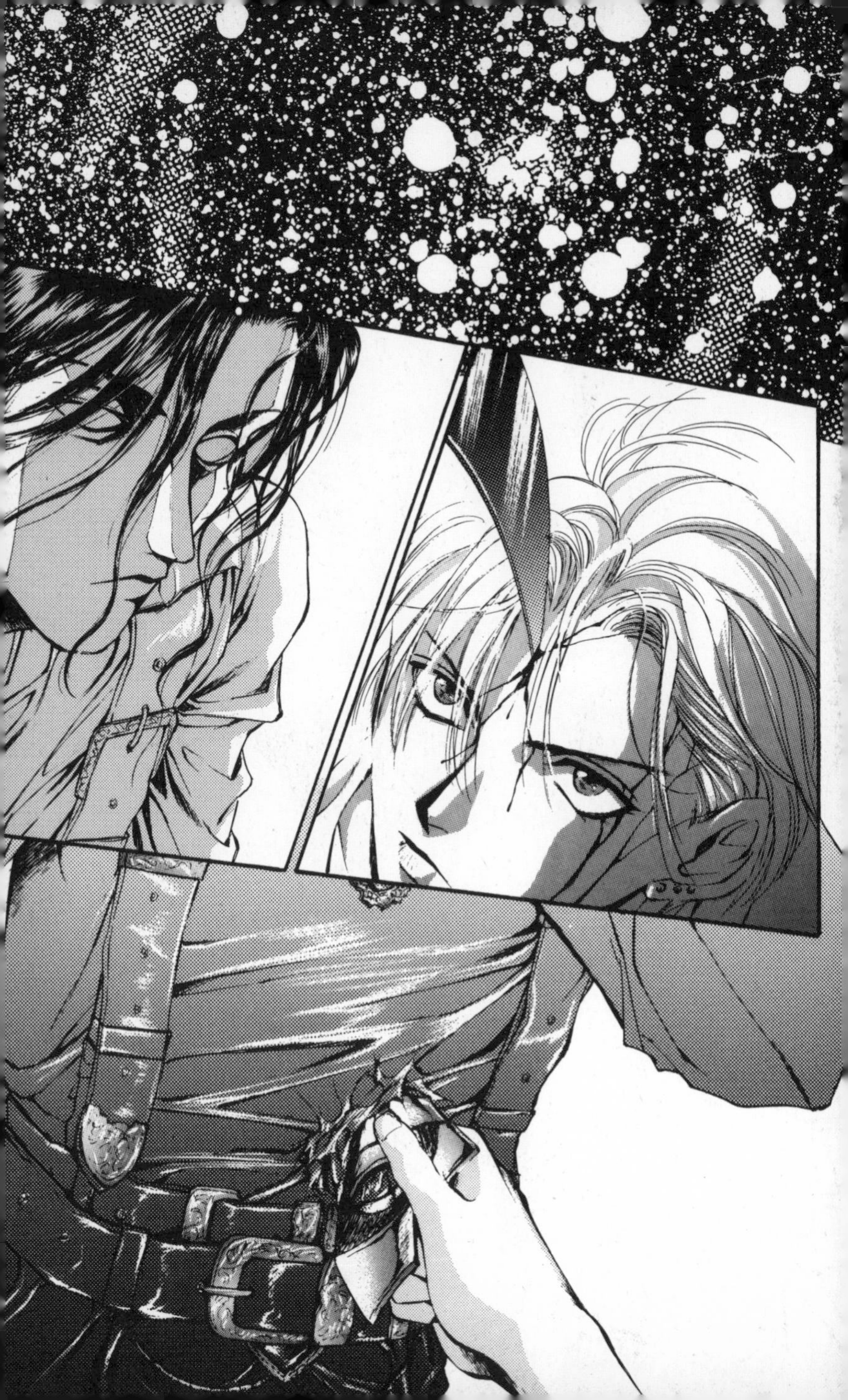

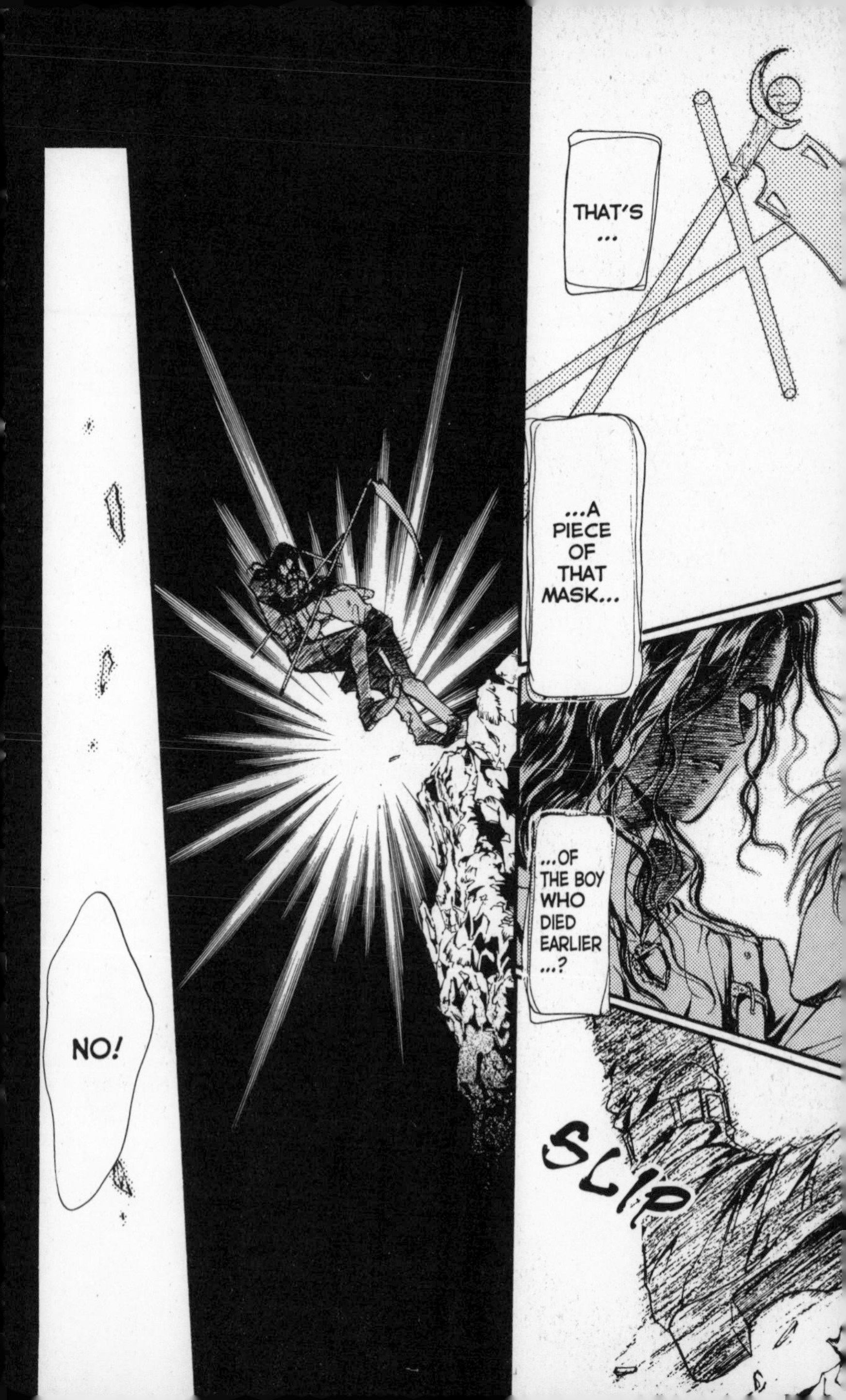
THAT'S ...
...A PIECE OF THAT MASK...
...OF THE BOY WHO DIED EARLIER ...?
SLIP
NO!

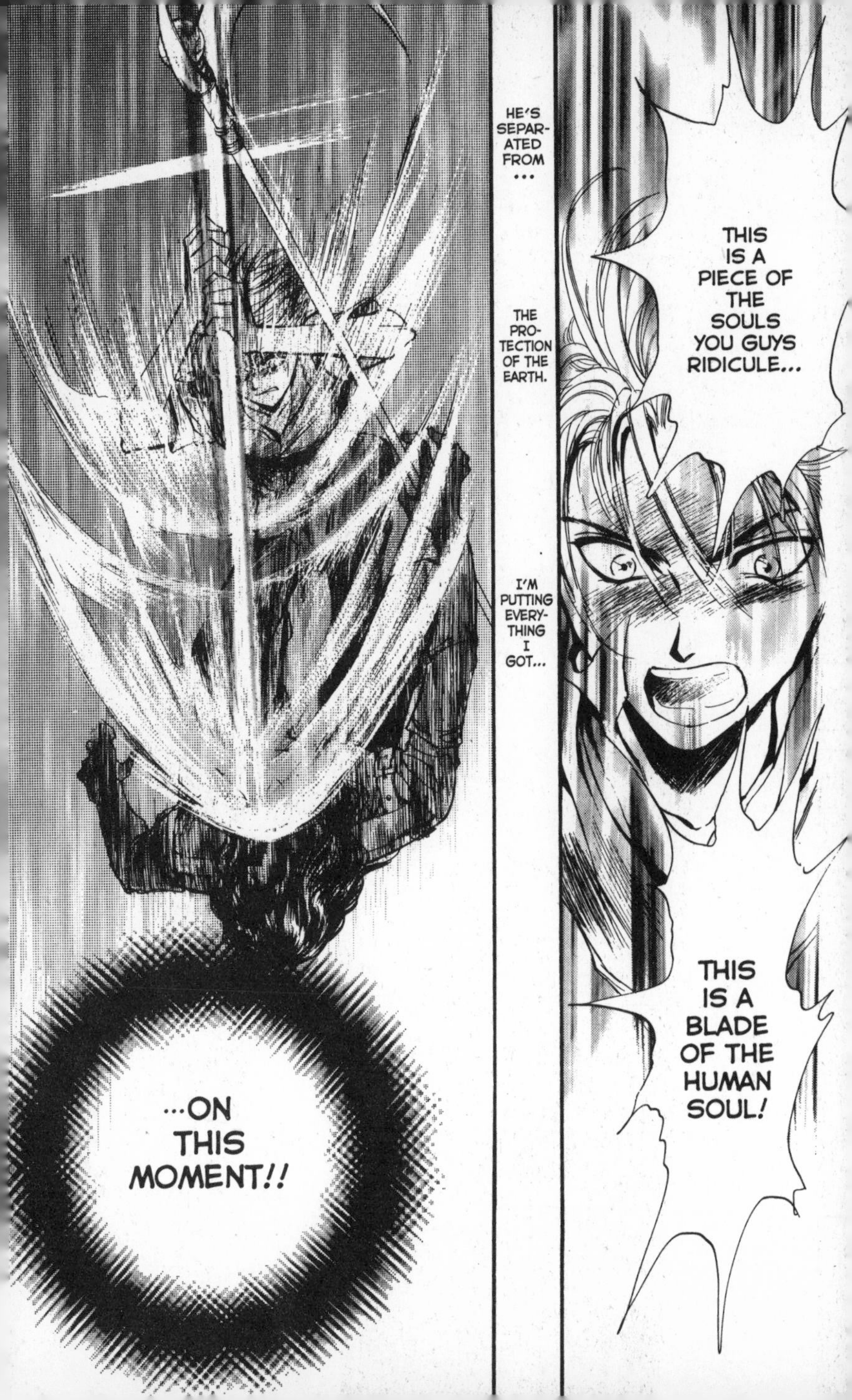
THIS IS A PIECE OF THE SOULS YOU GUYS RIDICULE...
THIS IS A BLADE OF THE HUMAN SOUL!
HE'S SEPARATED FROM...
THE PROTECTION OF THE EARTH.
I'M PUTTING EVERYTHING I GOT...
...ON THIS MOMENT!!

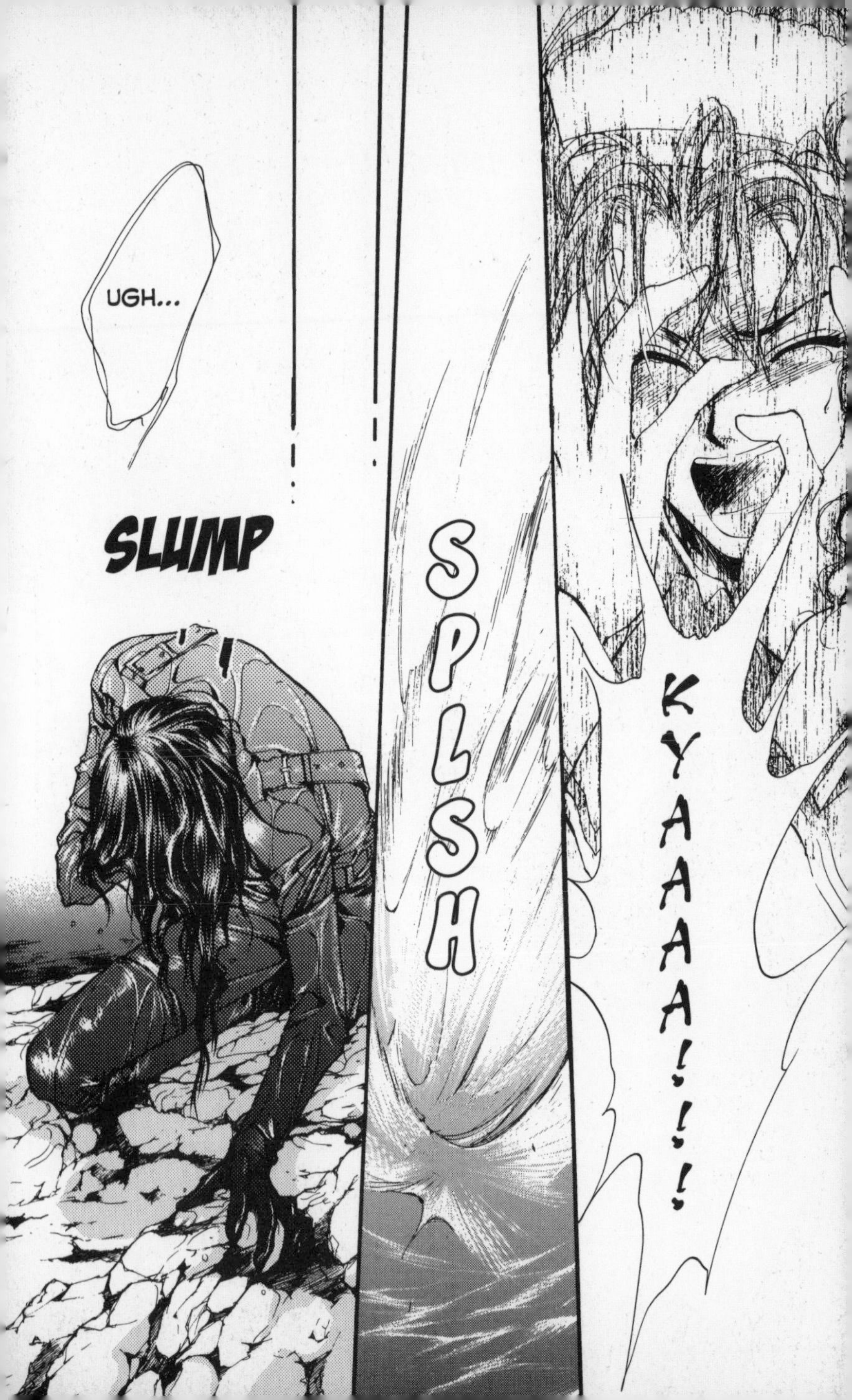
KYAAAA!!!
SPLSH
UGH...
SLUMP

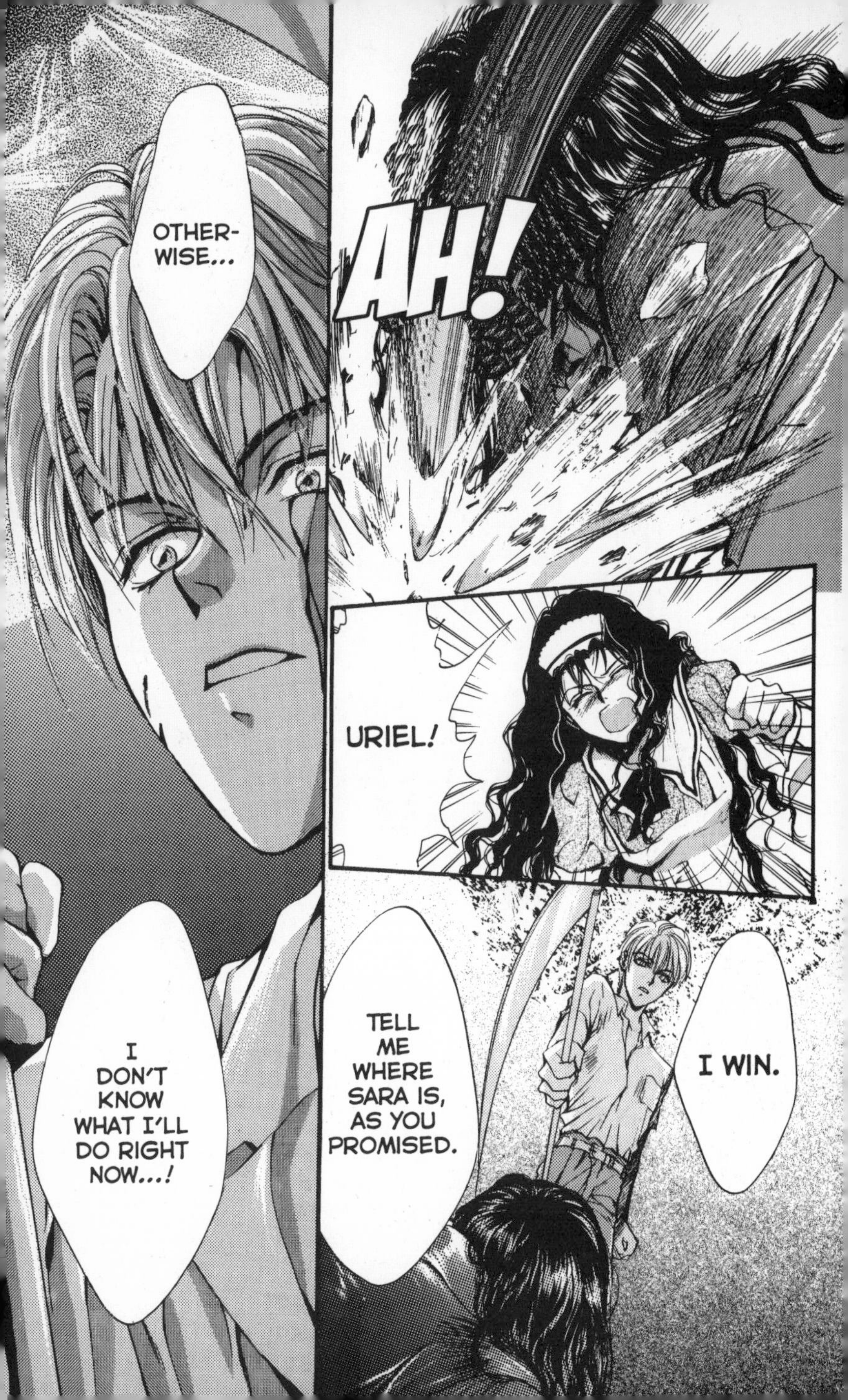
AH!
URIEL!
I WIN.
TELL ME WHERE SARA IS, AS YOU PROMISED.
OTHER-WISE...
I DON'T KNOW WHAT I'LL DO RIGHT NOW...!

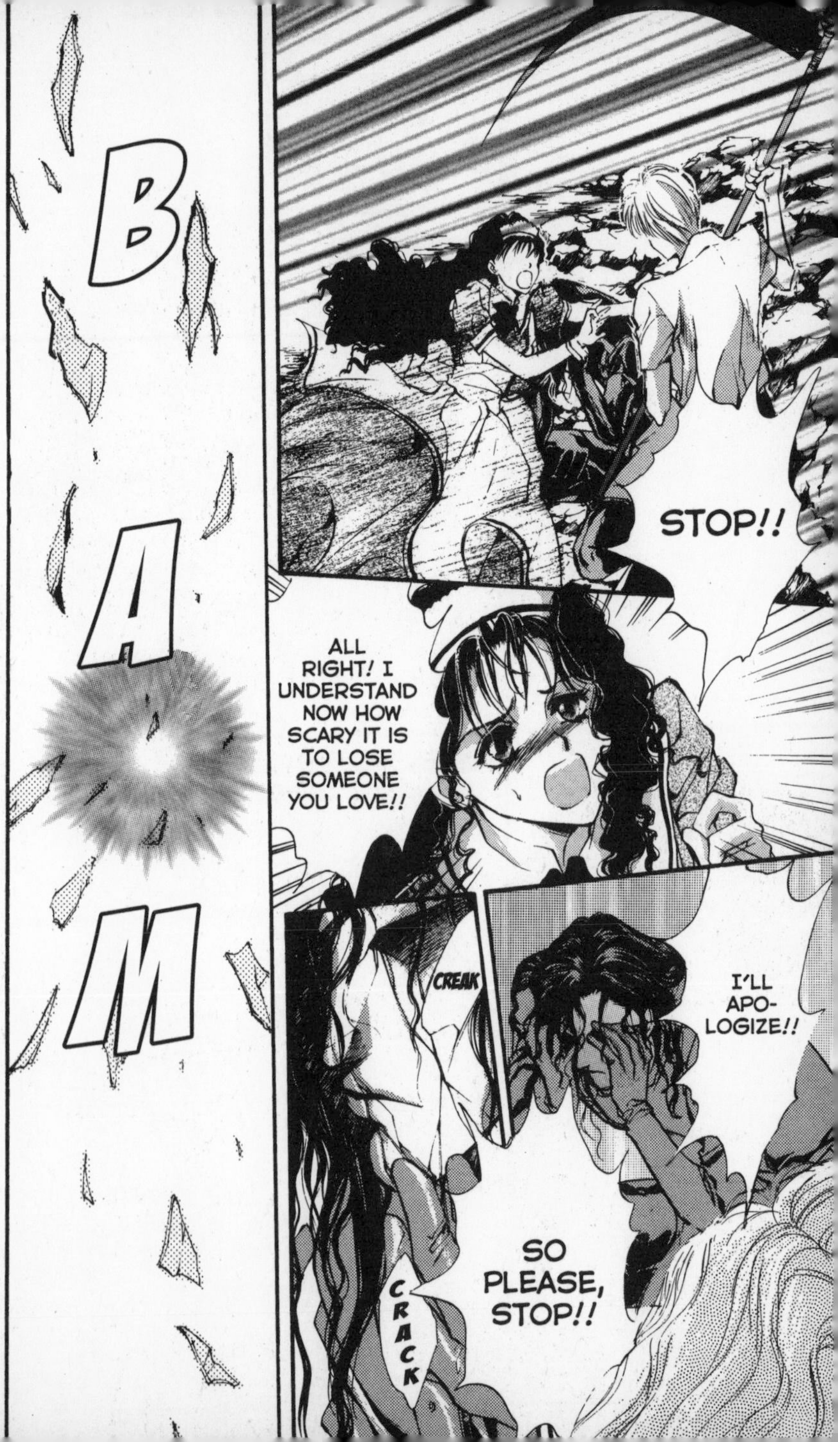
STOP!!
ALL RIGHT! I UNDERSTAND NOW HOW SCARY IT IS TO LOSE SOMEONE YOU LOVE!!
I'LL APOLOGIZE!!
SO PLEASE, STOP!!
CREAK
CRACK
BAM

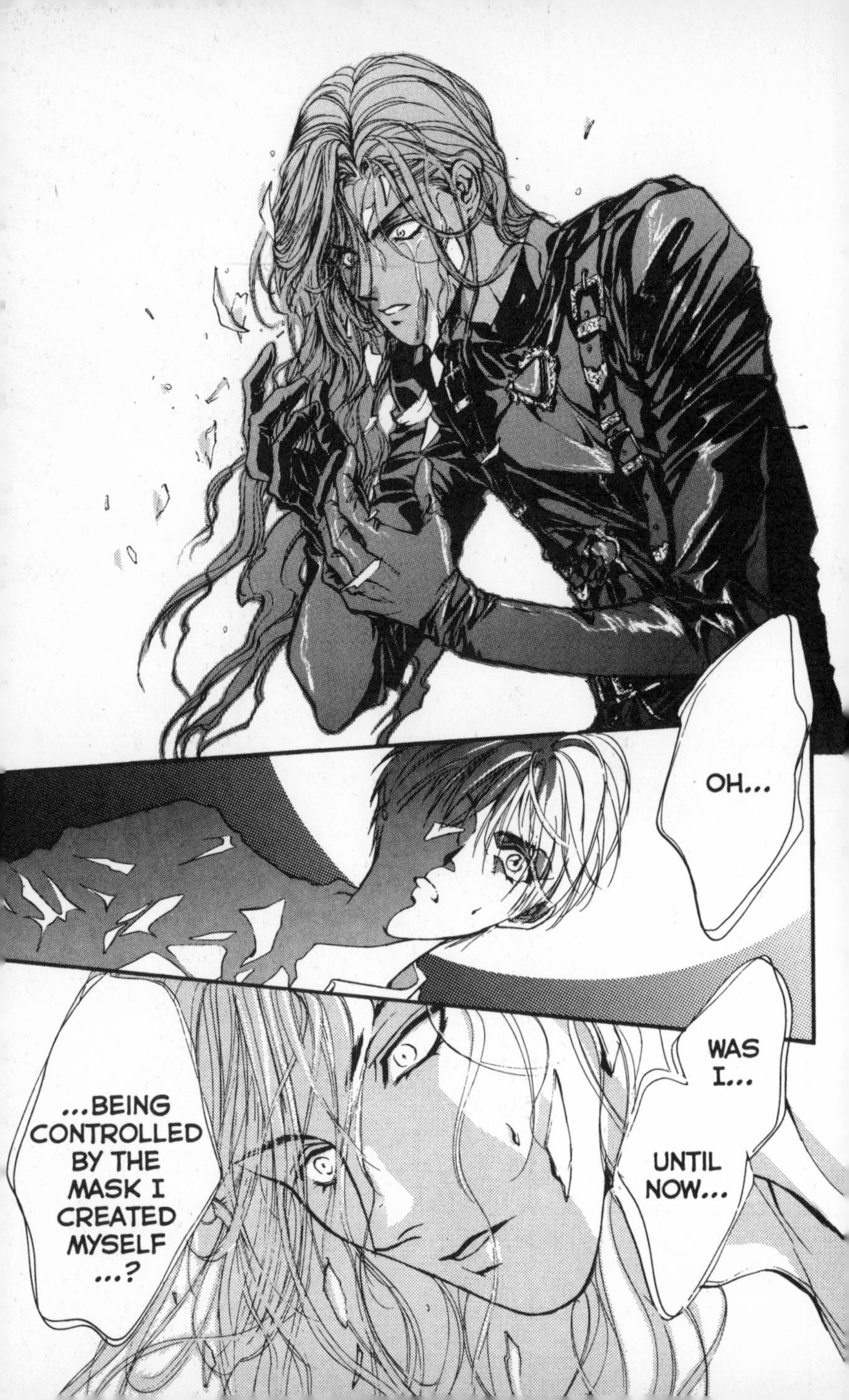
OH...
WAS I...
UNTIL NOW...
...BEING CONTROLLED BY THE MASK I CREATED MYSELF ...?

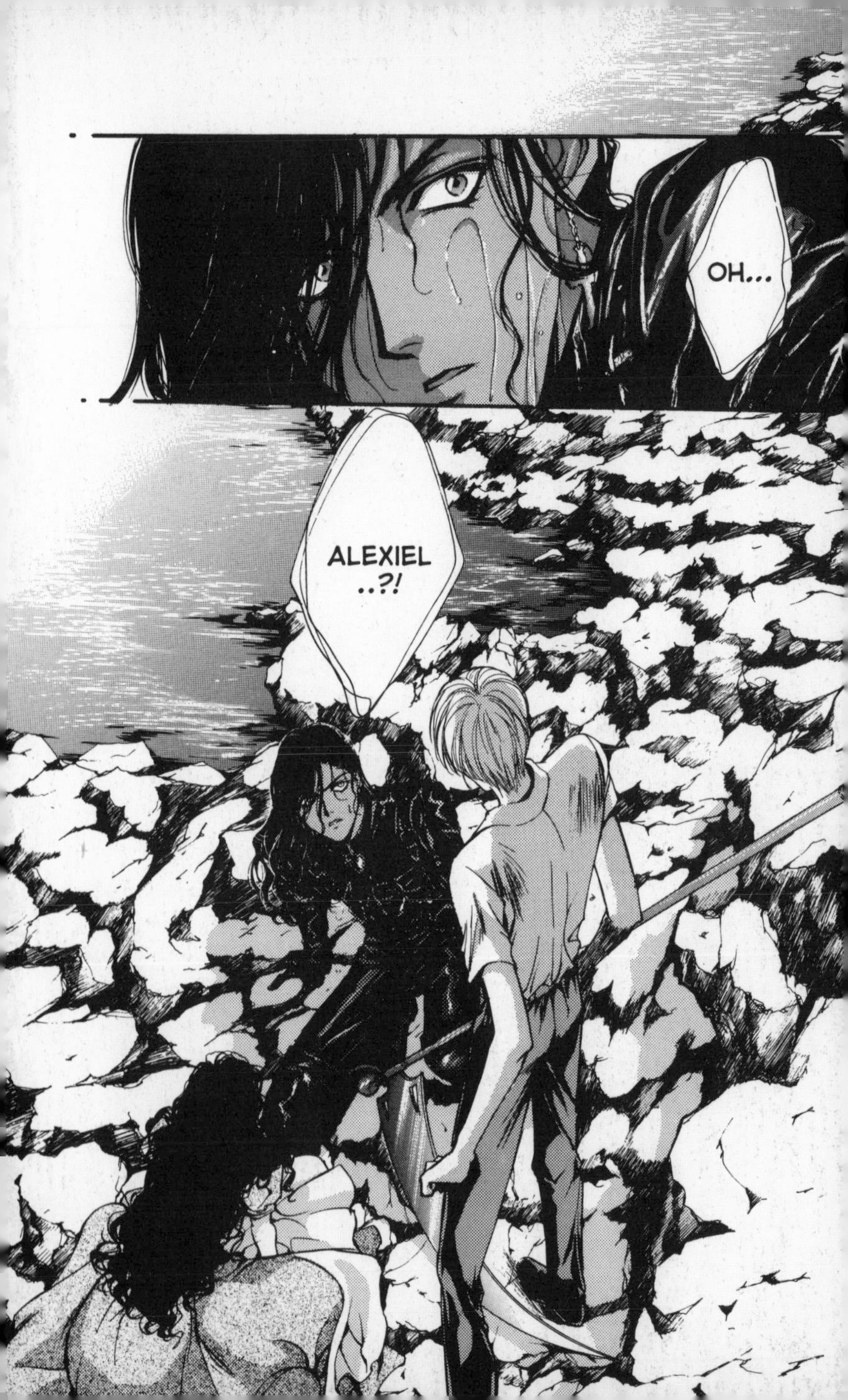
OH...
ALEXIEL ..?!

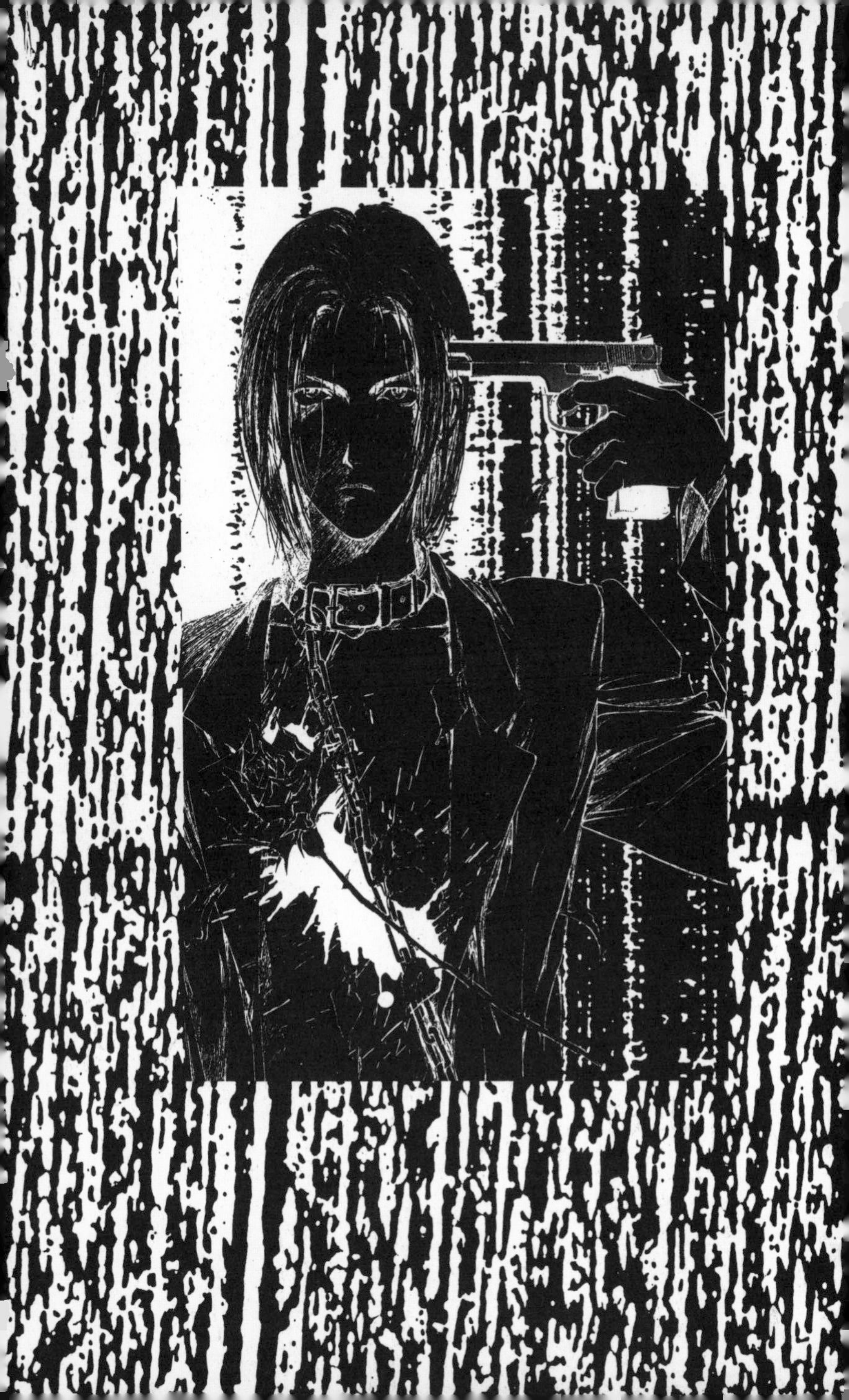

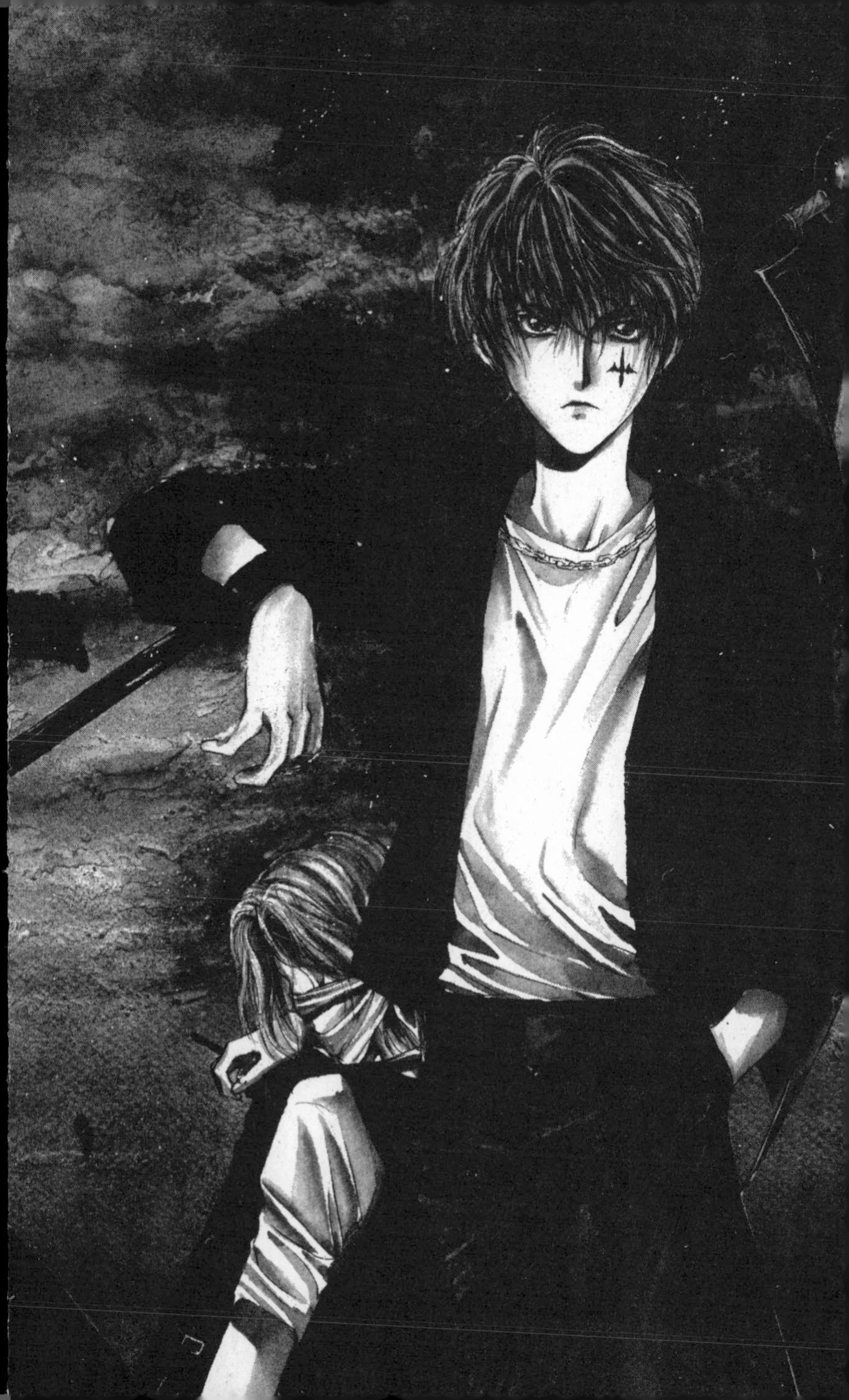

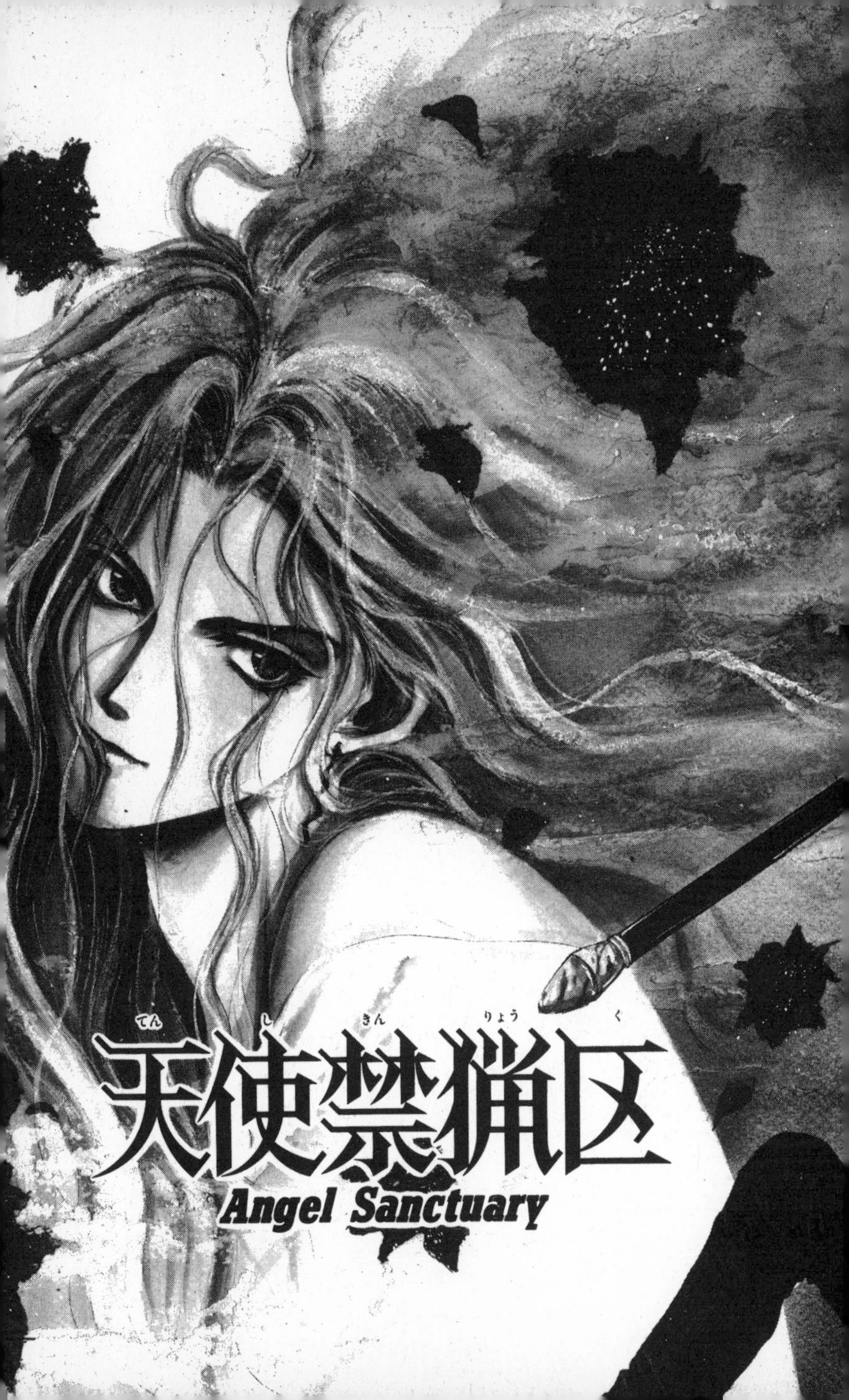
てん し きん りょう く
天使禁猟区
Angel Sanctuary

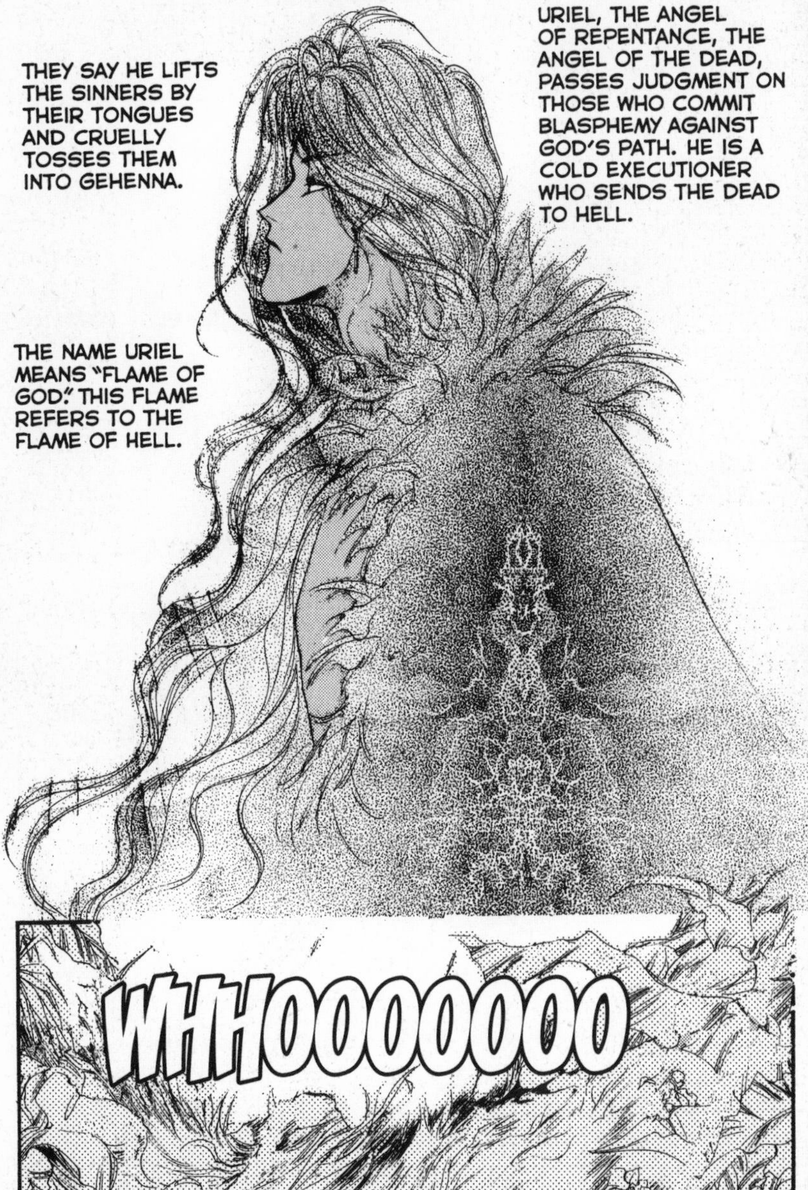
URIEL, THE ANGEL OF REPENTANCE, THE ANGEL OF THE DEAD, PASSES JUDGMENT ON THOSE WHO COMMIT BLASPHEMY AGAINST GOD'S PATH. HE IS A COLD EXECUTIONER WHO SENDS THE DEAD TO HELL.
THEY SAY HE LIFTS THE SINNERS BY THEIR TONGUES AND CRUELLY TOSSES THEM INTO GEHENNA.
THE NAME URIEL MEANS "FLAME OF GOD." THIS FLAME REFERS TO THE FLAME OF HELL.
WHHOOOOOOO

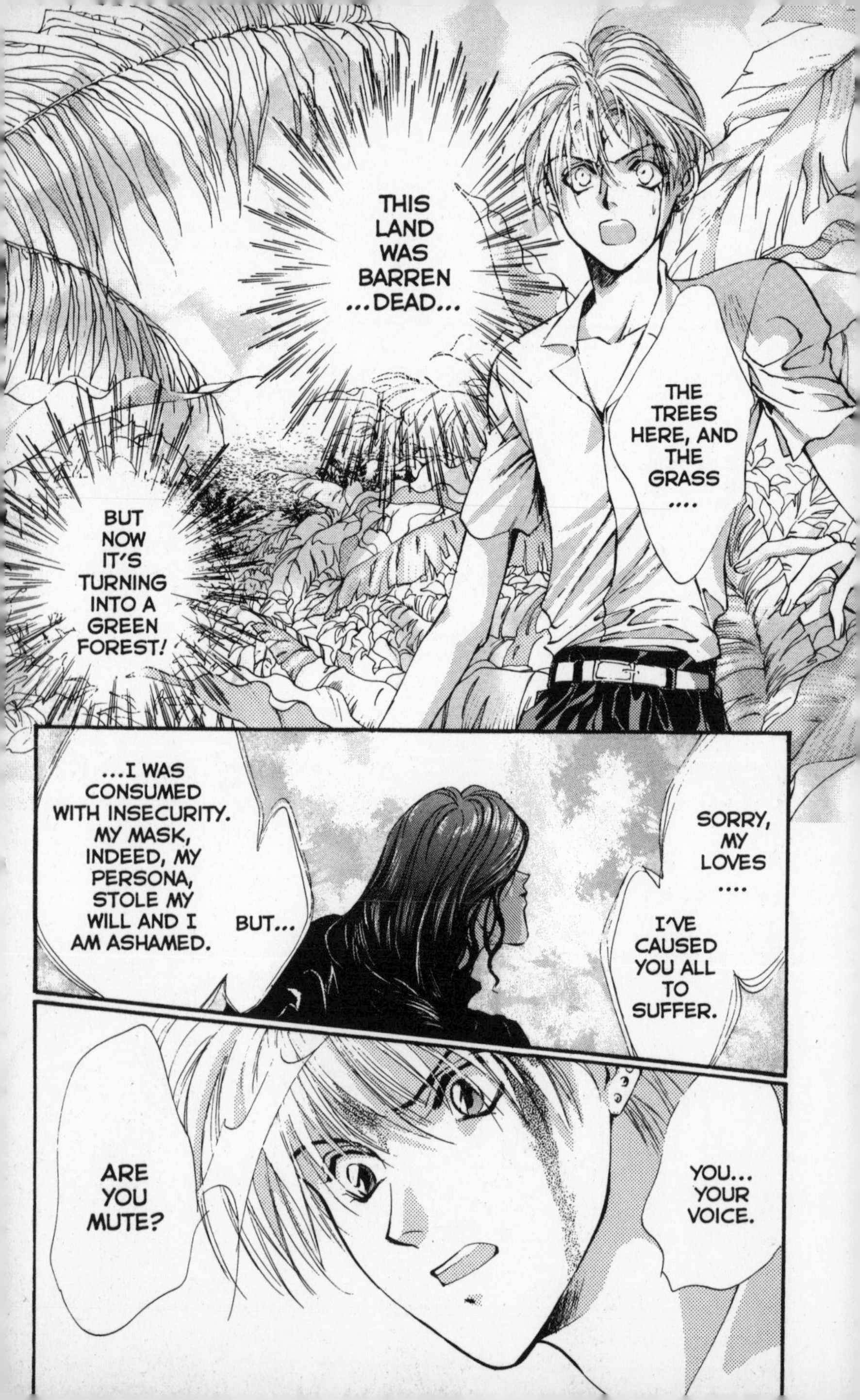
THIS LAND WAS BARREN ...DEAD...
THE TREES HERE, AND THE GRASS ....
BUT NOW IT'S TURNING INTO A GREEN FOREST!
SORRY, MY LOVES ....
I'VE CAUSED YOU ALL TO SUFFER.
BUT...
...I WAS CONSUMED WITH INSECURITY. MY MASK, INDEED, MY PERSONA, STOLE MY WILL AND I AM ASHAMED.
YOU... YOUR VOICE.
ARE YOU MUTE?

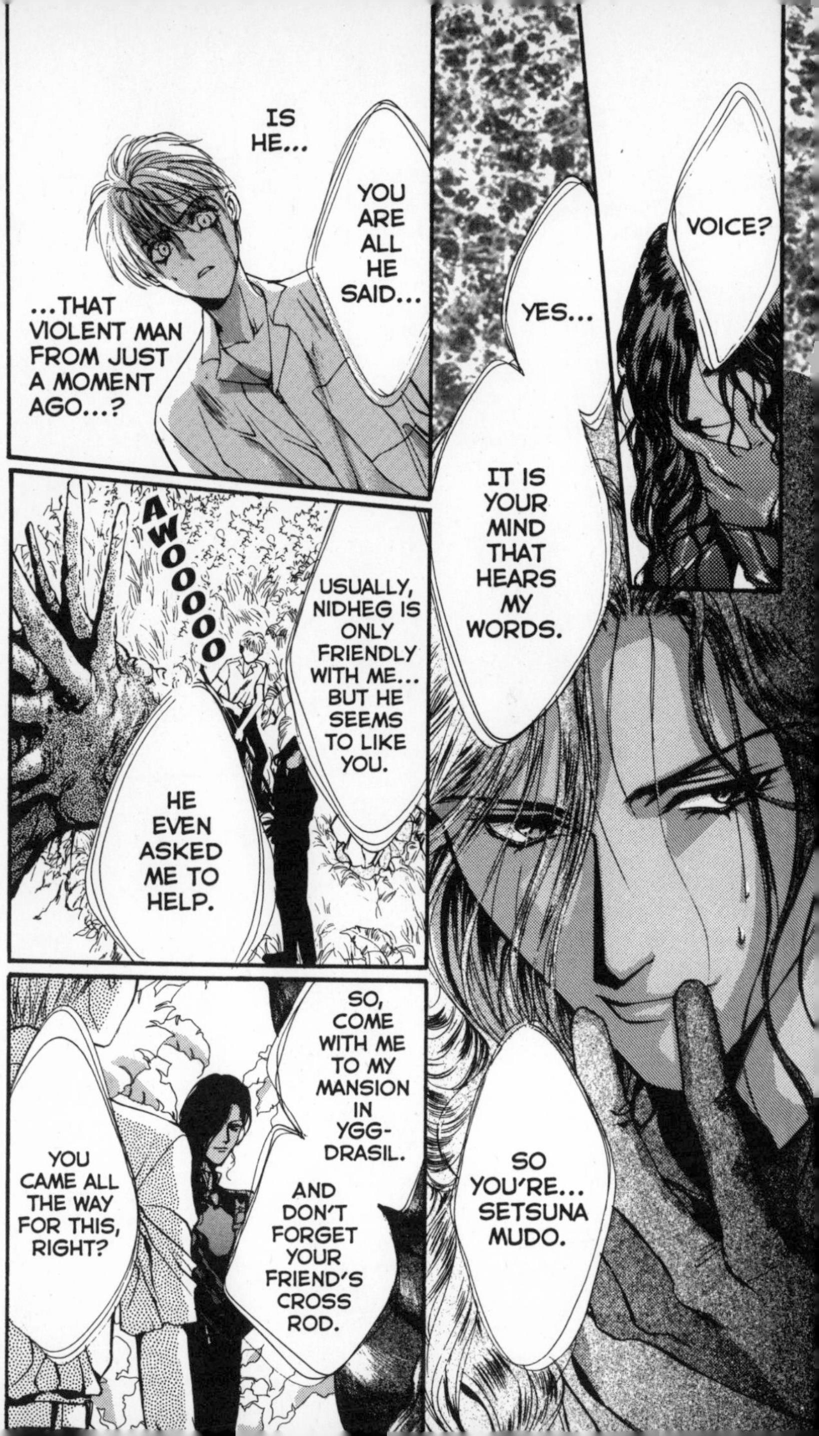
VOICE?
YES...
IT IS YOUR MIND THAT HEARS MY WORDS.
SO YOU'RE... SETSUNA MUDO.
YOU ARE ALL HE SAID...
IS HE...
...THAT VIOLENT MAN FROM JUST A MOMENT AGO...?
AWOOOOOO
USUALLY, NIDHEG IS ONLY FRIENDLY WITH ME... BUT HE SEEMS TO LIKE YOU.
HE EVEN ASKED ME TO HELP.
SO, COME WITH ME TO MY MANSION IN YGG-DRASIL.
AND DON'T FORGET YOUR FRIEND'S CROSS ROD.
YOU CAME ALL THE WAY FOR THIS, RIGHT?

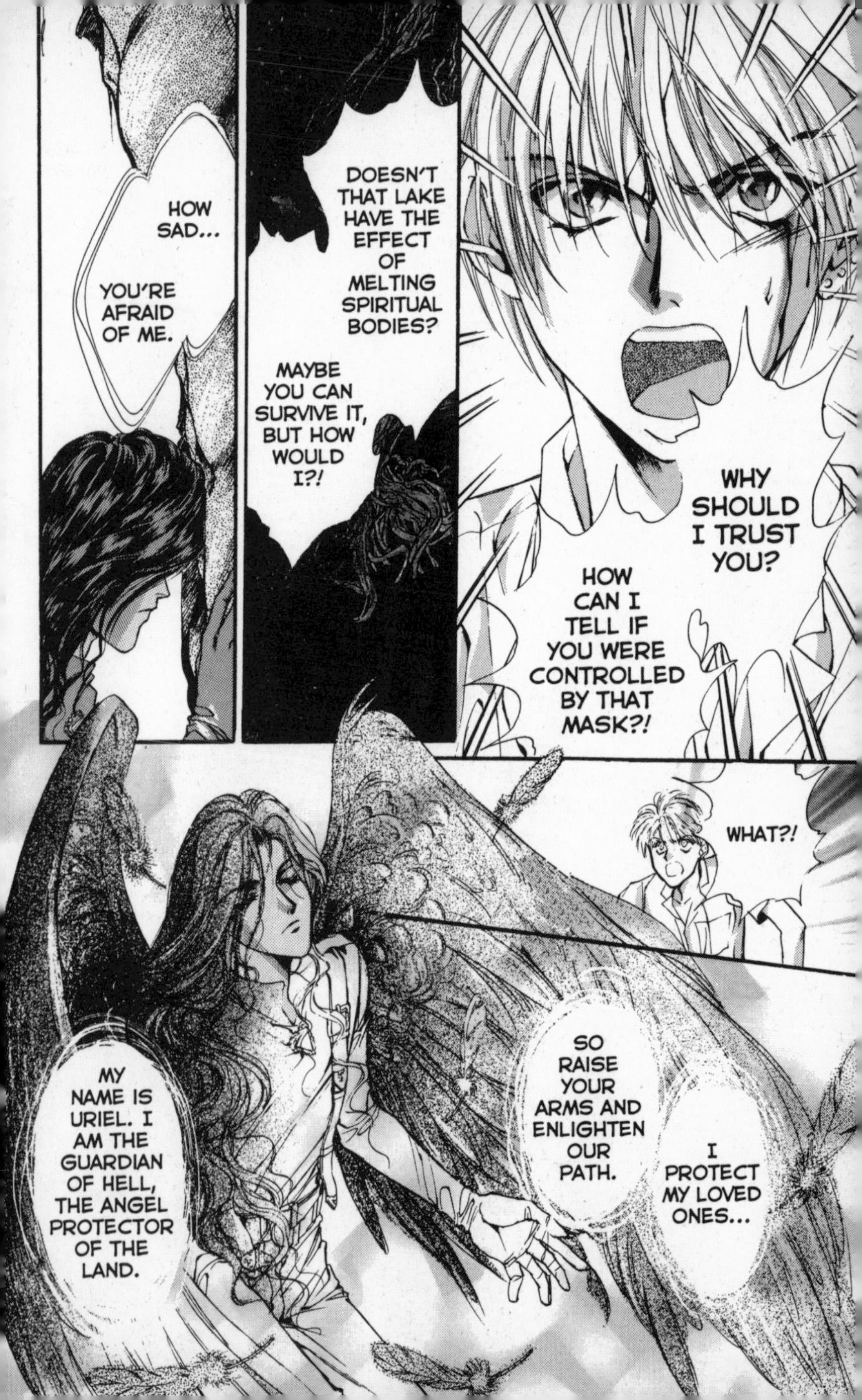
WHY SHOULD I TRUST YOU?
HOW CAN I TELL IF YOU WERE CONTROLLED BY THAT MASK?!
DOESN'T THAT LAKE HAVE THE EFFECT OF MELTING SPIRITUAL BODIES?
MAYBE YOU CAN SURVIVE IT, BUT HOW WOULD I?!
HOW SAD...
YOU'RE AFRAID OF ME.
WHAT?!
I PROTECT MY LOVED ONES...
SO RAISE YOUR ARMS AND ENLIGHTEN OUR PATH.
MY NAME IS URIEL. I AM THE GUARDIAN OF HELL, THE ANGEL PROTECTOR OF THE LAND.

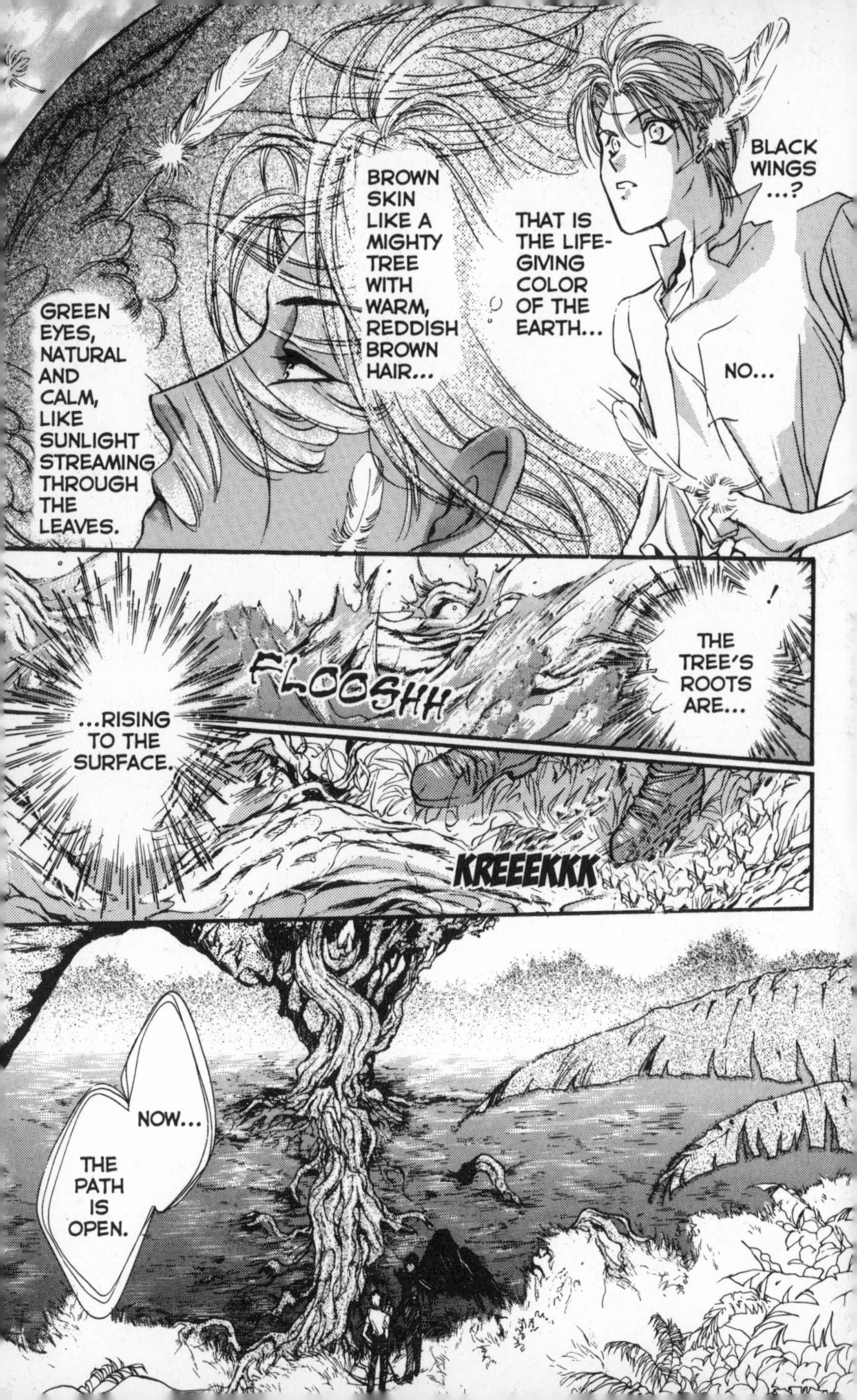
BLACK WINGS ...?
NO...
THAT IS THE LIFE-GIVING COLOR OF THE EARTH...
BROWN SKIN LIKE A MIGHTY TREE WITH WARM, REDDISH BROWN HAIR...
GREEN EYES, NATURAL AND CALM, LIKE SUNLIGHT STREAMING THROUGH THE LEAVES.
!
THE TREE'S ROOTS ARE...
FLOOSHH
...RISING TO THE SURFACE.
KREEEKKK
NOW...
THE PATH IS OPEN.

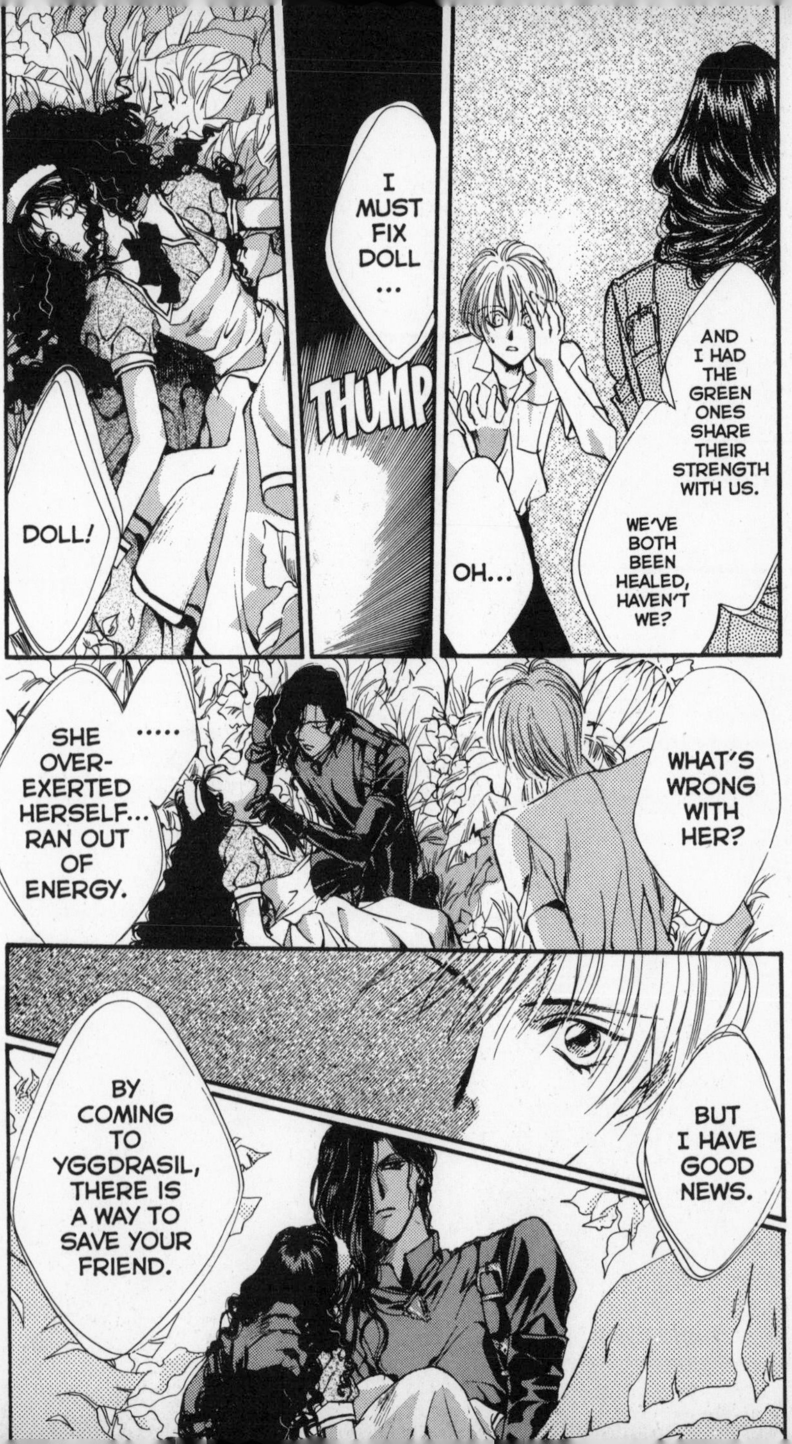
AND I HAD THE GREEN ONES SHARE THEIR STRENGTH WITH US.
WE'VE BOTH BEEN HEALED, HAVEN'T WE?
OH...
I MUST FIX DOLL ...
THUMP
DOLL!
WHAT'S WRONG WITH HER?
.....
SHE OVER-EXERTED HERSELF... RAN OUT OF ENERGY.
BUT I HAVE GOOD NEWS.
BY COMING TO YGGDRASIL, THERE IS A WAY TO SAVE YOUR FRIEND.

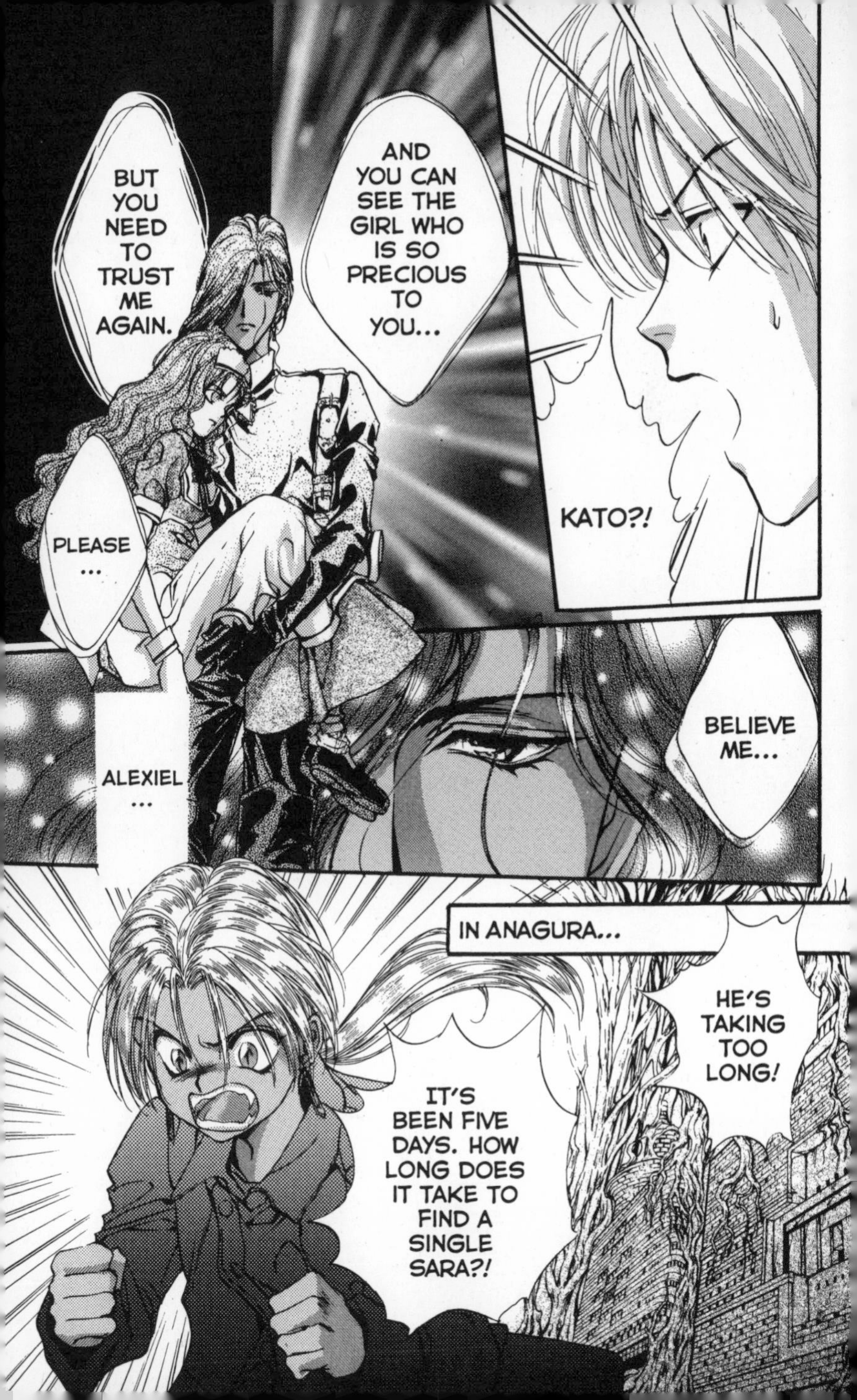
KATO?!
AND YOU CAN SEE THE GIRL WHO IS SO PRECIOUS TO YOU...
BUT YOU NEED TO TRUST ME AGAIN.
PLEASE...
BELIEVE ME...
ALEXIEL...
IN ANAGURA...
HE'S TAKING TOO LONG!
IT'S BEEN FIVE DAYS. HOW LONG DOES IT TAKE TO FIND A SINGLE SARA?!

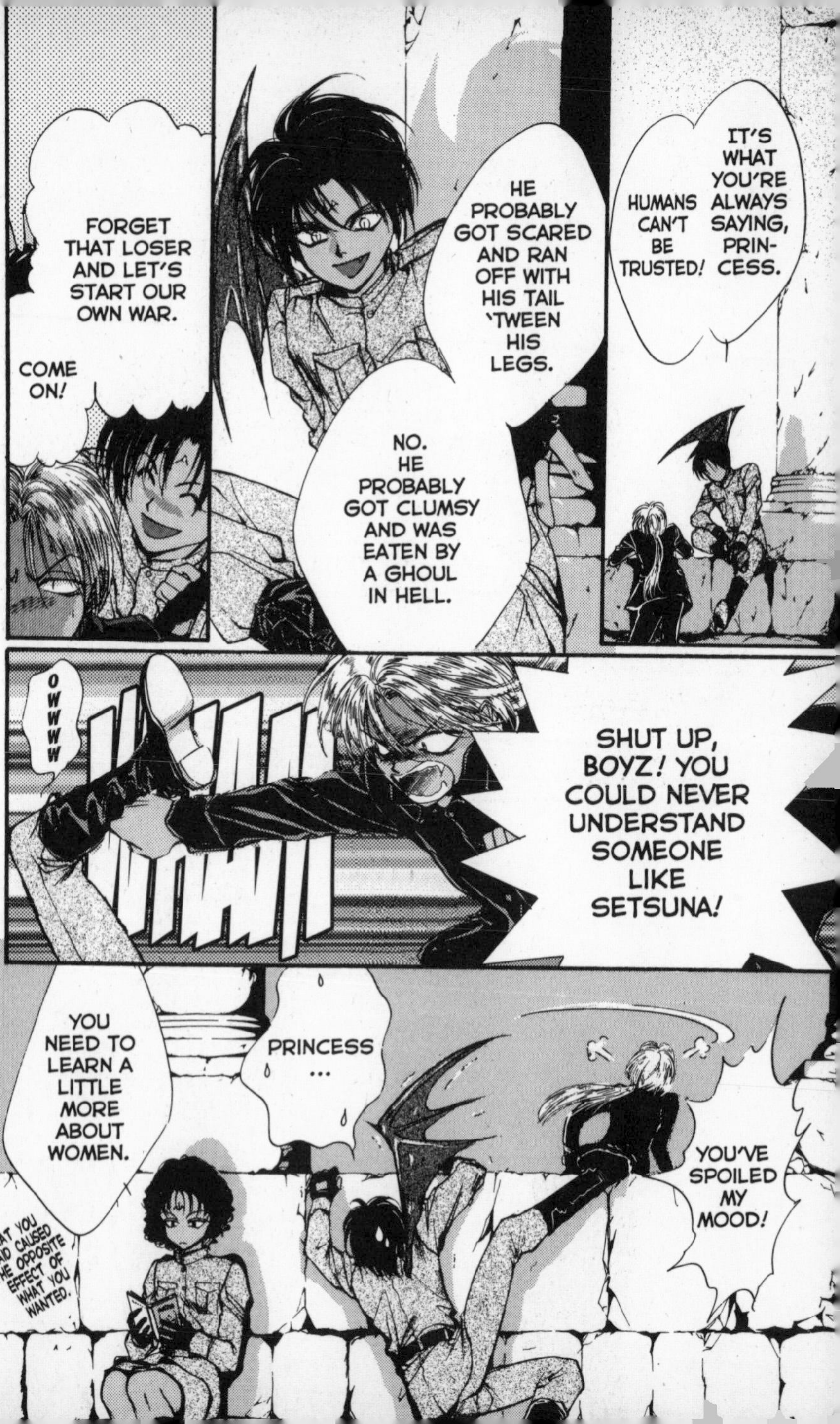
HUMANS CAN'T BE TRUSTED!
IT'S WHAT YOU'RE ALWAYS SAYING, PRINCESS.
HE PROBABLY GOT SCARED AND RAN OFF WITH HIS TAIL 'TWEEN HIS LEGS.
NO. HE PROBABLY GOT CLUMSY AND WAS EATEN BY A GHOUL IN HELL.
FORGET THAT LOSER AND LET'S START OUR OWN WAR.
COME ON!
SHUT UP, BOYZ! YOU COULD NEVER UNDERSTAND SOMEONE LIKE SETSUNA!
OWWWW
YOU'VE SPOILED MY MOOD!
PRINCESS...
YOU NEED TO LEARN A LITTLE MORE ABOUT WOMEN.
WHAT YOU SAID CAUSED THE OPPOSITE EFFECT OF WHAT YOU WANTED.

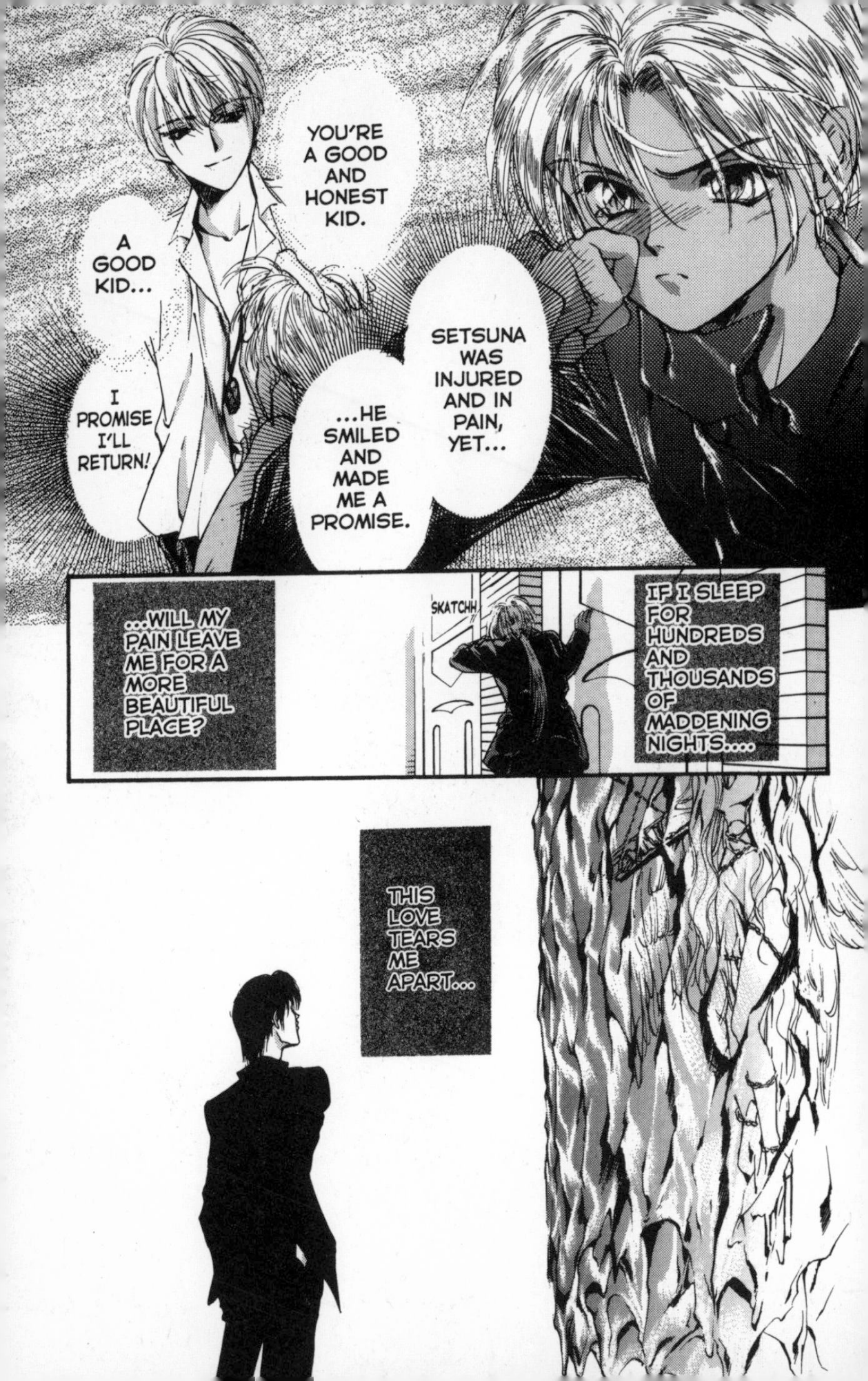
SETSUNA WAS INJURED AND IN PAIN, YET...
...HE SMILED AND MADE ME A PROMISE.
YOU'RE A GOOD AND HONEST KID.
A GOOD KID...
I PROMISE I'LL RETURN!
IF I SLEEP FOR HUNDREDS AND THOUSANDS OF MADDENING NIGHTS....
SKATCHH
...WILL MY PAIN LEAVE ME FOR A MORE BEAUTIFUL PLACE?
THIS LOVE TEARS ME APART...

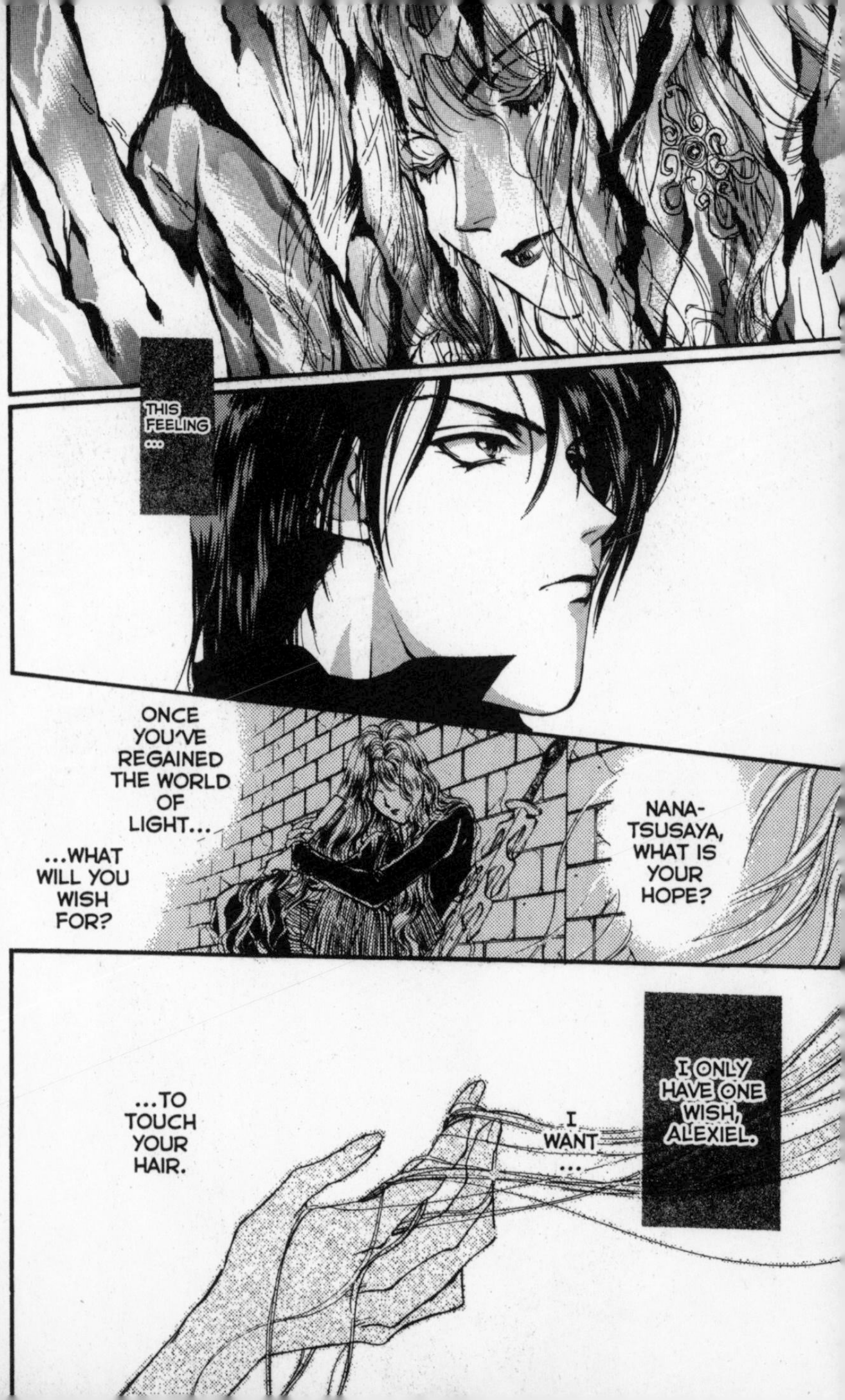
THIS FEELING...
NANA-TSUSAYA, WHAT IS YOUR HOPE?
ONCE YOU'VE REGAINED THE WORLD OF LIGHT...
...WHAT WILL YOU WISH FOR?
I ONLY HAVE ONE WISH, ALEXIEL.
I WANT...
...TO TOUCH YOUR HAIR.

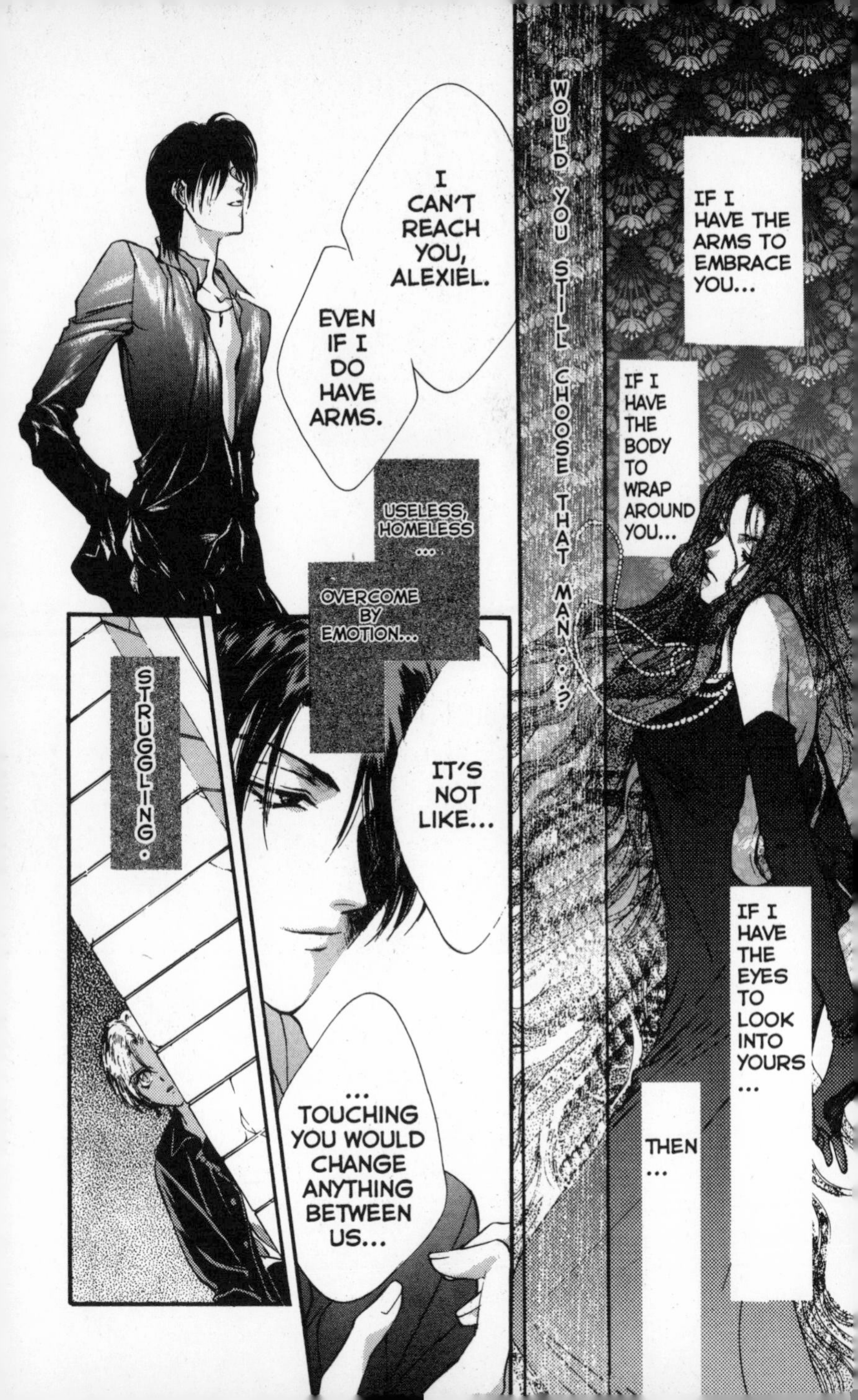

IF I HAVE THE ARMS TO EMBRACE YOU...
IF I HAVE THE BODY TO WRAP AROUND YOU...
IF I HAVE THE EYES TO LOOK INTO YOURS...
THEN...
WOULD YOU STILL CHOOSE THAT MAN...?
I CAN'T REACH YOU, ALEXIEL.
EVEN IF I DO HAVE ARMS.
USELESS, HOMELESS...
OVERCOME BY EMOTION...
STRUGGLING.
IT'S NOT LIKE...
...TOUCHING YOU WOULD CHANGE ANYTHING BETWEEN US...

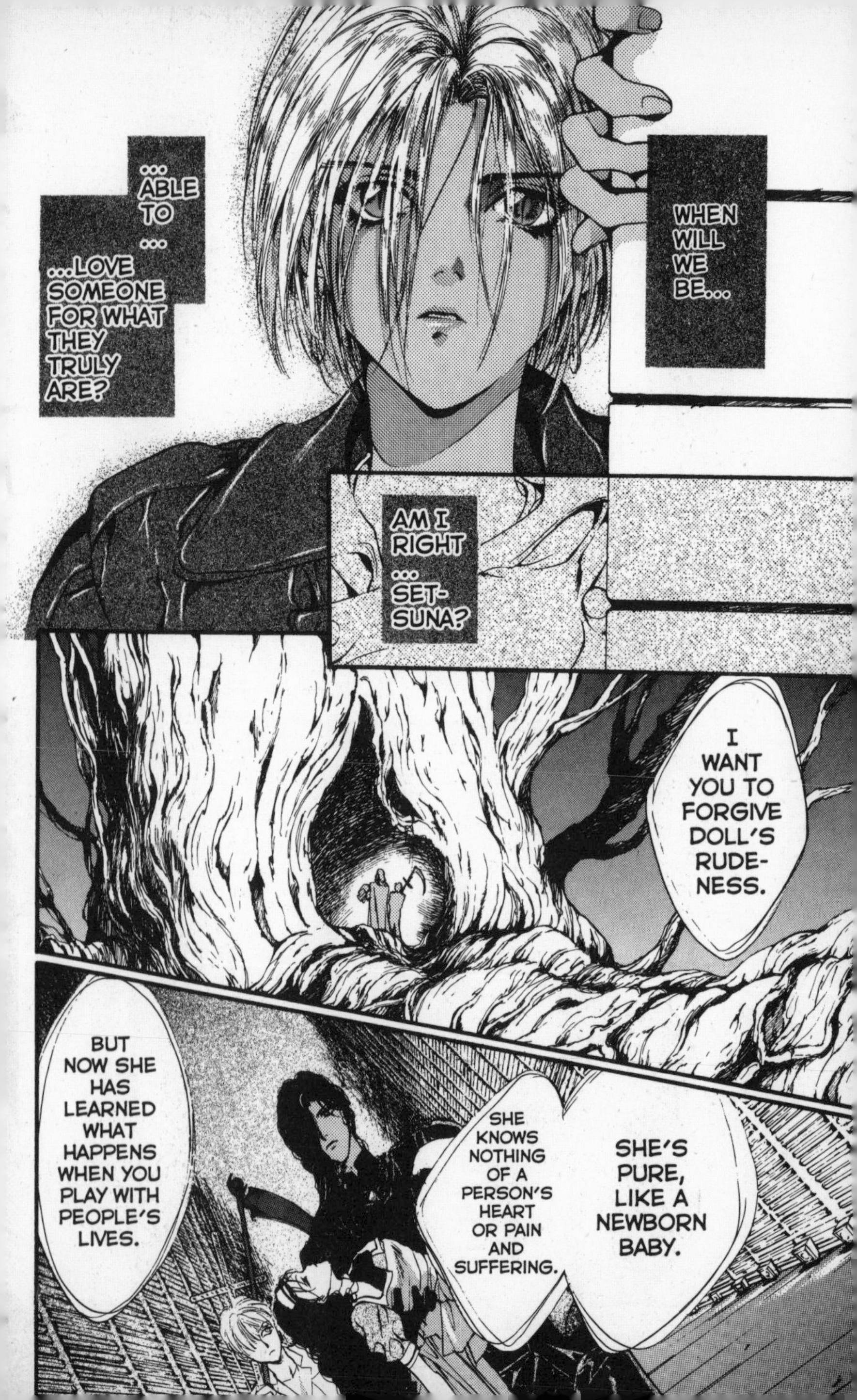

WHEN WILL WE BE...
...ABLE TO ... ...LOVE SOMEONE FOR WHAT THEY TRULY ARE?
AM I RIGHT ... SET-SUNA?
I WANT YOU TO FORGIVE DOLL'S RUDE-NESS.
SHE'S PURE, LIKE A NEWBORN BABY.
SHE KNOWS NOTHING OF A PERSON'S HEART OR PAIN AND SUFFERING.
BUT NOW SHE HAS LEARNED WHAT HAPPENS WHEN YOU PLAY WITH PEOPLE'S LIVES.

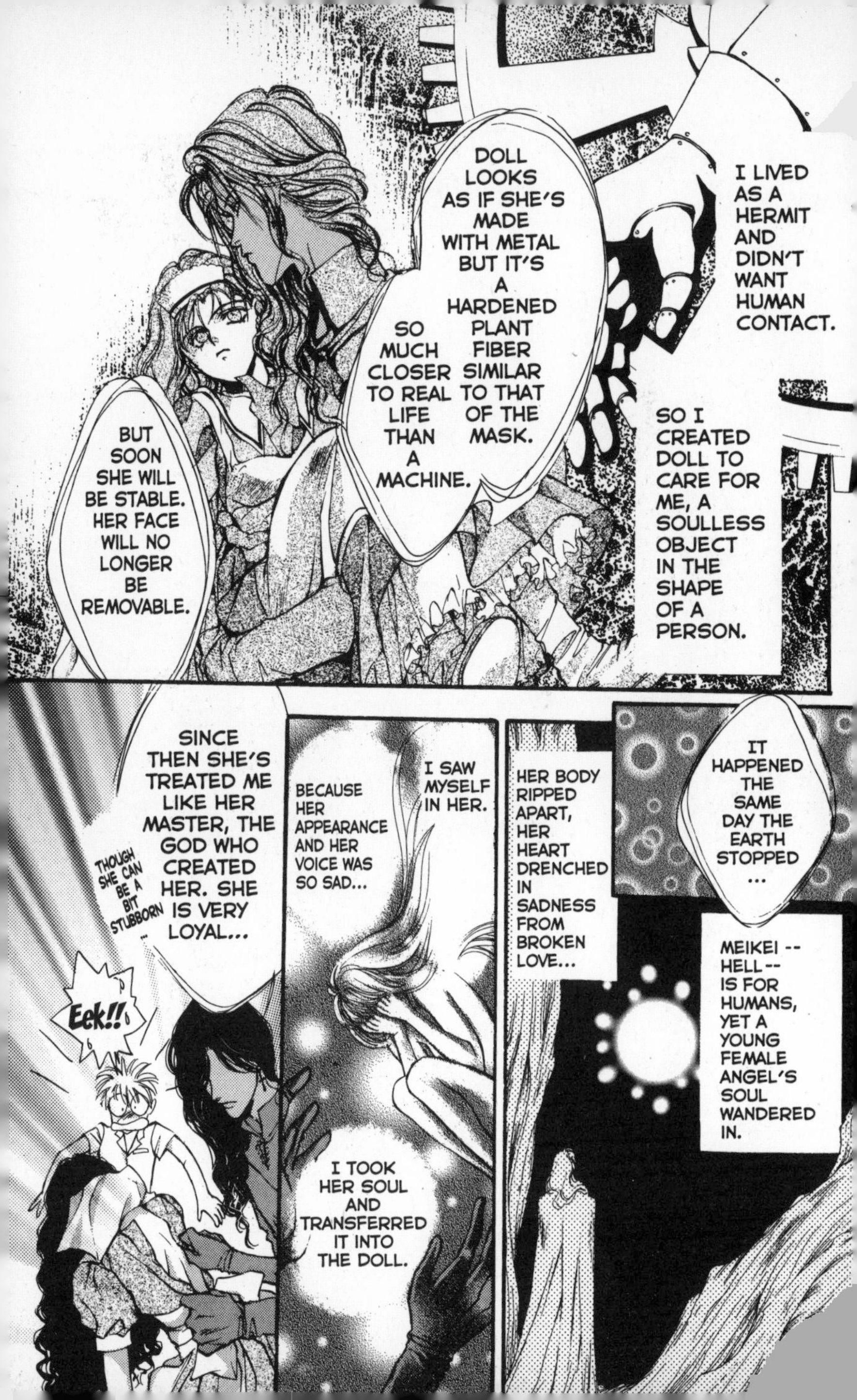
I LIVED AS A HERMIT AND DIDN'T WANT HUMAN CONTACT.
SO I CREATED DOLL TO CARE FOR ME, A SOULLESS OBJECT IN THE SHAPE OF A PERSON.
DOLL LOOKS AS IF SHE'S MADE WITH METAL BUT IT'S A HARDENED PLANT FIBER SIMILAR TO THAT OF THE MASK.
SO MUCH CLOSER TO REAL LIFE THAN A MACHINE.
BUT SOON SHE WILL BE STABLE. HER FACE WILL NO LONGER BE REMOVABLE.
IT HAPPENED THE SAME DAY THE EARTH STOPPED ...
MEIKEI -- HELL -- IS FOR HUMANS, YET A YOUNG FEMALE ANGEL'S SOUL WANDERED IN.
HER BODY RIPPED APART, HER HEART DRENCHED IN SADNESS FROM BROKEN LOVE...
I SAW MYSELF IN HER.
BECAUSE HER APPEARANCE AND HER VOICE WAS SO SAD...
I TOOK HER SOUL AND TRANSFERRED IT INTO THE DOLL.
SINCE THEN SHE'S TREATED ME LIKE HER MASTER, THE GOD WHO CREATED HER. SHE IS VERY LOYAL...
THOUGH SHE CAN BE A BIT STUBBORN ...
Eek!!

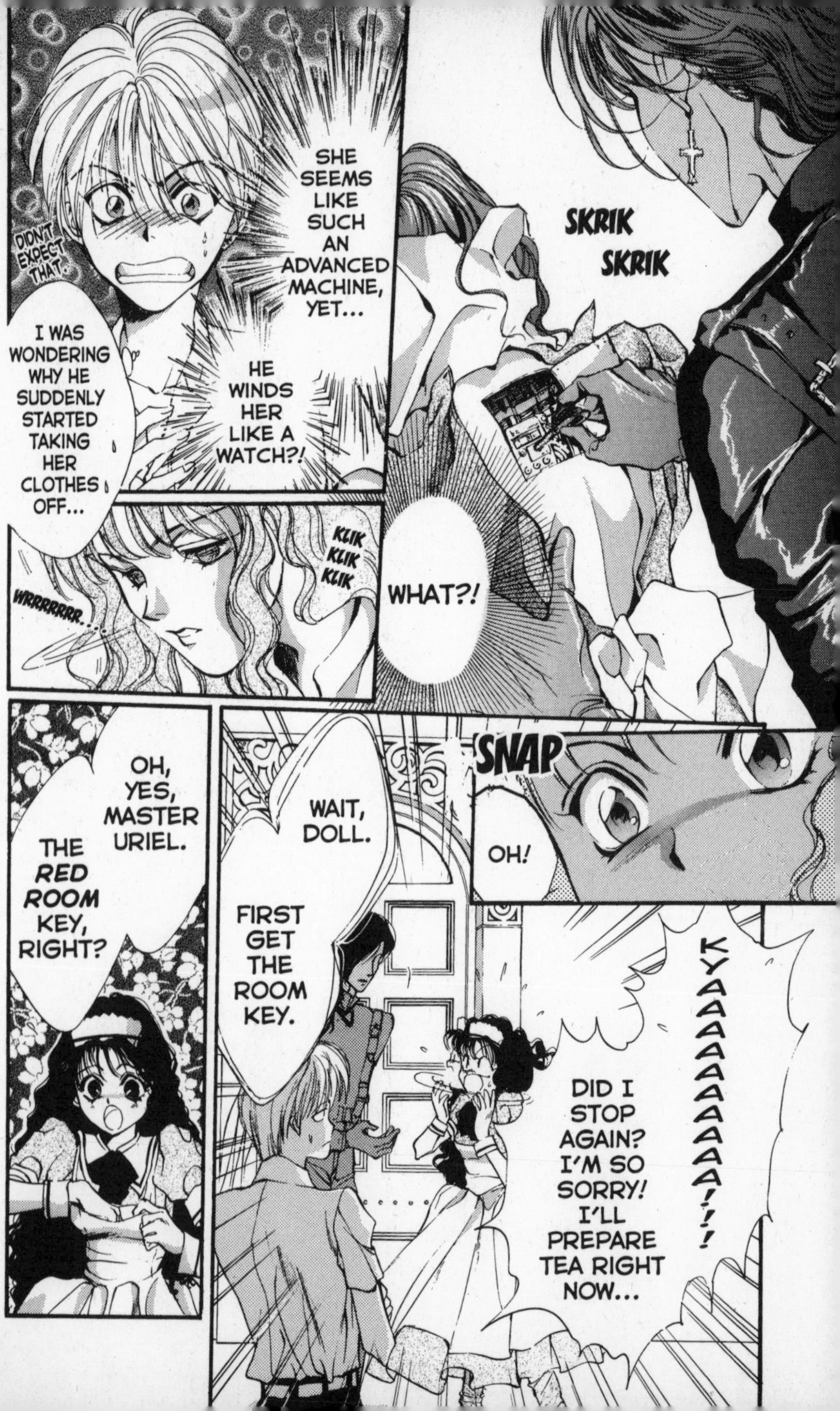
SKRIK SKRIK
WHAT?!
SHE SEEMS LIKE SUCH AN ADVANCED MACHINE, YET...
HE WINDS HER LIKE A WATCH?!
DIDN'T EXPECT THAT.
I WAS WONDERING WHY HE SUDDENLY STARTED TAKING HER CLOTHES OFF...
KLIK KLIK KLIK
WRRRRRRR...
SNAP
OH!
KYAAAAAAAAAAA!!!
DID I STOP AGAIN? I'M SO SORRY! I'LL PREPARE TEA RIGHT NOW...
WAIT, DOLL.
FIRST GET THE ROOM KEY.
OH, YES, MASTER URIEL.
THE *RED ROOM* KEY, RIGHT?

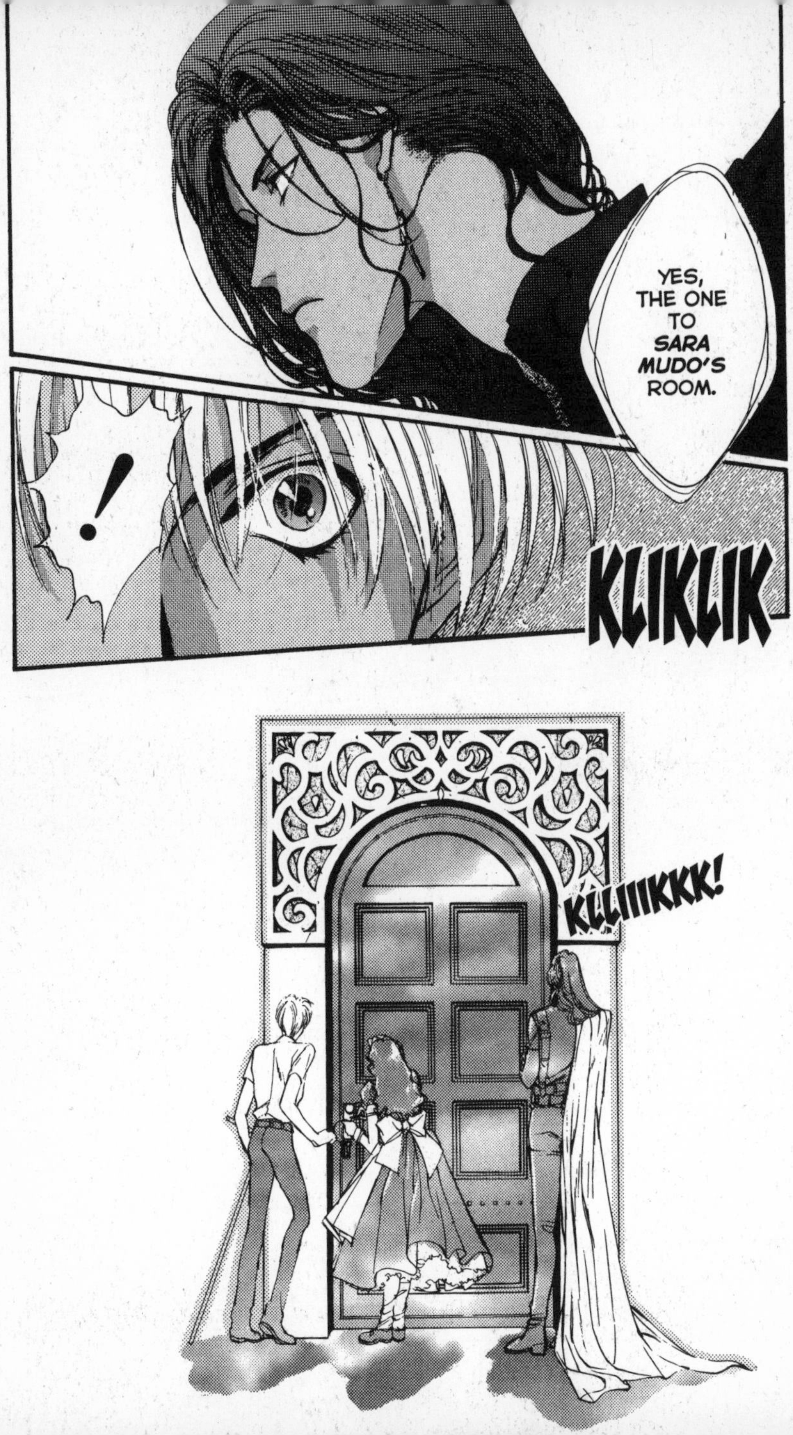
YES, THE ONE TO SARA MUDO'S ROOM.
!
KLIKLIK
KLIIIIKKK!

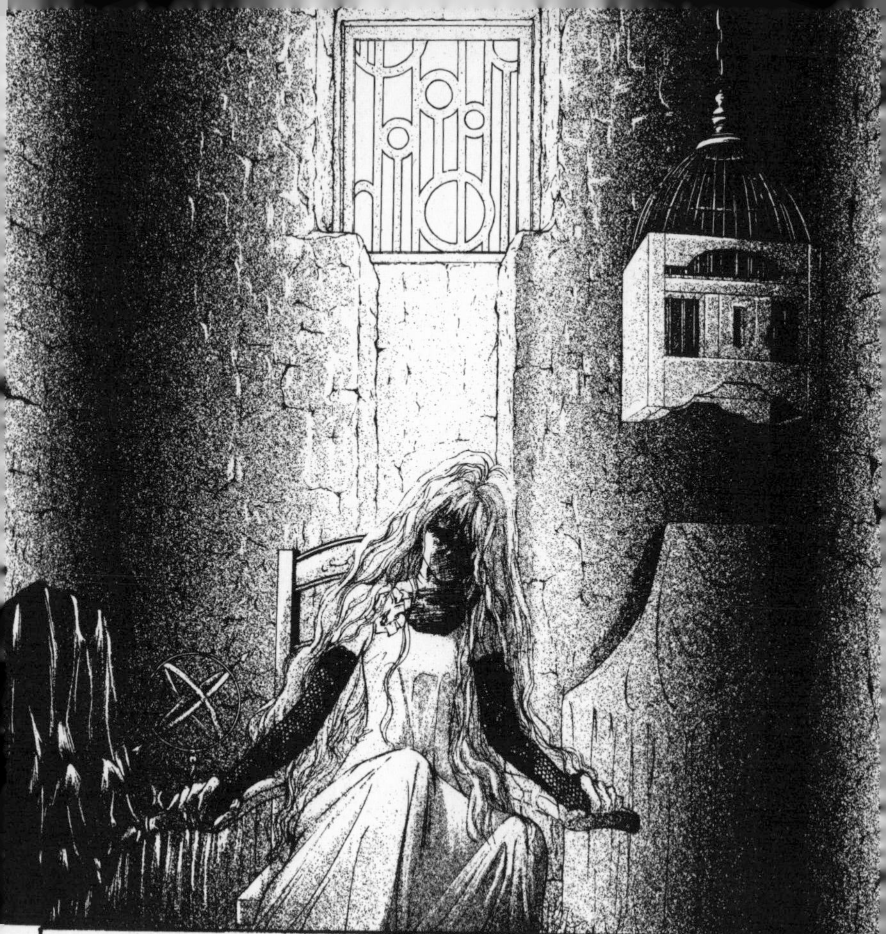
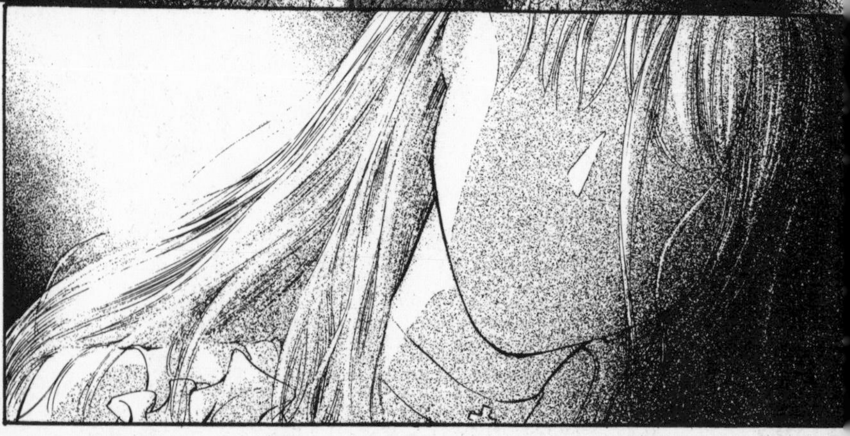

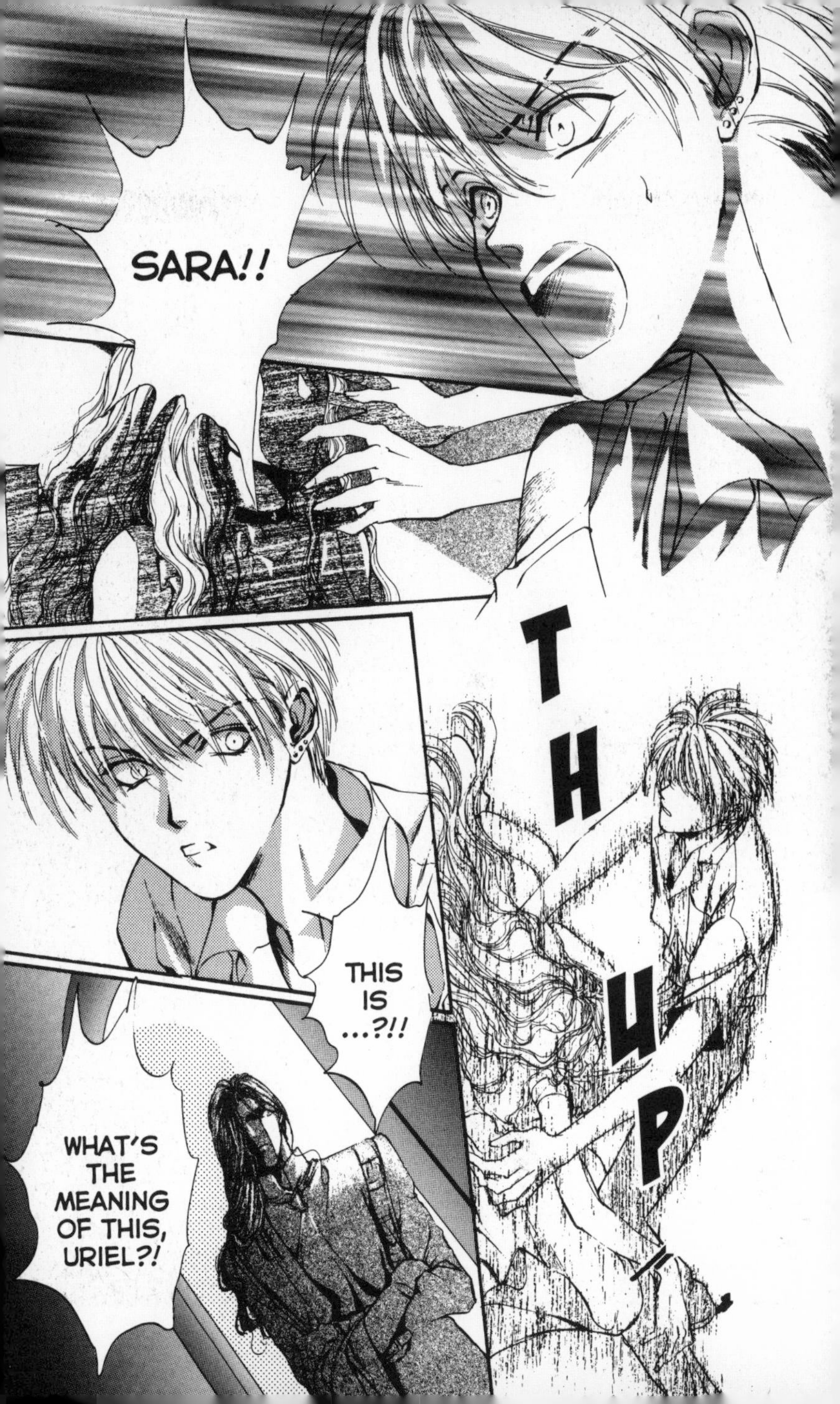
SARA!!
THUP
THIS IS ...?!!
WHAT'S THE MEANING OF THIS, URIEL?!

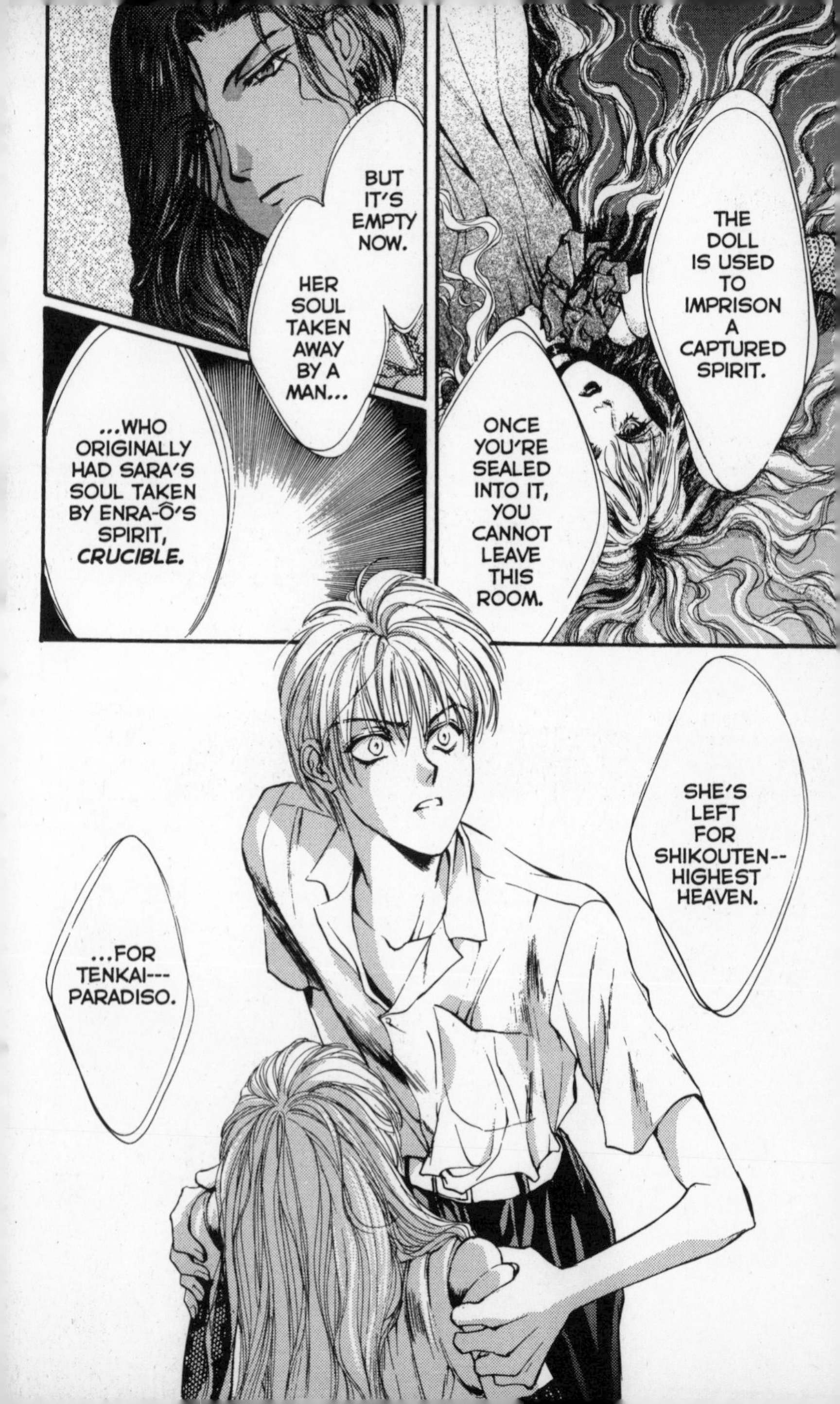
THE DOLL IS USED TO IMPRISON A CAPTURED SPIRIT.
ONCE YOU'RE SEALED INTO IT, YOU CANNOT LEAVE THIS ROOM.
BUT IT'S EMPTY NOW.
HER SOUL TAKEN AWAY BY A MAN...
...WHO ORIGINALLY HAD SARA'S SOUL TAKEN BY ENRA-Ô'S SPIRIT, *CRUCIBLE.*
SHE'S LEFT FOR SHIKOUTEN-- HIGHEST HEAVEN.
...FOR TENKAI--- PARADISO.

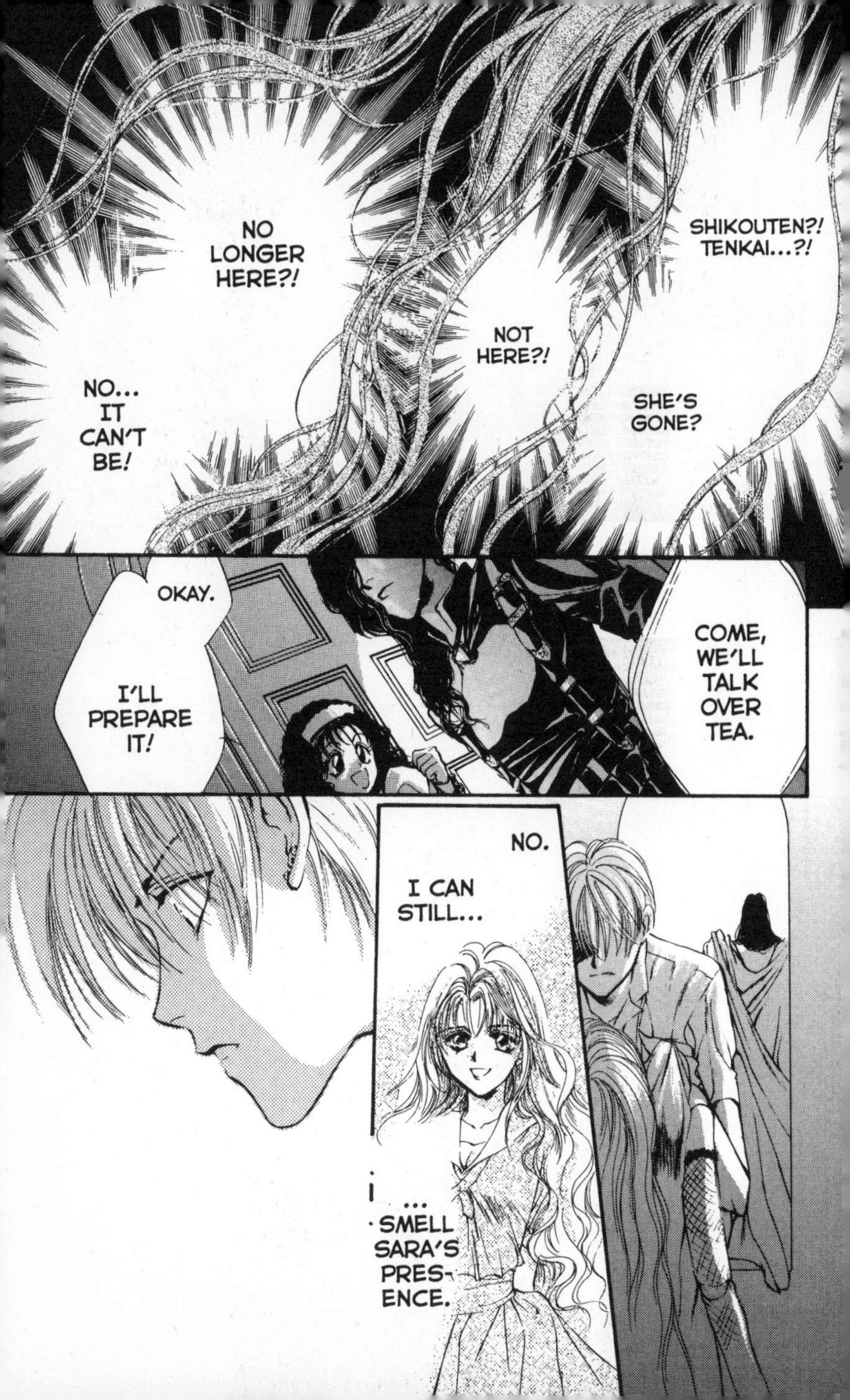
SHIKOUTEN?! TENKAI...?!
SHE'S GONE?
NOT HERE?!
NO LONGER HERE?!
NO... IT CAN'T BE!
COME, WE'LL TALK OVER TEA.
OKAY.
I'LL PREPARE IT!
NO.
I CAN STILL...
...SMELL SARA'S PRES-ENCE.

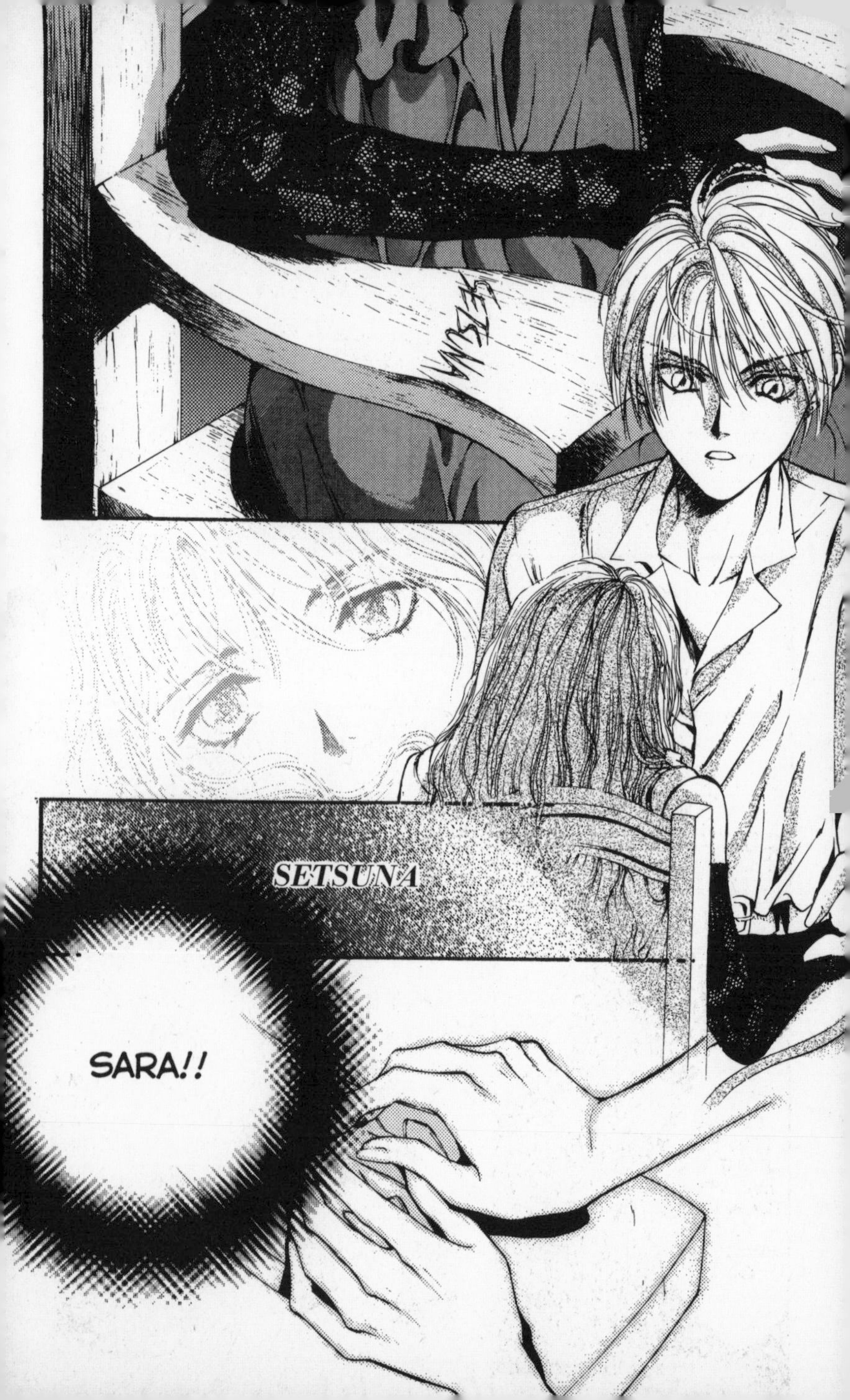
SETSUNA
SETSUNA
SARA!!

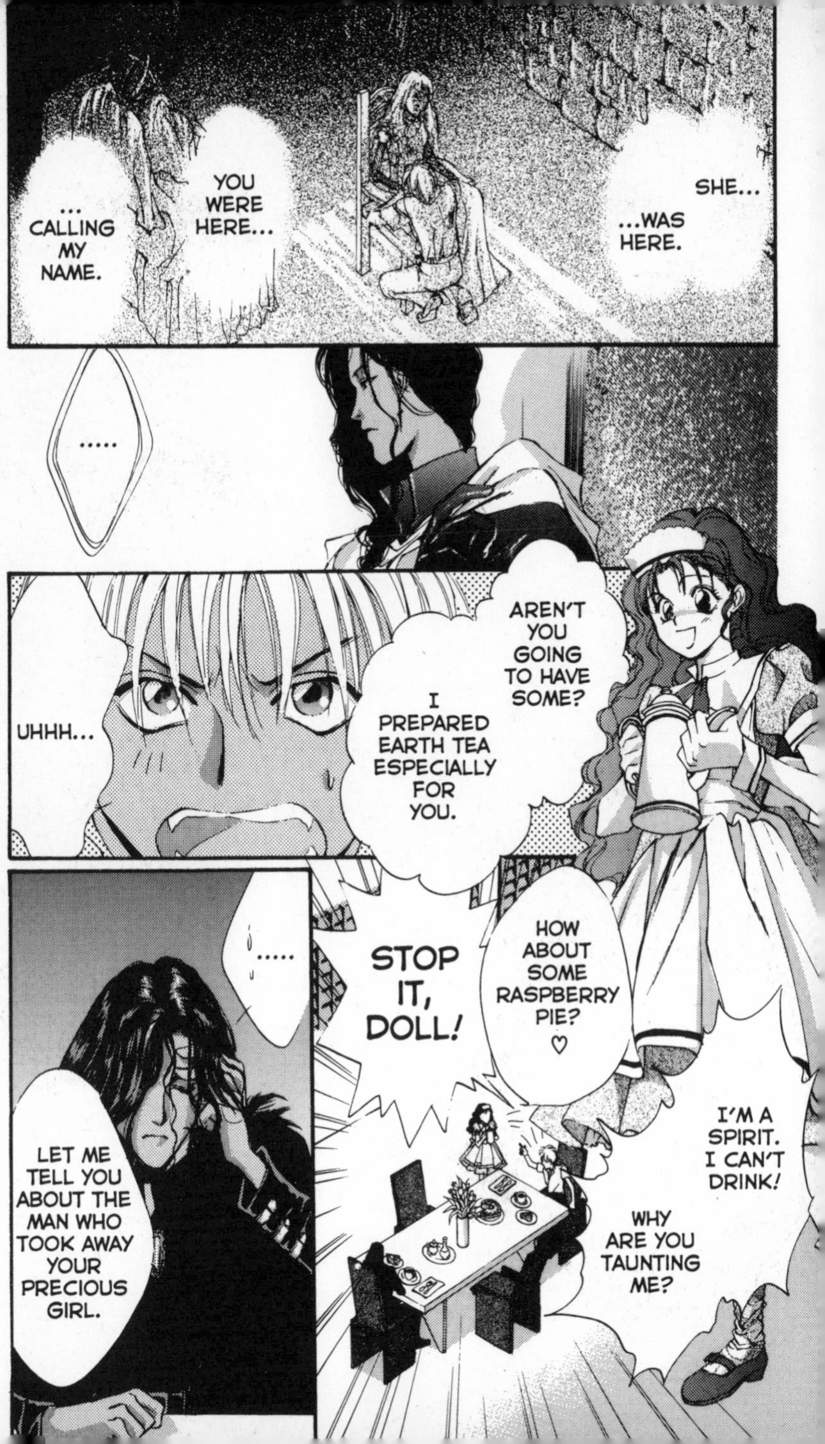
SHE...
...WAS HERE.
YOU WERE HERE...
... CALLING MY NAME.
.....
AREN'T YOU GOING TO HAVE SOME?
I PREPARED EARTH TEA ESPECIALLY FOR YOU.
UHHH...
HOW ABOUT SOME RASPBERRY PIE? ♡
STOP IT, DOLL!
I'M A SPIRIT. I CAN'T DRINK!
WHY ARE YOU TAUNTING ME?
.....
LET ME TELL YOU ABOUT THE MAN WHO TOOK AWAY YOUR PRECIOUS GIRL.

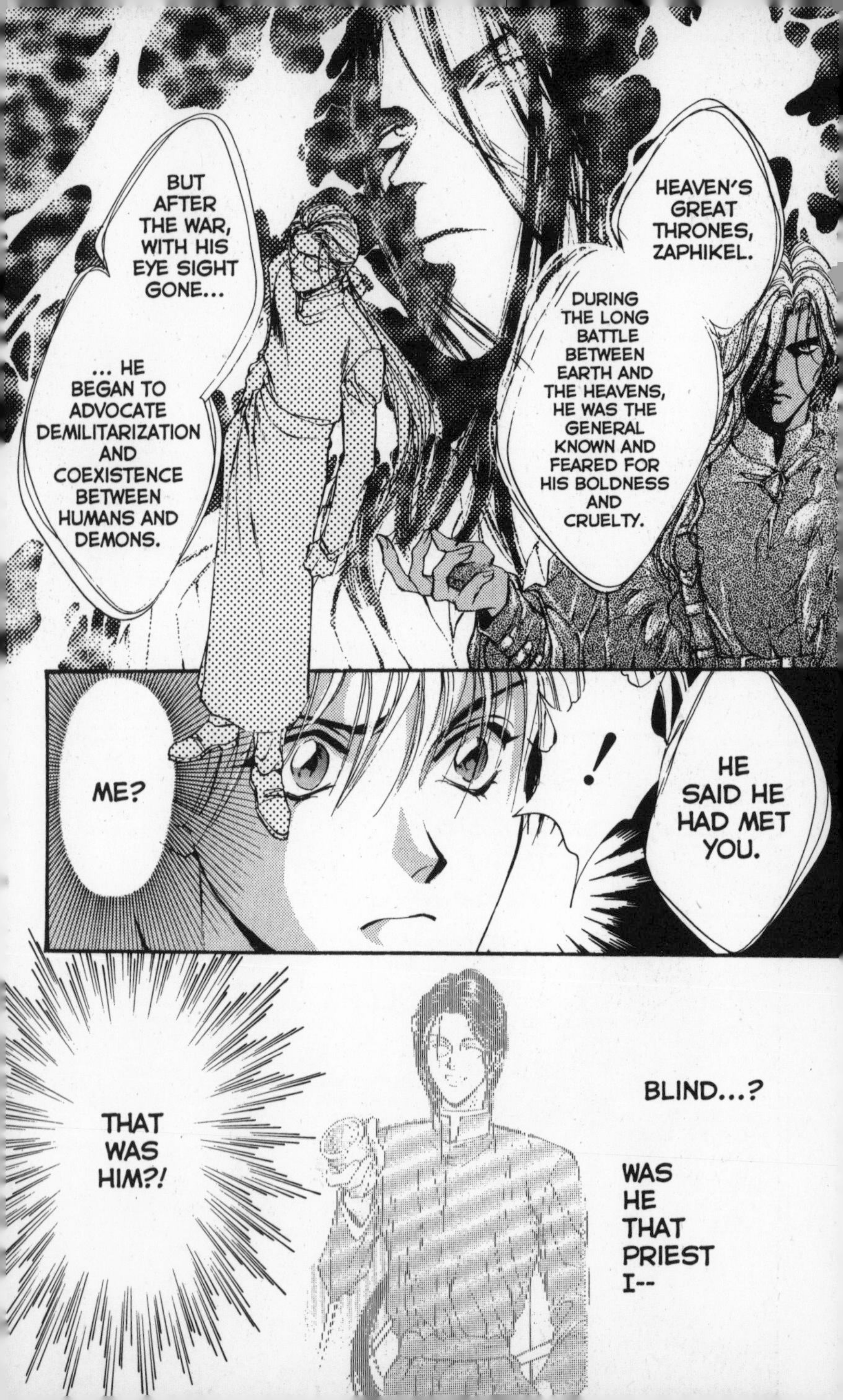
HEAVEN'S GREAT THRONES, ZAPHIKEL.
DURING THE LONG BATTLE BETWEEN EARTH AND THE HEAVENS, HE WAS THE GENERAL KNOWN AND FEARED FOR HIS BOLDNESS AND CRUELTY.
BUT AFTER THE WAR, WITH HIS EYE SIGHT GONE...
... HE BEGAN TO ADVOCATE DEMILITARIZATION AND COEXISTENCE BETWEEN HUMANS AND DEMONS.
HE SAID HE HAD MET YOU.
!
ME?
BLIND...?
WAS HE THAT PRIEST I--
THAT WAS HIM?!

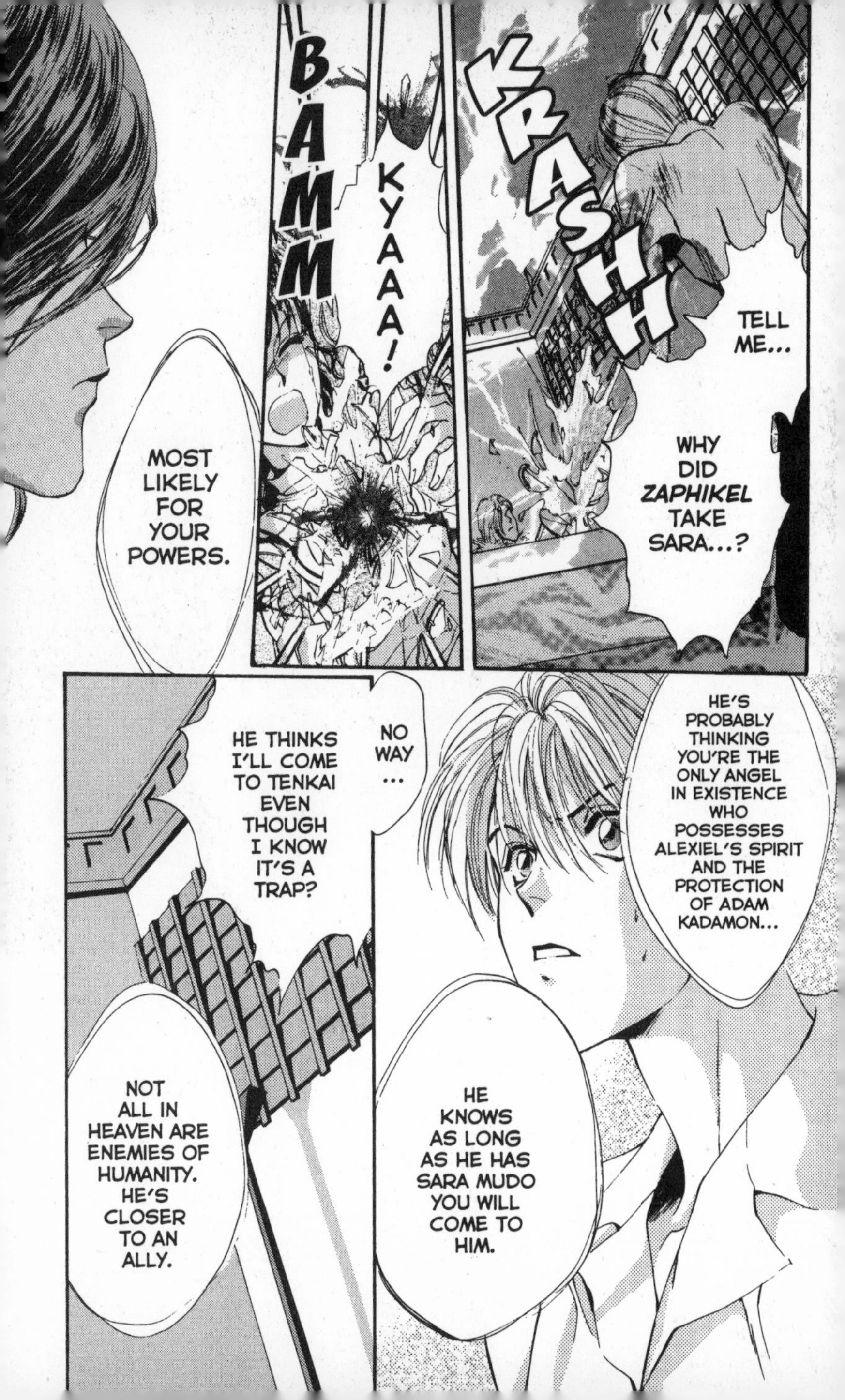
KRASHH
TELL ME...
WHY DID *ZAPHIKEL* TAKE SARA...?
BAMM
KYAAA!
MOST LIKELY FOR YOUR POWERS.
HE'S PROBABLY THINKING YOU'RE THE ONLY ANGEL IN EXISTENCE WHO POSSESSES ALEXIEL'S SPIRIT AND THE PROTECTION OF ADAM KADAMON...
HE KNOWS AS LONG AS HE HAS SARA MUDO YOU WILL COME TO HIM.
NO WAY ...
HE THINKS I'LL COME TO TENKAI EVEN THOUGH I KNOW IT'S A TRAP?
NOT ALL IN HEAVEN ARE ENEMIES OF HUMANITY. HE'S CLOSER TO AN ALLY.

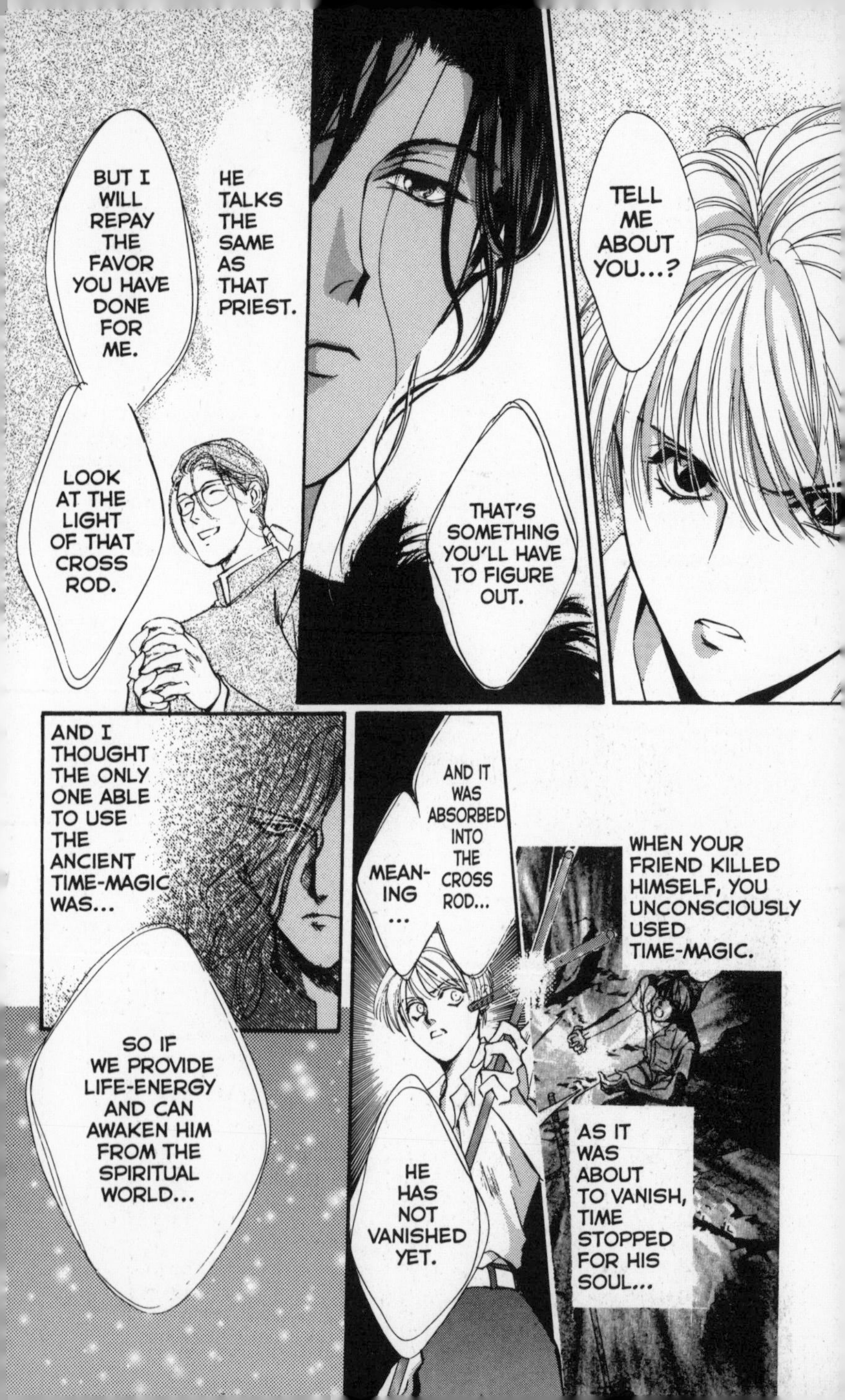
TELL ME ABOUT YOU...?
THAT'S SOMETHING YOU'LL HAVE TO FIGURE OUT.
HE TALKS THE SAME AS THAT PRIEST.
BUT I WILL REPAY THE FAVOR YOU HAVE DONE FOR ME.
LOOK AT THE LIGHT OF THAT CROSS ROD.
WHEN YOUR FRIEND KILLED HIMSELF, YOU UNCONSCIOUSLY USED TIME-MAGIC.
AS IT WAS ABOUT TO VANISH, TIME STOPPED FOR HIS SOUL...
AND IT WAS ABSORBED INTO THE CROSS ROD...
MEAN-ING...
HE HAS NOT VANISHED YET.
AND I THOUGHT THE ONLY ONE ABLE TO USE THE ANCIENT TIME-MAGIC WAS...
SO IF WE PROVIDE LIFE-ENERGY AND CAN AWAKEN HIM FROM THE SPIRITUAL WORLD...

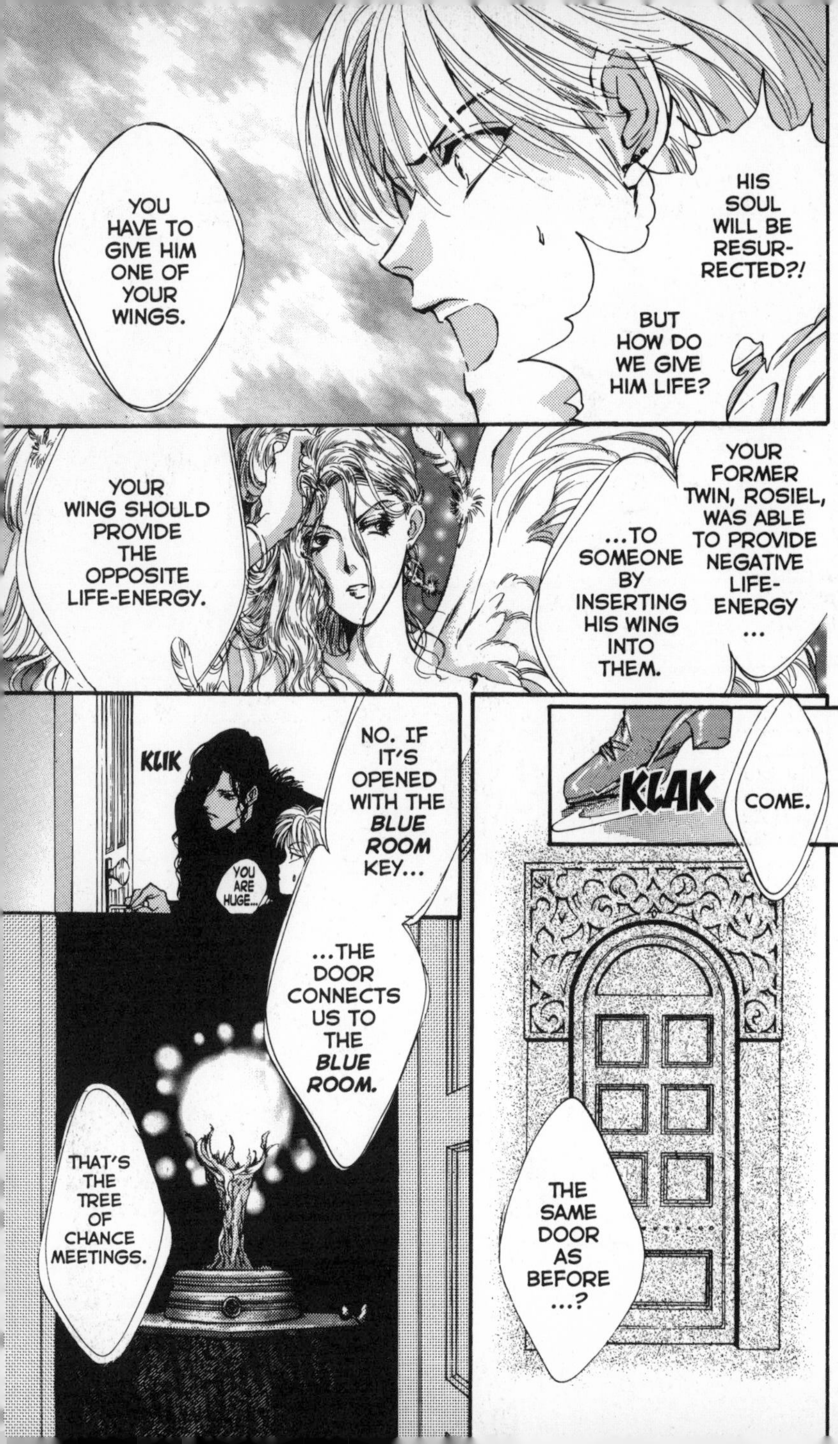
HIS SOUL WILL BE RESURRECTED?!
BUT HOW DO WE GIVE HIM LIFE?
YOU HAVE TO GIVE HIM ONE OF YOUR WINGS.
YOUR FORMER TWIN, ROSIEL, WAS ABLE TO PROVIDE NEGATIVE LIFE-ENERGY ...
...TO SOMEONE BY INSERTING HIS WING INTO THEM.
YOUR WING SHOULD PROVIDE THE OPPOSITE LIFE-ENERGY.
KLAK
COME.
THE SAME DOOR AS BEFORE ...?
KLIK
NO. IF IT'S OPENED WITH THE *BLUE ROOM* KEY...
YOU ARE HUGE...
...THE DOOR CONNECTS US TO THE *BLUE ROOM.*
THAT'S THE TREE OF CHANCE MEETINGS.

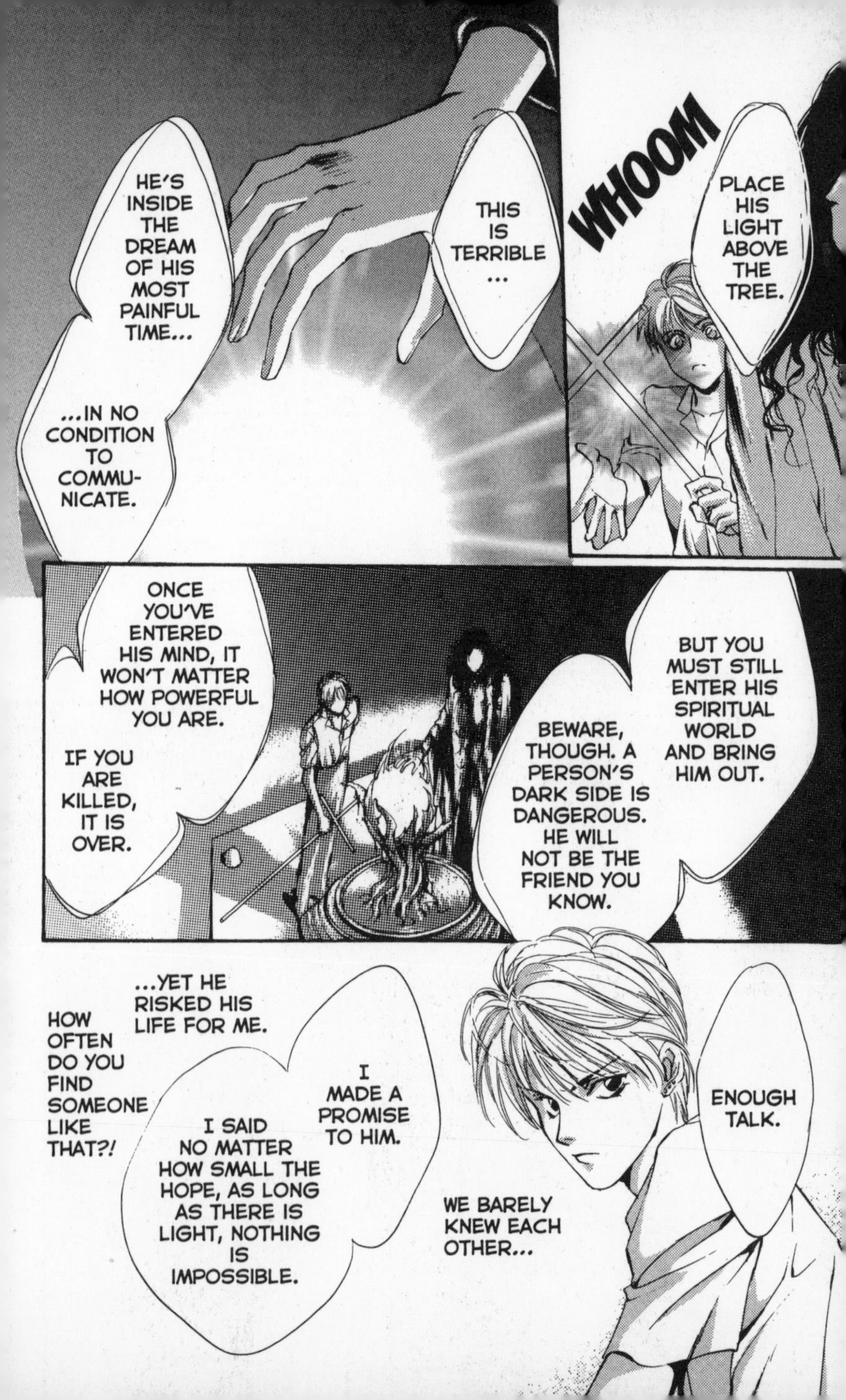
WHOOM
PLACE HIS LIGHT ABOVE THE TREE.
THIS IS TERRIBLE...
HE'S INSIDE THE DREAM OF HIS MOST PAINFUL TIME...
...IN NO CONDITION TO COMMUNICATE.
BUT YOU MUST STILL ENTER HIS SPIRITUAL WORLD AND BRING HIM OUT.
BEWARE, THOUGH. A PERSON'S DARK SIDE IS DANGEROUS. HE WILL NOT BE THE FRIEND YOU KNOW.
ONCE YOU'VE ENTERED HIS MIND, IT WON'T MATTER HOW POWERFUL YOU ARE.
IF YOU ARE KILLED, IT IS OVER.
ENOUGH TALK.
WE BARELY KNEW EACH OTHER...
...YET HE RISKED HIS LIFE FOR ME.
HOW OFTEN DO YOU FIND SOMEONE LIKE THAT?!
I MADE A PROMISE TO HIM.
I SAID NO MATTER HOW SMALL THE HOPE, AS LONG AS THERE IS LIGHT, NOTHING IS IMPOSSIBLE.

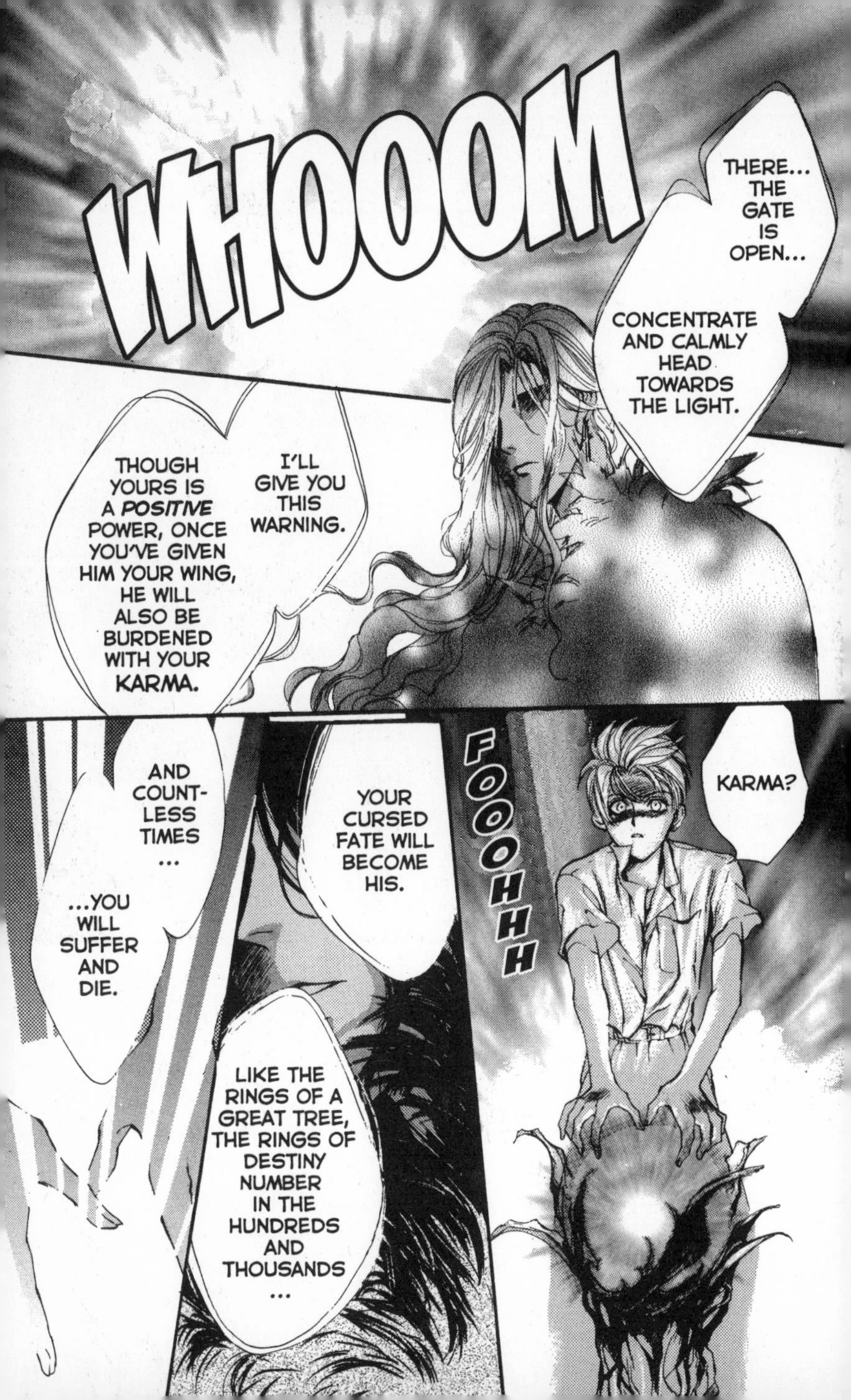
WHOOOM
THERE... THE GATE IS OPEN...
CONCENTRATE AND CALMLY HEAD TOWARDS THE LIGHT.
I'LL GIVE YOU THIS WARNING.
THOUGH YOURS IS A *POSITIVE* POWER, ONCE YOU'VE GIVEN HIM YOUR WING, HE WILL ALSO BE BURDENED WITH YOUR KARMA.
KARMA?
FOOOOHHH
YOUR CURSED FATE WILL BECOME HIS.
LIKE THE RINGS OF A GREAT TREE, THE RINGS OF DESTINY NUMBER IN THE HUNDREDS AND THOUSANDS ...
AND COUNT-LESS TIMES ...
...YOU WILL SUFFER AND DIE.

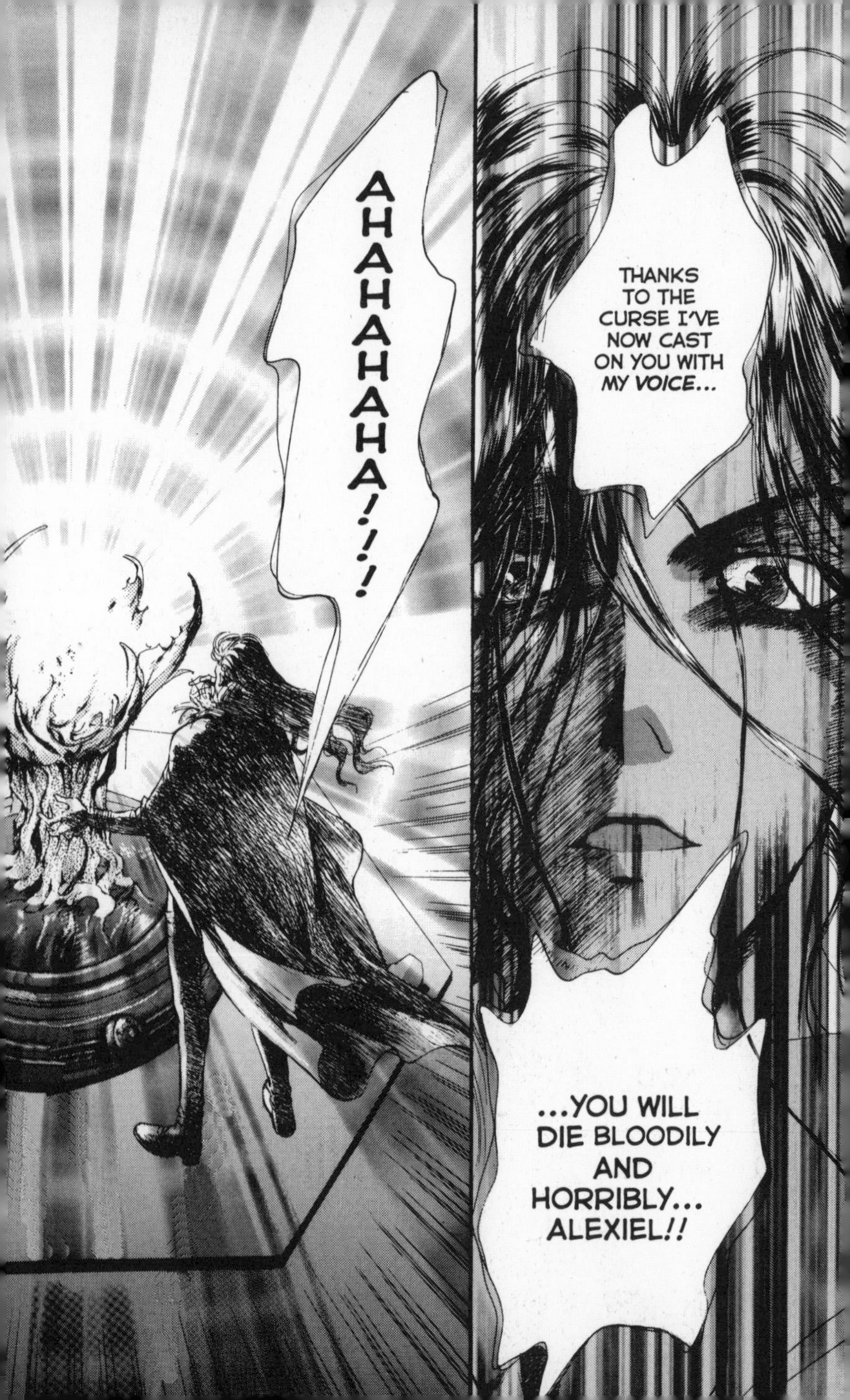
THANKS TO THE CURSE I'VE NOW CAST ON YOU WITH *MY VOICE*...
...YOU WILL DIE BLOODILY AND HORRIBLY... ALEXIEL!!
AHAHAHAHA!!!

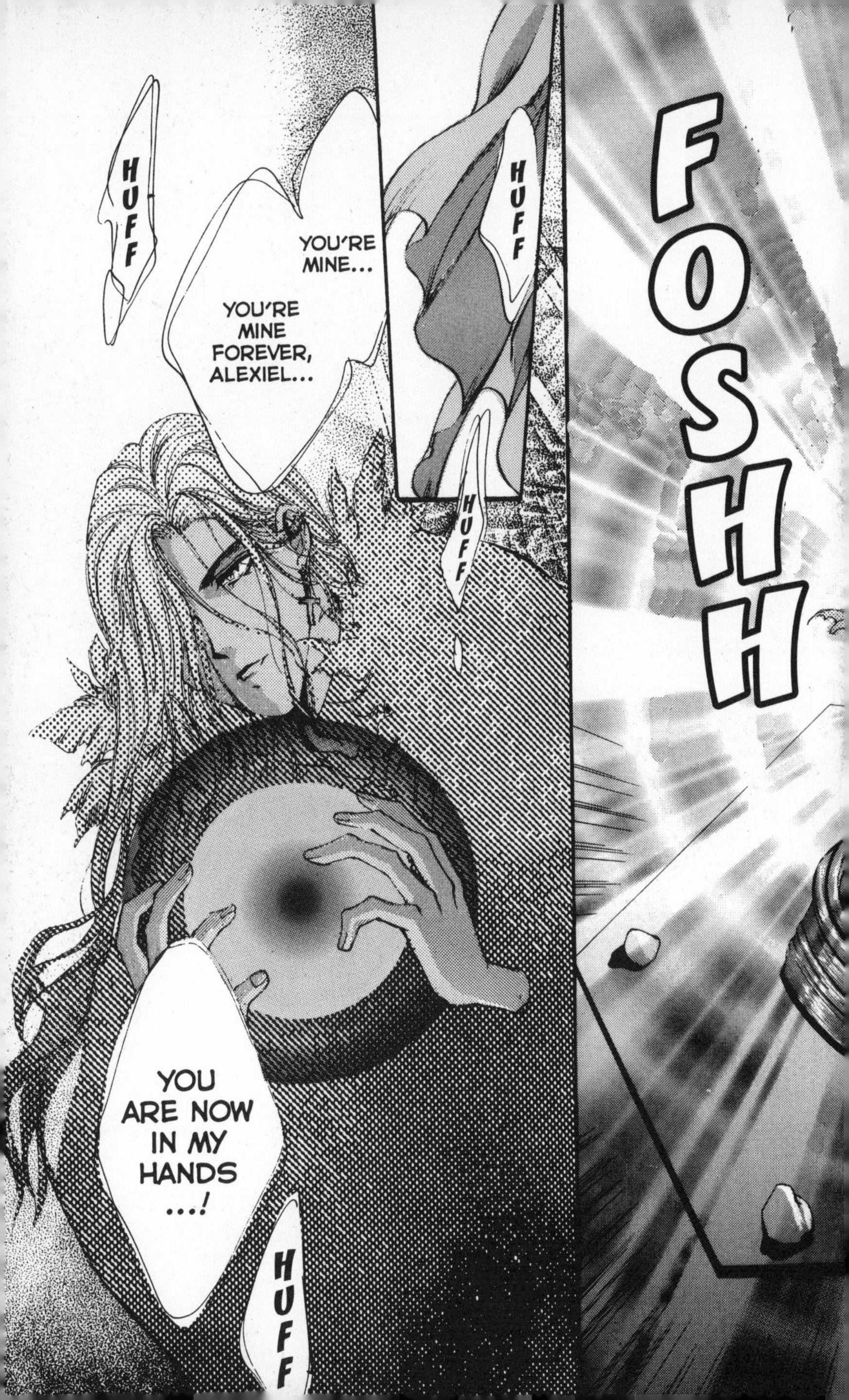
FOSHH
HUFF
HUFF
YOU'RE MINE...
YOU'RE MINE FOREVER, ALEXIEL...
HUFF
YOU ARE NOW IN MY HANDS ...!
HUFF

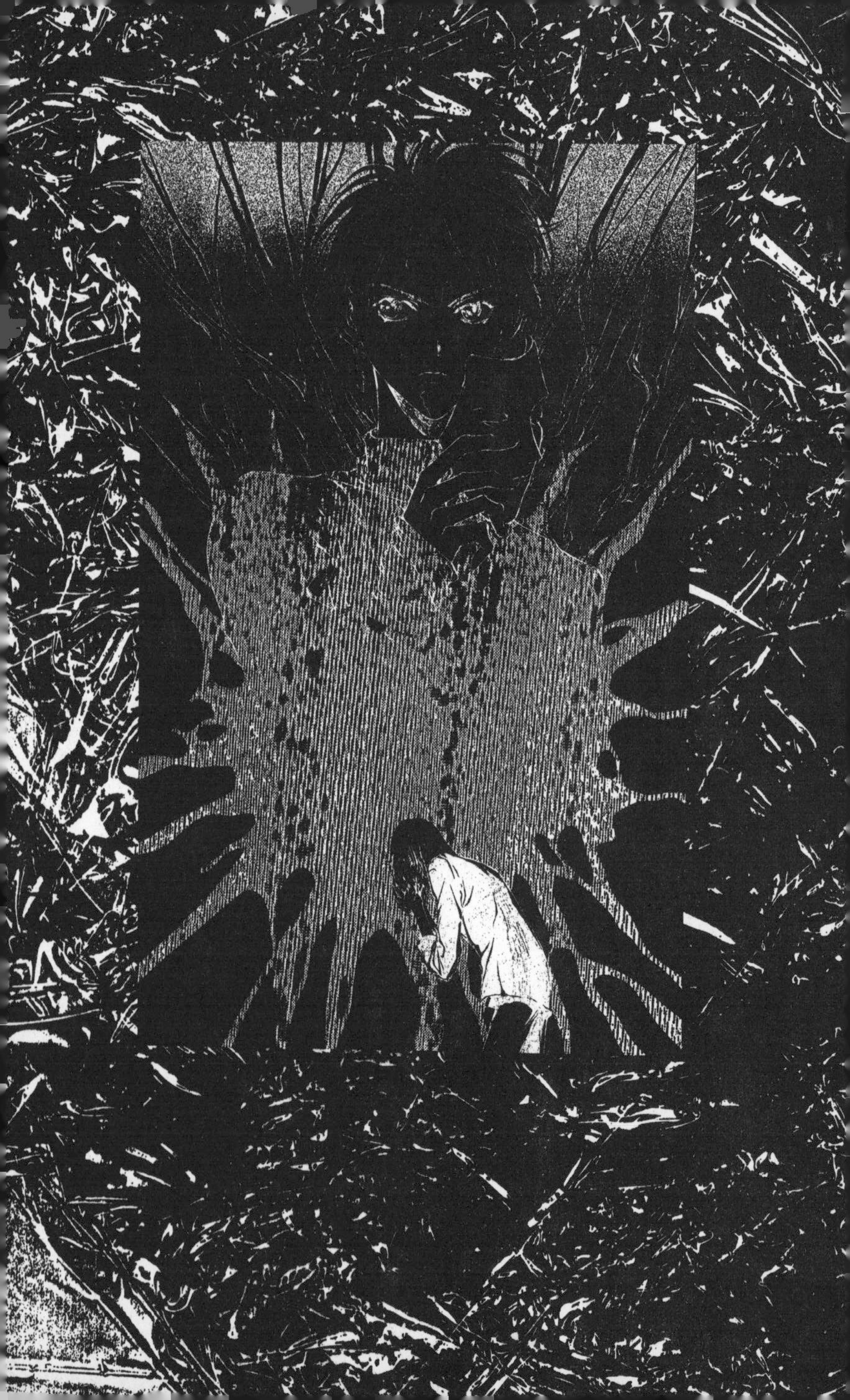

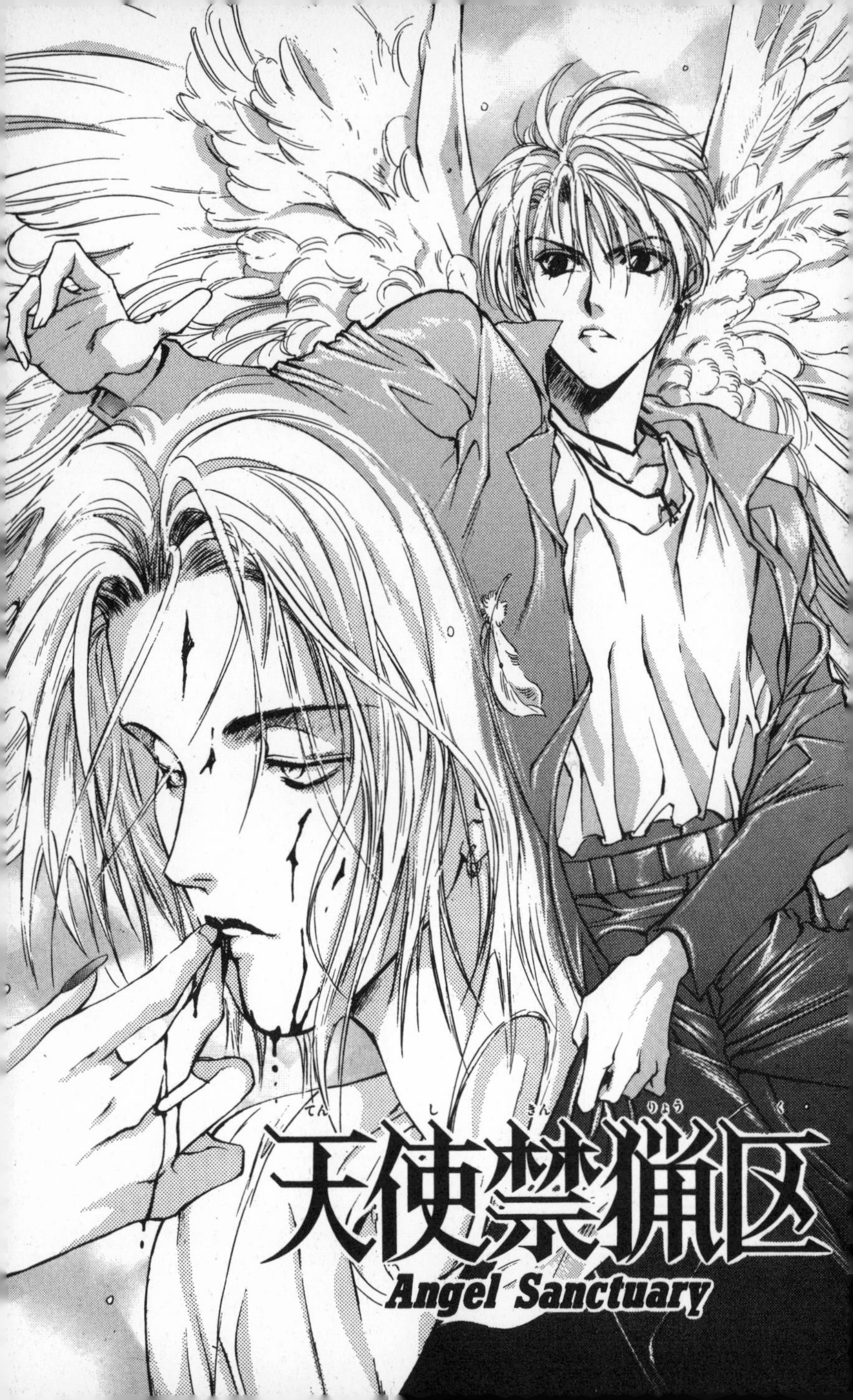
天使禁猟区
Angel Sanctuary

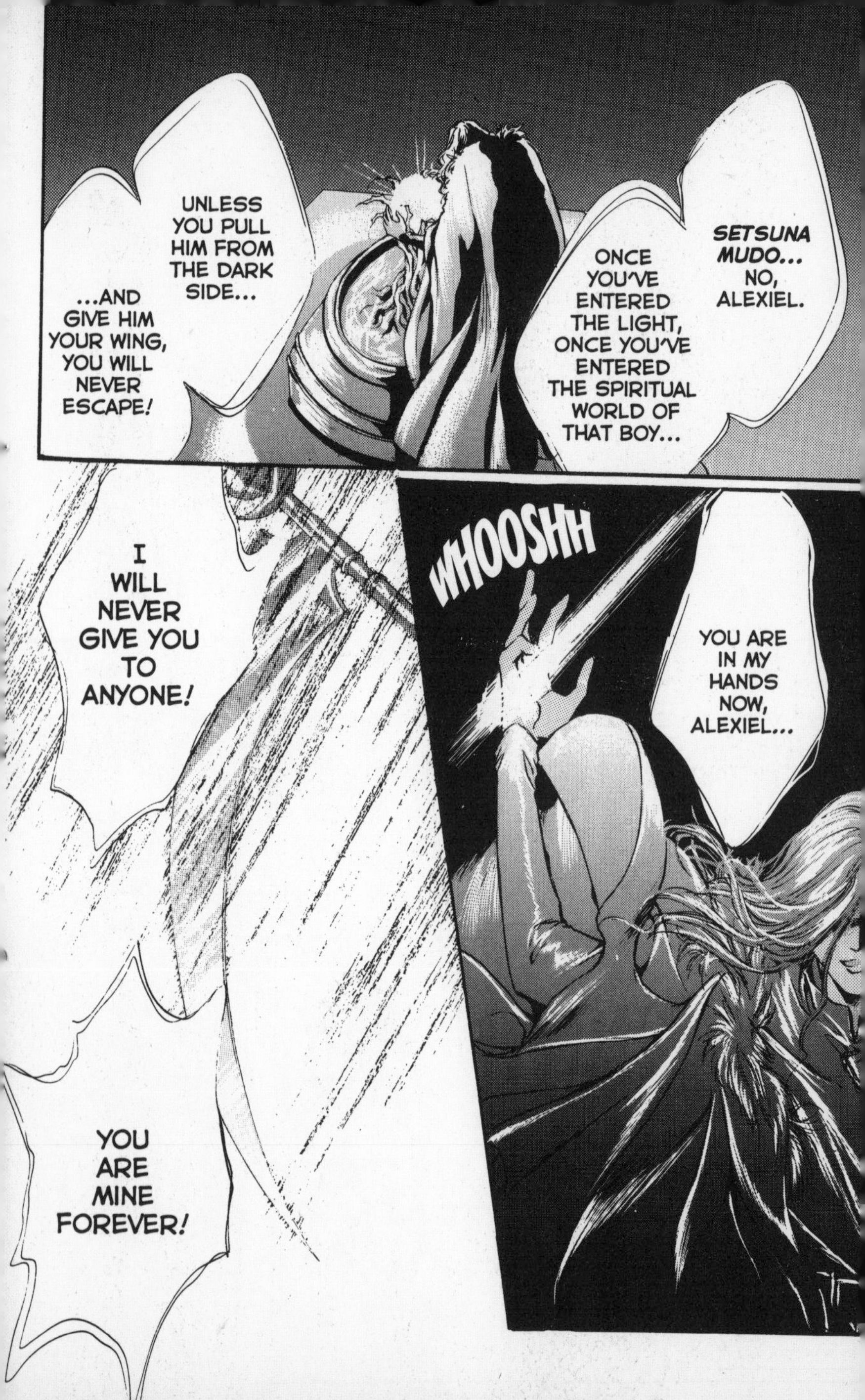
SETSUNA MUDO... NO, ALEXIEL.
ONCE YOU'VE ENTERED THE LIGHT, ONCE YOU'VE ENTERED THE SPIRITUAL WORLD OF THAT BOY...
UNLESS YOU PULL HIM FROM THE DARK SIDE...
...AND GIVE HIM YOUR WING, YOU WILL NEVER ESCAPE!
WHOOSHH
YOU ARE IN MY HANDS NOW, ALEXIEL...
I WILL NEVER GIVE YOU TO ANYONE!
YOU ARE MINE FOREVER!

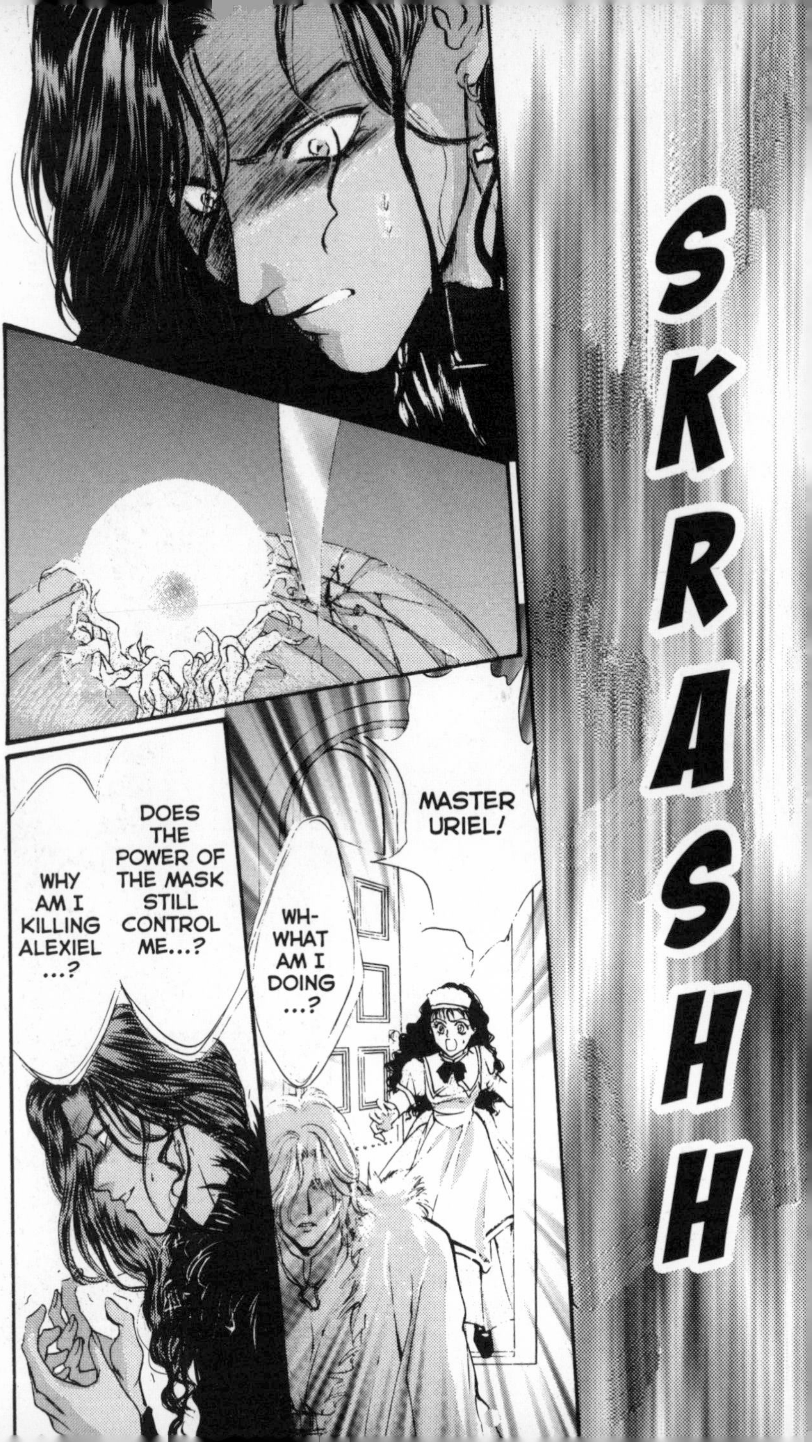
SKRASHH
MASTER URIEL!
WH- WHAT AM I DOING ...?
DOES THE POWER OF THE MASK STILL CONTROL ME...?
WHY AM I KILLING ALEXIEL ...?

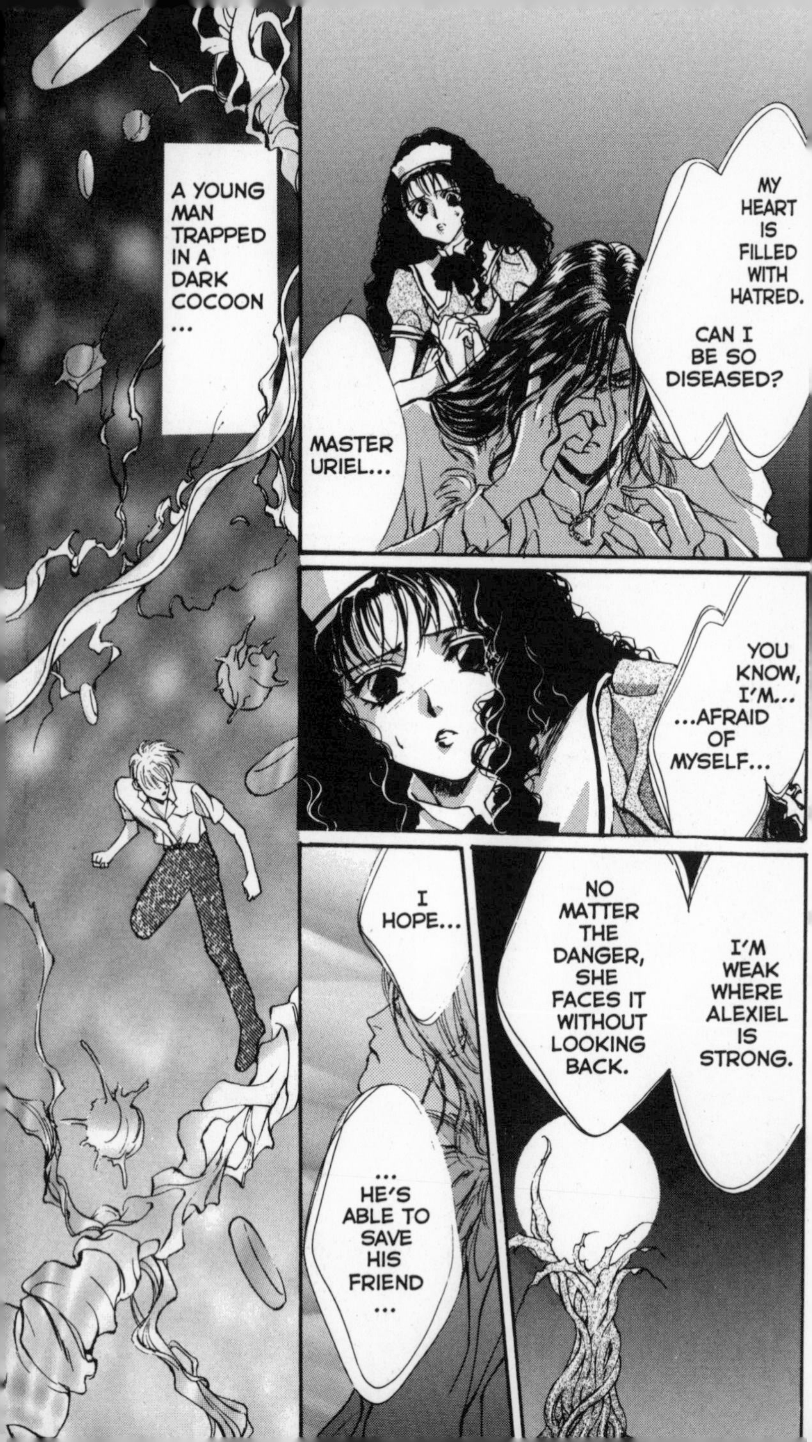
MY HEART IS FILLED WITH HATRED.
CAN I BE SO DISEASED?
MASTER URIEL...
YOU KNOW, I'M... ...AFRAID OF MYSELF...
I'M WEAK WHERE ALEXIEL IS STRONG.
NO MATTER THE DANGER, SHE FACES IT WITHOUT LOOKING BACK.
I HOPE...
...HE'S ABLE TO SAVE HIS FRIEND...
A YOUNG MAN TRAPPED IN A DARK COCOON...

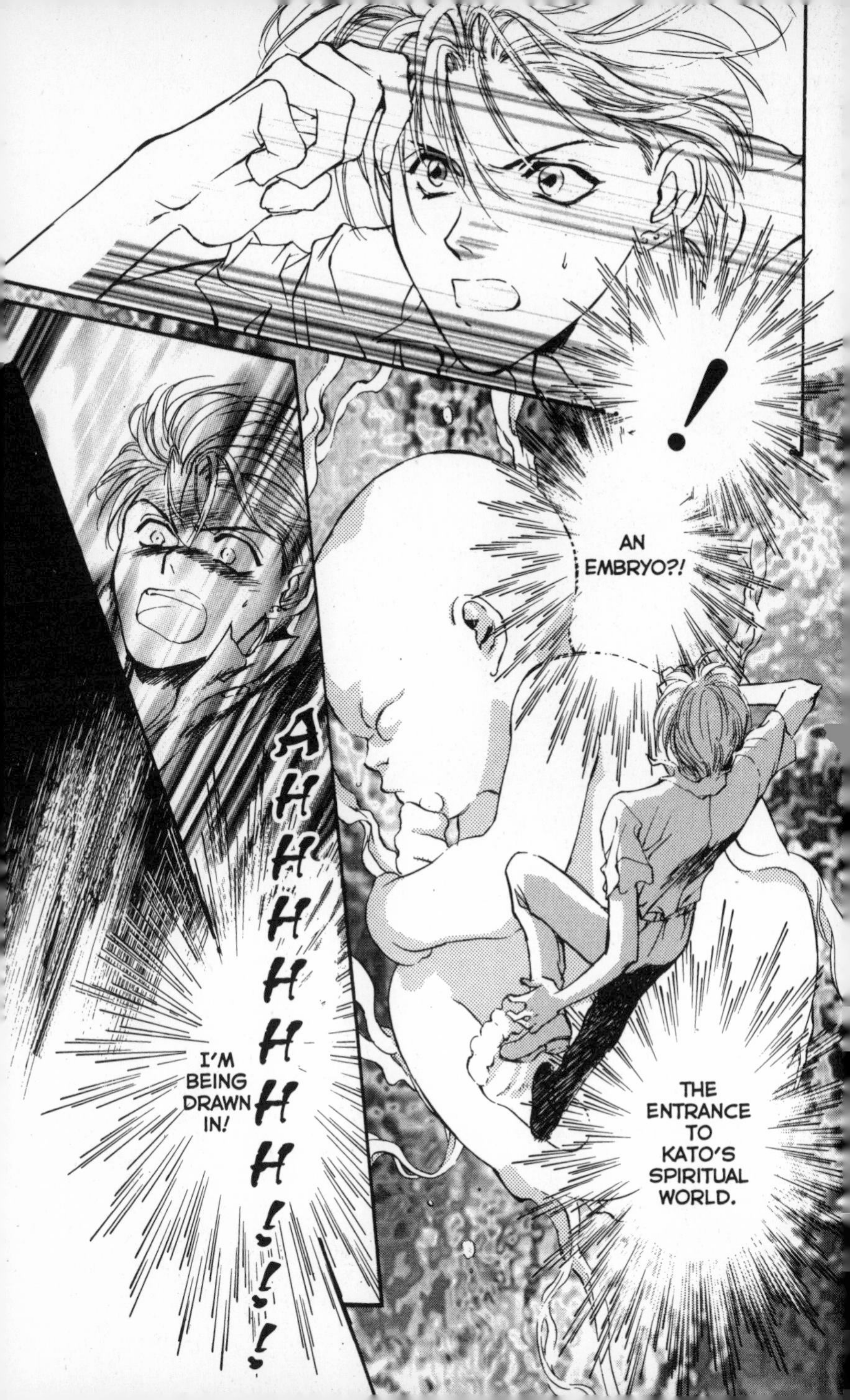
!
AN EMBRYO?!
THE ENTRANCE TO KATO'S SPIRITUAL WORLD.
AHHHHHHHH!!!
I'M BEING DRAWN IN!

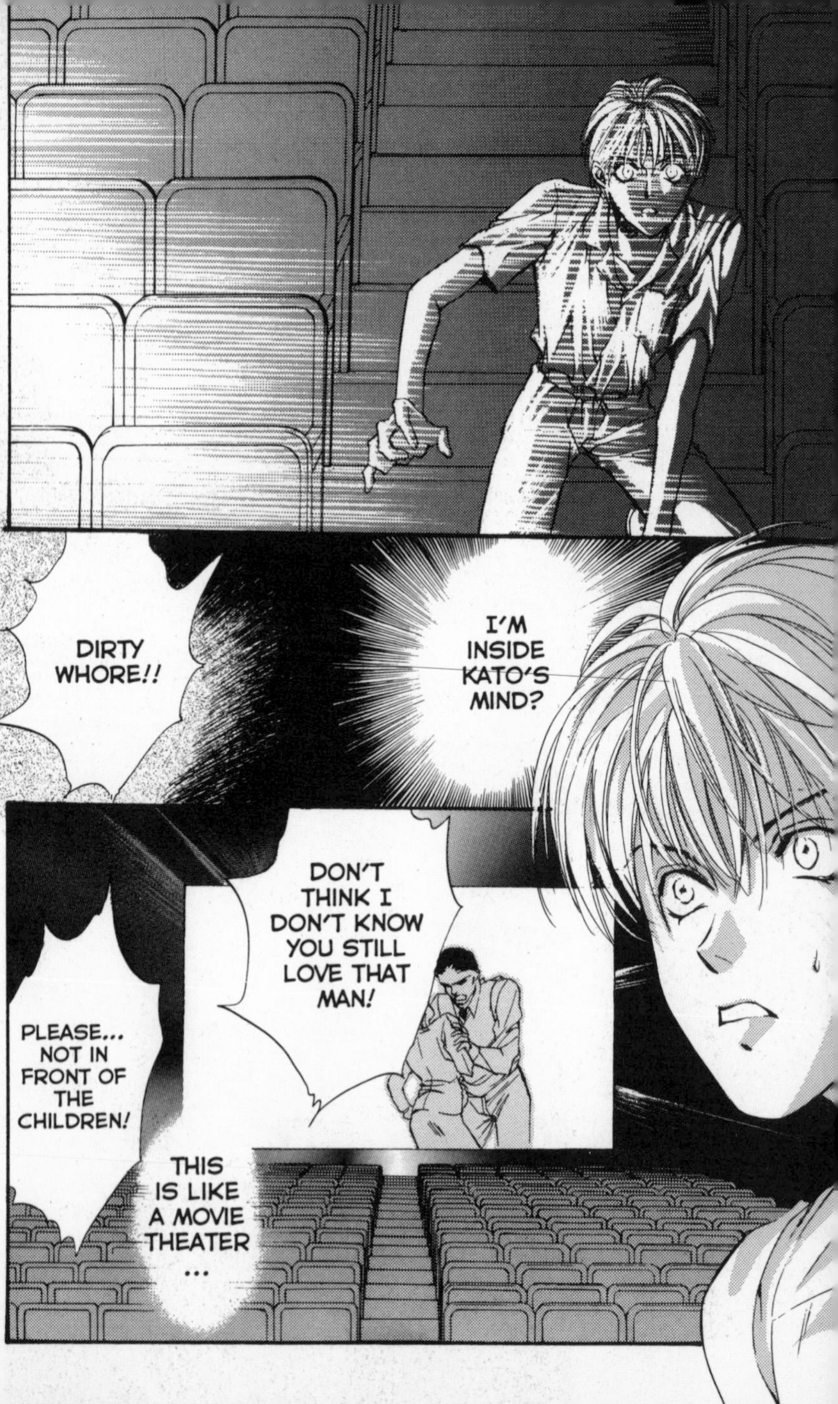
I'M INSIDE KATO'S MIND?
DIRTY WHORE!!
DON'T THINK I DON'T KNOW YOU STILL LOVE THAT MAN!
PLEASE... NOT IN FRONT OF THE CHILDREN!
THIS IS LIKE A MOVIE THEATER ...

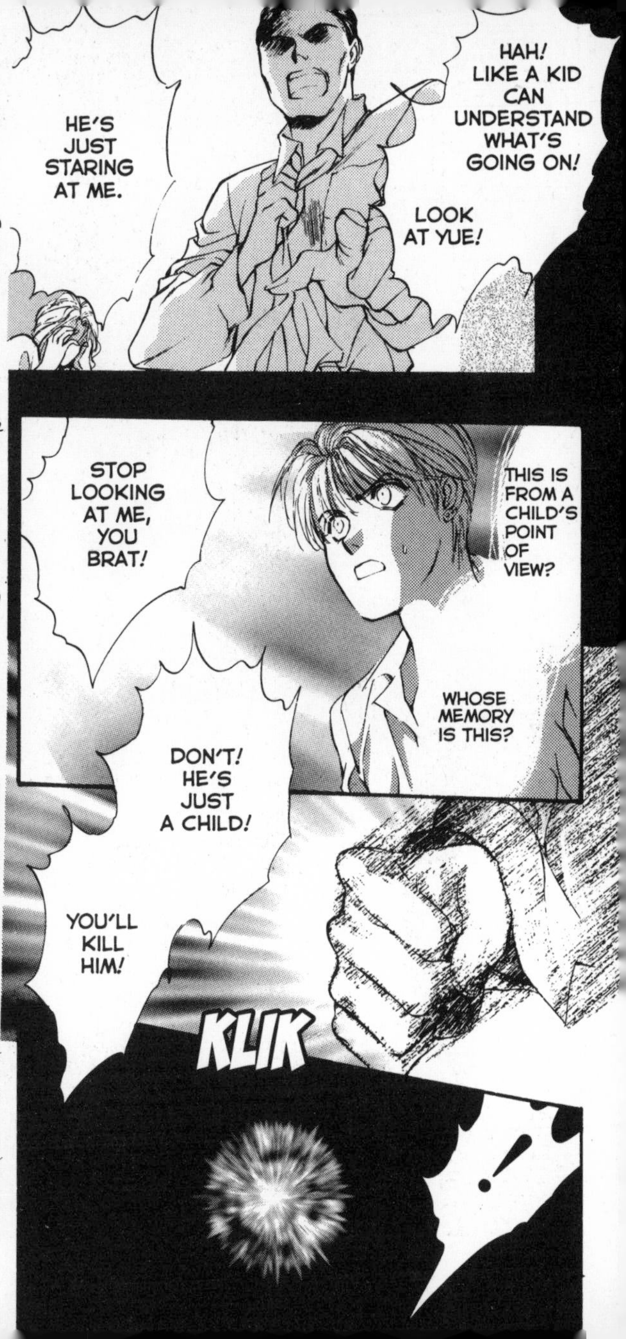
HAH! LIKE A KID CAN UNDERSTAND WHAT'S GOING ON!
LOOK AT YUE!
HE'S JUST STARING AT ME.
THIS IS FROM A CHILD'S POINT OF VIEW?
STOP LOOKING AT ME, YOU BRAT!
WHOSE MEMORY IS THIS?
DON'T! HE'S JUST A CHILD!
YOU'LL KILL HIM!
KLIK
!

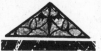

Hi. The reason I didn't have any notes for the last chapter was because I forgot to include space to put them in. How could I forget...?! Anyway, Kato is taking the spotlight again. I needed to fill some pages so this flashback got pretty detailed. But reader reaction seemed positive so I'm very happy. The name 'Yue' is strange but doesn't it sound nice? Kato is always busy disappearing and such but I get a lot of letters saying 'Don't kill him.' I mean, he's already dead anyway... or won't that excuse work? Still, with parents like his, you can understand why he became bad, right?

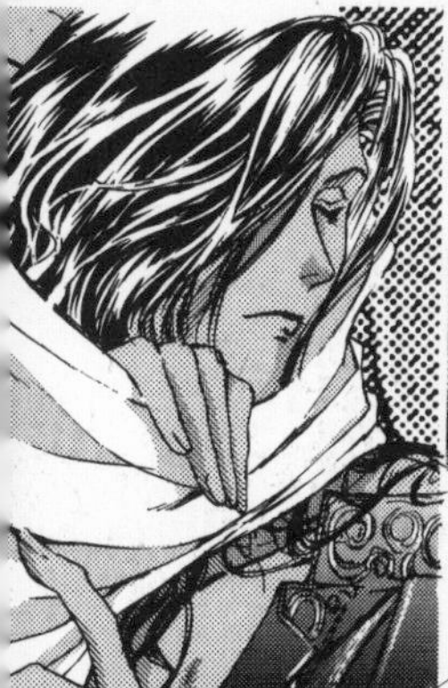

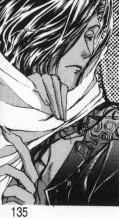

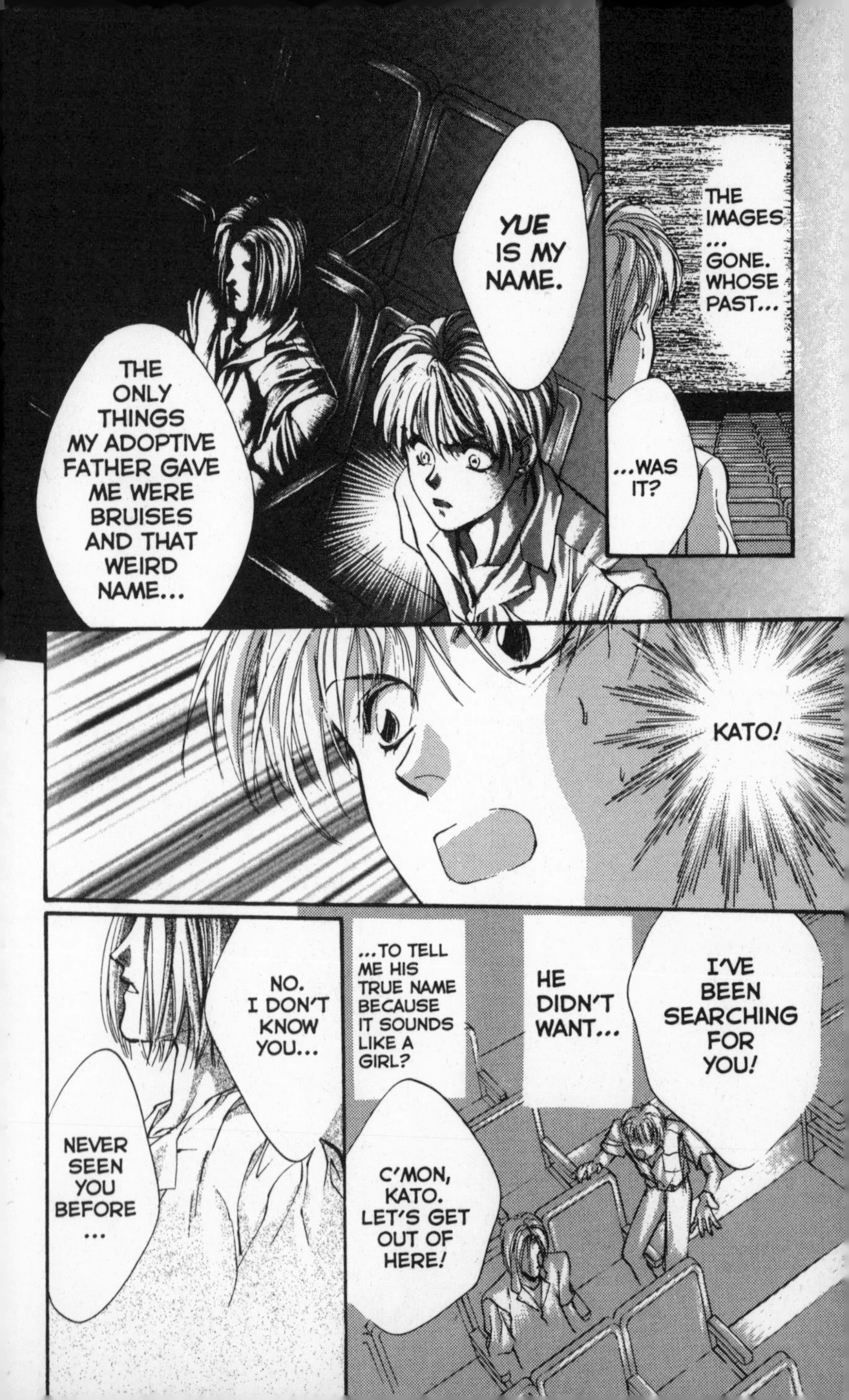
THE IMAGES ... GONE. WHOSE PAST...
...WAS IT?
YUE IS MY NAME.
THE ONLY THINGS MY ADOPTIVE FATHER GAVE ME WERE BRUISES AND THAT WEIRD NAME...
KATO!
I'VE BEEN SEARCHING FOR YOU!
HE DIDN'T WANT...
...TO TELL ME HIS TRUE NAME BECAUSE IT SOUNDS LIKE A GIRL?
C'MON, KATO. LET'S GET OUT OF HERE!
NO. I DON'T KNOW YOU...
NEVER SEEN YOU BEFORE ...

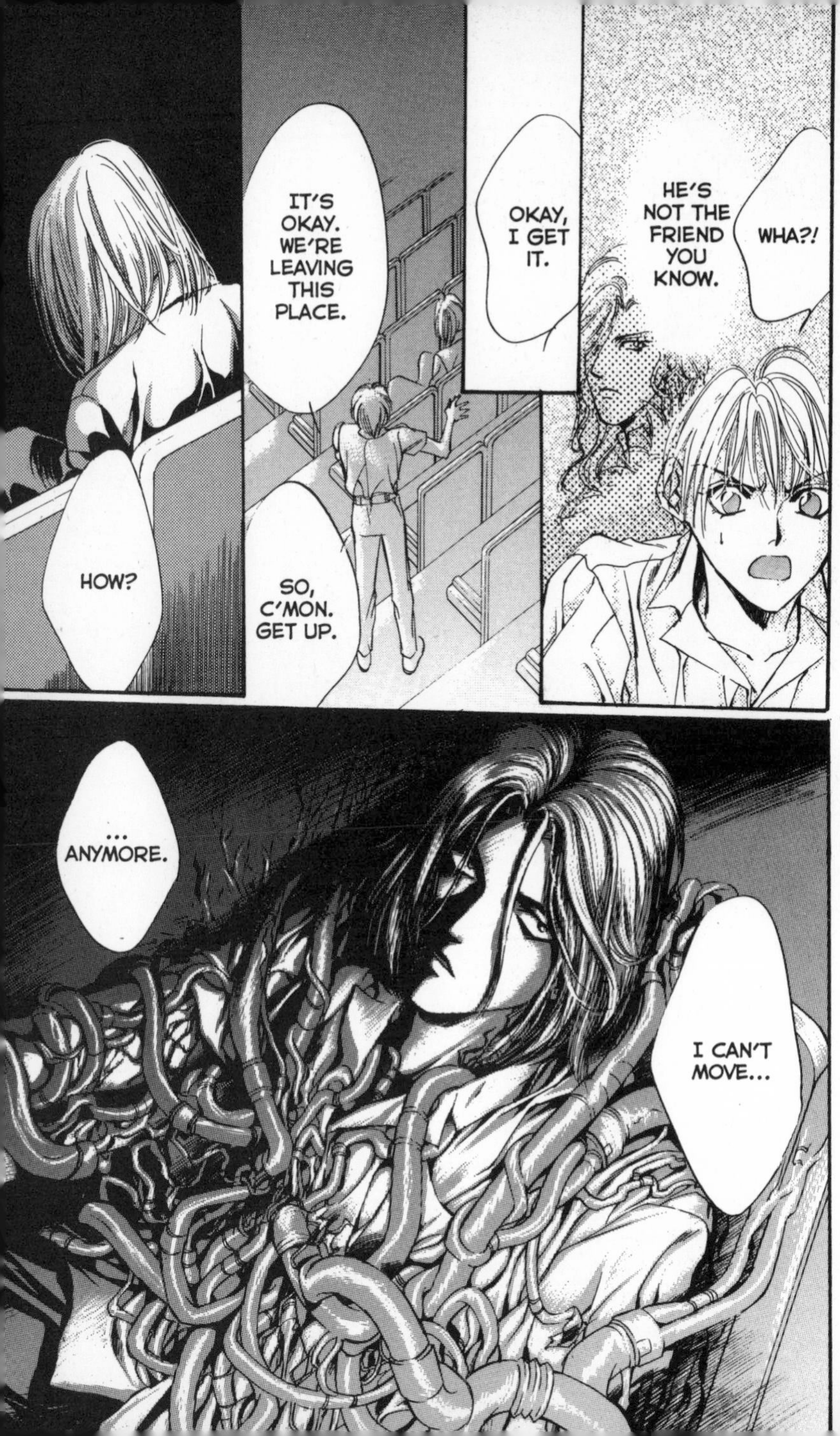
WHA?!
HE'S NOT THE FRIEND YOU KNOW.
OKAY, I GET IT.
IT'S OKAY. WE'RE LEAVING THIS PLACE.
SO, C'MON. GET UP.
HOW?
I CAN'T MOVE...
... ANYMORE.

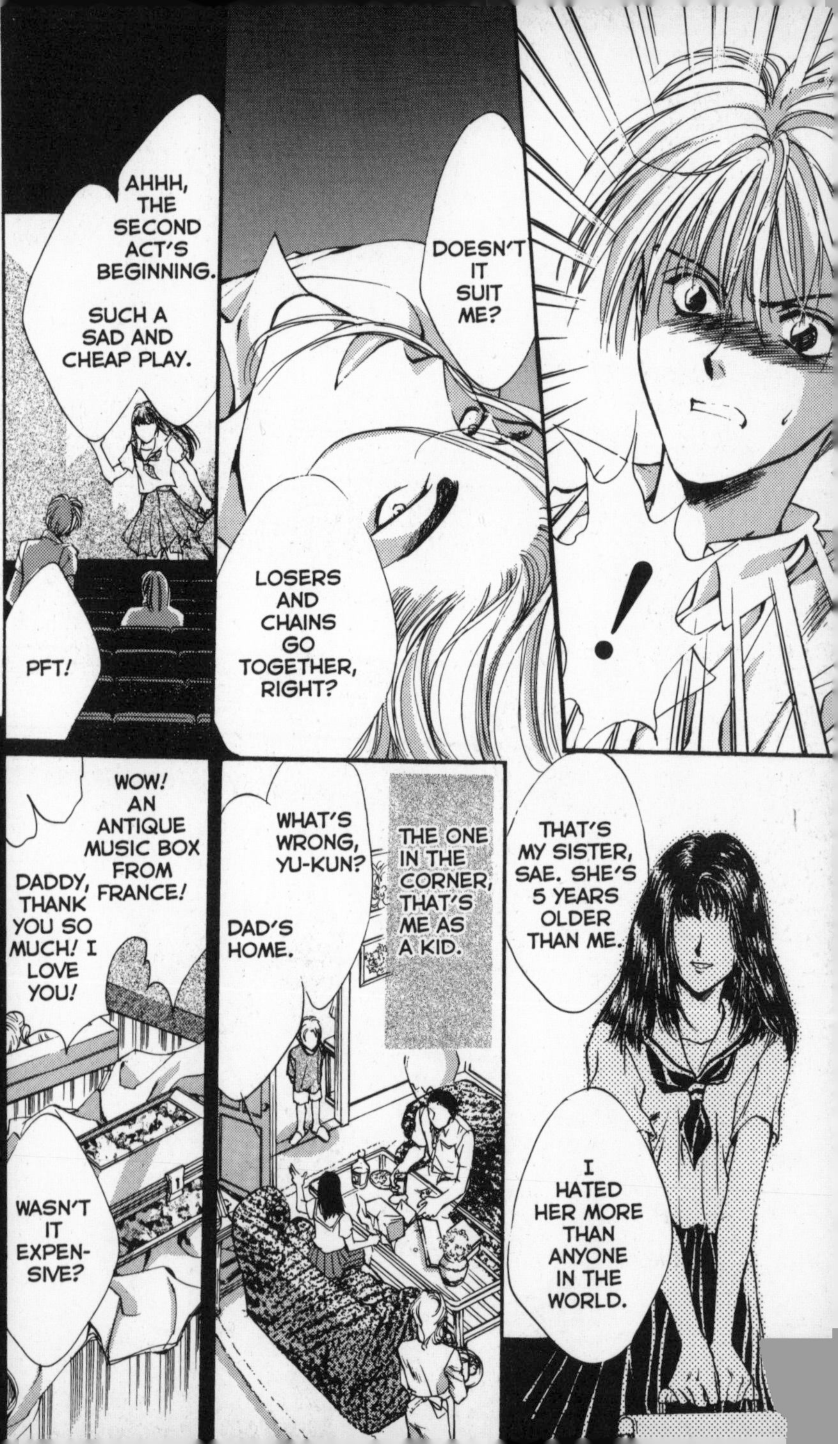
!
DOESN'T IT SUIT ME?
LOSERS AND CHAINS GO TOGETHER, RIGHT?
AHHH, THE SECOND ACT'S BEGINNING.
SUCH A SAD AND CHEAP PLAY.
PFT!
THAT'S MY SISTER, SAE. SHE'S 5 YEARS OLDER THAN ME.
I HATED HER MORE THAN ANYONE IN THE WORLD.
THE ONE IN THE CORNER, THAT'S ME AS A KID.
WHAT'S WRONG, YU-KUN?
DAD'S HOME.
WOW! AN ANTIQUE MUSIC BOX FROM FRANCE!
DADDY, THANK YOU SO MUCH! I LOVE YOU!
WASN'T IT EXPENSIVE?

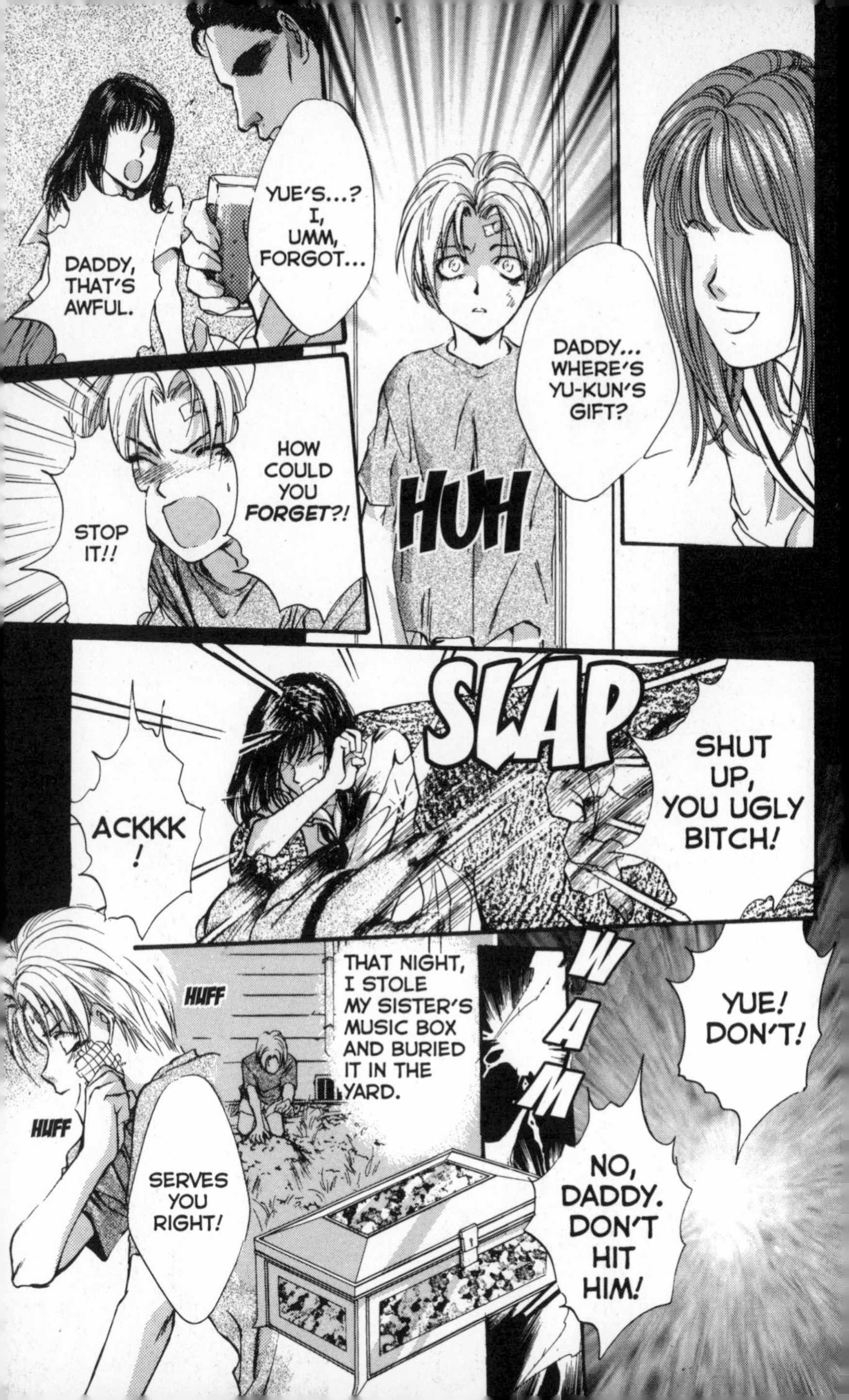
DADDY... WHERE'S YU-KUN'S GIFT?
HUH
YUE'S...? I, UMM, FORGOT...
DADDY, THAT'S AWFUL.
HOW COULD YOU FORGET?!
STOP IT!!
SHUT UP, YOU UGLY BITCH!
SLAP
ACKKK!
YUE! DON'T!
WHAM
NO, DADDY. DON'T HIT HIM!
THAT NIGHT, I STOLE MY SISTER'S MUSIC BOX AND BURIED IT IN THE YARD.
HUFF
HUFF
SERVES YOU RIGHT!

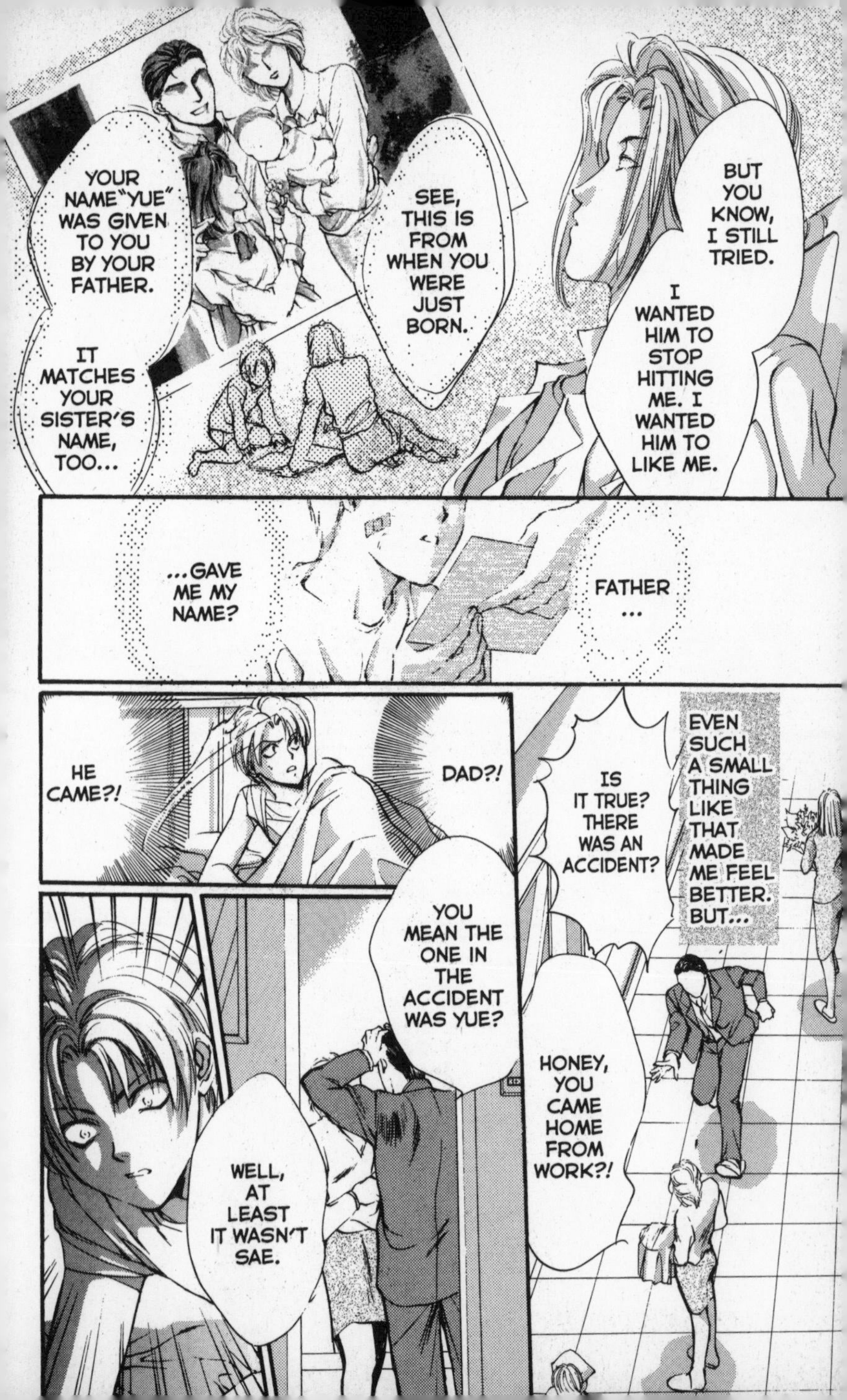
BUT YOU KNOW, I STILL TRIED.
I WANTED HIM TO STOP HITTING ME. I WANTED HIM TO LIKE ME.
SEE, THIS IS FROM WHEN YOU WERE JUST BORN.
YOUR NAME "YUE" WAS GIVEN TO YOU BY YOUR FATHER.
IT MATCHES YOUR SISTER'S NAME, TOO...
FATHER ...
...GAVE ME MY NAME?
EVEN SUCH A SMALL THING LIKE THAT MADE ME FEEL BETTER. BUT...
IS IT TRUE? THERE WAS AN ACCIDENT?
HONEY, YOU CAME HOME FROM WORK?!
DAD?!
HE CAME?!
YOU MEAN THE ONE IN THE ACCIDENT WAS YUE?
WELL, AT LEAST IT WASN'T SAE.

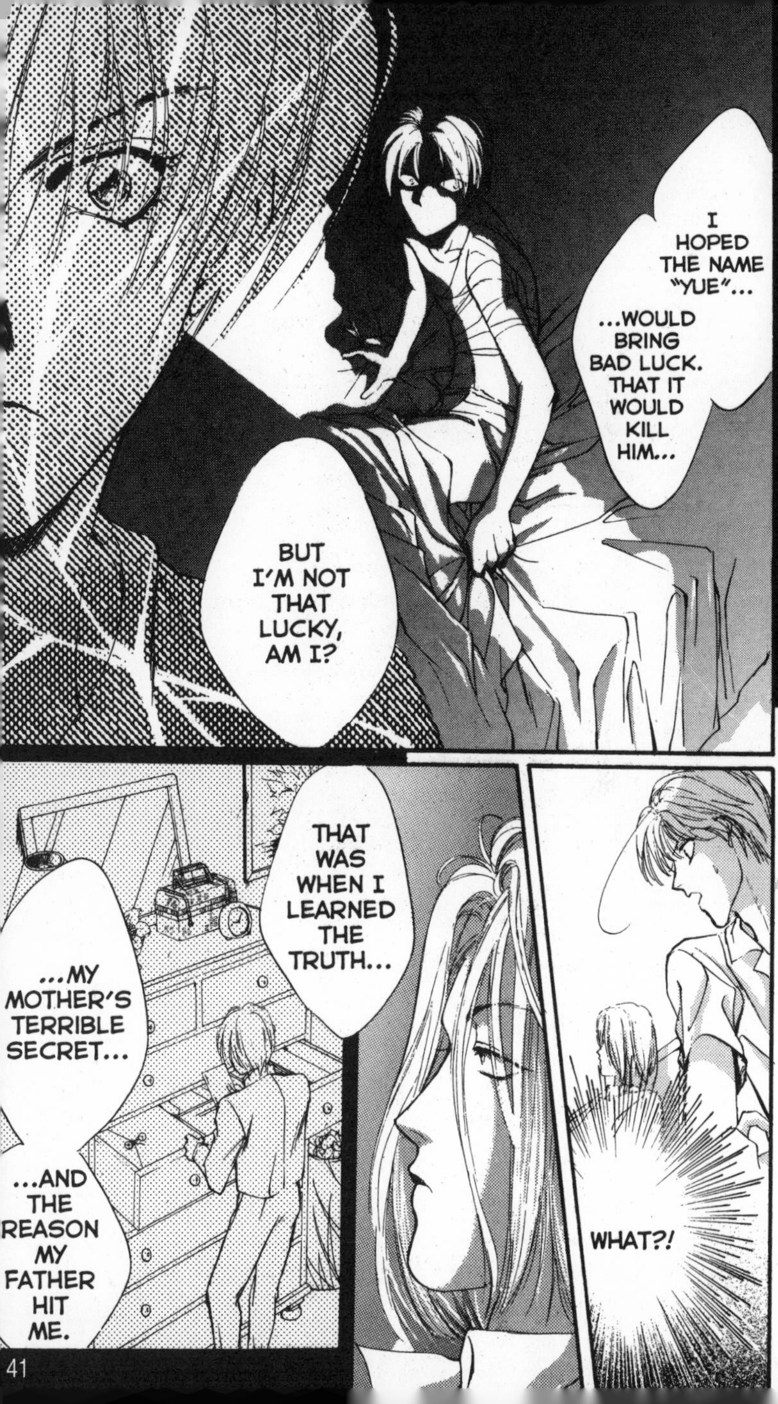
I HOPED THE NAME "YUE"...
...WOULD BRING BAD LUCK. THAT IT WOULD KILL HIM...
BUT I'M NOT THAT LUCKY, AM I?
WHAT?!
THAT WAS WHEN I LEARNED THE TRUTH...
...MY MOTHER'S TERRIBLE SECRET...
...AND THE REASON MY FATHER HIT ME.

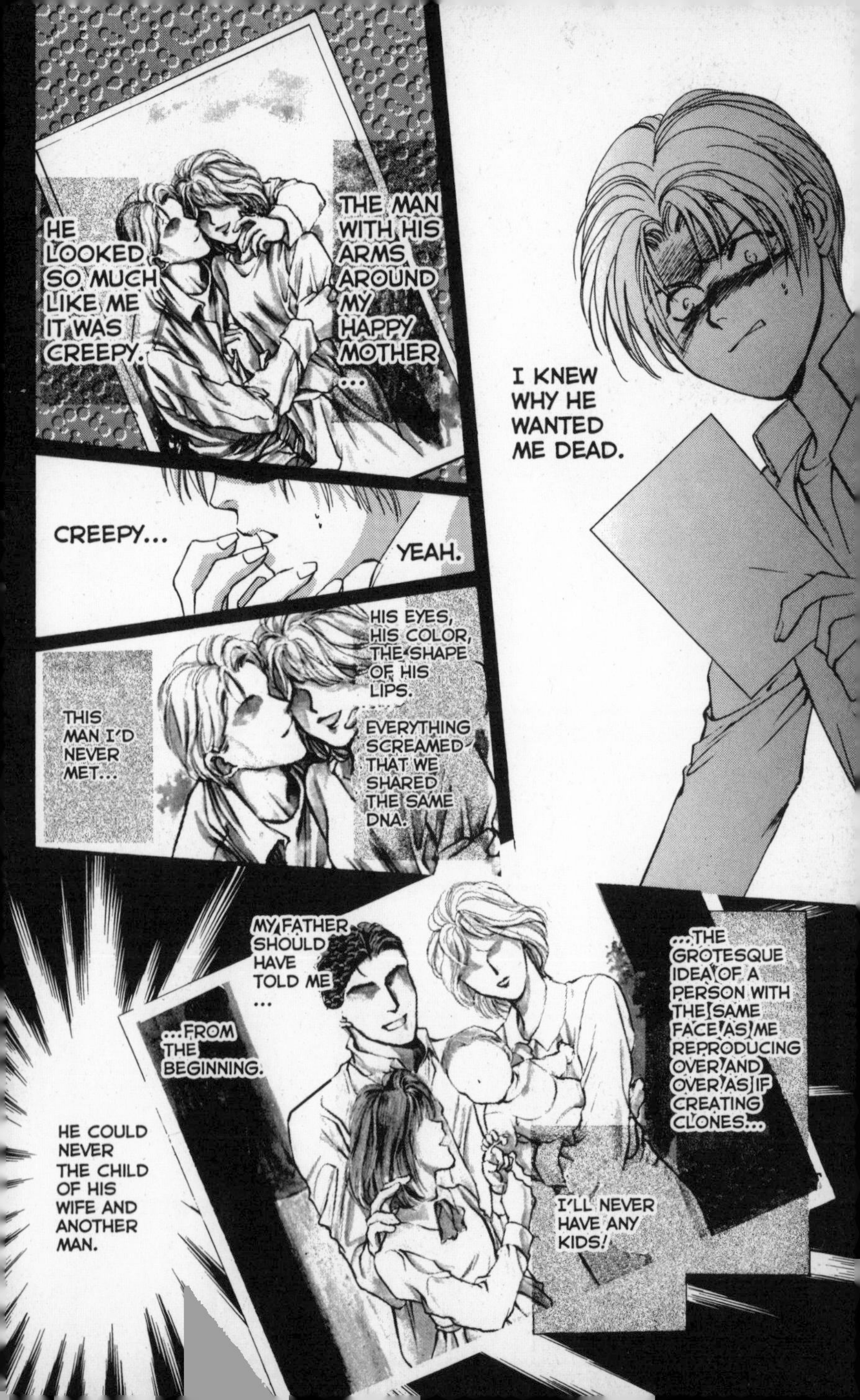
I KNEW WHY HE WANTED ME DEAD.
THE MAN WITH HIS ARMS AROUND MY HAPPY MOTHER ...
HE LOOKED SO MUCH LIKE ME IT WAS CREEPY.
CREEPY...
YEAH.
HIS EYES, HIS COLOR, THE SHAPE OF HIS LIPS.
THIS MAN I'D NEVER MET...
EVERYTHING SCREAMED THAT WE SHARED THE SAME DNA.
...THE GROTESQUE IDEA OF A PERSON WITH THE SAME FACE AS ME REPRODUCING OVER AND OVER AS IF CREATING CLONES...
MY FATHER SHOULD HAVE TOLD ME ...
...FROM THE BEGINNING.
I'LL NEVER HAVE ANY KIDS!
HE COULD NEVER THE CHILD OF HIS WIFE AND ANOTHER MAN.

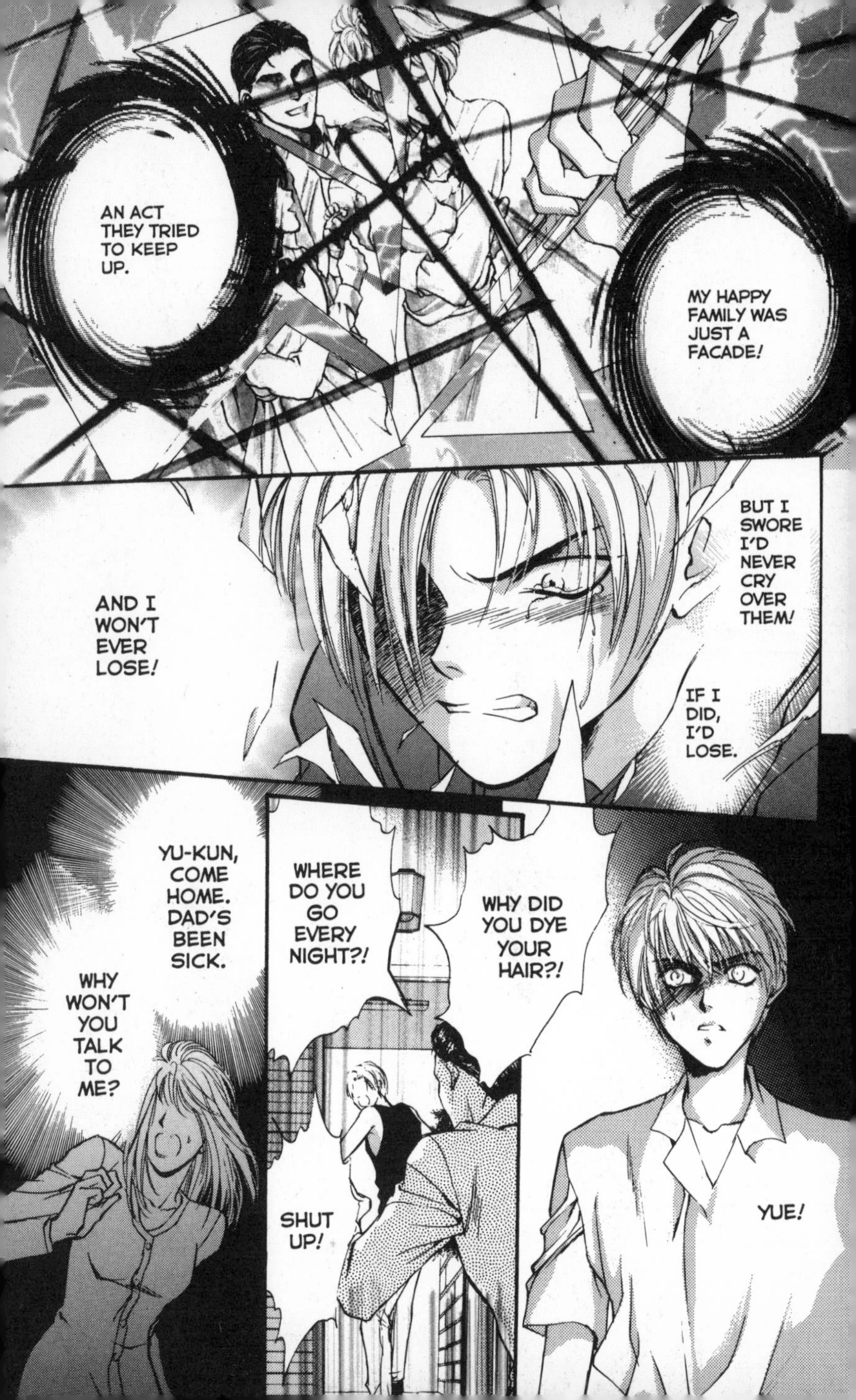
MY HAPPY FAMILY WAS JUST A FACADE!
AN ACT THEY TRIED TO KEEP UP.
BUT I SWORE I'D NEVER CRY OVER THEM!
IF I DID, I'D LOSE.
AND I WON'T EVER LOSE!
WHY DID YOU DYE YOUR HAIR?!
WHERE DO YOU GO EVERY NIGHT?!
YUE!
SHUT UP!
YU-KUN, COME HOME. DAD'S BEEN SICK.
WHY WON'T YOU TALK TO ME?

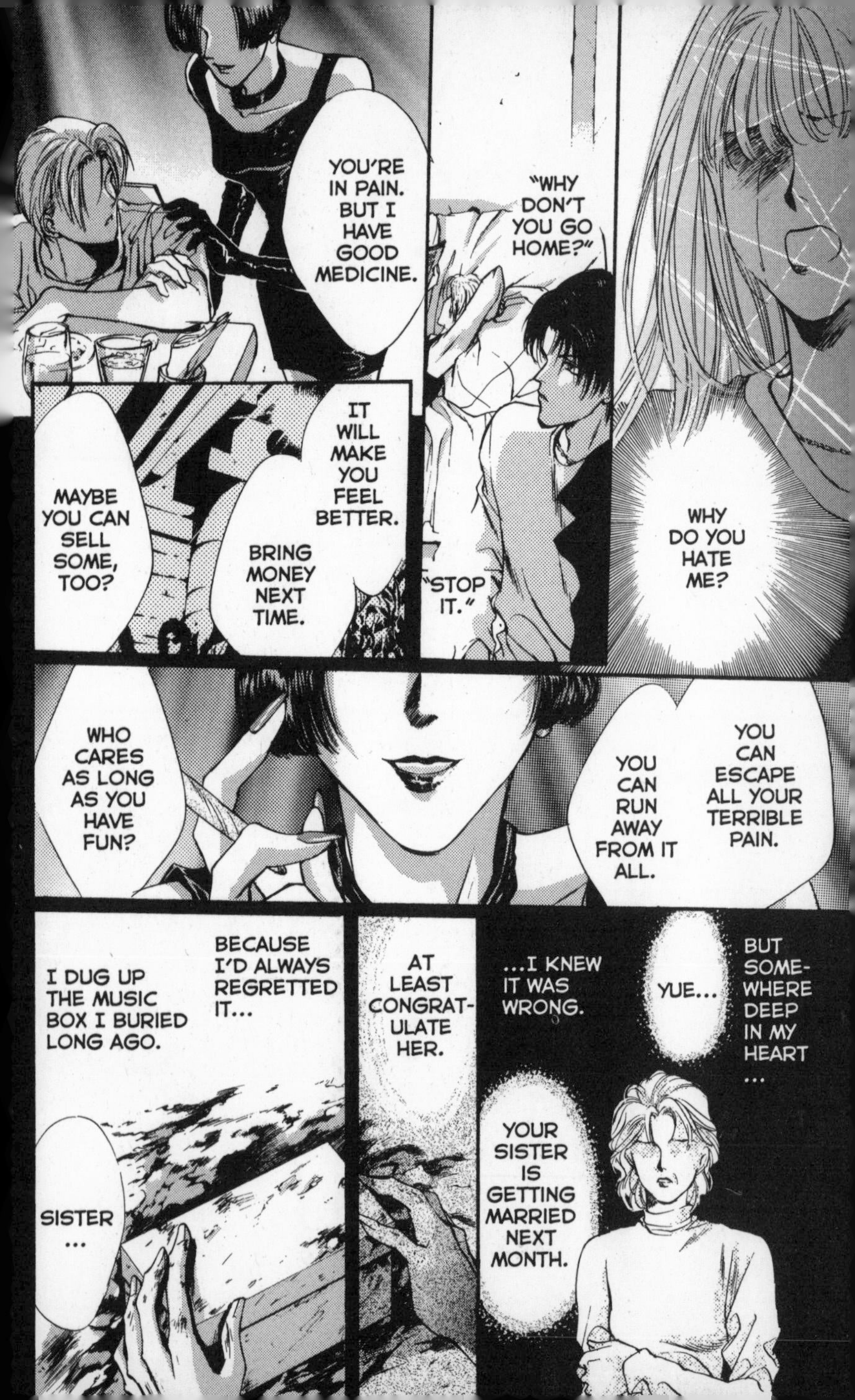
WHY DO YOU HATE ME?
"WHY DON'T YOU GO HOME?"
"STOP IT."
YOU'RE IN PAIN. BUT I HAVE GOOD MEDICINE.
IT WILL MAKE YOU FEEL BETTER.
BRING MONEY NEXT TIME.
MAYBE YOU CAN SELL SOME, TOO?
YOU CAN ESCAPE ALL YOUR TERRIBLE PAIN.
YOU CAN RUN AWAY FROM IT ALL.
WHO CARES AS LONG AS YOU HAVE FUN?
BUT SOMEWHERE DEEP IN MY HEART ...
YUE...
...I KNEW IT WAS WRONG.
YOUR SISTER IS GETTING MARRIED NEXT MONTH.
AT LEAST CONGRAT-ULATE HER.
BECAUSE I'D ALWAYS REGRETTED IT...
I DUG UP THE MUSIC BOX I BURIED LONG AGO.
SISTER ...

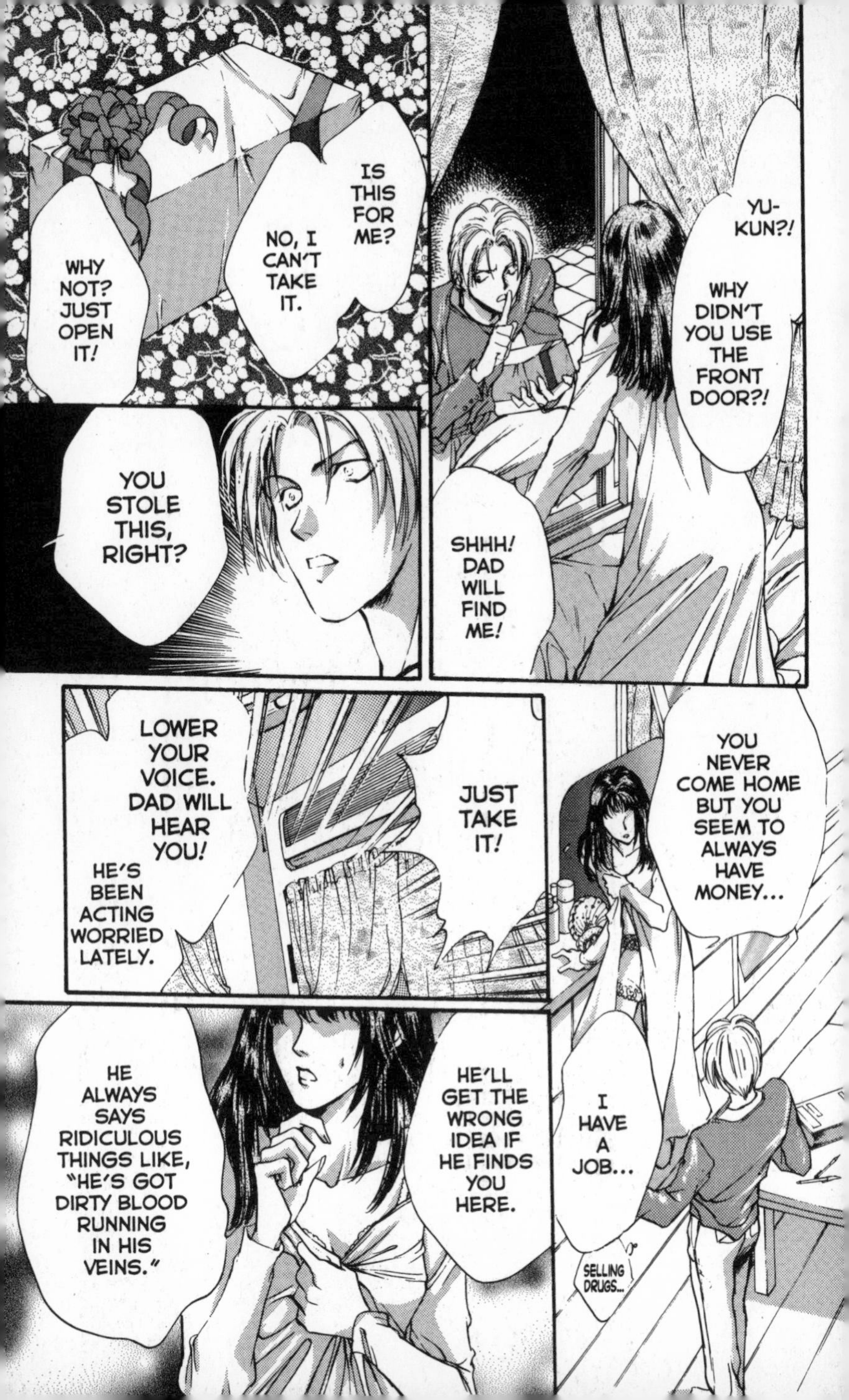
YU-KUN?!
WHY DIDN'T YOU USE THE FRONT DOOR?!
SHHH! DAD WILL FIND ME!
IS THIS FOR ME?
NO, I CAN'T TAKE IT.
WHY NOT? JUST OPEN IT!
YOU STOLE THIS, RIGHT?
YOU NEVER COME HOME BUT YOU SEEM TO ALWAYS HAVE MONEY...
JUST TAKE IT!
LOWER YOUR VOICE. DAD WILL HEAR YOU!
HE'S BEEN ACTING WORRIED LATELY.
I HAVE A JOB...
SELLING DRUGS...
HE'LL GET THE WRONG IDEA IF HE FINDS YOU HERE.
HE ALWAYS SAYS RIDICULOUS THINGS LIKE, "HE'S GOT DIRTY BLOOD RUNNING IN HIS VEINS."

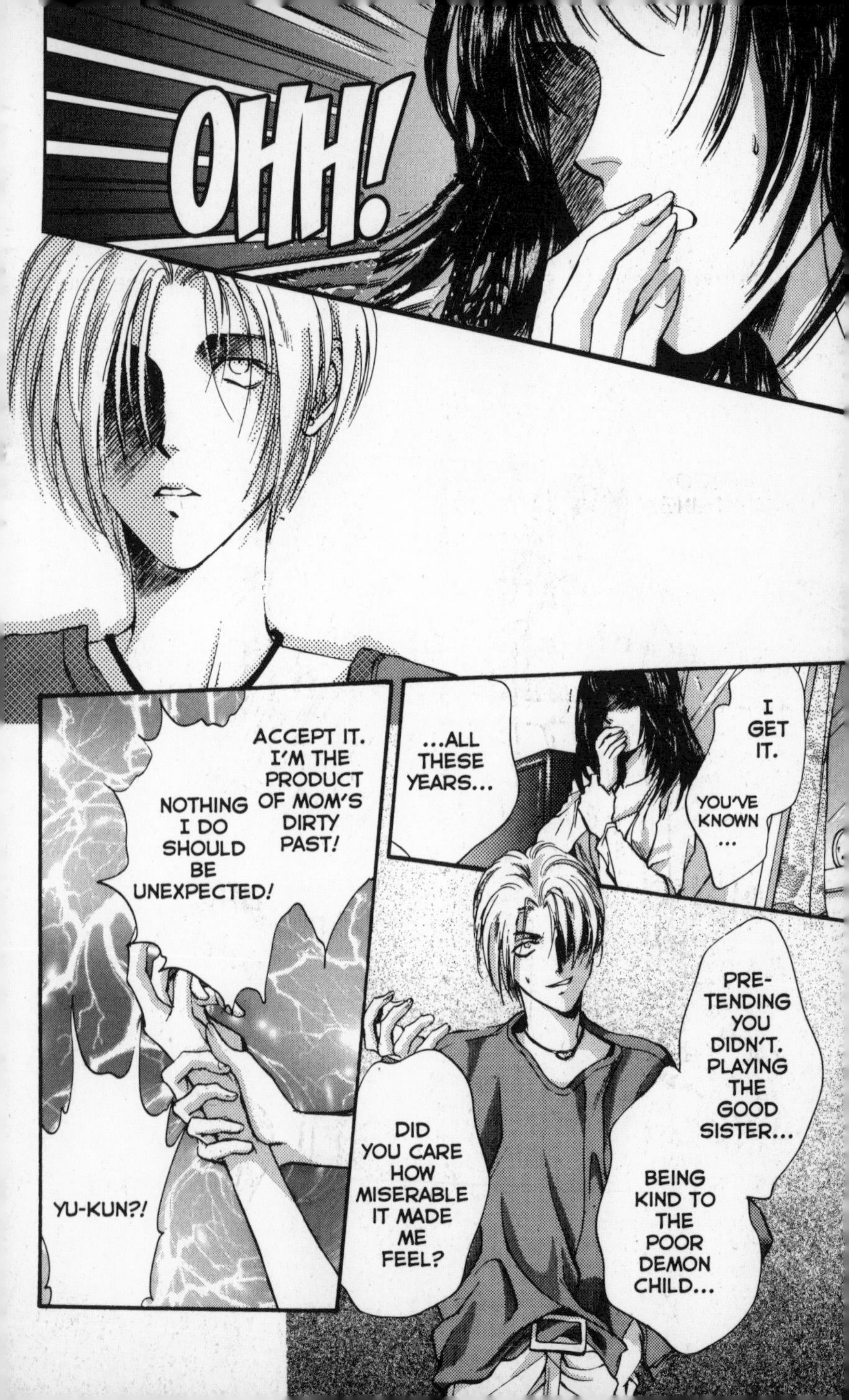
OHH!
I GET IT.
YOU'VE KNOWN...
...ALL THESE YEARS...
PRE-TENDING YOU DIDN'T. PLAYING THE GOOD SISTER...
BEING KIND TO THE POOR DEMON CHILD...
DID YOU CARE HOW MISERABLE IT MADE ME FEEL?
ACCEPT IT. I'M THE PRODUCT OF MOM'S DIRTY PAST!
NOTHING I DO SHOULD BE UNEXPECTED!
YU-KUN?!

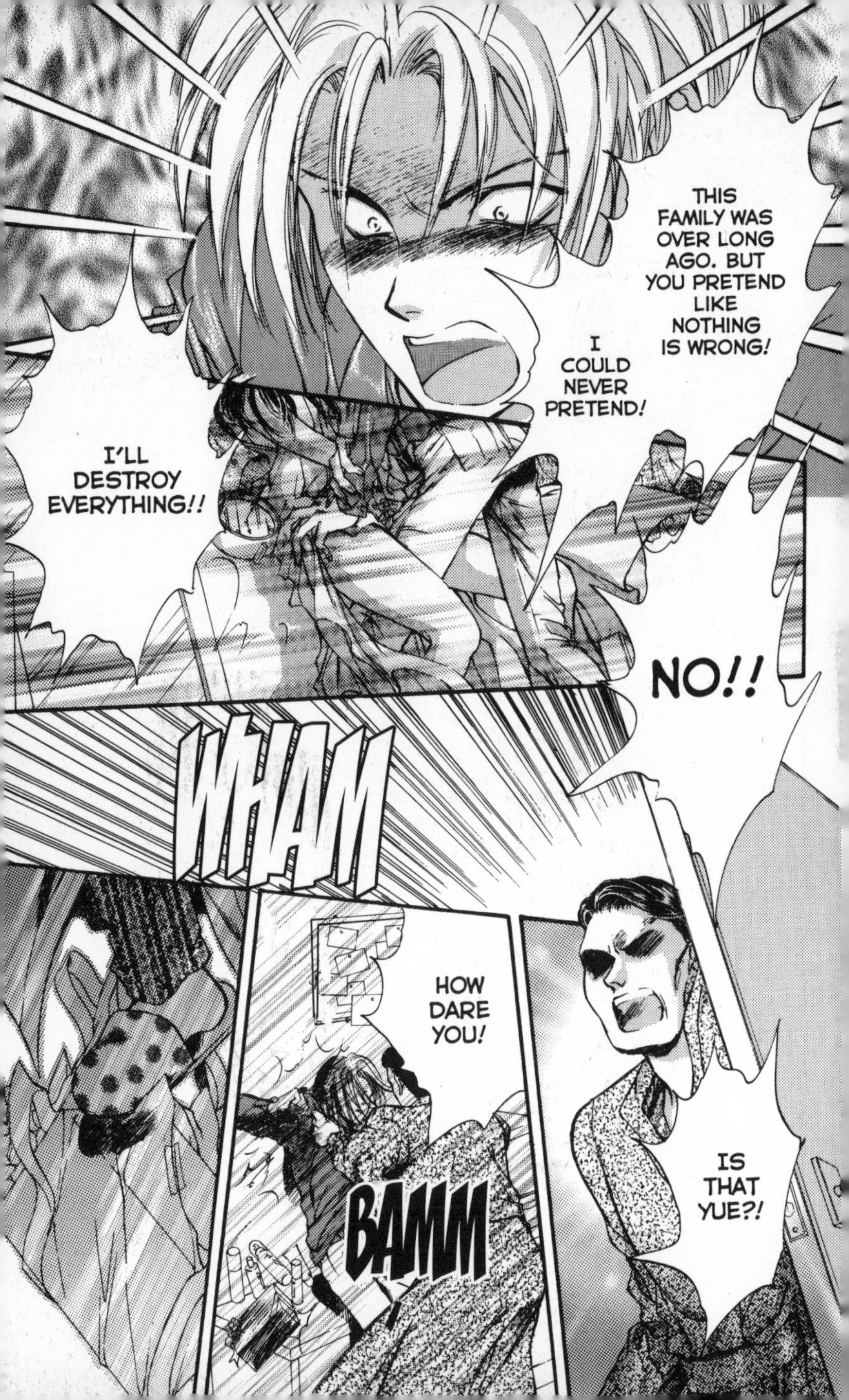
THIS FAMILY WAS OVER LONG AGO. BUT YOU PRETEND LIKE NOTHING IS WRONG!
I COULD NEVER PRETEND!
I'LL DESTROY EVERYTHING!!
NO!!
WHAM
IS THAT YUE?!
HOW DARE YOU!
BAMM

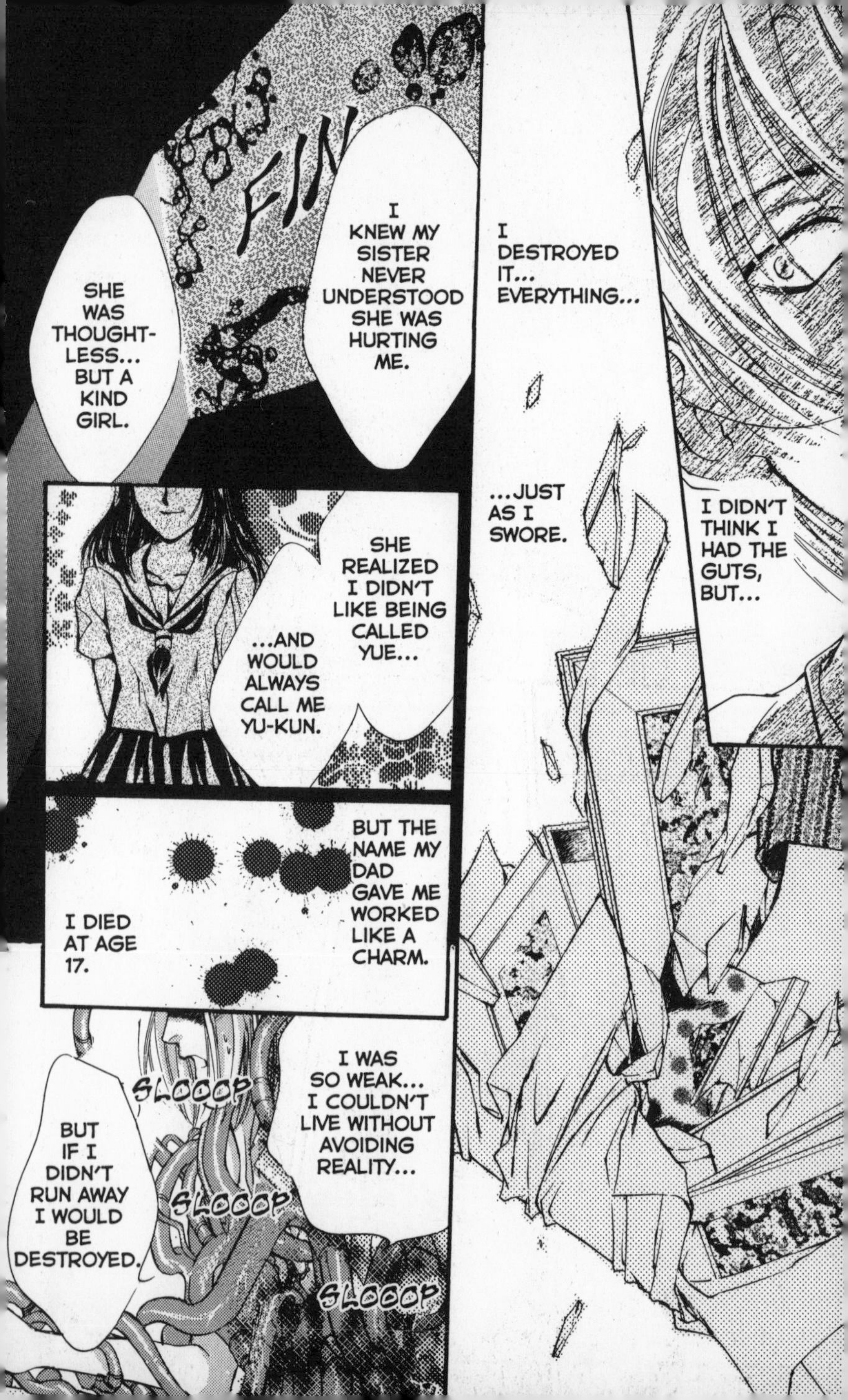
I DIDN'T THINK I HAD THE GUTS, BUT...
I DESTROYED IT... EVERYTHING...
...JUST AS I SWORE.
FIN
I KNEW MY SISTER NEVER UNDERSTOOD SHE WAS HURTING ME.
SHE WAS THOUGHTLESS... BUT A KIND GIRL.
SHE REALIZED I DIDN'T LIKE BEING CALLED YUE...
...AND WOULD ALWAYS CALL ME YU-KUN.
BUT THE NAME MY DAD GAVE ME WORKED LIKE A CHARM.
I DIED AT AGE 17.
I WAS SO WEAK... I COULDN'T LIVE WITHOUT AVOIDING REALITY...
SLOOOP
BUT IF I DIDN'T RUN AWAY I WOULD BE DESTROYED.
SLOOOP
SLOOOP

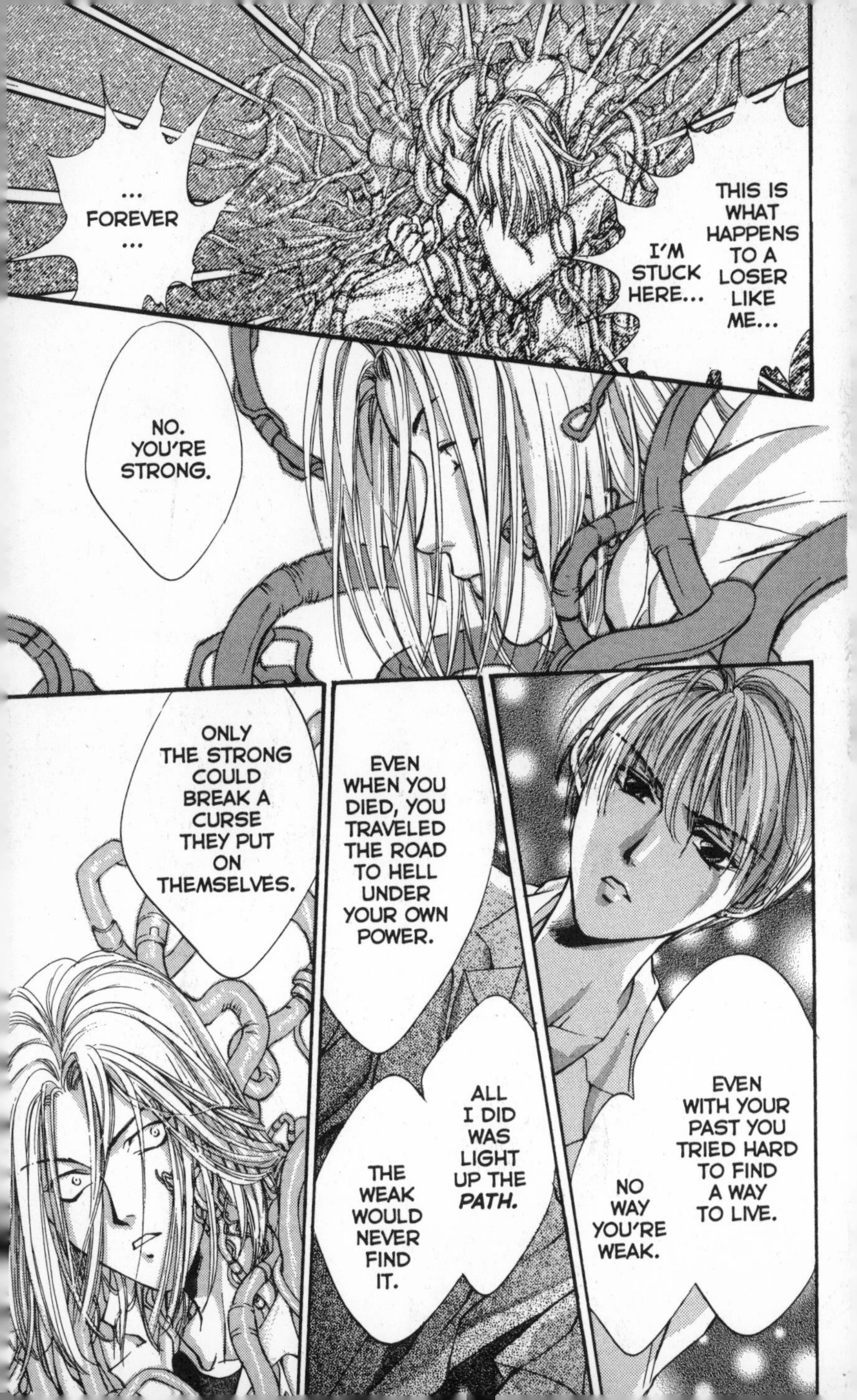
THIS IS WHAT HAPPENS TO A LOSER LIKE ME...
I'M STUCK HERE...
... FOREVER ...
NO. YOU'RE STRONG.
EVEN WITH YOUR PAST YOU TRIED HARD TO FIND A WAY TO LIVE.
NO WAY YOU'RE WEAK.
EVEN WHEN YOU DIED, YOU TRAVELED THE ROAD TO HELL UNDER YOUR OWN POWER.
ALL I DID WAS LIGHT UP THE *PATH.*
THE WEAK WOULD NEVER FIND IT.
ONLY THE STRONG COULD BREAK A CURSE THEY PUT ON THEMSELVES.

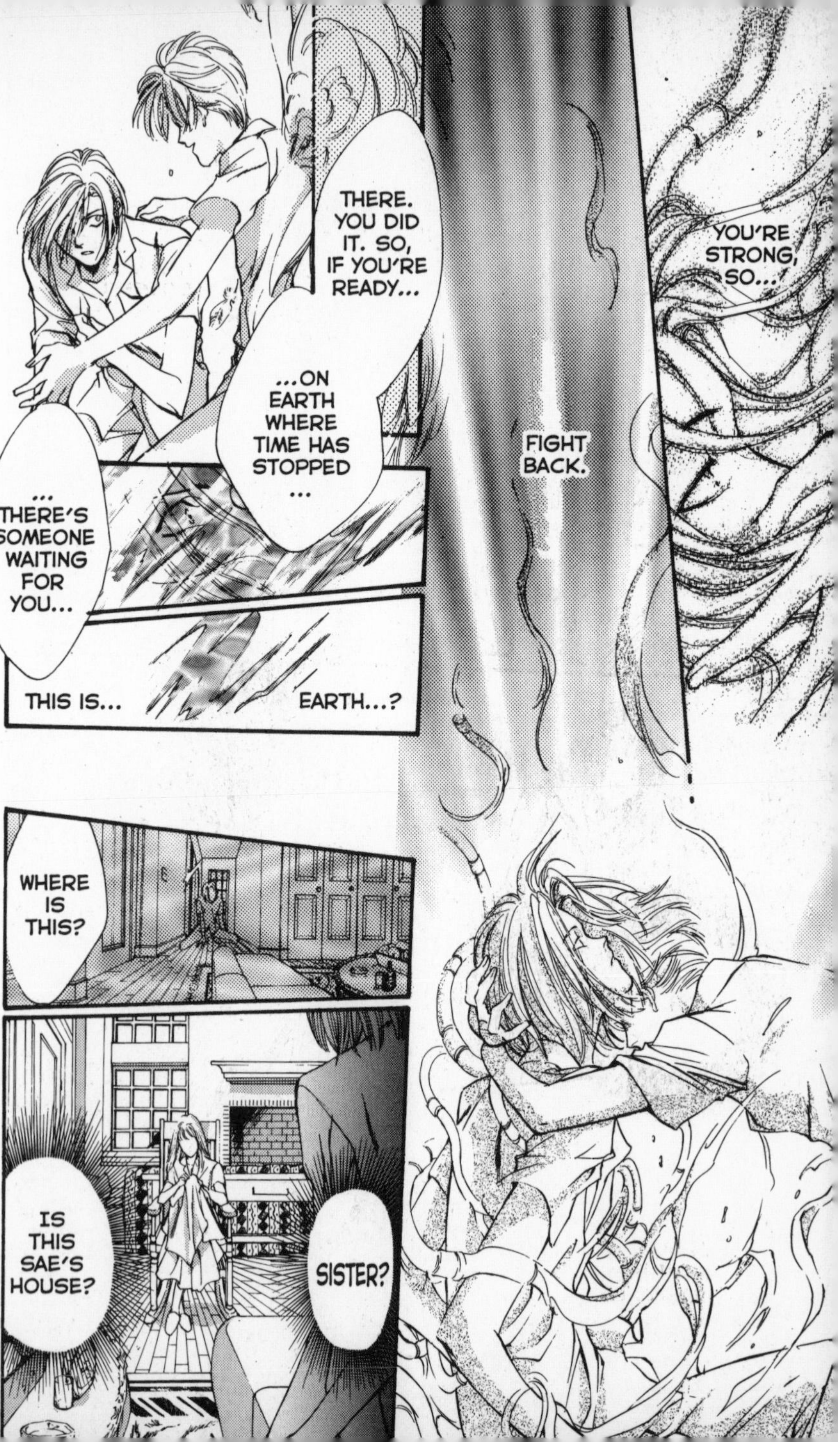

YOU'RE STRONG, SO...
FIGHT BACK.
THERE. YOU DID IT. SO, IF YOU'RE READY...
...ON EARTH WHERE TIME HAS STOPPED...
...THERE'S SOMEONE WAITING FOR YOU...
THIS IS...
EARTH...?
WHERE IS THIS?
IS THIS SAE'S HOUSE?
SISTER?

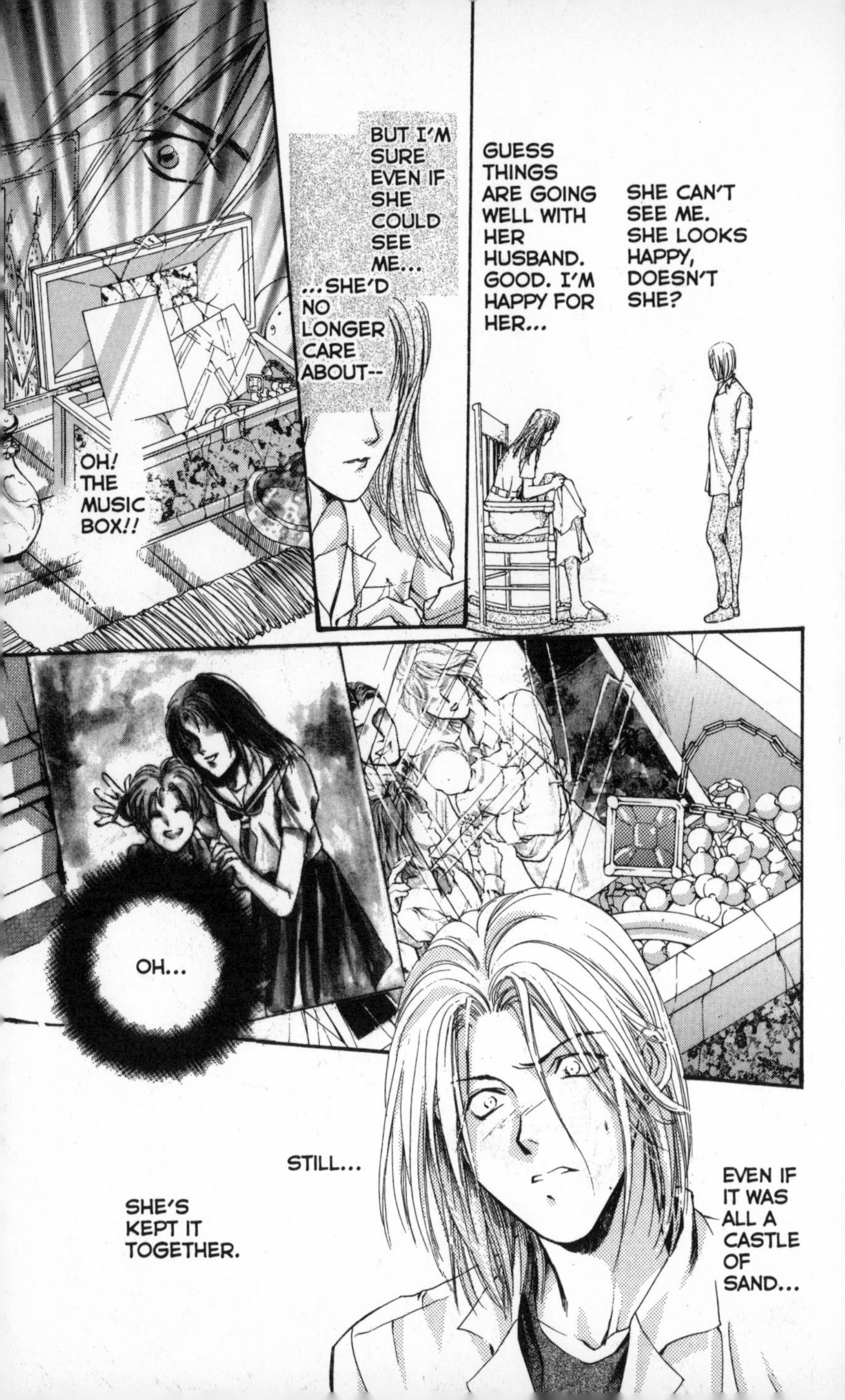
SHE CAN'T SEE ME. SHE LOOKS HAPPY, DOESN'T SHE?
GUESS THINGS ARE GOING WELL WITH HER HUSBAND. GOOD. I'M HAPPY FOR HER...
BUT I'M SURE EVEN IF SHE COULD SEE ME...
...SHE'D NO LONGER CARE ABOUT--
OH! THE MUSIC BOX!!
EVEN IF IT WAS ALL A CASTLE OF SAND...
STILL...
SHE'S KEPT IT TOGETHER.
OH...

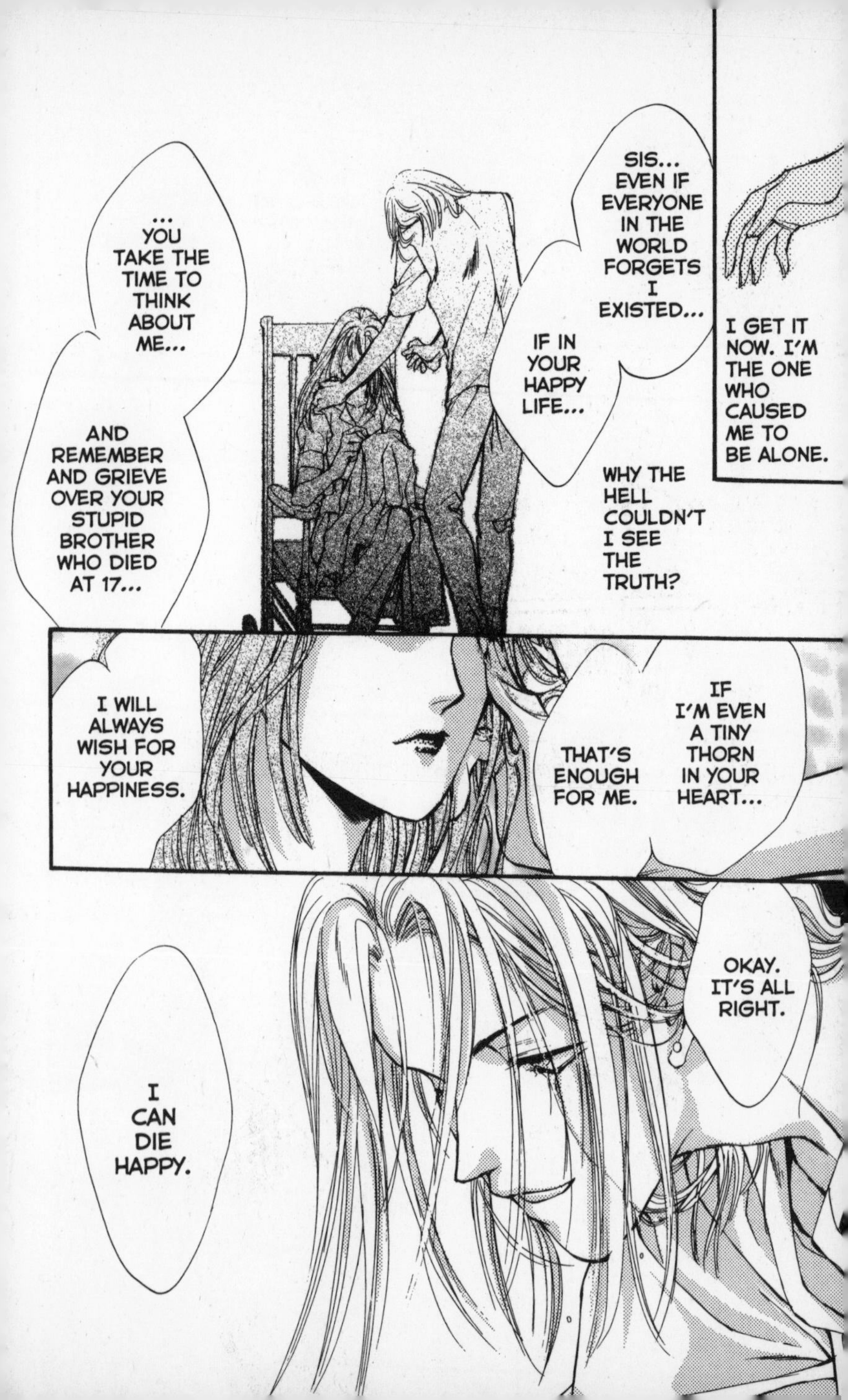
I GET IT NOW. I'M THE ONE WHO CAUSED ME TO BE ALONE.
WHY THE HELL COULDN'T I SEE THE TRUTH?
SIS... EVEN IF EVERYONE IN THE WORLD FORGETS I EXISTED...
IF IN YOUR HAPPY LIFE...
...YOU TAKE THE TIME TO THINK ABOUT ME...
AND REMEMBER AND GRIEVE OVER YOUR STUPID BROTHER WHO DIED AT 17...
IF I'M EVEN A TINY THORN IN YOUR HEART...
THAT'S ENOUGH FOR ME.
I WILL ALWAYS WISH FOR YOUR HAPPINESS.
OKAY. IT'S ALL RIGHT.
I CAN DIE HAPPY.

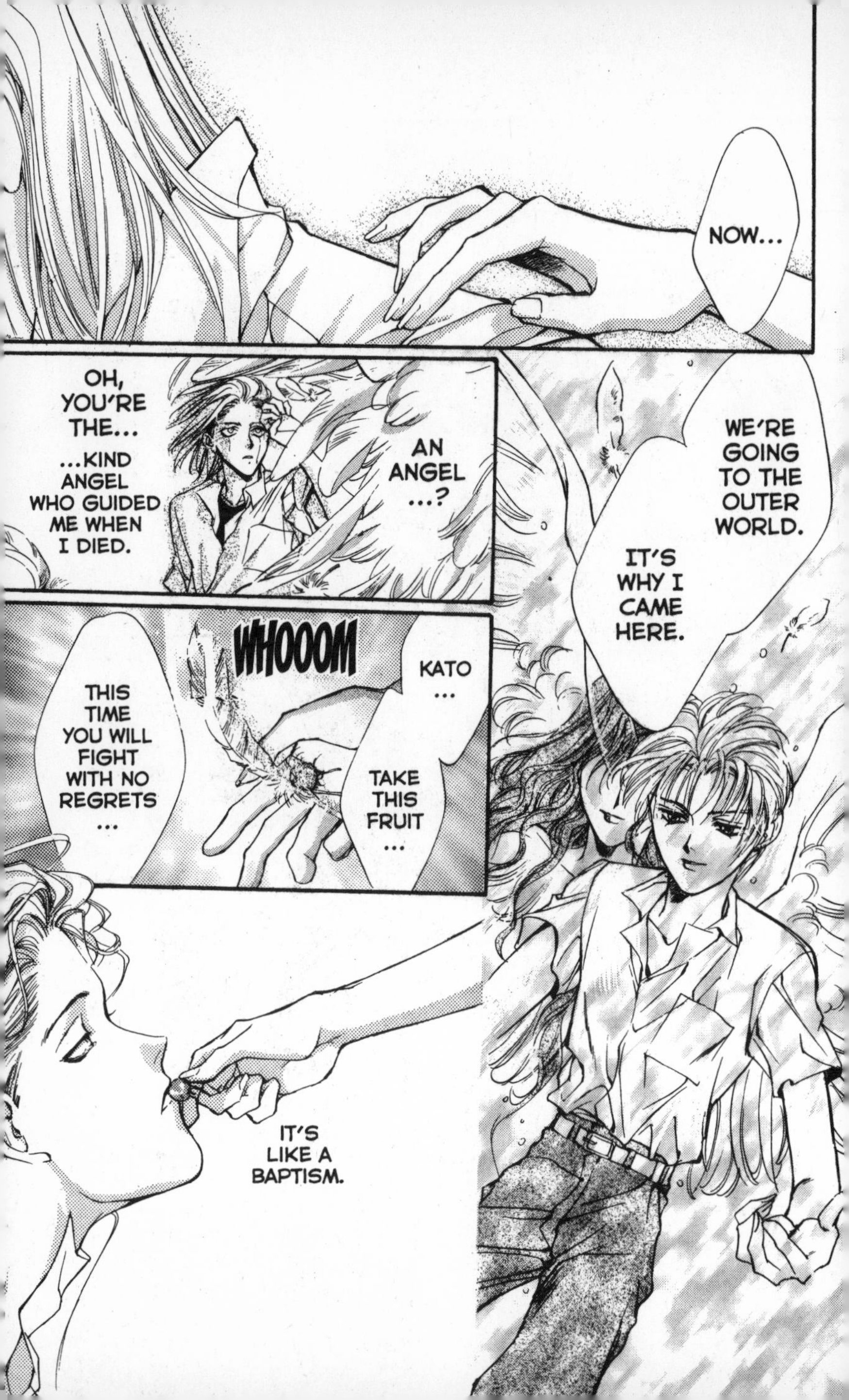
NOW...
WE'RE GOING TO THE OUTER WORLD.
IT'S WHY I CAME HERE.
AN ANGEL ...?
OH, YOU'RE THE...
...KIND ANGEL WHO GUIDED ME WHEN I DIED.
KATO ...
WHOOOM
TAKE THIS FRUIT ...
THIS TIME YOU WILL FIGHT WITH NO REGRETS ...
IT'S LIKE A BAPTISM.

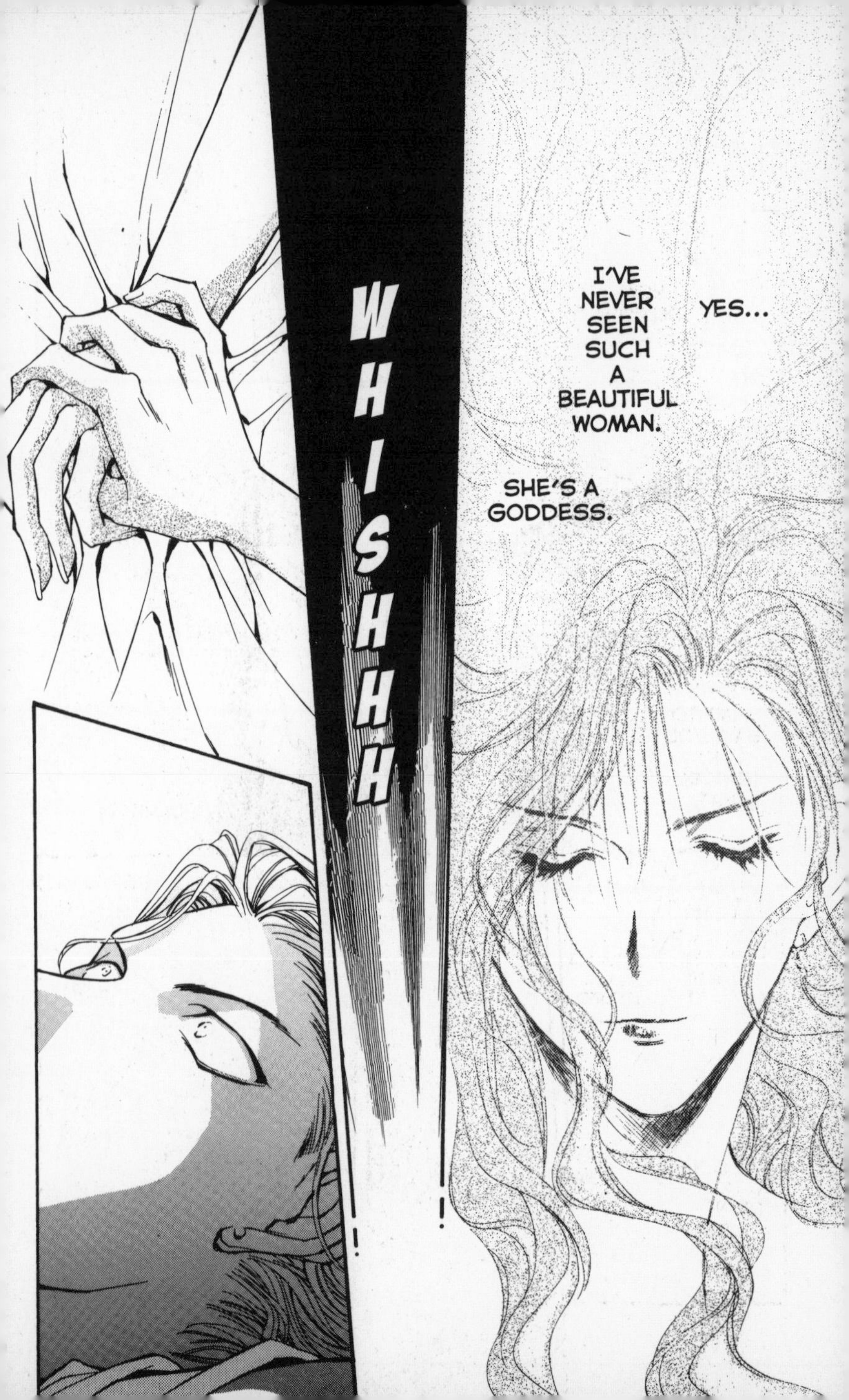
YES...
I'VE NEVER SEEN SUCH A BEAUTIFUL WOMAN.
SHE'S A GODDESS.
WHISHHH

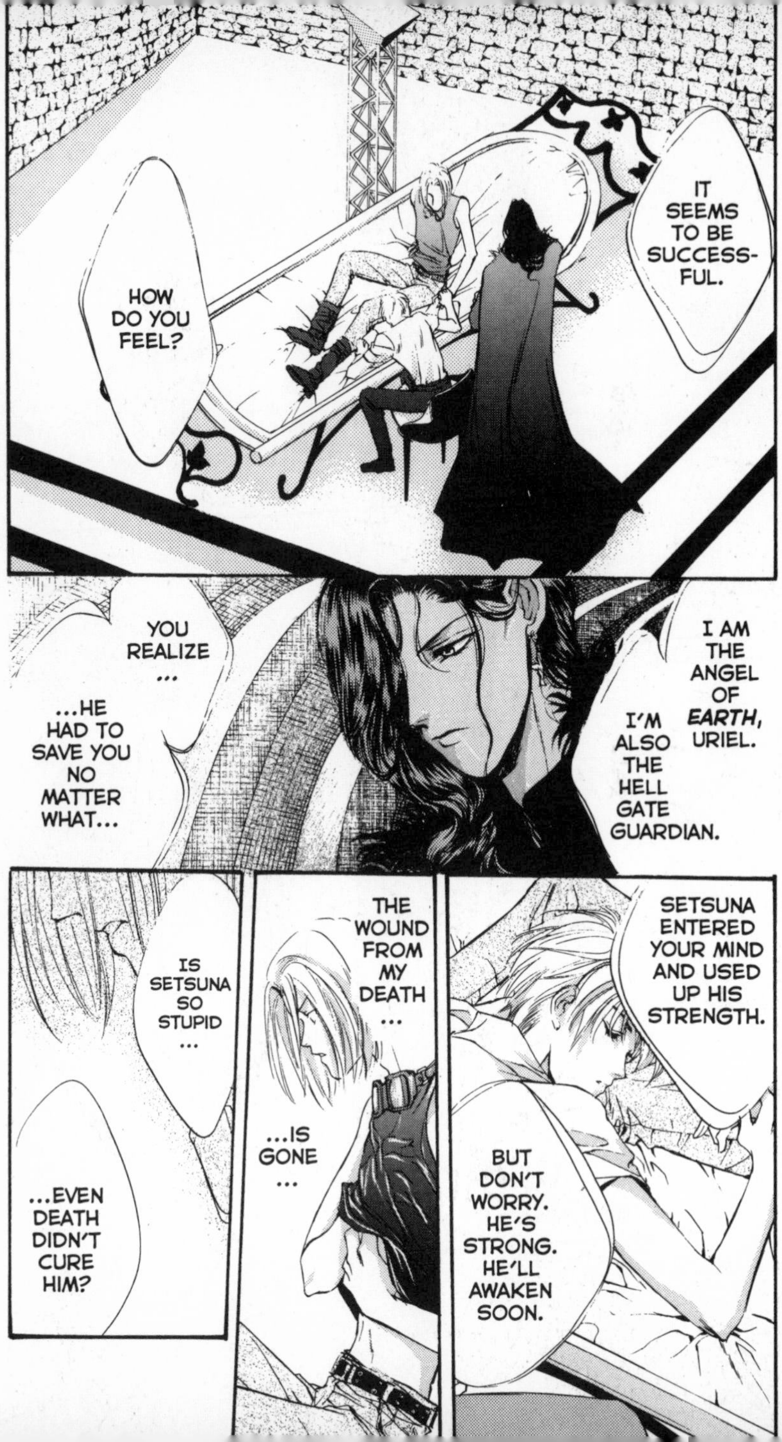
IT SEEMS TO BE SUCCESSFUL.
HOW DO YOU FEEL?
I AM THE ANGEL OF *EARTH*, URIEL.
I'M ALSO THE HELL GATE GUARDIAN.
YOU REALIZE ...
...HE HAD TO SAVE YOU NO MATTER WHAT...
SETSUNA ENTERED YOUR MIND AND USED UP HIS STRENGTH.
BUT DON'T WORRY. HE'S STRONG. HE'LL AWAKEN SOON.
THE WOUND FROM MY DEATH ...
...IS GONE ...
IS SETSUNA SO STUPID ...
...EVEN DEATH DIDN'T CURE HIM?

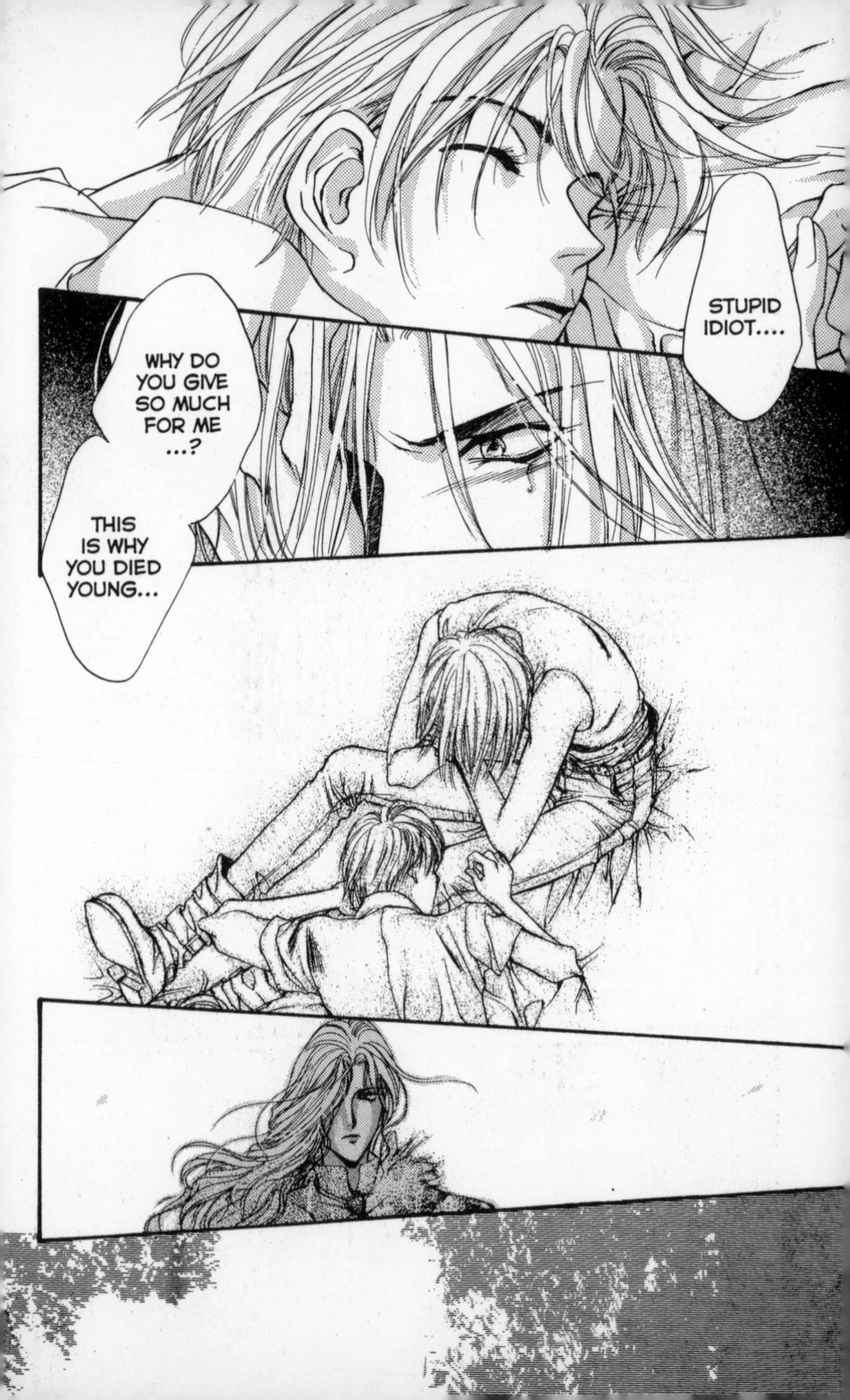
STUPID IDIOT....
WHY DO YOU GIVE SO MUCH FOR ME ...?
THIS IS WHY YOU DIED YOUNG...

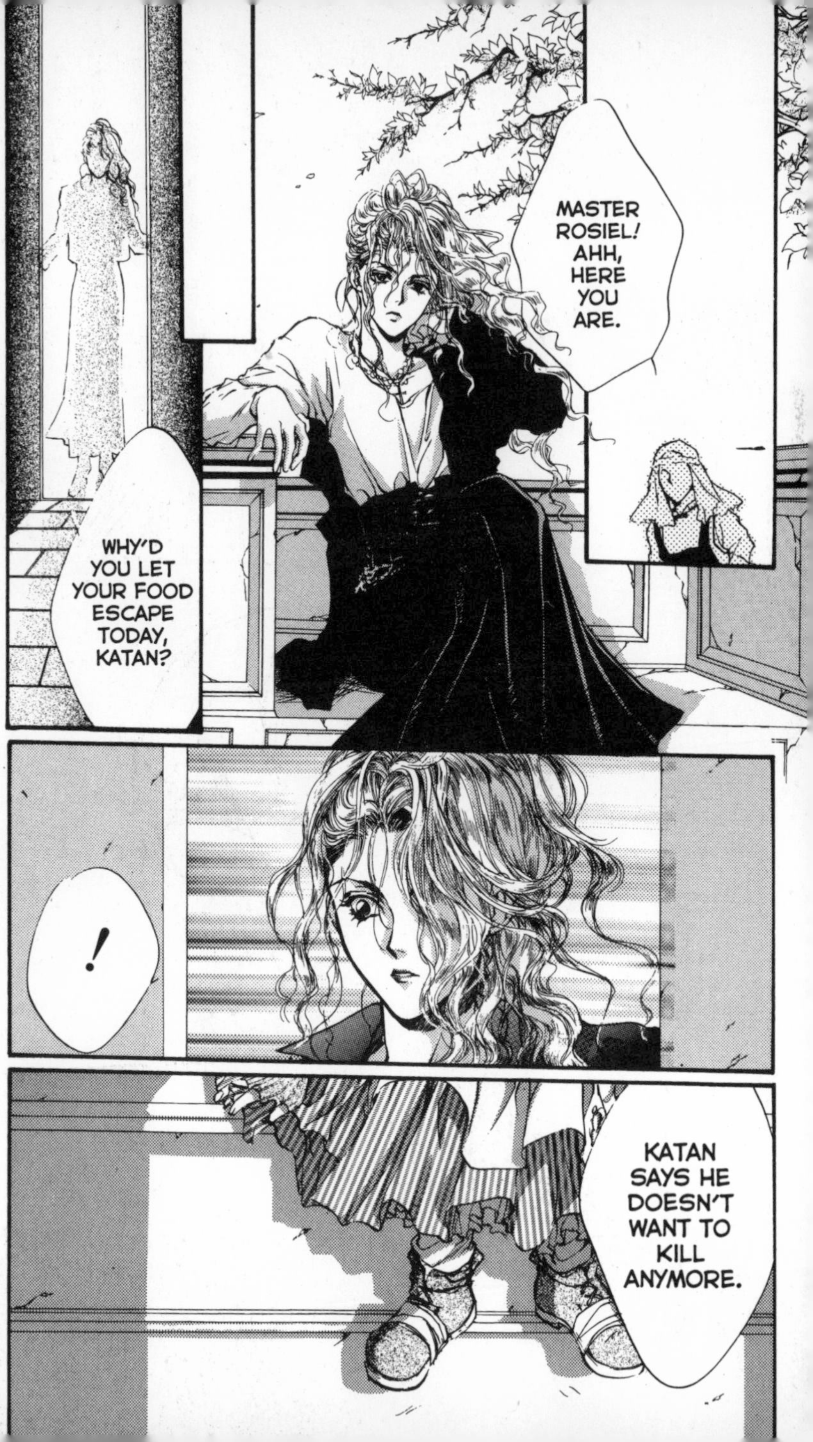
MASTER ROSIEL! AHH, HERE YOU ARE.
WHY'D YOU LET YOUR FOOD ESCAPE TODAY, KATAN?
!
KATAN SAYS HE DOESN'T WANT TO KILL ANYMORE.

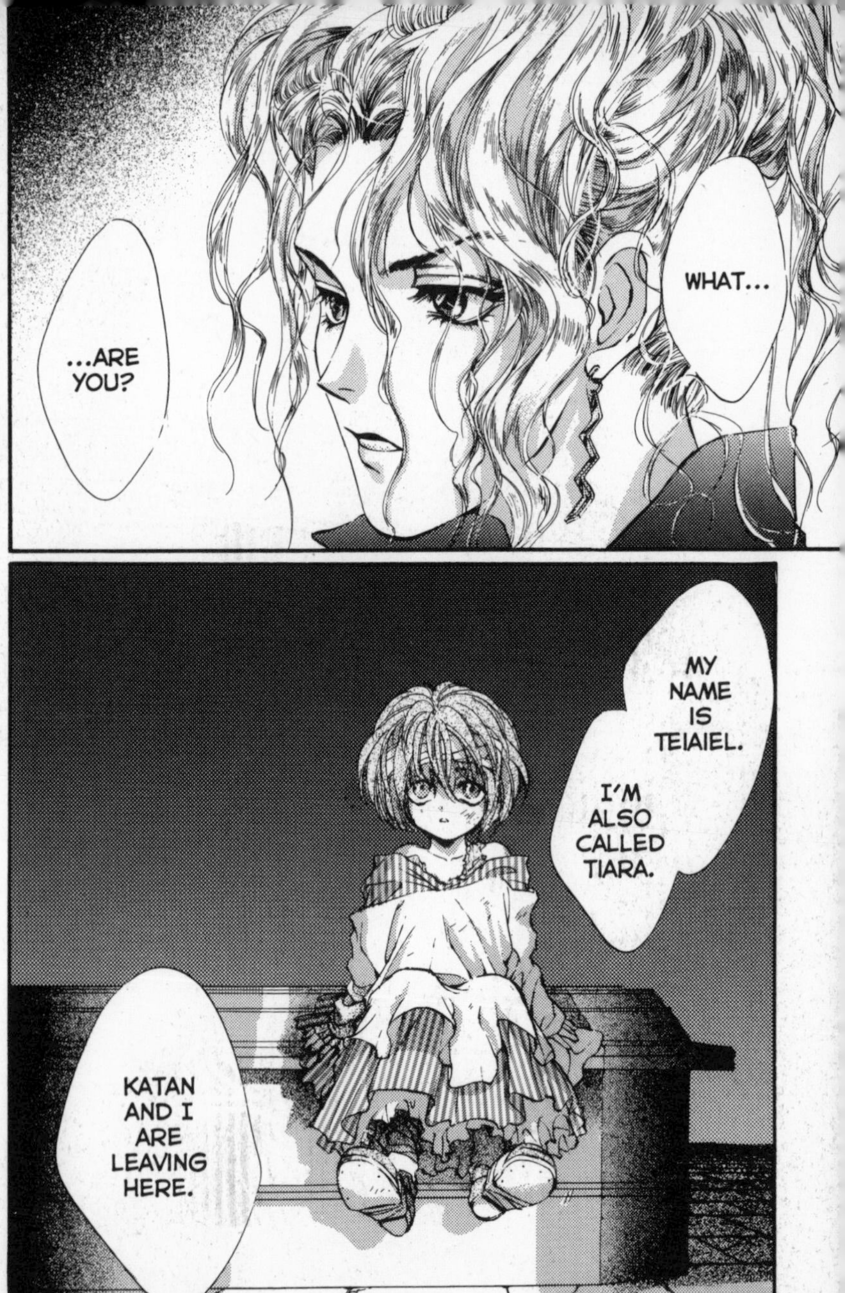
WHAT...
...ARE YOU?
MY NAME IS TEIAIEL.
I'M ALSO CALLED TIARA.
KATAN AND I ARE LEAVING HERE.

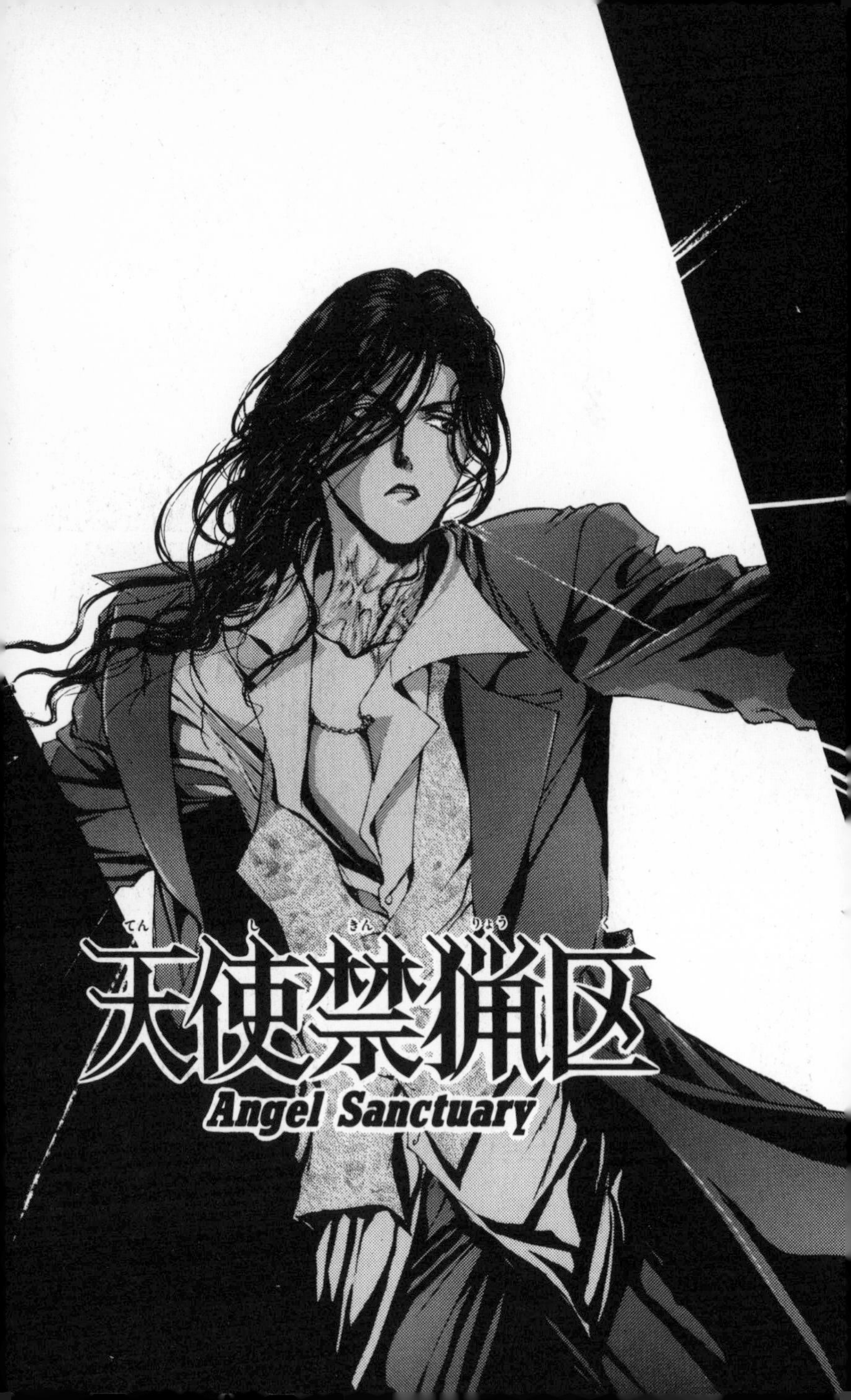
天使禁猟区
Angel Sanctuary

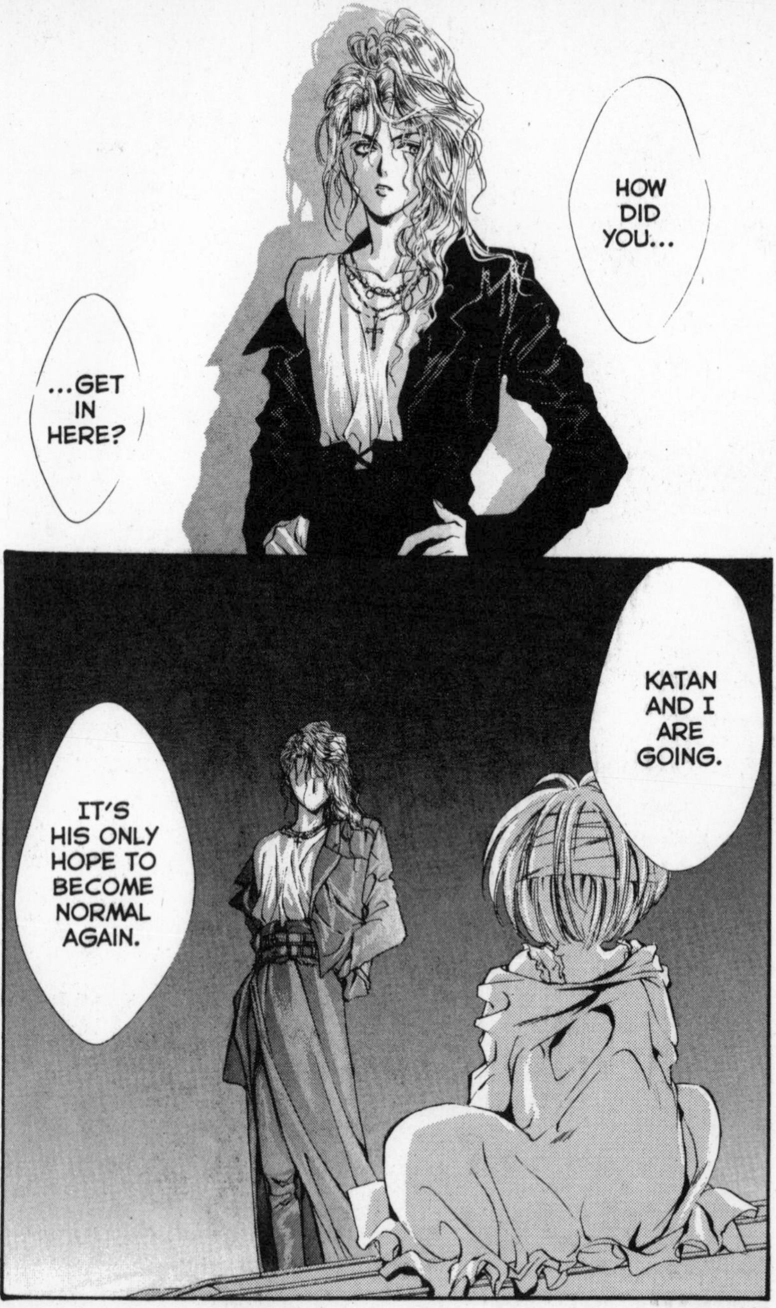
HOW DID YOU...
...GET IN HERE?
KATAN AND I ARE GOING.
IT'S HIS ONLY HOPE TO BECOME NORMAL AGAIN.

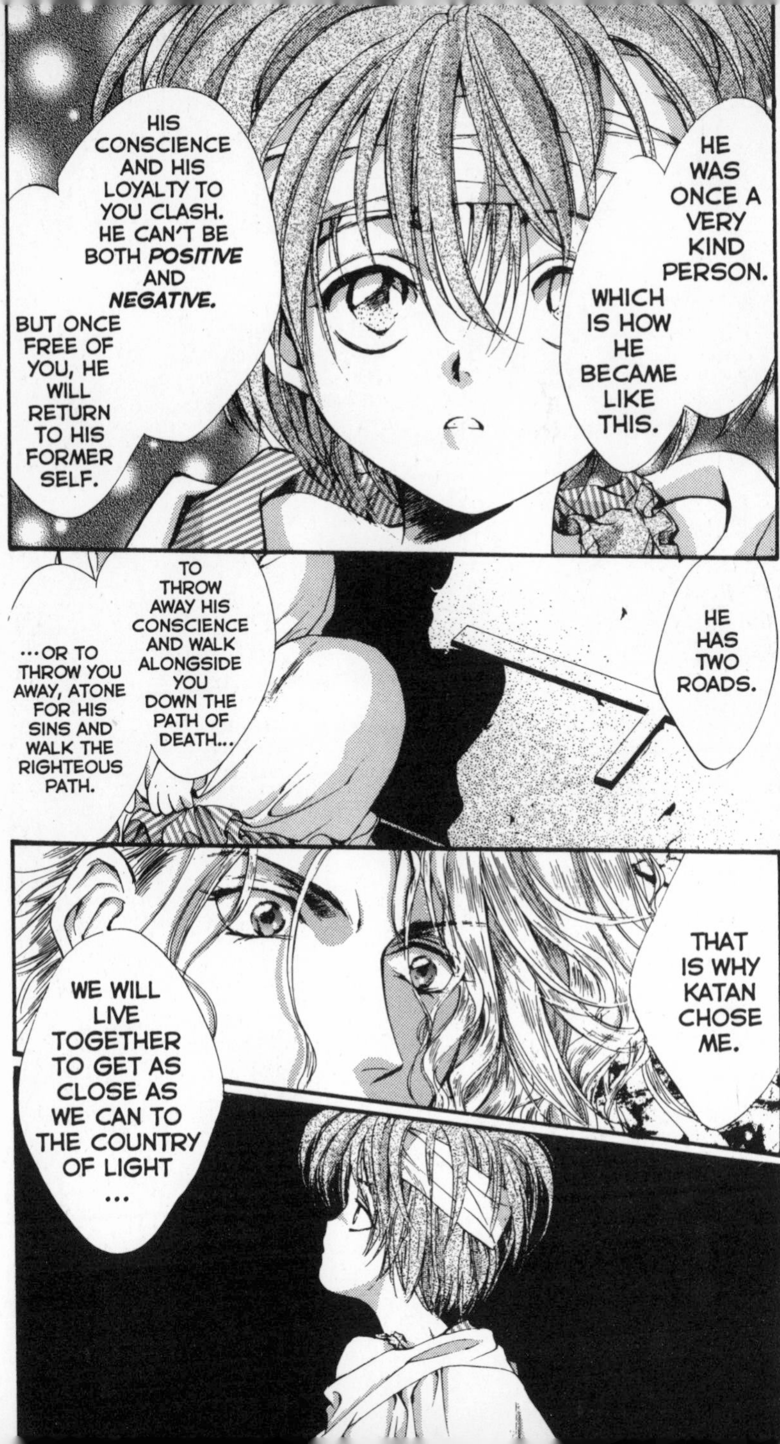
HE WAS ONCE A VERY KIND PERSON.
WHICH IS HOW HE BECAME LIKE THIS.
HIS CONSCIENCE AND HIS LOYALTY TO YOU CLASH. HE CAN'T BE BOTH *POSITIVE* AND *NEGATIVE.*
BUT ONCE FREE OF YOU, HE WILL RETURN TO HIS FORMER SELF.
HE HAS TWO ROADS.
TO THROW AWAY HIS CONSCIENCE AND WALK ALONGSIDE YOU DOWN THE PATH OF DEATH...
...OR TO THROW YOU AWAY, ATONE FOR HIS SINS AND WALK THE RIGHTEOUS PATH.
THAT IS WHY KATAN CHOSE ME.
WE WILL LIVE TOGETHER TO GET AS CLOSE AS WE CAN TO THE COUNTRY OF LIGHT ...

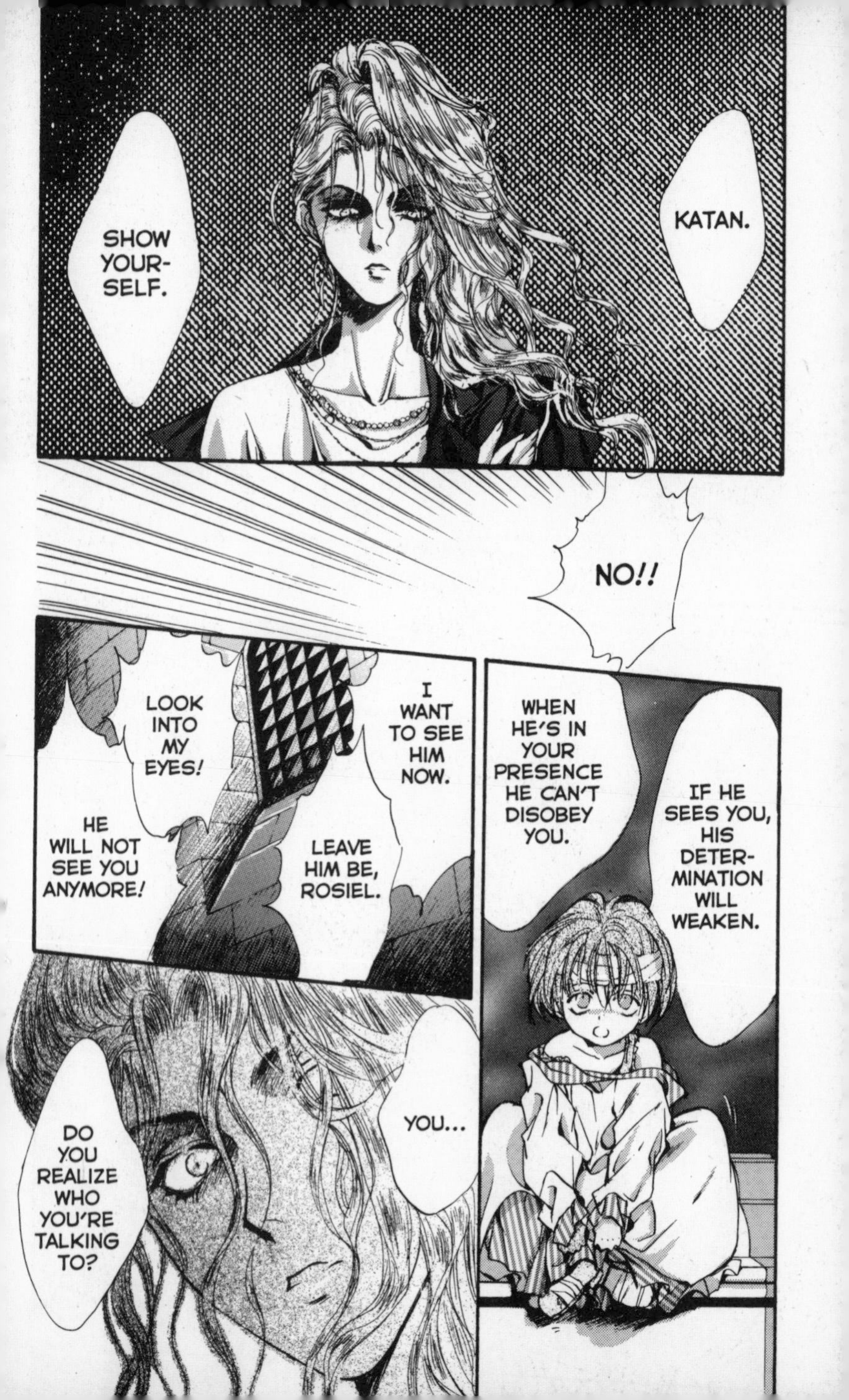
KATAN.
SHOW YOURSELF.
NO!!
IF HE SEES YOU, HIS DETERMINATION WILL WEAKEN.
WHEN HE'S IN YOUR PRESENCE HE CAN'T DISOBEY YOU.
I WANT TO SEE HIM NOW.
LOOK INTO MY EYES!
LEAVE HIM BE, ROSIEL.
HE WILL NOT SEE YOU ANYMORE!
YOU...
DO YOU REALIZE WHO YOU'RE TALKING TO?

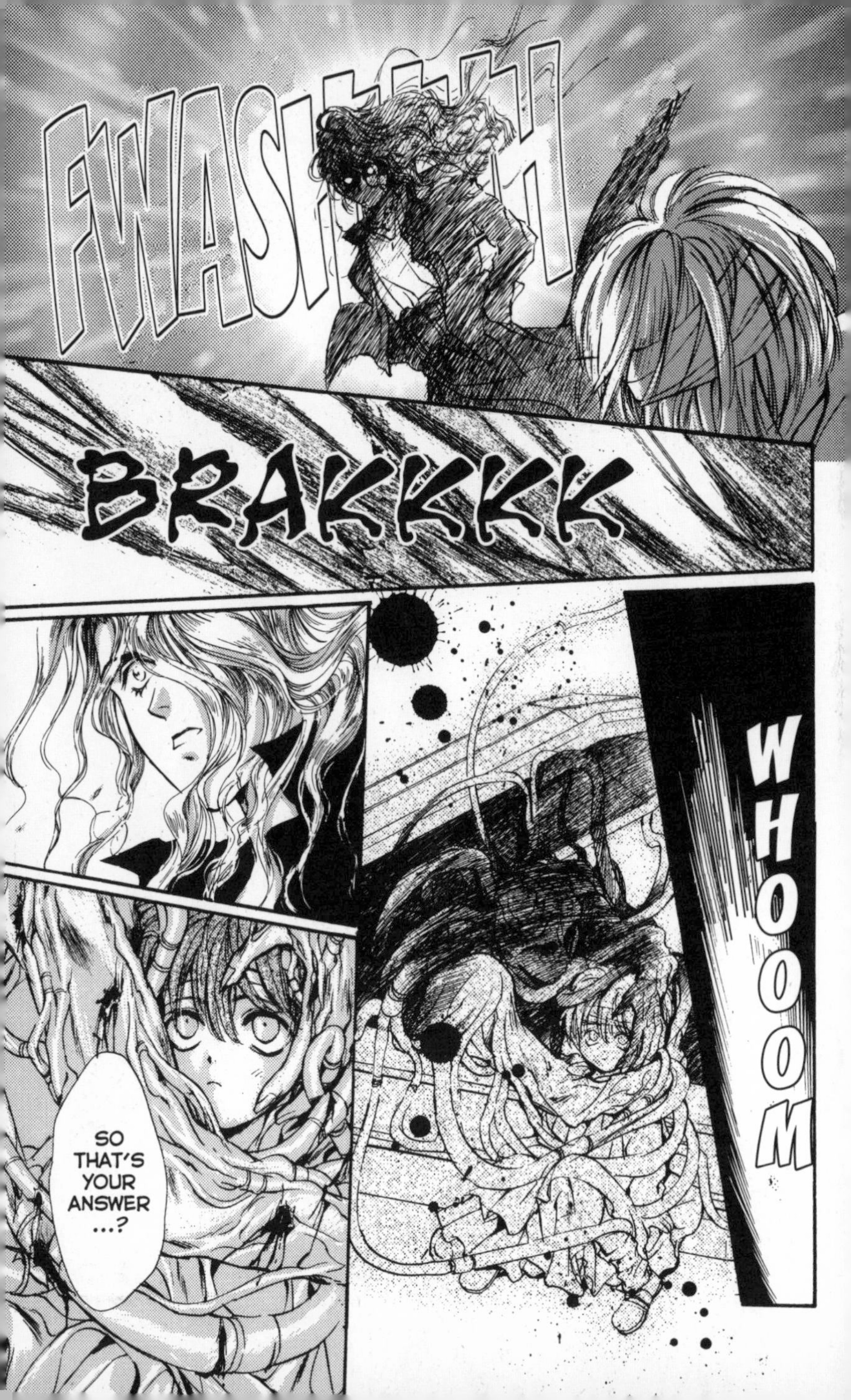
FWASH
BRAKKKK
WHOOOOM
SO THAT'S YOUR ANSWER ...?

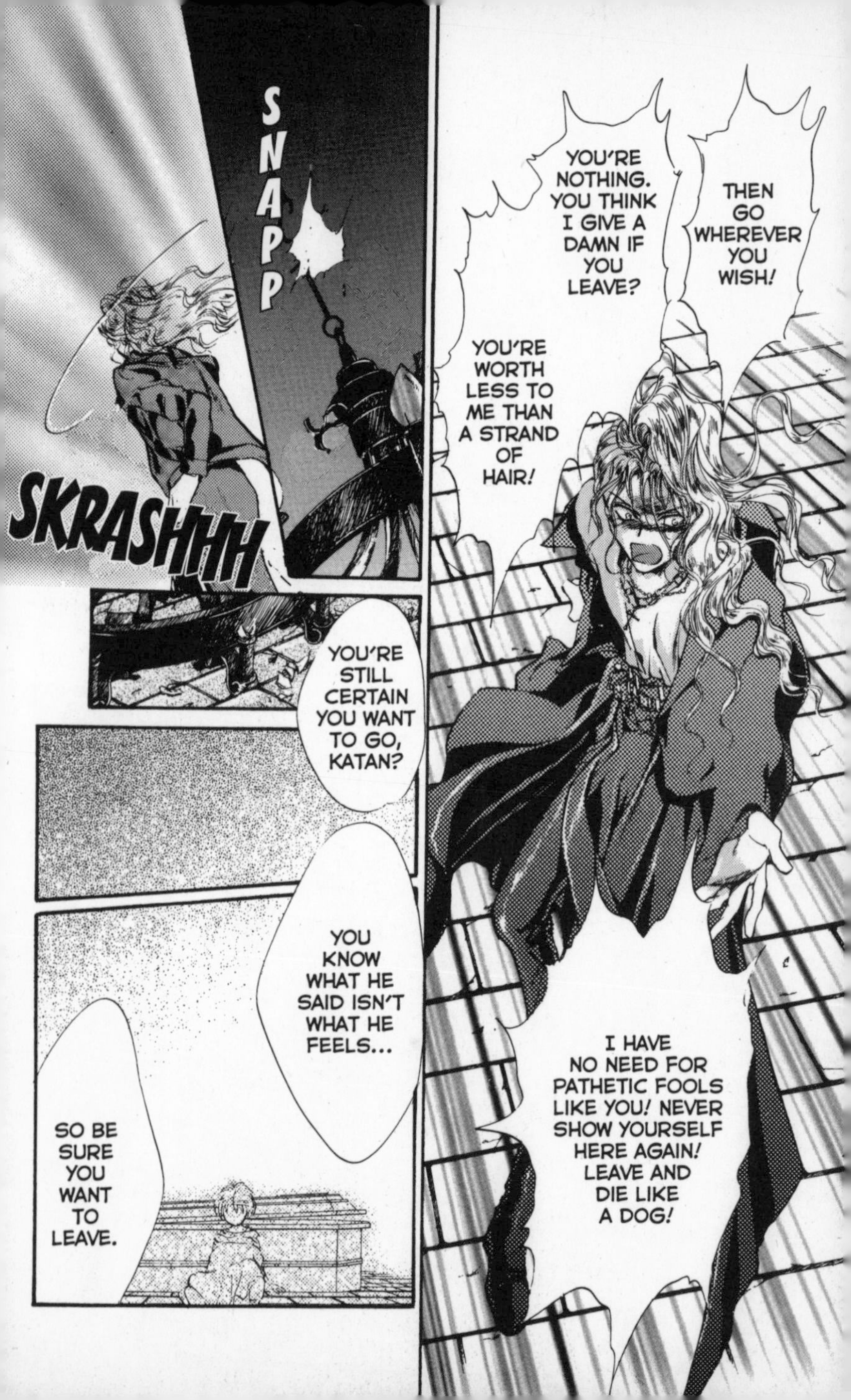
THEN GO WHEREVER YOU WISH!
YOU'RE NOTHING. YOU THINK I GIVE A DAMN IF YOU LEAVE?
YOU'RE WORTH LESS TO ME THAN A STRAND OF HAIR!
I HAVE NO NEED FOR PATHETIC FOOLS LIKE YOU! NEVER SHOW YOURSELF HERE AGAIN! LEAVE AND DIE LIKE A DOG!
SNAPP
SKRASHHH
YOU'RE STILL CERTAIN YOU WANT TO GO, KATAN?
YOU KNOW WHAT HE SAID ISN'T WHAT HE FEELS...
SO BE SURE YOU WANT TO LEAVE.

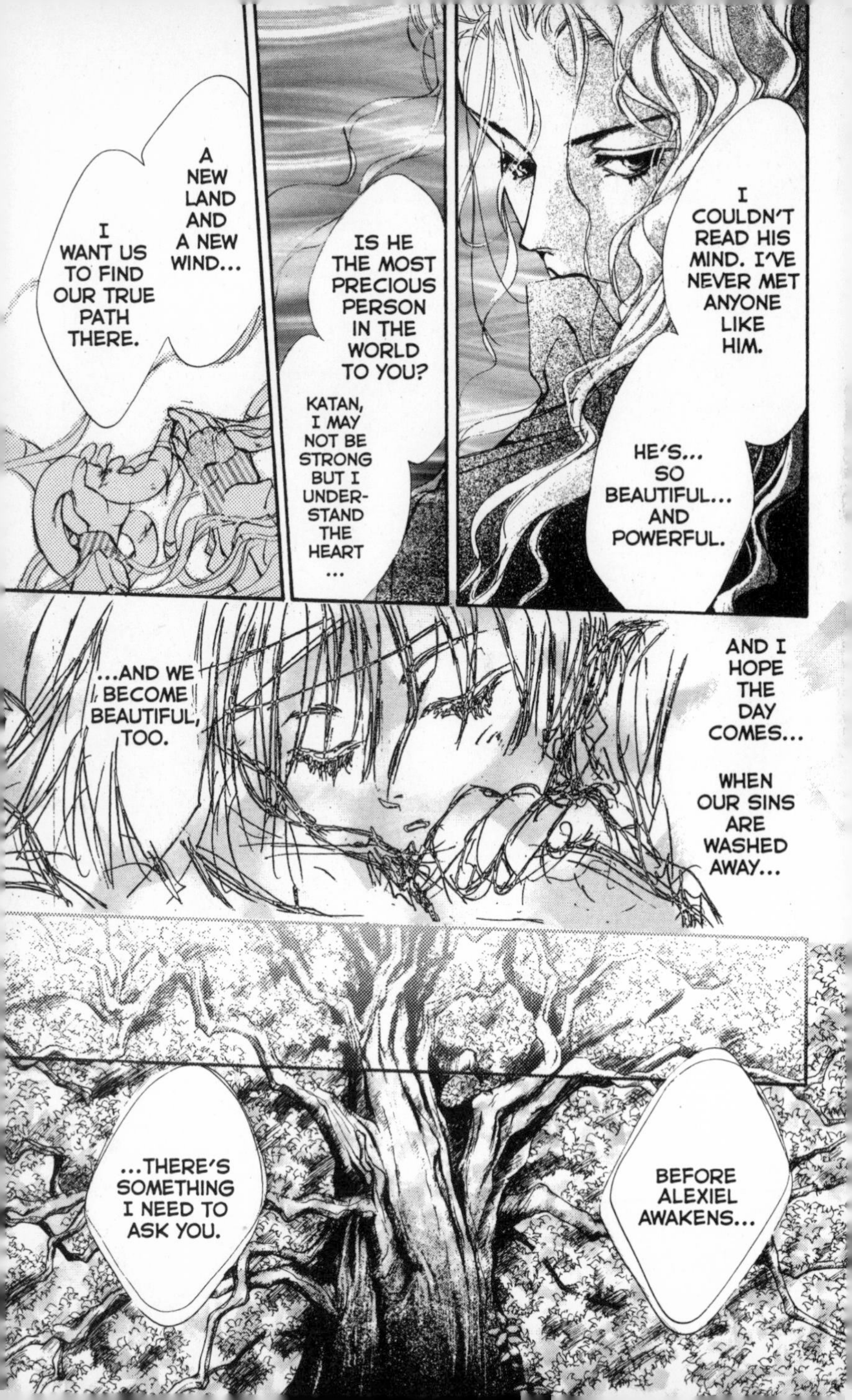

I COULDN'T READ HIS MIND. I'VE NEVER MET ANYONE LIKE HIM.
HE'S... SO BEAUTIFUL... AND POWERFUL.
IS HE THE MOST PRECIOUS PERSON IN THE WORLD TO YOU?
KATAN, I MAY NOT BE STRONG BUT I UNDER-STAND THE HEART ...
A NEW LAND AND A NEW WIND...
I WANT US TO FIND OUR TRUE PATH THERE.
AND I HOPE THE DAY COMES...
WHEN OUR SINS ARE WASHED AWAY...
...AND WE BECOME BEAUTIFUL, TOO.
BEFORE ALEXIEL AWAKENS...
...THERE'S SOMETHING I NEED TO ASK YOU.

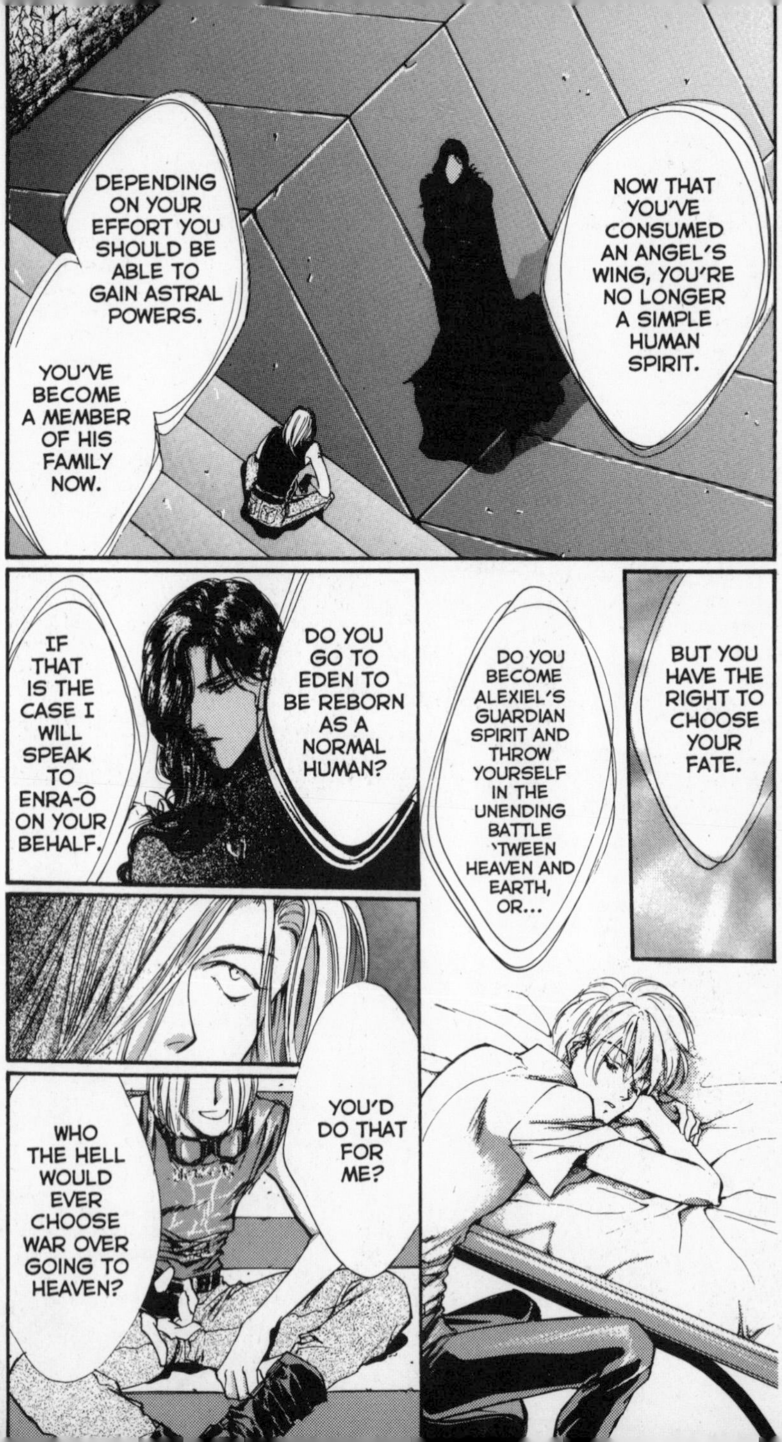
NOW THAT YOU'VE CONSUMED AN ANGEL'S WING, YOU'RE NO LONGER A SIMPLE HUMAN SPIRIT.
DEPENDING ON YOUR EFFORT YOU SHOULD BE ABLE TO GAIN ASTRAL POWERS.
YOU'VE BECOME A MEMBER OF HIS FAMILY NOW.
BUT YOU HAVE THE RIGHT TO CHOOSE YOUR FATE.
DO YOU BECOME ALEXIEL'S GUARDIAN SPIRIT AND THROW YOURSELF IN THE UNENDING BATTLE 'TWEEN HEAVEN AND EARTH, OR...
DO YOU GO TO EDEN TO BE REBORN AS A NORMAL HUMAN?
IF THAT IS THE CASE I WILL SPEAK TO ENRA-Ô ON YOUR BEHALF.
YOU'D DO THAT FOR ME?
WHO THE HELL WOULD EVER CHOOSE WAR OVER GOING TO HEAVEN?

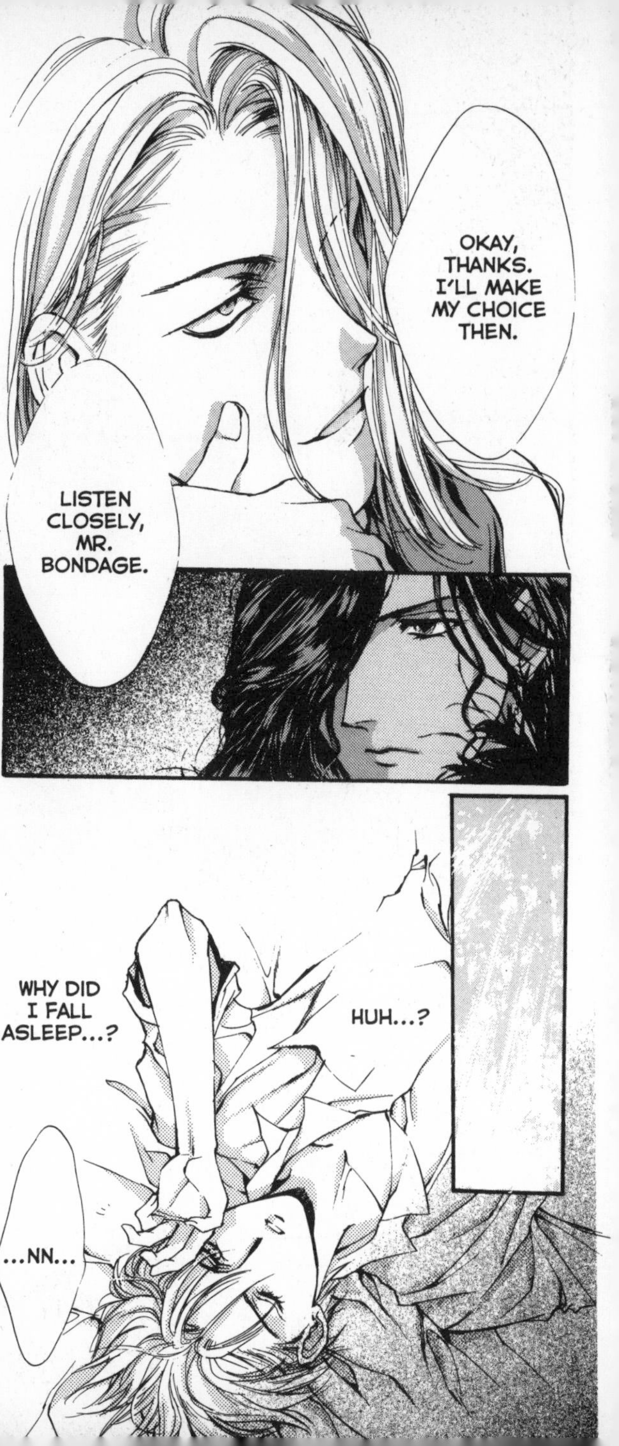
OKAY, THANKS. I'LL MAKE MY CHOICE THEN.
LISTEN CLOSELY, MR. BONDAGE.
HUH...?
WHY DID I FALL ASLEEP...?
...NN...

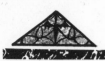

Tiara was actually really popular. I didn't draw her that cute but... Misfortune seems to suit her. You can see it in her eyes. Her clothes are all ripped...

Well, I liked that about her...

I also got a good laugh out of how a number of people, as if planned, suddenly started calling Uriel 'Uri-Uri.' Uriel is suppose to represent a giant tree so I made him as tall as a volleyball player. And as many have realized, Doll is the soul of Kirie. She's once again serving a strange master but this one must be better than Rosiel. Well, either way she's always in the company of good looking guys, isn't she?!

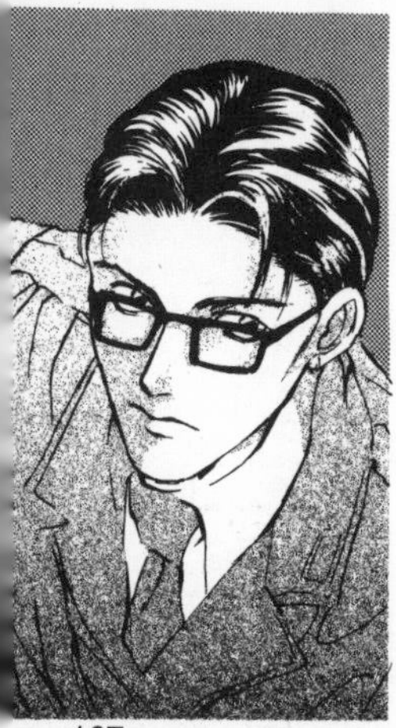

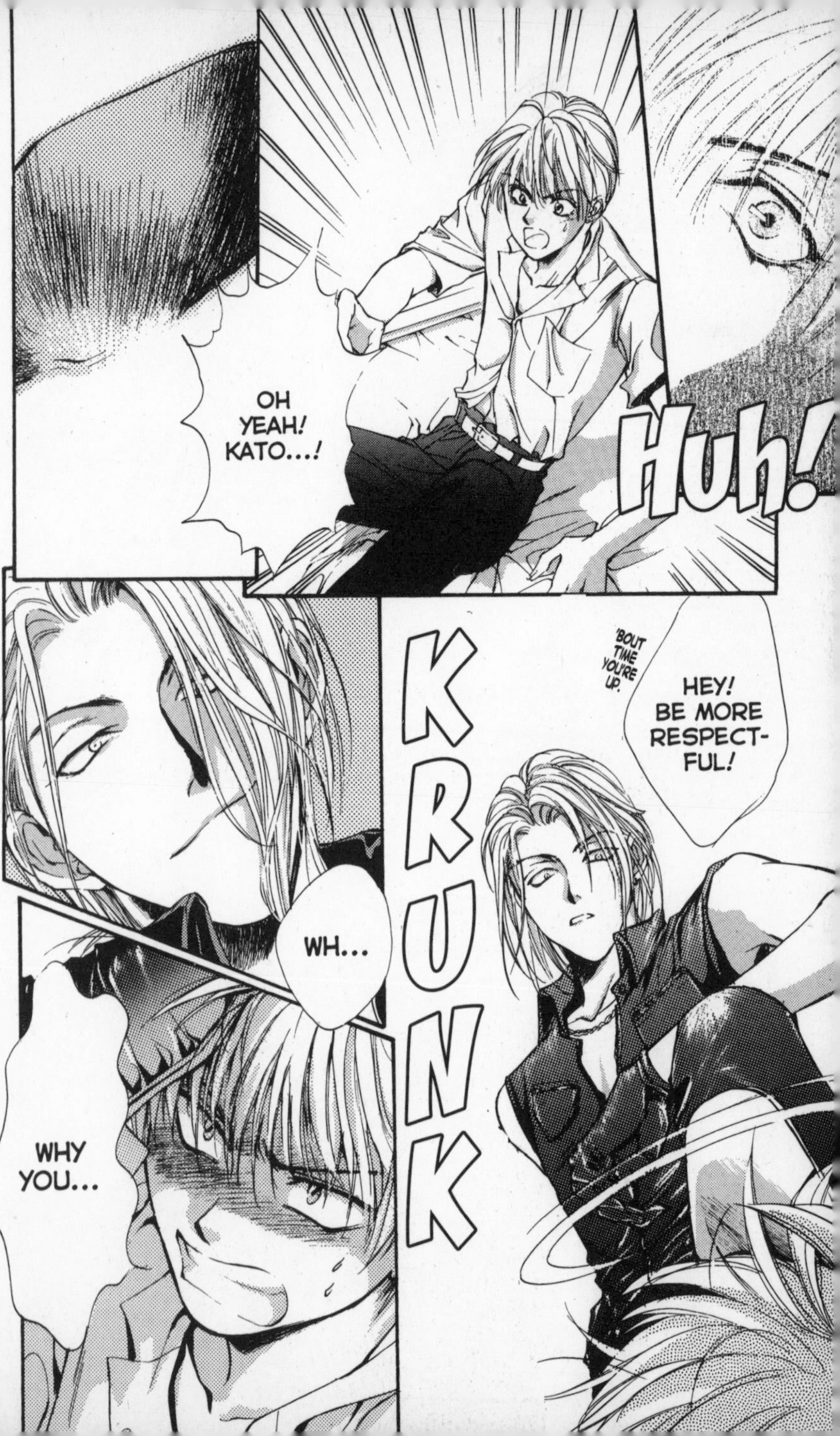
Huh!
OH YEAH! KATO...!
HEY! BE MORE RESPECT-FUL!
'BOUT TIME YOU'RE UP.
KRUNK
WH...
WHY YOU...

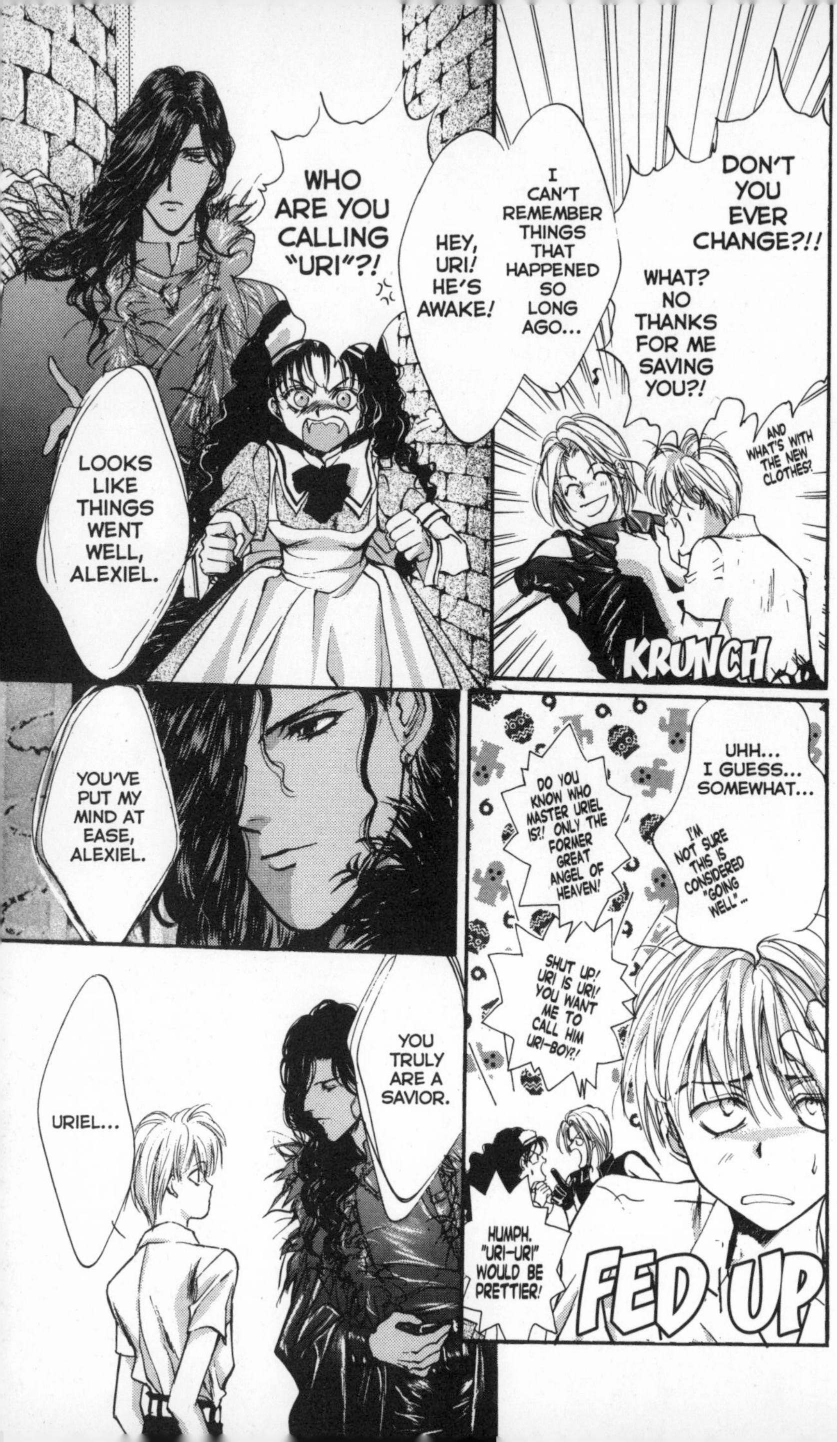
DON'T YOU EVER CHANGE?!!
WHAT? NO THANKS FOR ME SAVING YOU?!
AND WHAT'S WITH THE NEW CLOTHES?
I CAN'T REMEMBER THINGS THAT HAPPENED SO LONG AGO...
KRUNCH
HEY, URI! HE'S AWAKE!
WHO ARE YOU CALLING "URI"?!
LOOKS LIKE THINGS WENT WELL, ALEXIEL.
UHH... I GUESS... SOMEWHAT...
I'M NOT SURE THIS IS CONSIDERED "GOING WELL"...
DO YOU KNOW WHO MASTER URIEL IS?! ONLY THE FORMER GREAT ANGEL OF HEAVEN!
SHUT UP! URI IS URI! YOU WANT ME TO CALL HIM URI-BOY?!
HUMPH. "URI-URI" WOULD BE PRETTIER!
FED UP
YOU'VE PUT MY MIND AT EASE, ALEXIEL.
YOU TRULY ARE A SAVIOR.
URIEL...

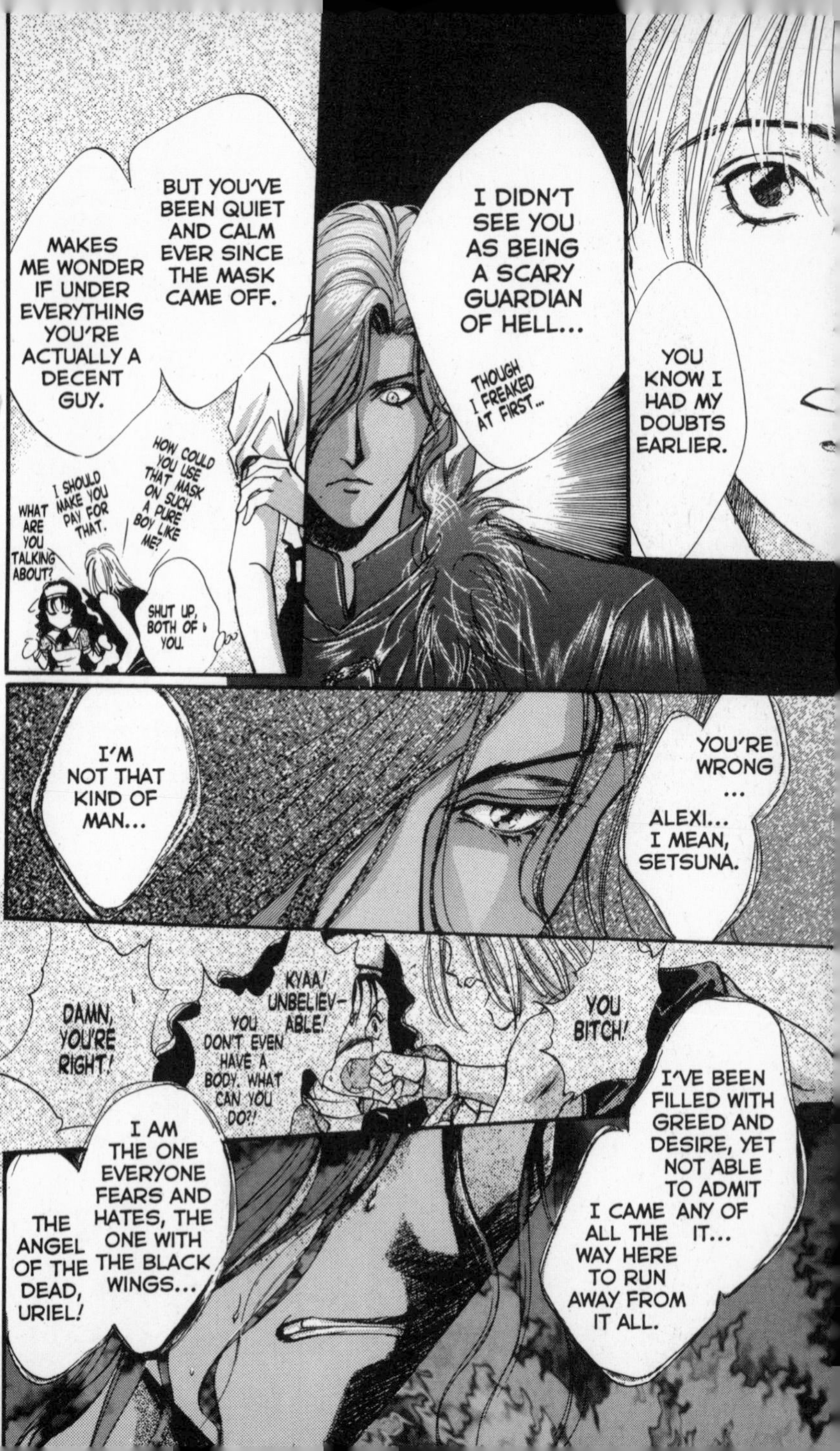
YOU KNOW I HAD MY DOUBTS EARLIER.
I DIDN'T SEE YOU AS BEING A SCARY GUARDIAN OF HELL...
THOUGH I FREAKED AT FIRST...
BUT YOU'VE BEEN QUIET AND CALM EVER SINCE THE MASK CAME OFF.
MAKES ME WONDER IF UNDER EVERYTHING YOU'RE ACTUALLY A DECENT GUY.
HOW COULD YOU USE THAT MASK ON SUCH A PURE BOY LIKE ME?
I SHOULD MAKE YOU PAY FOR THAT.
WHAT ARE YOU TALKING ABOUT?
SHUT UP, BOTH OF YOU.
YOU'RE WRONG ... ALEXI... I MEAN, SETSUNA.
I'M NOT THAT KIND OF MAN...
YOU BITCH!
KYAA! UNBELIEVABLE!
YOU DON'T EVEN HAVE A BODY. WHAT CAN YOU DO?!
DAMN, YOU'RE RIGHT!
I'VE BEEN FILLED WITH GREED AND DESIRE, YET NOT ABLE TO ADMIT ANY OF IT...
I CAME ALL THE WAY HERE TO RUN AWAY FROM IT ALL.
I AM THE ONE EVERYONE FEARS AND HATES, THE ONE WITH THE BLACK WINGS...
THE ANGEL OF THE DEAD, URIEL!

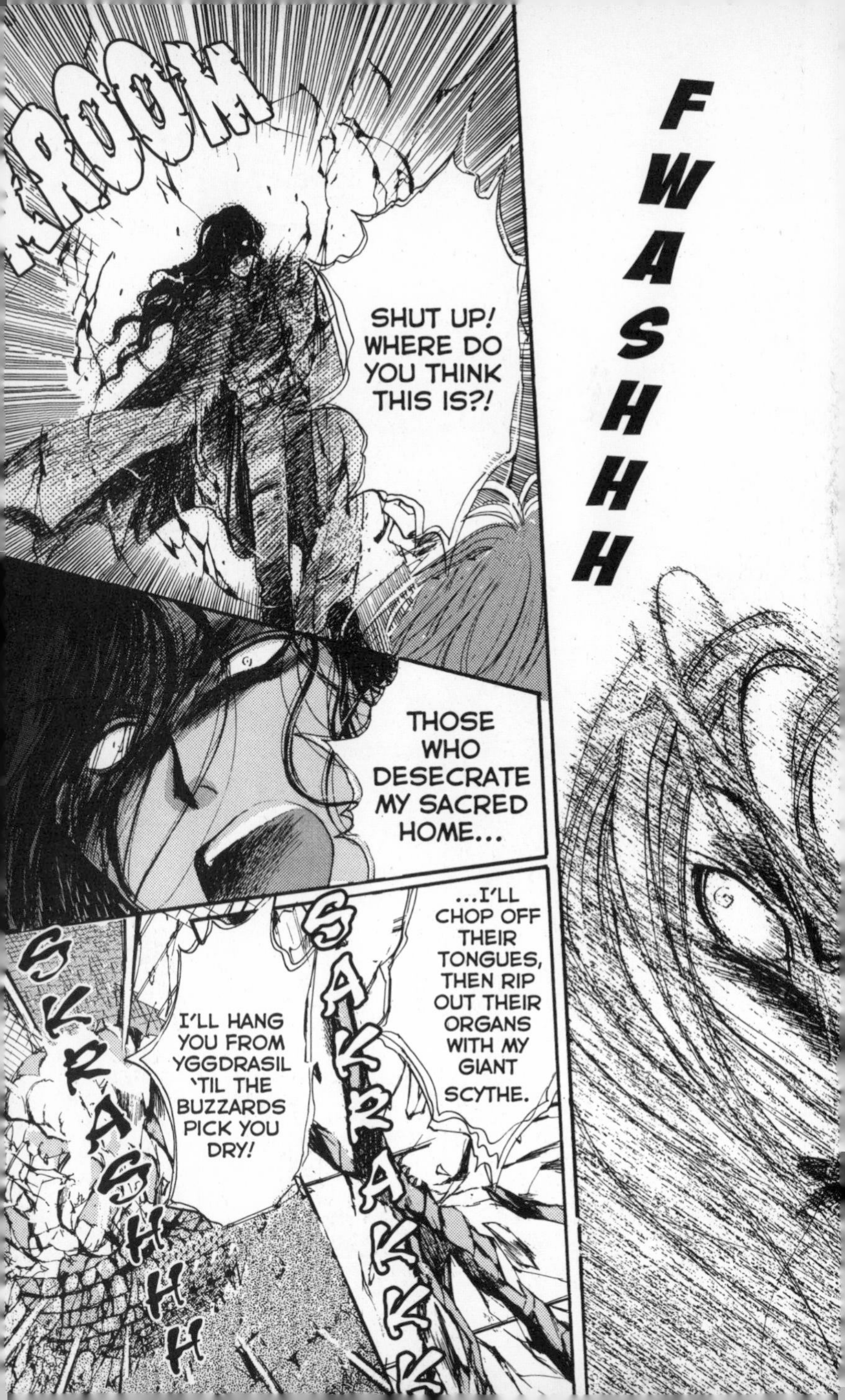
FWASHHH
KROOM
SHUT UP! WHERE DO YOU THINK THIS IS?!
THOSE WHO DESECRATE MY SACRED HOME...
...I'LL CHOP OFF THEIR TONGUES, THEN RIP OUT THEIR ORGANS WITH MY GIANT SCYTHE.
SAKRAKAKK
I'LL HANG YOU FROM YGGDRASIL 'TIL THE BUZZARDS PICK YOU DRY!
SKRASHHH

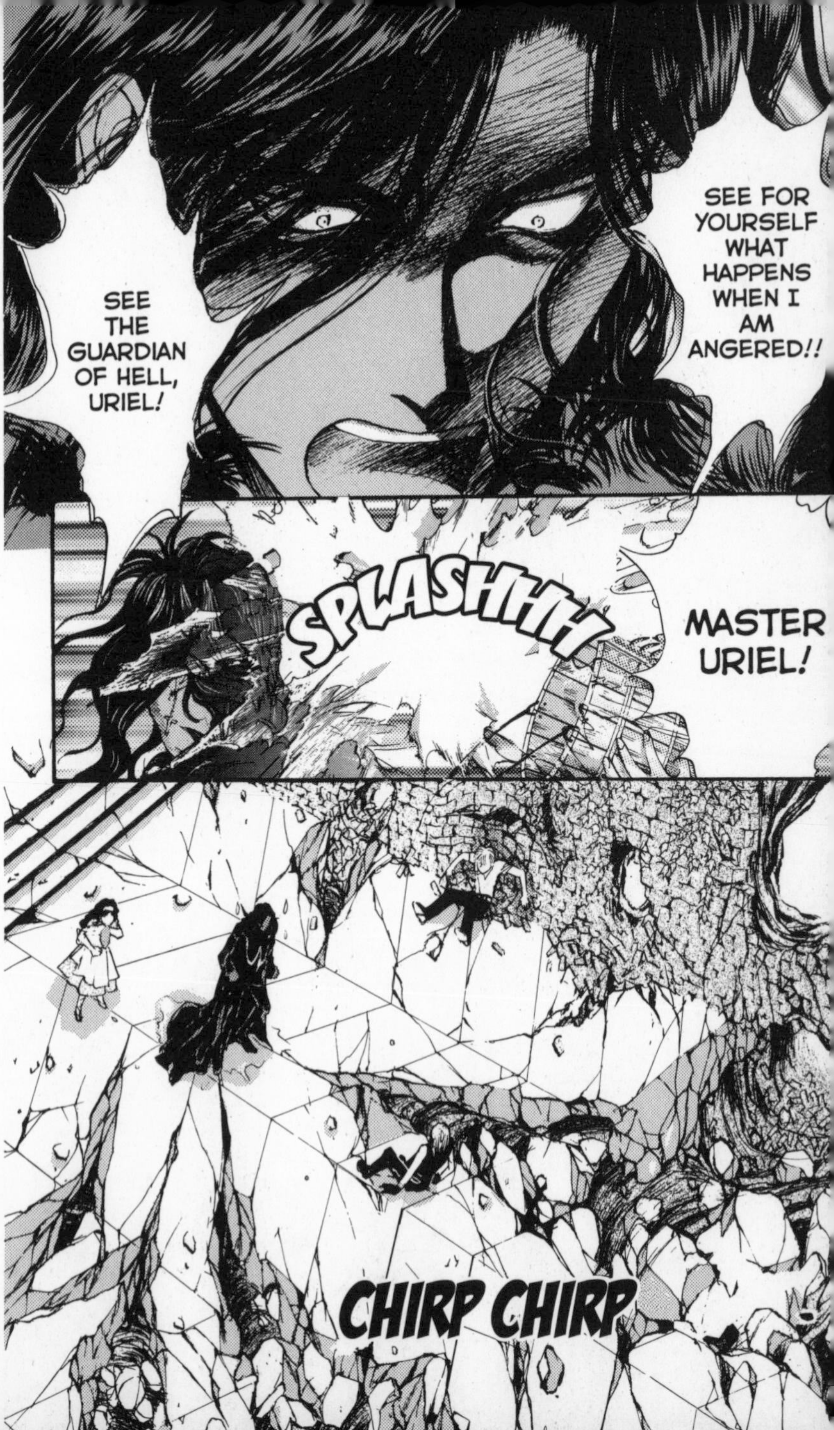
SEE FOR YOURSELF WHAT HAPPENS WHEN I AM ANGERED!!
SEE THE GUARDIAN OF HELL, URIEL!
MASTER URIEL!
SPLASHHH!
CHIRP CHIRP

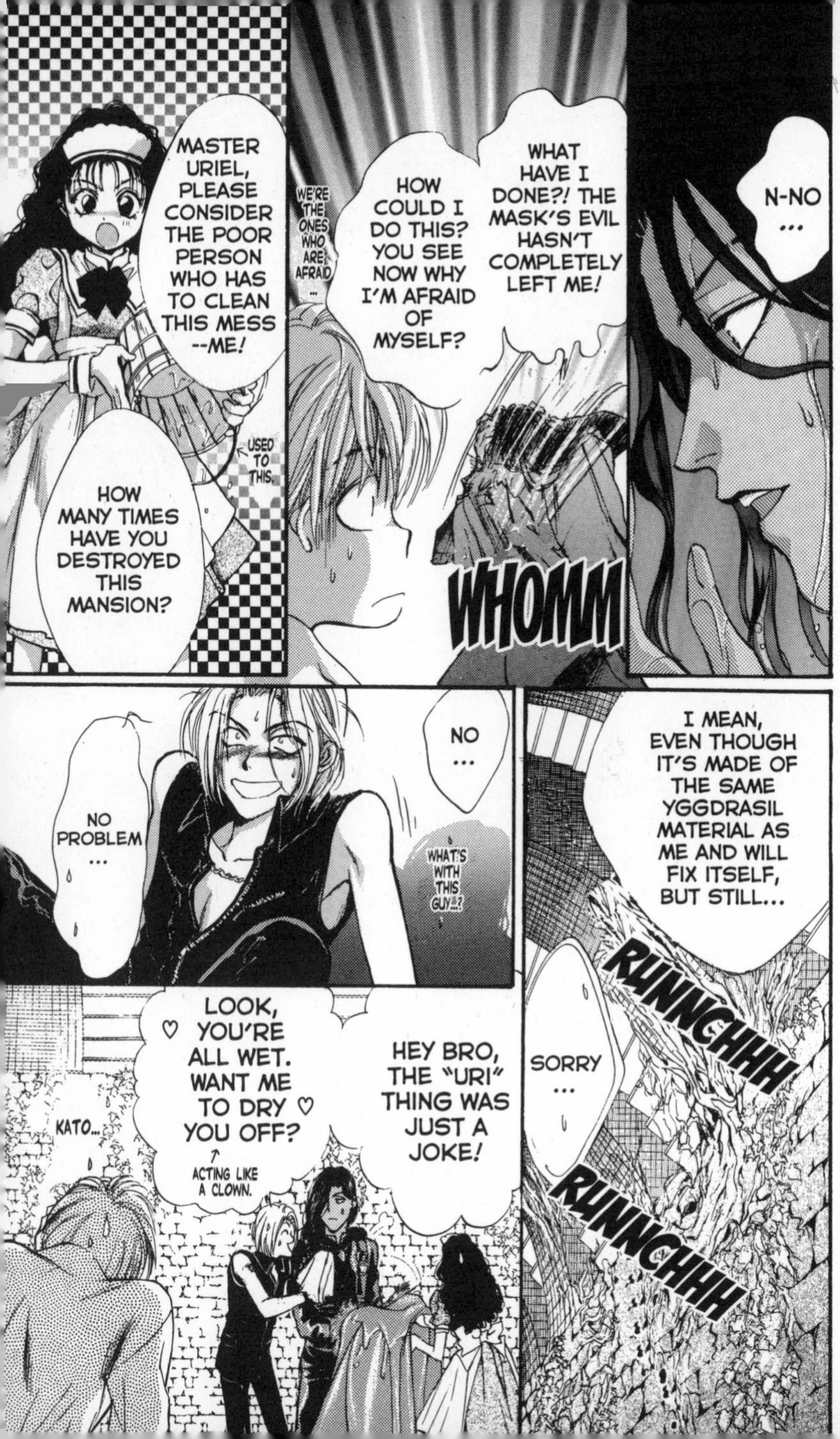
N-NO ...
WHAT HAVE I DONE?! THE MASK'S EVIL HASN'T COMPLETELY LEFT ME!
HOW COULD I DO THIS? YOU SEE NOW WHY I'M AFRAID OF MYSELF?
WE'RE THE ONES WHO ARE AFRAID ...
WHOMM
MASTER URIEL, PLEASE CONSIDER THE POOR PERSON WHO HAS TO CLEAN THIS MESS --ME!
USED TO THIS.
HOW MANY TIMES HAVE YOU DESTROYED THIS MANSION?
I MEAN, EVEN THOUGH IT'S MADE OF THE SAME YGGDRASIL MATERIAL AS ME AND WILL FIX ITSELF, BUT STILL...
RUNNCHHH
SORRY ...
RUNNCHHH
NO ...
WHAT'S WITH THIS GUY...?
NO PROBLEM ...
HEY BRO, THE "URI" THING WAS JUST A JOKE!
♡ LOOK, YOU'RE ALL WET. WANT ME TO DRY ♡ YOU OFF?
ACTING LIKE A CLOWN.
KATO...

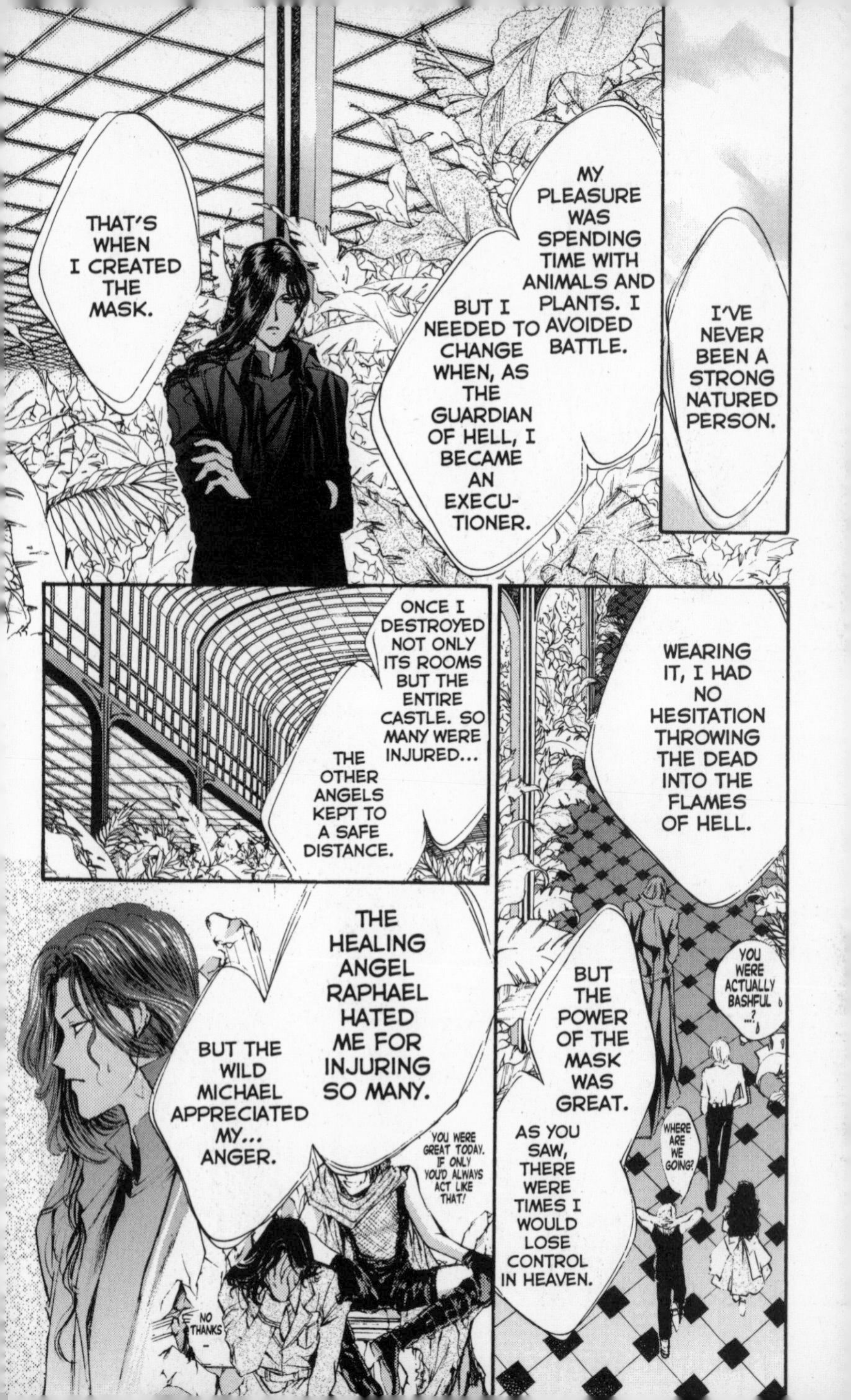
I'VE NEVER BEEN A STRONG NATURED PERSON.
MY PLEASURE WAS SPENDING TIME WITH ANIMALS AND PLANTS. I AVOIDED BATTLE.
BUT I NEEDED TO CHANGE WHEN, AS THE GUARDIAN OF HELL, I BECAME AN EXECUTIONER.
THAT'S WHEN I CREATED THE MASK.
WEARING IT, I HAD NO HESITATION THROWING THE DEAD INTO THE FLAMES OF HELL.
BUT THE POWER OF THE MASK WAS GREAT.
YOU WERE ACTUALLY BASHFUL ...?
WHERE ARE WE GOING?
AS YOU SAW, THERE WERE TIMES I WOULD LOSE CONTROL IN HEAVEN.
ONCE I DESTROYED NOT ONLY ITS ROOMS BUT THE ENTIRE CASTLE. SO MANY WERE INJURED...
THE OTHER ANGELS KEPT TO A SAFE DISTANCE.
THE HEALING ANGEL RAPHAEL HATED ME FOR INJURING SO MANY.
BUT THE WILD MICHAEL APPRECIATED MY... ANGER.
YOU WERE GREAT TODAY. IF ONLY YOU'D ALWAYS ACT LIKE THAT!
NO THANKS -

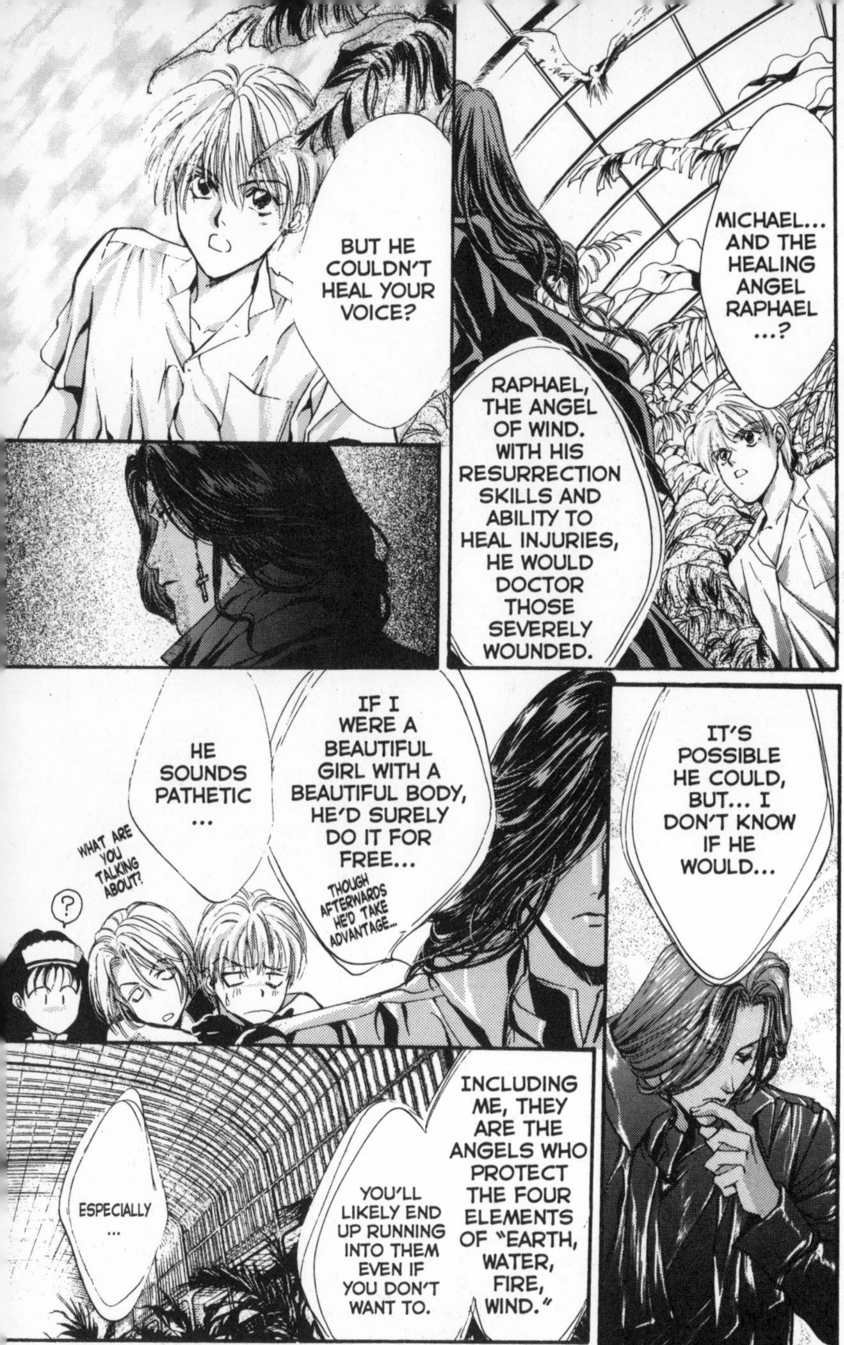
MICHAEL... AND THE HEALING ANGEL RAPHAEL ...?
RAPHAEL, THE ANGEL OF WIND. WITH HIS RESURRECTION SKILLS AND ABILITY TO HEAL INJURIES, HE WOULD DOCTOR THOSE SEVERELY WOUNDED.
BUT HE COULDN'T HEAL YOUR VOICE?
IT'S POSSIBLE HE COULD, BUT... I DON'T KNOW IF HE WOULD...
IF I WERE A BEAUTIFUL GIRL WITH A BEAUTIFUL BODY, HE'D SURELY DO IT FOR FREE...
THOUGH AFTERWARDS HE'D TAKE ADVANTAGE...
HE SOUNDS PATHETIC ...
WHAT ARE YOU TALKING ABOUT?
?
INCLUDING ME, THEY ARE THE ANGELS WHO PROTECT THE FOUR ELEMENTS OF "EARTH, WATER, FIRE, WIND."
YOU'LL LIKELY END UP RUNNING INTO THEM EVEN IF YOU DON'T WANT TO.
ESPECIALLY ...

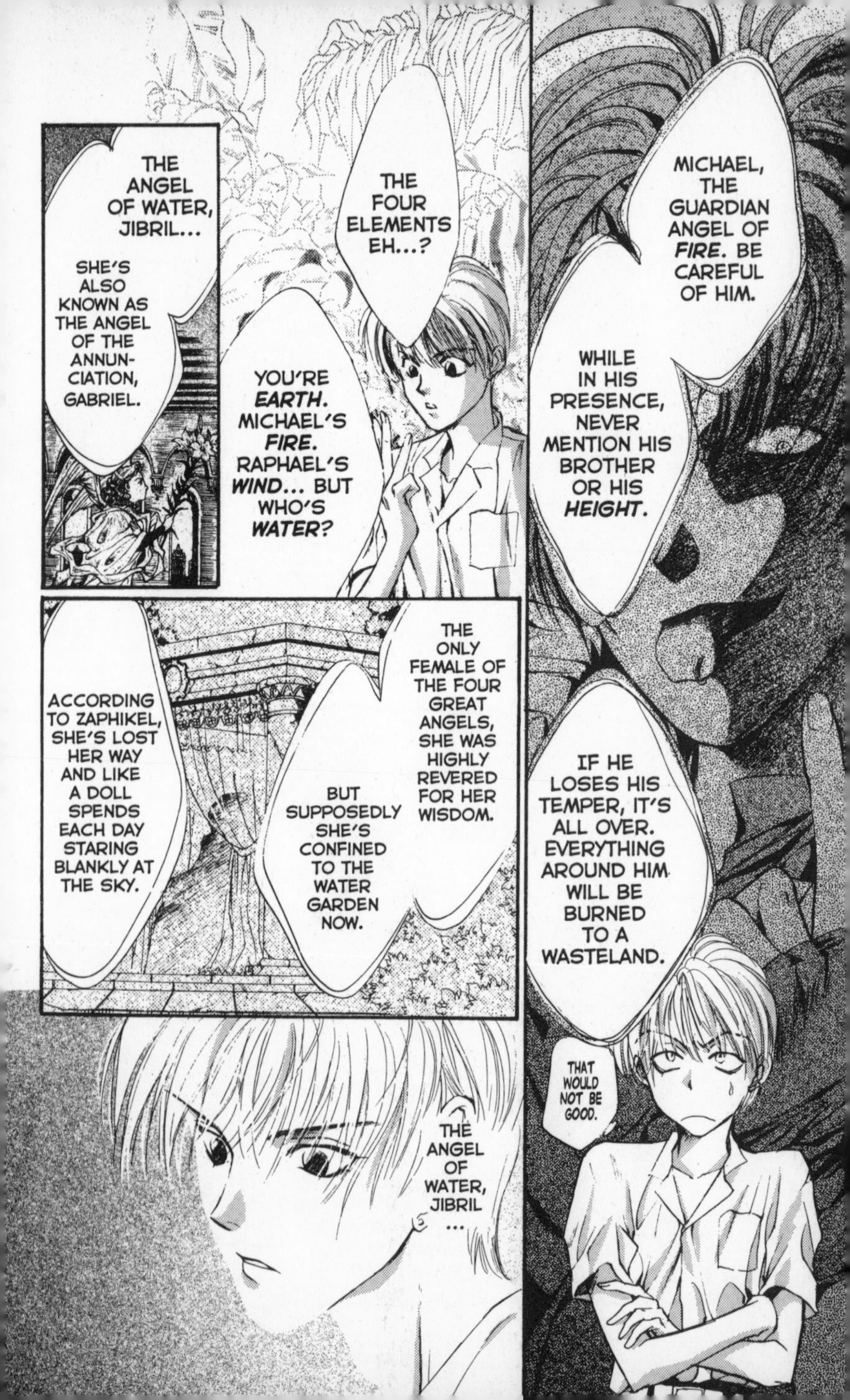
MICHAEL, THE GUARDIAN ANGEL OF *FIRE*. BE CAREFUL OF HIM.
WHILE IN HIS PRESENCE, NEVER MENTION HIS BROTHER OR HIS *HEIGHT*.
IF HE LOSES HIS TEMPER, IT'S ALL OVER. EVERYTHING AROUND HIM WILL BE BURNED TO A WASTELAND.
THAT WOULD NOT BE GOOD.
THE FOUR ELEMENTS EH...?
YOU'RE *EARTH*. MICHAEL'S *FIRE*. RAPHAEL'S *WIND*... BUT WHO'S *WATER?*
THE ANGEL OF WATER, JIBRIL...
SHE'S ALSO KNOWN AS THE ANGEL OF THE ANNUNCIATION, GABRIEL.
THE ONLY FEMALE OF THE FOUR GREAT ANGELS, SHE WAS HIGHLY REVERED FOR HER WISDOM.
BUT SUPPOSEDLY SHE'S CONFINED TO THE WATER GARDEN NOW.
ACCORDING TO ZAPHIKEL, SHE'S LOST HER WAY AND LIKE A DOLL SPENDS EACH DAY STARING BLANKLY AT THE SKY.
THE ANGEL OF WATER, JIBRIL ...

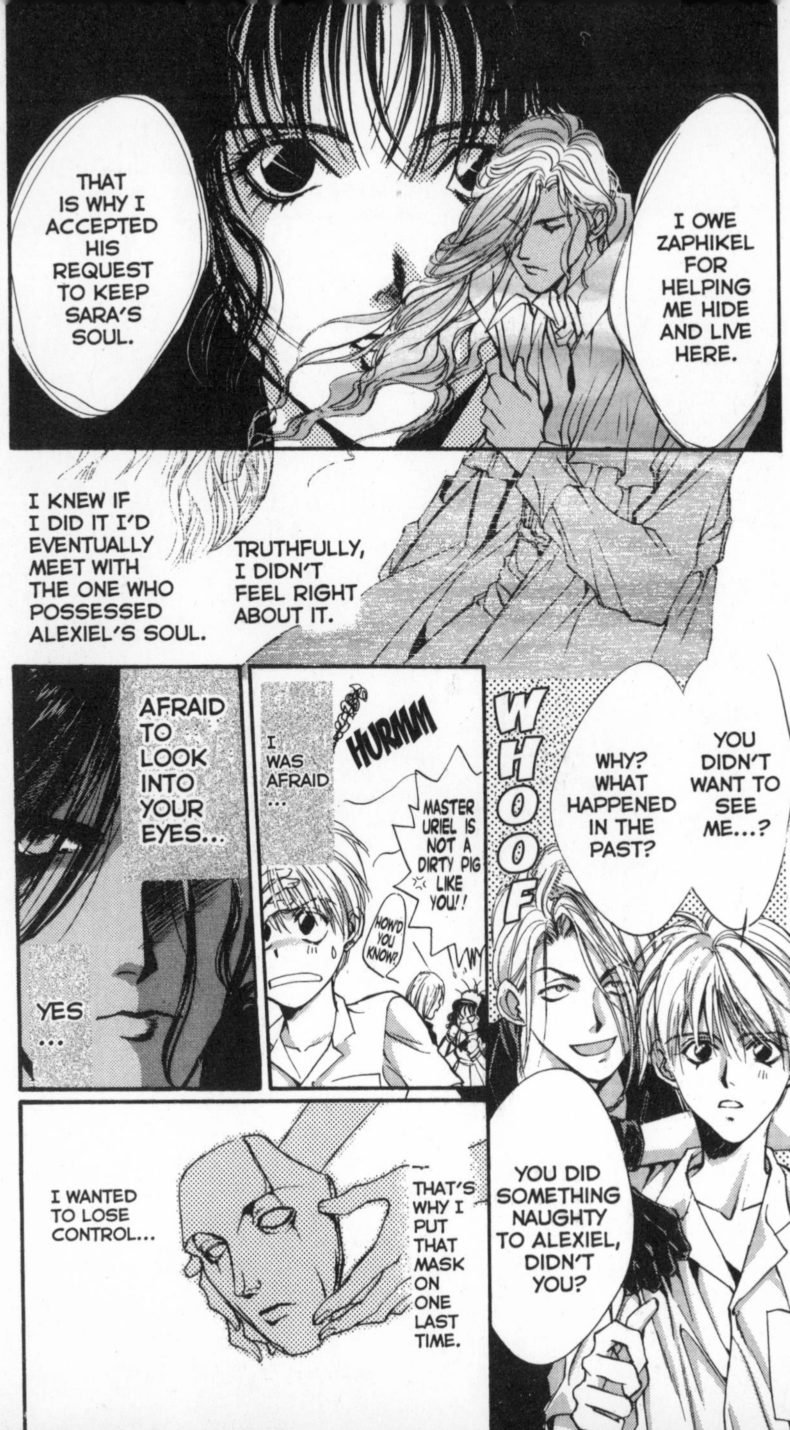
I OWE ZAPHIKEL FOR HELPING ME HIDE AND LIVE HERE.
THAT IS WHY I ACCEPTED HIS REQUEST TO KEEP SARA'S SOUL.
TRUTHFULLY, I DIDN'T FEEL RIGHT ABOUT IT.
I KNEW IF I DID IT I'D EVENTUALLY MEET WITH THE ONE WHO POSSESSED ALEXIEL'S SOUL.
YOU DIDN'T WANT TO SEE ME...?
WHY? WHAT HAPPENED IN THE PAST?
WHOOF
YOU DID SOMETHING NAUGHTY TO ALEXIEL, DIDN'T YOU?
I WAS AFRAID ...
HURMM
MASTER URIEL IS NOT A DIRTY PIG LIKE YOU!!
HOW'D YOU KNOW?
AFRAID TO LOOK INTO YOUR EYES...
YES ...
—THAT'S WHY I PUT THAT MASK ON ONE LAST TIME.
I WANTED TO LOSE CONTROL...

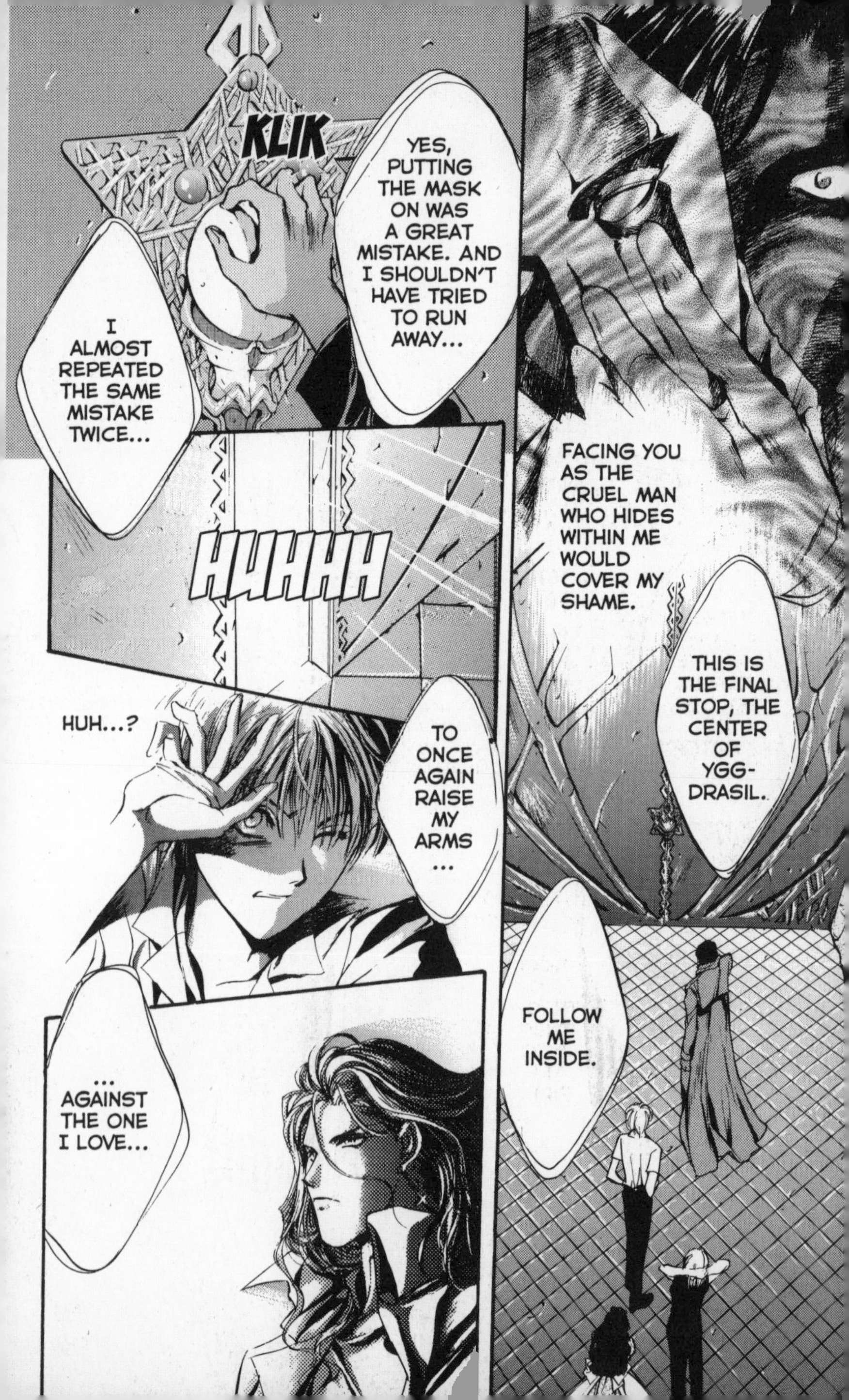
FACING YOU AS THE CRUEL MAN WHO HIDES WITHIN ME WOULD COVER MY SHAME.
THIS IS THE FINAL STOP, THE CENTER OF YGG-DRASIL.
KLIK
YES, PUTTING THE MASK ON WAS A GREAT MISTAKE. AND I SHOULDN'T HAVE TRIED TO RUN AWAY...
I ALMOST REPEATED THE SAME MISTAKE TWICE...
HUHHH
TO ONCE AGAIN RAISE MY ARMS ...
HUH...?
FOLLOW ME INSIDE.
... AGAINST THE ONE I LOVE...

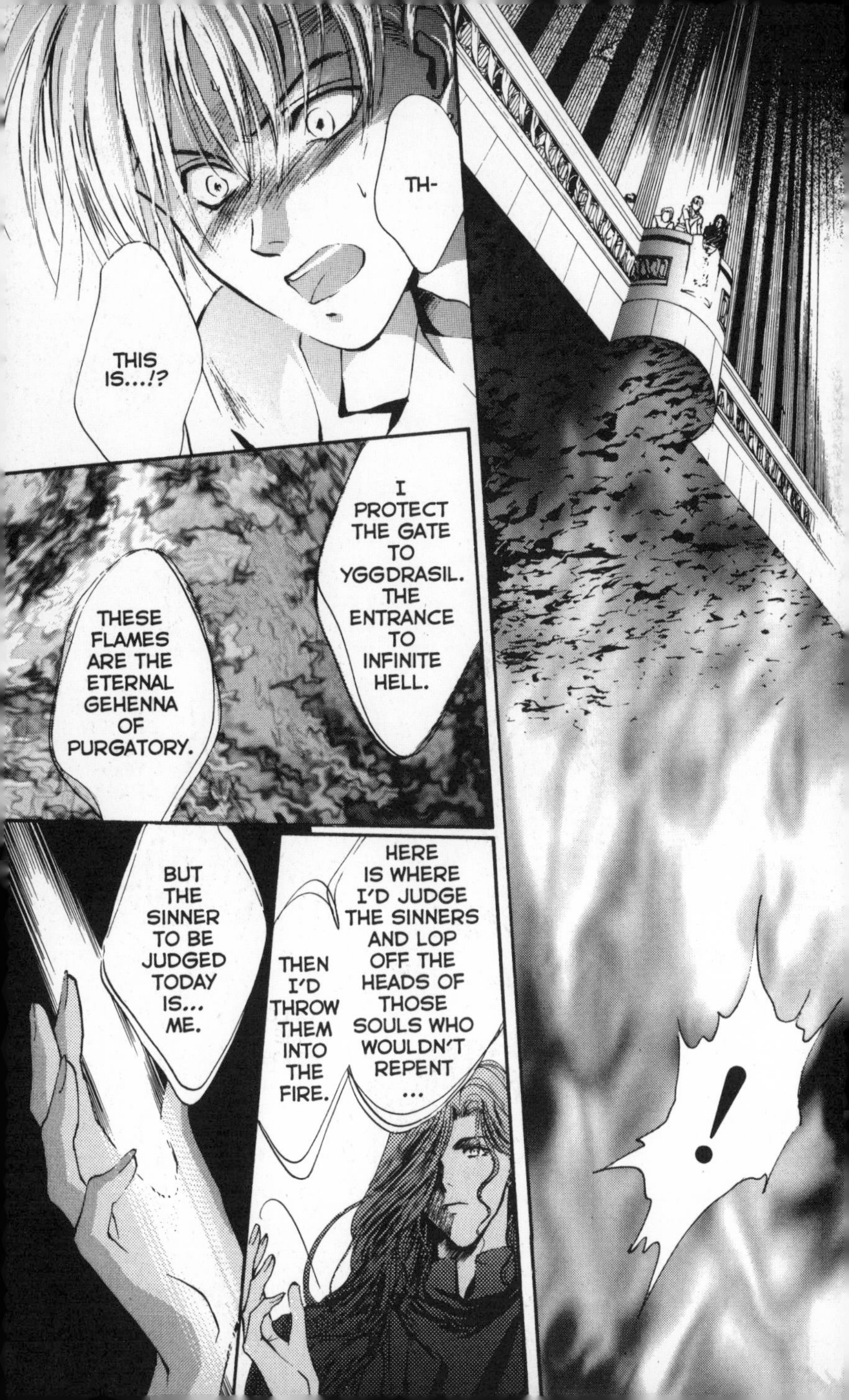
!
TH-
THIS IS...!?
I PROTECT THE GATE TO YGGDRASIL. THE ENTRANCE TO INFINITE HELL.
THESE FLAMES ARE THE ETERNAL GEHENNA OF PURGATORY.
HERE IS WHERE I'D JUDGE THE SINNERS AND LOP OFF THE HEADS OF THOSE SOULS WHO WOULDN'T REPENT ...
THEN I'D THROW THEM INTO THE FIRE.
BUT THE SINNER TO BE JUDGED TODAY IS... ME.

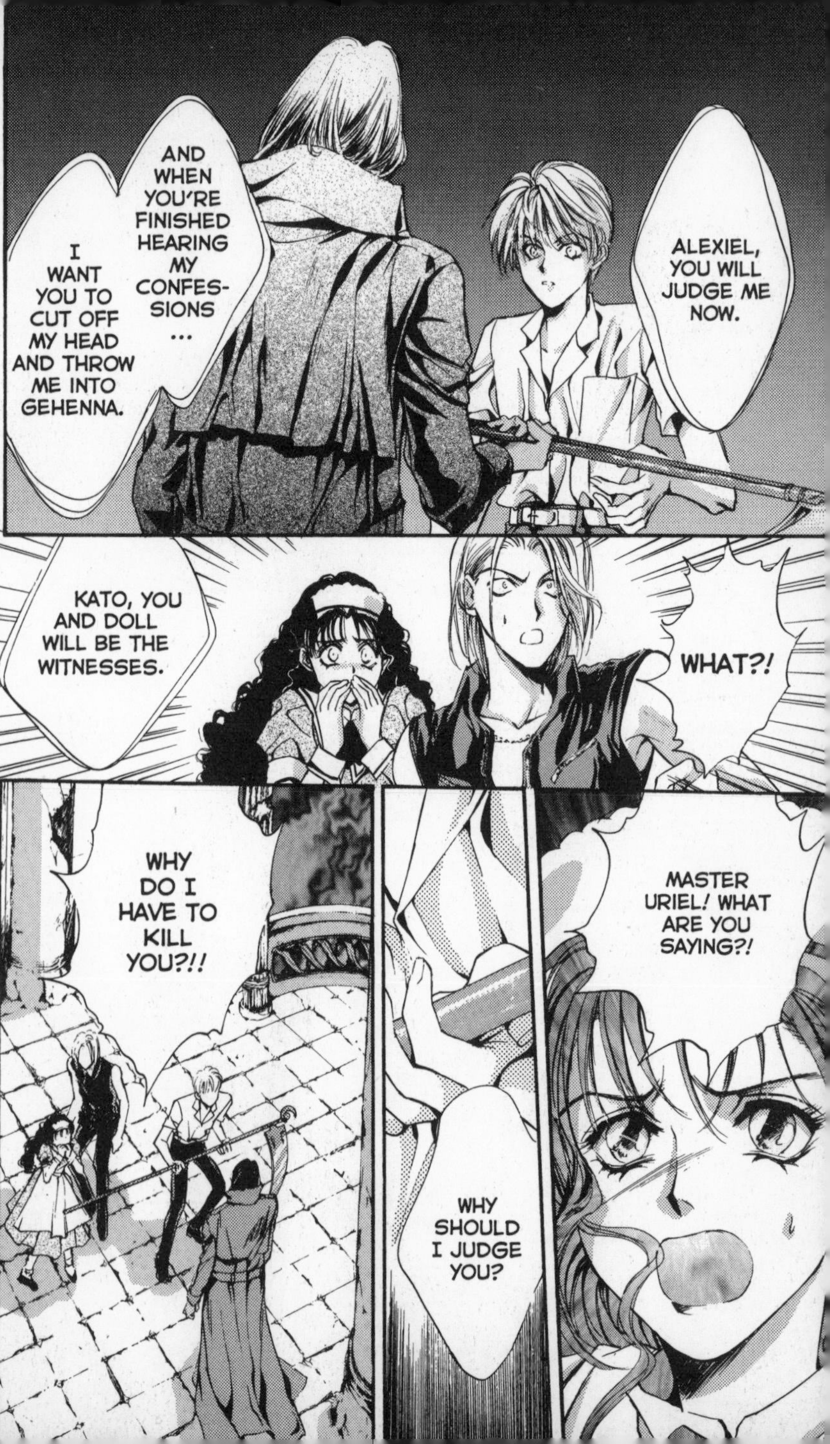
ALEXIEL, YOU WILL JUDGE ME NOW.
AND WHEN YOU'RE FINISHED HEARING MY CONFESSIONS ...
I WANT YOU TO CUT OFF MY HEAD AND THROW ME INTO GEHENNA.
WHAT?!
KATO, YOU AND DOLL WILL BE THE WITNESSES.
MASTER URIEL! WHAT ARE YOU SAYING?!
WHY SHOULD I JUDGE YOU?
WHY DO I HAVE TO KILL YOU?!!

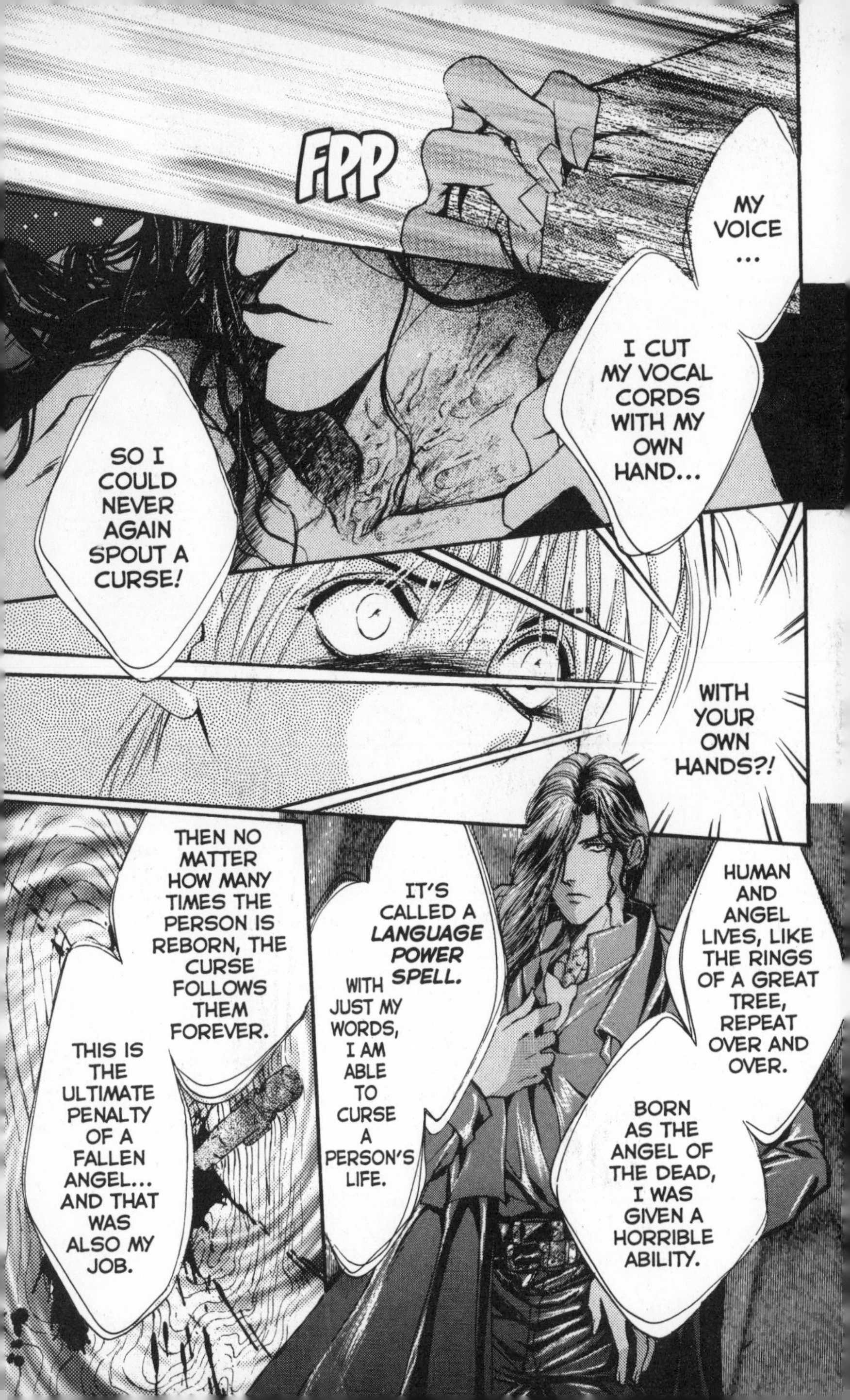
FPP
MY VOICE ...
I CUT MY VOCAL CORDS WITH MY OWN HAND...
SO I COULD NEVER AGAIN SPOUT A CURSE!
WITH YOUR OWN HANDS?!
HUMAN AND ANGEL LIVES, LIKE THE RINGS OF A GREAT TREE, REPEAT OVER AND OVER.
BORN AS THE ANGEL OF THE DEAD, I WAS GIVEN A HORRIBLE ABILITY.
IT'S CALLED A *LANGUAGE POWER SPELL.*
WITH JUST MY WORDS, I AM ABLE TO CURSE A PERSON'S LIFE.
THEN NO MATTER HOW MANY TIMES THE PERSON IS REBORN, THE CURSE FOLLOWS THEM FOREVER.
THIS IS THE ULTIMATE PENALTY OF A FALLEN ANGEL... AND THAT WAS ALSO MY JOB.

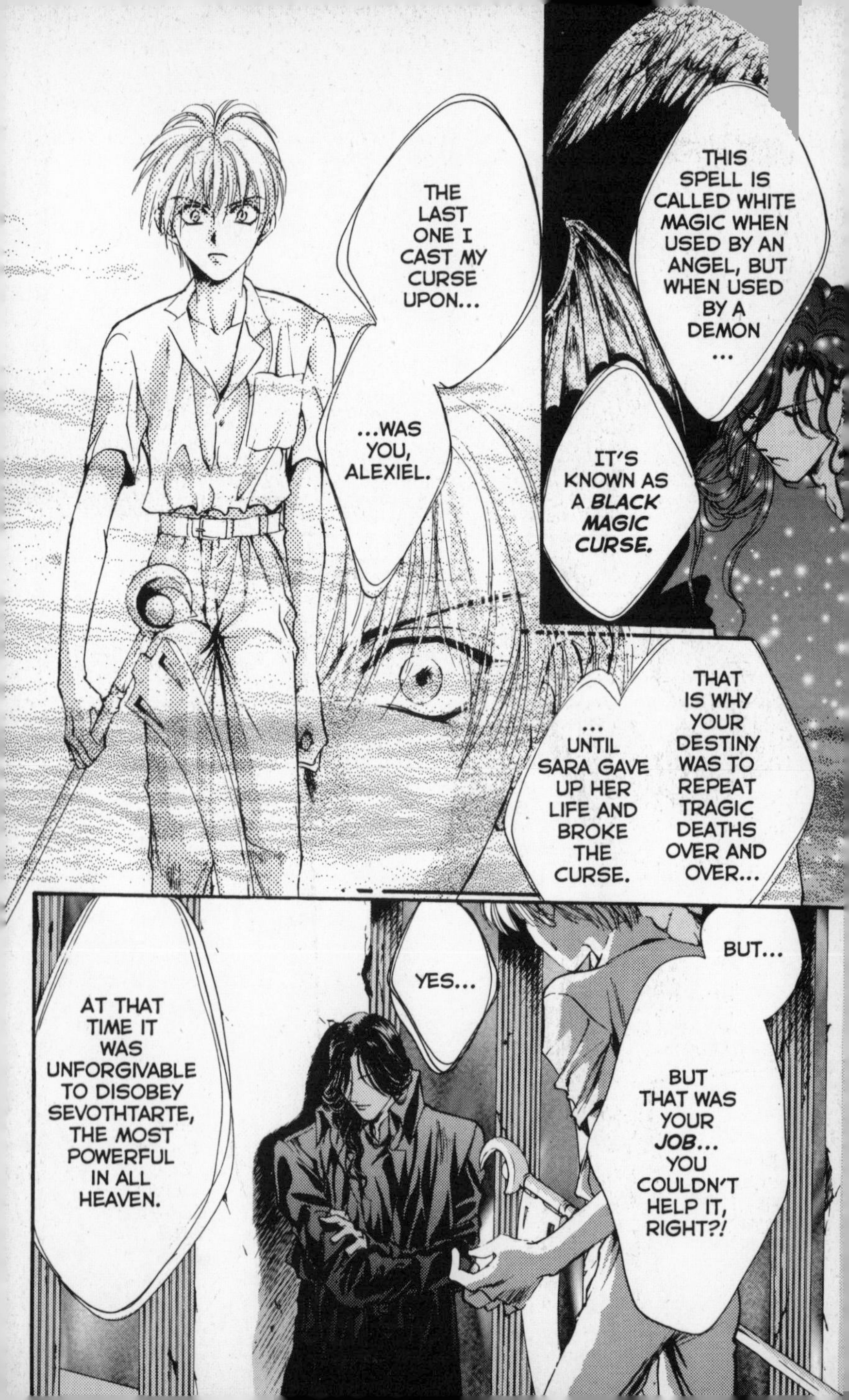
THIS SPELL IS CALLED WHITE MAGIC WHEN USED BY AN ANGEL, BUT WHEN USED BY A DEMON ...
IT'S KNOWN AS A *BLACK MAGIC CURSE.*
THE LAST ONE I CAST MY CURSE UPON...
...WAS YOU, ALEXIEL.
THAT IS WHY YOUR DESTINY WAS TO REPEAT TRAGIC DEATHS OVER AND OVER...
... UNTIL SARA GAVE UP HER LIFE AND BROKE THE CURSE.
BUT...
BUT THAT WAS YOUR *JOB*... YOU COULDN'T HELP IT, RIGHT?!
YES...
AT THAT TIME IT WAS UNFORGIVABLE TO DISOBEY SEVOTHTARTE, THE MOST POWERFUL IN ALL HEAVEN.

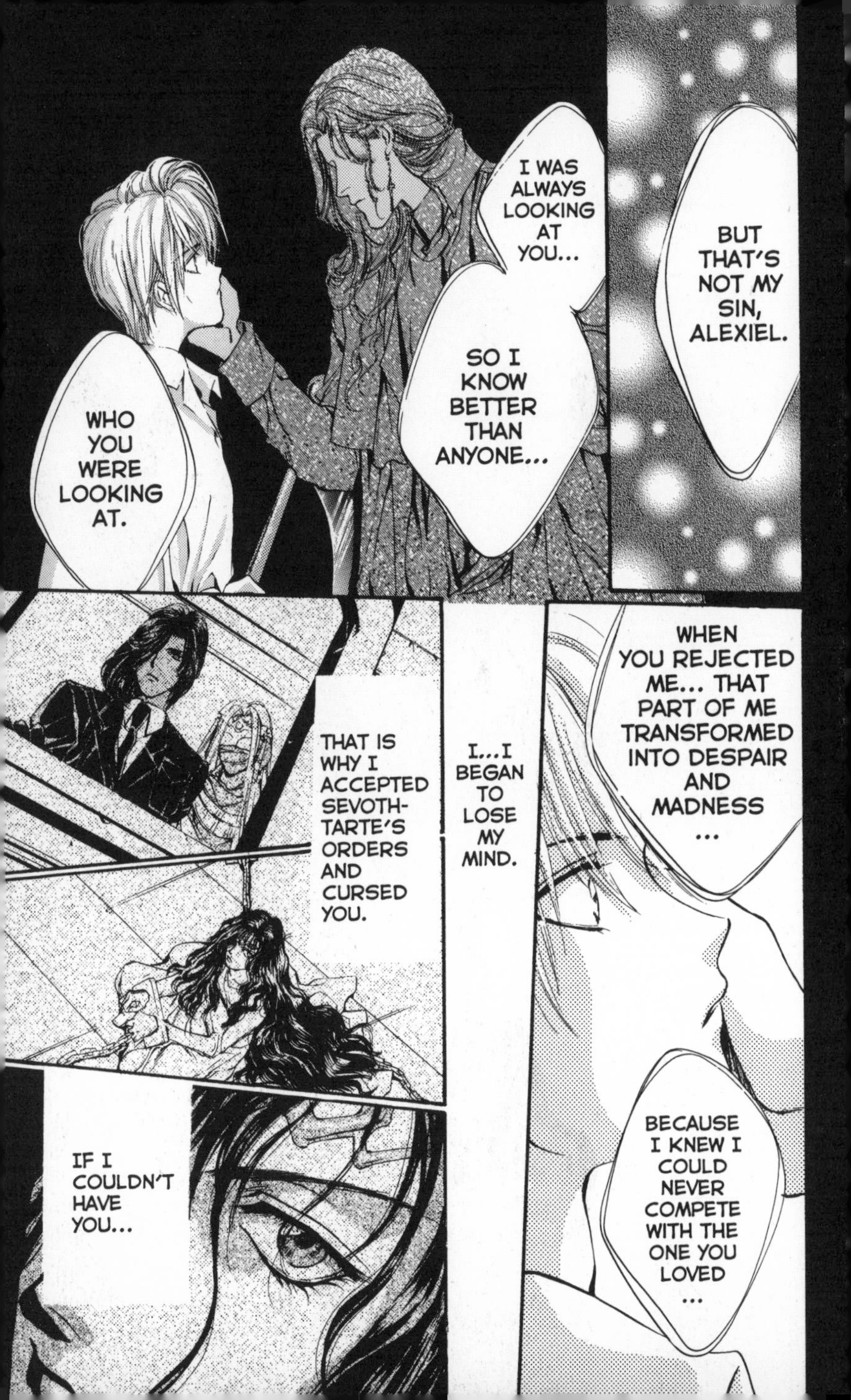
BUT THAT'S NOT MY SIN, ALEXIEL.
I WAS ALWAYS LOOKING AT YOU...
SO I KNOW BETTER THAN ANYONE...
WHO YOU WERE LOOKING AT.
WHEN YOU REJECTED ME... THAT PART OF ME TRANSFORMED INTO DESPAIR AND MADNESS ...
BECAUSE I KNEW I COULD NEVER COMPETE WITH THE ONE YOU LOVED ...
I...I BEGAN TO LOSE MY MIND.
THAT IS WHY I ACCEPTED SEVOTH-TARTE'S ORDERS AND CURSED YOU.
IF I COULDN'T HAVE YOU...

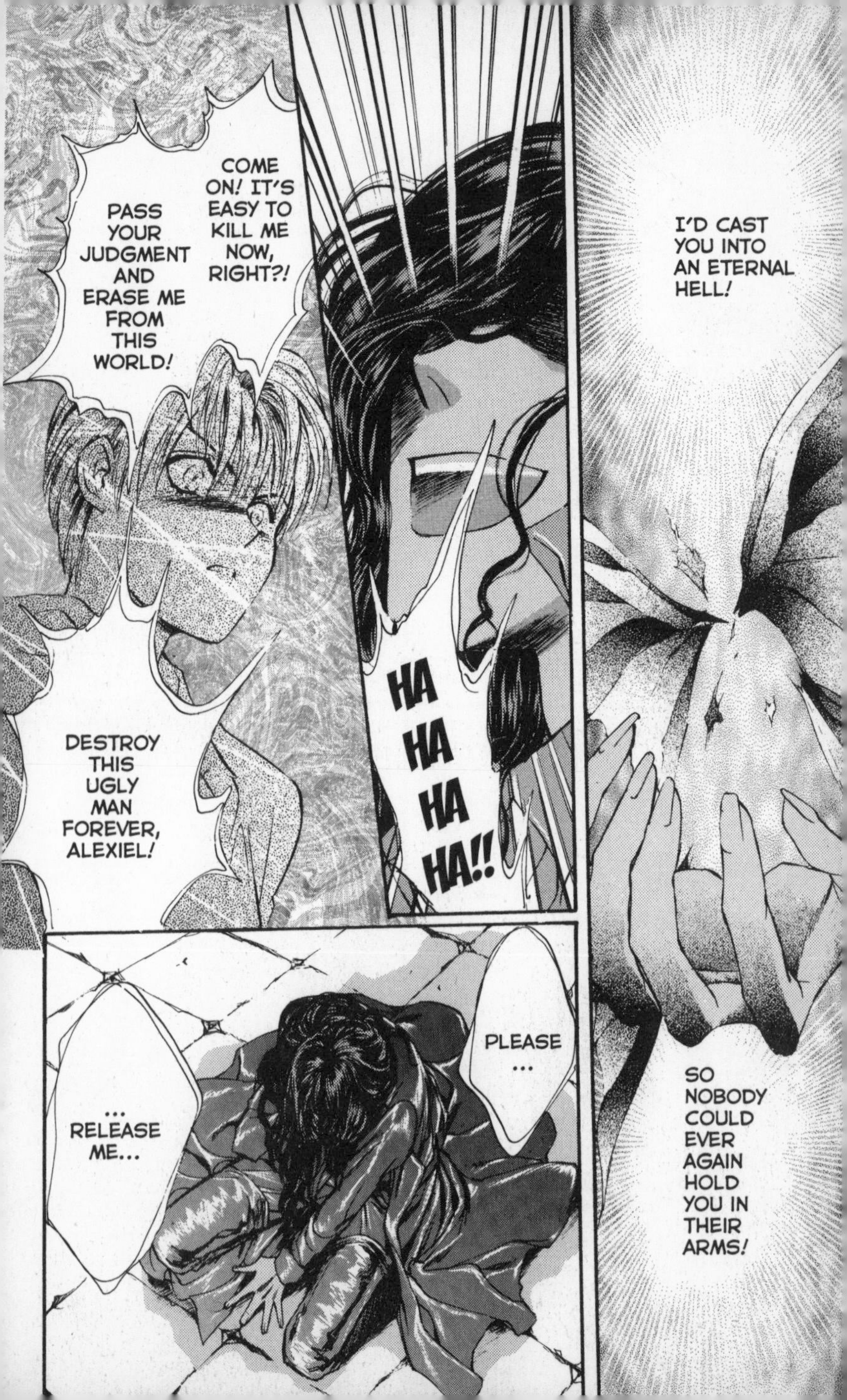
I'D CAST YOU INTO AN ETERNAL HELL!
SO NOBODY COULD EVER AGAIN HOLD YOU IN THEIR ARMS!
HA HA HA HA!!
COME ON! IT'S EASY TO KILL ME NOW, RIGHT?!
PASS YOUR JUDGMENT AND ERASE ME FROM THIS WORLD!
DESTROY THIS UGLY MAN FOREVER, ALEXIEL!
PLEASE ...
... RELEASE ME...

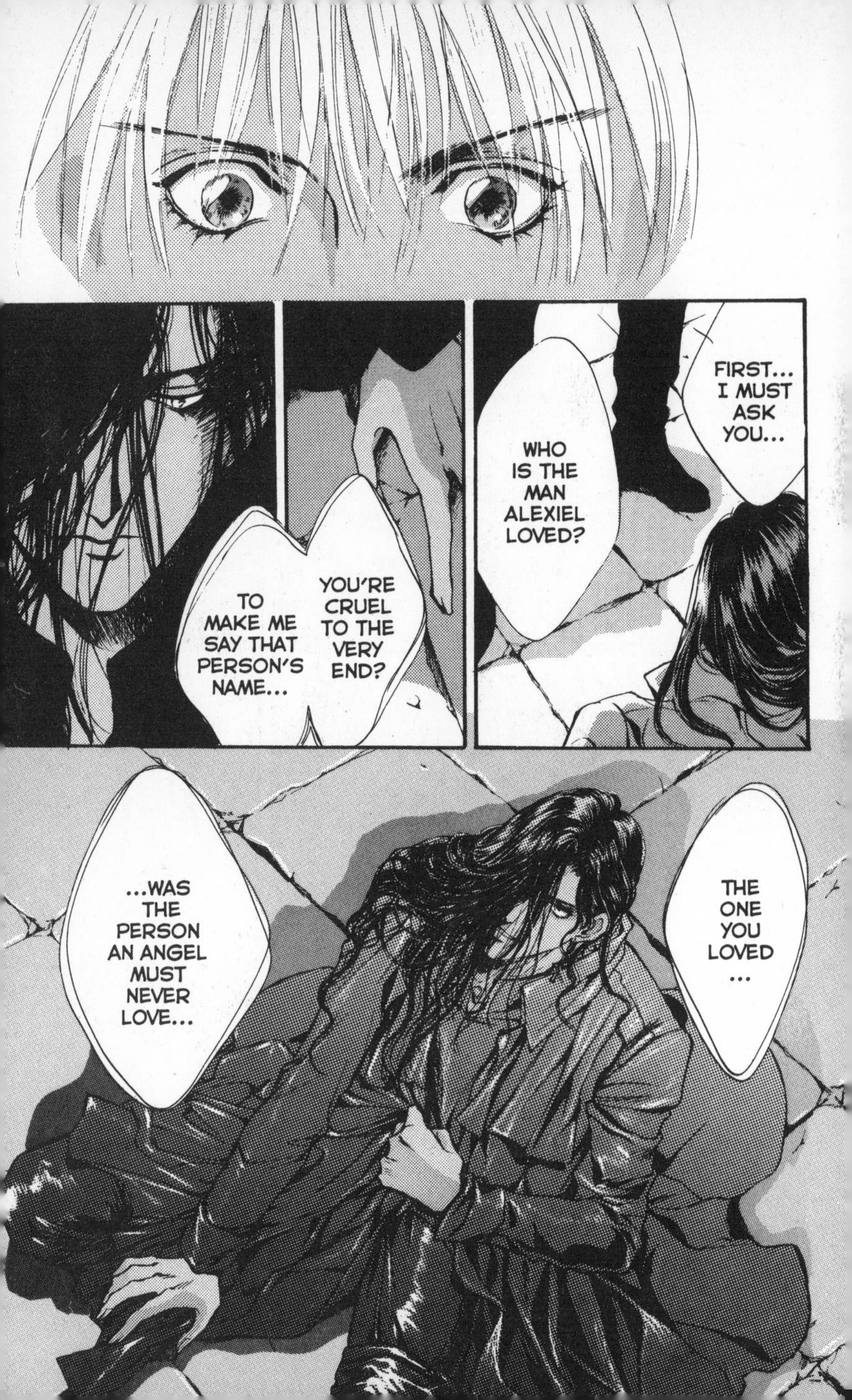
FIRST... I MUST ASK YOU...
WHO IS THE MAN ALEXIEL LOVED?
YOU'RE CRUEL TO THE VERY END?
TO MAKE ME SAY THAT PERSON'S NAME...
THE ONE YOU LOVED ...
...WAS THE PERSON AN ANGEL MUST NEVER LOVE...

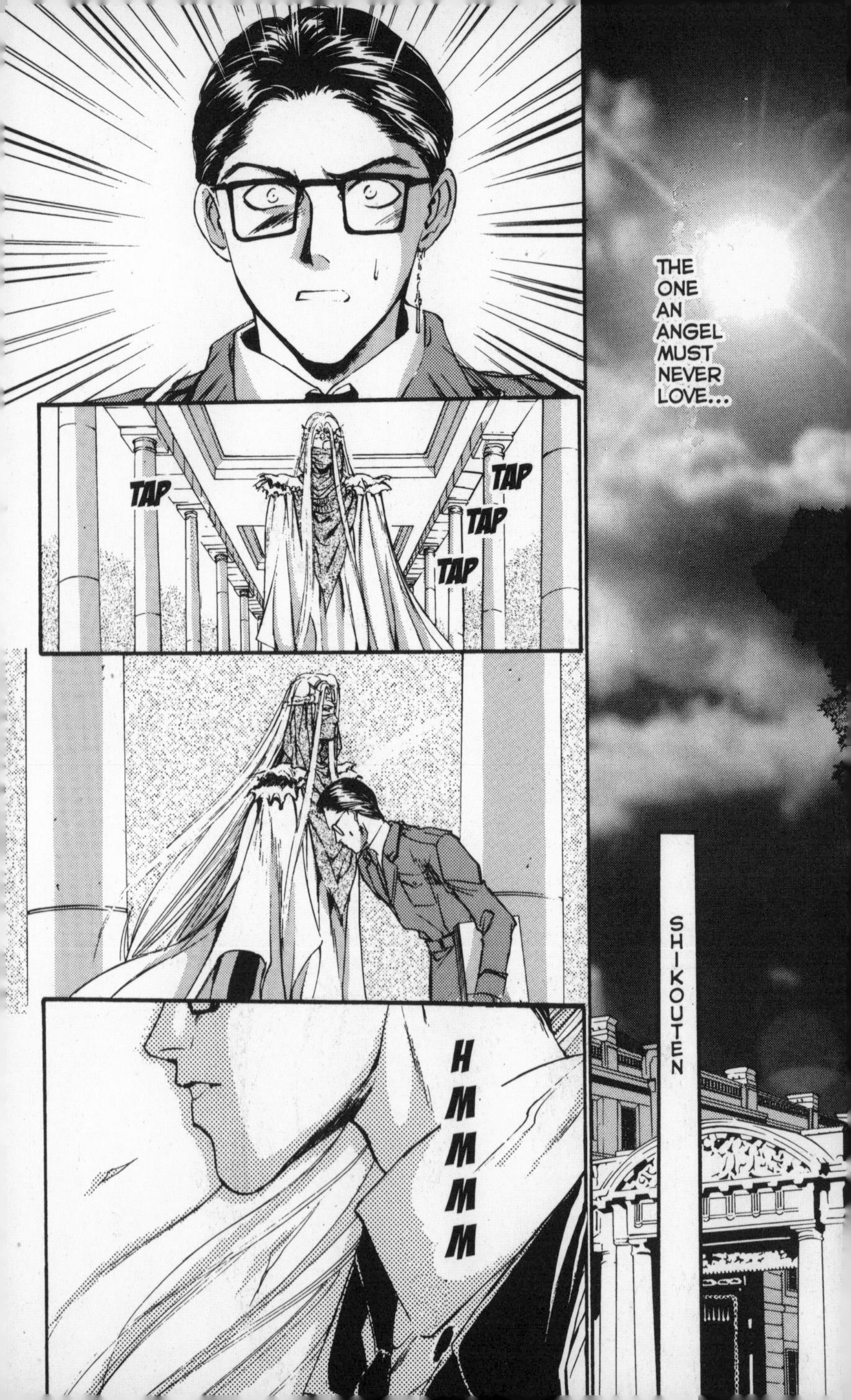
THE ONE AN ANGEL MUST NEVER LOVE...
SHIKOUTEN
TAP
TAP
TAP
TAP
HMMMM

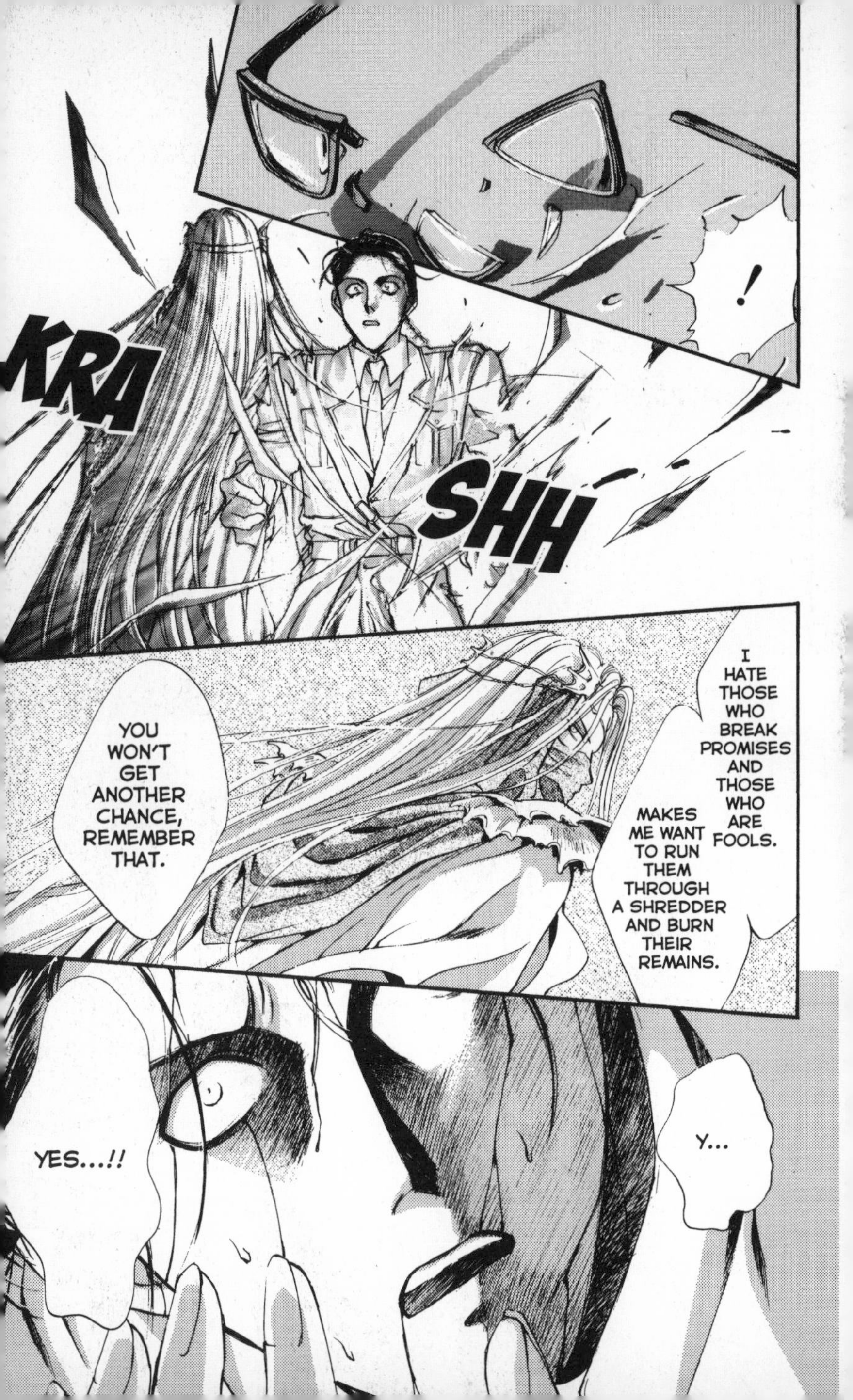
!
KRA
SHH
I HATE THOSE WHO BREAK PROMISES AND THOSE WHO ARE FOOLS.
MAKES ME WANT TO RUN THEM THROUGH A SHREDDER AND BURN THEIR REMAINS.
YOU WON'T GET ANOTHER CHANCE, REMEMBER THAT.
Y...
YES...!!

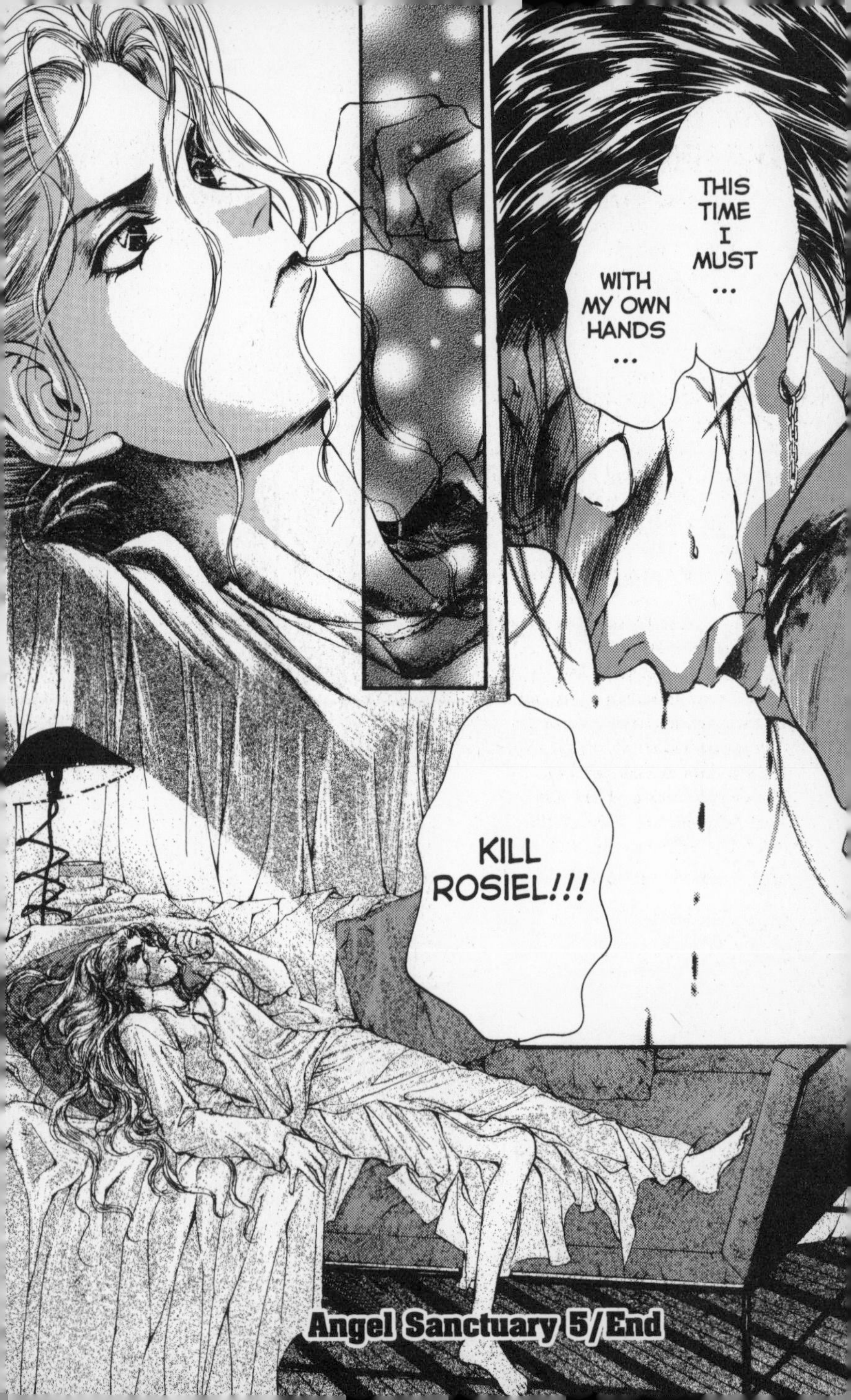
THIS TIME I MUST ...
WITH MY OWN HANDS ...
KILL ROSIEL!!!
Angel Sanctuary 5/End

ANGEL REPORT: A DEVIL'S FLATTERY

Once again I don't have much space, so let's start right off with a recap from last time...Yes! For this corner in book 4, I covered up the name of the band I like and I received letters from so many people who wanted to know. HOWEVER... So few people got it correct! OH! MY GOD! (This is strange since 99% of you guessed the person Rosiel looks like.) I gave so many hints on that page... I thought it was be easy. Sorry for all the trouble, it wasn't supposed to be this much of a struggle. But the people who got it right shared a lot of info with me on the band and I really enjoyed that. Some sent me books, which I thought was a bomb... Hey, it was thick and heavy! But thanks for the books. They were great! Now I know all about Egawa-san and Jizou-san. (Hint hint) Anyway, doesn't Kato look like a certain someone? When he reentered the series, (blank)-san's name or face wasn't revealed yet... Oh, and I've gotten lots of letters saying things like 'Age doesn't matter when it comes to becoming a fan, right?' or 'I became a fan at the same time as you!' Thank you so much for all the letters. I started liking the band when a reader sent me a tape. I listened to the song a lot and didn't find out what they looked like until well after that. Who would have known they'd be that hot?! They're guys yet they are prettier than girls...

This has nothing to do with anything but I can't get my hands on the songs from when Raru(blank) was an indies band. And I love them so much. Oh, the tag line for that chapter title was written by my editor and not me.

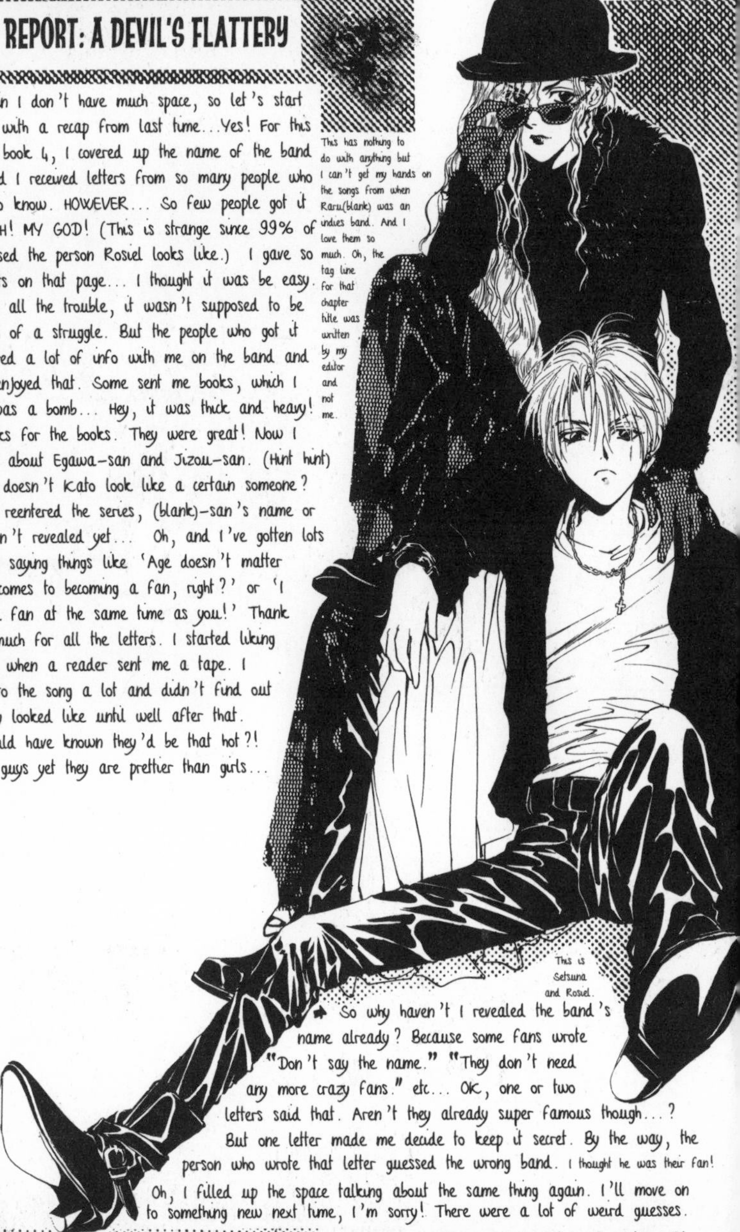

This is Setsuna and Rosiel.

I really wanted to draw them here.

So why haven't I revealed the band's name already? Because some fans wrote "Don't say the name." "They don't need any more crazy fans." etc... OK, one or two letters said that. Aren't they already super famous though...? But one letter made me decide to keep it secret. By the way, the person who wrote that letter guessed the wrong band. I thought he was their fan! Oh, I filled up the space talking about the same thing again. I'll move on to something new next time, I'm sorry! There were a lot of weird guesses.

What was that Ski one? Skidrow?! You have it all wrong!

shôjo

AT THE HEART OF THE MATTER

- Alice 19th
- Angel Sanctuary
- Banana Fish
- Basara
- B.B. Explosion
- Boys Over Flowers *
- Ceres, Celestial Legend *
- Descendants of Darkness
- Dolls
- From Far Away
- Fushigi Yûgi
- Hana-Kimi
- Here Is Greenwood
- Hot Gimmick
- Imadoki
- Kare First Love
- Please Save My Earth *
- Red River
- Revolutionary Girl Utena
- Sensual Phrase
- W Juliet
- Wedding Peach
- Wild Com.
- X/1999

Start Your Shôjo Graphic Novel Collection Today!